Get the eBook FREE!
(PDF, ePub, Kindle, and liveBook all included)

We believe that once you buy a book from us, you should be able to read it in any format we have available. To get electronic versions of this book at no additional cost to you, purchase and then register this book at the Manning website.

Go to https://www.manning.com/freebook and follow the instructions to complete your pBook registration.

That's it!
Thanks from Manning!

Effective Software Testing

Effective
Software Testing

A DEVELOPER'S GUIDE

MAURÍCIO ANICHE

Forewords by ARIE VAN DEURSEN and STEVE FREEMAN

MANNING

SHELTER ISLAND

Manning Publications Co.
20 Baldwin Road
PO Box 761
Shelter Island, NY 11964

Development editors:	Kristen Watterson and Toni Arritola
Technical development editor:	Frances Buontempo
Review editor:	Mihaela Batinić
Production editor:	Andy Marinkovich
Copy editor:	Tiffany Taylor
Proofreader:	Jason Everett
Technical proofreader:	Kevin Orr
Typesetter:	Dennis Dalinnik
Cover designer:	Marija Tudor

ISBN: 9781633439931

Printed and bound by CPI Group (UK) Ltd, Croydon, CR0 4YY

brief contents

contents

forewords

In modern software development, software testing steers the design, implementation, evolution, quality assurance, and deployment of software systems. To be an effective developer, you must become an effective software tester. This book helps you to achieve that goal.

Put simply, testing is nothing but executing a piece of software to see if it behaves as expected. But testing is also hard. Its difficulty surfaces when thinking about the full set of test cases to be designed and executed. Out of the infinitely many possible test cases, which one should you write? Did you do enough testing to move the system to production? What extra tests do you need? Why these tests? And, if you need to change the system, how should you set up the test suite so that it supports rather than impedes future change?

This book doesn't shy away from such complex questions. It covers key testing techniques like design by contract, property-based testing, boundary testing, test adequacy criteria, mutation testing, and the proper use of mock objects. Where relevant, it gives pointers to additional research papers on the topic.

At the same time, this book succeeds in making sure the test cases themselves and the testing process remain as simple as can be justified. It does so by always taking the perspective of the developer who is actually designing and running the tests. The book is full of examples, ensuring that the reader can get started with applying the techniques in their own projects straight away.

This book emerged out of a course taught at Delft University of Technology for many years. In 2003 I introduced a course on software testing in the undergraduate curriculum. In 2016, Maurício Aniche joined me in teaching the course, and in 2019 he took over the course entirely. Maurício is a superb lecturer, and in 2021 the students elected him as *Teacher of the Year* of the faculty of Electrical Engineering, Mathematics, and Computer Science.

At TU Delft, we teach testing in the very first year of our Computer Science and Engineering bachelor program. It has been difficult finding a book that aligns with our vision that an effective software engineer must be an effective software tester. Many academic textbooks focus on research results. Many developer-oriented texts focus on specific tools or processes.

Maurício Aniche's *Effective Software Testing* fills that gap by finding the sweet spot between theory and practice. It is written with the working developer in mind, offering you state-of-the-art software testing techniques. At the same time, it is perfect for undergraduate university courses, training the next generations of computer scientists to become effective software testers.

—Dr. Arie van Deursen, Professor in Software Engineering,
Delft University of Technology, The Netherlands

Effective Software Testing by Maurício Aniche is a practical introductory book that helps developers test their code. It's a compact tour through the essentials of software testing that covers major topics every developer should know about. The book's combination of theory and practice shows the depth of Maurício's experience as an academic and as a working programmer.

My own path into software was rather haphazard: some programming courses at university, ad-hoc training on the job, and eventually a conversion course leading to a PhD. This left me envious of programmers who had taken the right courses at the right time and had the theoretical depth that I lacked. I periodically discovered that one of my ideas, usually with a half-baked implementation, turned out to be an established concept that I hadn't heard of. That's why I think it's important to read introductory material, such as this book.

Throughout much of my software life, I saw testing as a necessary evil that mostly involved the tedium of following text instructions by hand. Nowadays it's obvious to most that test automation is best done by computers, but it's taken decades for that to become so widely accepted. That's why, to me, test-driven development, when I first came across it, initially seemed crazy—and then essential.

That said, I see a lot of test code in the wild that really isn't clear. Obviously, this is easier to see in hindsight, without the immediate pressure of deadlines or after the domain model has settled. But I believe that this test code would be improved if more programmers used the techniques described in this book to structure and reason about the problems they're working on. This doesn't mean that we all must turn into academics, but the light application of a few concepts can make a big difference. For example, I find design-by-contract helpful when working with components that maintain state. I might not always add explicit pre- and post-conditions to my code, but the concepts help me to think about, or discuss, what the code should do.

Obviously, software testing is a huge subject for developers, but this book is a good way to get started. And, for those of us who've been around a bit longer, it's a good reminder of techniques that we've neglected or maybe missed the first time around. It's also good to see sections on software testing as a practice, in particular the brief introduction to larger-scale testing and, my favorite, sustaining test code quality. So many real-life test suites turn into a source of frustration because they haven't been maintained.

Maurício's experience shows in the practical guidance and heuristics that he includes in the explanation of each technique. He is careful to provide the tools, but lets the reader find their own path (although it's probably a good idea to take his advice). And, of course, the contents of the book itself have been thoroughly tested as it was originally developed in the open for his course at TU Delft.

On a personal note, I used to meet Maurício when I guest lectured for his course, after which we would stop for pickled herrings (a taste that is uniquely appealing to Northern European palates) at a historic market stall in the town center. We would discuss programming and testing techniques, and life in the Netherlands. I was impressed with his care to do his best for his students, and with his ideas for his research. I look forward to the day when I can get on the train to Delft again.

—DR. STEVE FREEMAN, author of *Growing Object-Oriented Software,*
Guided by Tests (Addison-Wesley Professional)

preface

Every software developer remembers a specific bug that affected their career. Let me tell you about mine. In 2006, I was the technical lead for a small development team that was building an application to control payments at gas stations. At the time, I was finishing my computer science undergraduate studies and beginning my career as a software developer. I had only worked on two serious web applications previously. And as the lead developer, I took my responsibility very seriously.

The system needed to communicate directly with gas pumps. As soon as a customer finished refueling, the gas pump notified our system, and the application started its process: gathering information about the purchase (type of fuel, quantity in liters), calculating the final price, taking the user through the payment process, and storing the information for future reporting.

The software system had to run on a dedicated device with a 200 MHz processor, 2 MB of RAM, and a few megabytes of permanent storage. This was the first time anyone had tried to use the device for a business application. So, there was no previous project from which we could learn or borrow code. We also could not reuse any external libraries, and we even had to implement our own simplistic database.

The system required refuelings, and simulating them became a vital part of our development flow. We would implement a new feature, run the system, run the simulator, simulate a few gas purchases, and manually check that the system responded correctly.

After a few months, we had implemented the important features. Our (manual) tests, including tests performed by the company, succeeded. We had a version that could be tested in the wild! But real-world testing was not simple: an engineering team had to make physical changes at a gas station so the pumps could talk to our software. To my surprise, the company decided to schedule the first pilot in the Dominican Republic. I was excited not only to see my project go live but also to visit such a beautiful country.

I was the only developer who traveled to the Dominican Republic for the pilot, so I was responsible for fixing any last-minute bugs. I watched the installation and followed along when the software ran for the first time. I spent the entire day monitoring the system, and everything seemed fine.

That night we went out to celebrate. The beer was cold, and I was proud of myself. I went to bed early so I would be ready to meet the stakeholders the next morning and discuss the project's next steps. But at 6:00 a.m., my hotel telephone rang. It was the owner of the pilot gas station: "The software apparently crashed during the night. The night workers did not know what to do, and the gas pumps were not delivering a single drop of fuel, so the station could not sell anything the entire night!" I was shaken. How could that have happened?

I went straight to the site and started debugging the system. The bug was caused by a situation we had not tested: more refuelings than the system could handle. We knew we were using an embedded device with limited memory, so we had taken precautions. But we never tested what would happen if the limit was reached—and there was a bug!

Our tests were all done manually: to simulate refueling, we went to the simulator, clicked a button on a pump, started pumping gas, waited some number of seconds (on the simulator, the longer we waited, the more liters of fuel we purchased), and then stopped the refueling process. If we wanted to simulate 100 gas purchases, we had to click 100 times in the simulator. Doing so was slow and painful. So, at development time, we tried only two or three refuelings. We probably tested the exception-handling mechanism once, but that was not enough.

The first software system for which I was the lead developer did not even work a full day! What could I have done to prevent the bug? It was time for me to change how I was building software—and this led me to learn more about software testing. Sure, in college I had learned about many testing techniques and the importance of software testing, but you only recognize the value of some things when you need them.

Today, I cannot imagine building a system without building an automated test suite along with it. The automated test suite can tell me in seconds whether the code I wrote is right or wrong, so I am much more productive. This book is my attempt to help developers avoid the mistakes I made.

acknowledgments

This is not my first technical book, but it is the first one I have put my heart into. And it was only possible due to the help and inspiration of many people.

First, by far the most important person who led me to write this book is Prof. Dr. Arie van Deursen. Arie was my post-doc supervisor and later my colleague in the Software Engineering Research Group (SERG) at Delft University of Technology. In 2017, he invited me to co-teach his software testing course for first-year computer science students (yes, Delft teaches software testing from the start!). While co-teaching with him, I learned a great deal about his views on theoretical and practical software testing. Arie's passion for educating people on this topic inspired me, and I keep working to improve TU Delft's software testing course (which is now my full responsibility). This book is a natural result of the interest he triggered in me years ago.

Other colleagues at TU Delft have also influenced me significantly. Frank Mulder, who now co-teaches software testing with me, is a very experienced software developer and not afraid to challenge the software development status quo. I have lost count of how many discussions we have had about different practices over the years. We also take these discussions into the lecture hall, and our students have almost as much fun as we do as we present our views. Many of the pragmatic discussions in this book began as conversations with Frank.

My thanks go to Wouter Polet. Wouter has been my teaching assistant for many years. When the Covid pandemic began, I told Wouter that we should make the lecture notes available for students who couldn't attend class. He took that as a mission and quickly built a website containing transcripts of videos I had made a few years earlier.

These transcripts became my lecture notes, which later became this book. Without Wouter's support, I do not think this book would have come to be. My thanks also go to Sára Juhošová, who joined us as a head teaching assistant and has been instrumental in the course. I don't know if anyone else will read this book as thoroughly as she did. Sára also spent a lot of time fine-tuning my poorly written sentences—the book would not have been the same without her help. Finally, I thank Nadine Kuo and the dozens of teaching assistants over the years who have helped me improve the course material. There are many others who helped me (too many to list here), but they all played a role in the development of this book.

Thank you to Prof. Dr. Andy Zaidman and Dr. Annibale Panichella. Andy has been a colleague of mine for years and was a role model for me before that. I read his papers with passion and interest. Andy's love for empirical software testing inspired me to come to Delft for my post-doc. Annibale was my office mate for many years and is, by far, the best software engineering researcher I know. Annibale is a world-class expert on search-based software testing and I have learned a great deal about the topic from him (much of it over beers). Although I don't talk much about it in the book, Annibale has shown me how far artificial intelligence can go in software testing, and has influenced me to reflect on what should be done by (human) developers.

People outside TU Delft have also influenced me and made this book possible. First, I want to thank Alberto Souza. Alberto is one of my best friends and one of the most pragmatic developers I know. When I decided to embark on the lengthy process of writing a book, I needed positive reinforcement, and Alberto provided it. Without his constant positive feedback, I am not sure I would have finished the book.

I also want to thank Steve Freeman. Steve is one of the authors of the well-known book, *Growing Object-Oriented Systems, Guided by Tests* (Addison-Wesley Professional, 2009). When I gave my first-ever academic talk at a workshop on test-driven development (TDD) in 2011, Steve was the keynote speaker. Today, Steve gives a guest lecture each year as part of my testing course. I am a big fan of how Steve sees software development, and his book is one of the most influential I have ever read. I also have fun discussing software development topics with him because he is passionate and opinionated. Although my chapters on TDD and mocking do not reflect the way Steve thinks, he has definitely influenced my views on testing.

I also want to thank the people at Manning Publications. They have helped me shape my ideas from day one, and the final version of the book is much different (and better) than the initial proposal. My thanks to Kristen Watterson, Tiffany Taylor, Toni Arritola, Rebecca Rinehart, Melissa Ice, Ivan Martinovic, Paul Wells, Christopher Kaufmann, Andy Marinkovich, Aira Ducic, Jason Everett, Azra Dedic, and Michael Stephens. I also thank Frances Buontempo, the developer assigned to follow my book from start to finish. Her timely, rich feedback led to many improvements in the book.

To all the reviewers: Amit Lamba, Atul S Khot, David Cabrero Souto, Francesco Basile, James Liu, James McKean Wood, Jereme Allen, Joel Holmes, Kevin Orr, Matteo Battista, Michael Holmes, Nelson H. Ferrari, Prabhuti Prakash, Robert Edwards,

Shawn Lam, Stephen Byrne, Timothy Wooldridge, and Tom Madden, your suggestions helped make this a better book.

Finally, I thank my beloved wife, Laura. I signed the deal with Manning a few weeks before our baby was born. She was incredibly patient and supportive throughout this time. Without her, I could not have written this book (or done many other things in life). Our baby is now seven months old, and although he does not know much about testing yet, he is the reason I want to make the world a better place.

about this book

Like most software engineering, software testing is an art. Over the past decade, our community has learned that automated tests are the best way to test software. Computers can run hundreds of tests in a split second, and such test suites allow companies to confidently ship software dozens of times a day.

A huge number of resources (books, tutorials, and online courses) are available that explain how to automate tests. No matter what language you are working in or what type of software you are developing, you can find information about the right tool to use. But we are missing resources related to engineering effective test cases. Automation executes tests that a developer designed. If the tests are not good or do not exercise parts of the code that contain bugs, the test suite is less useful.

The development community treats software testing like an art form, where inspired and creative developers create more effective test suites than developers who are less creative or experienced. But I challenge that attitude in this book and show that software testing does not need to depend on expertise, experience, or creativity: it can, for the most part, be systematized.

By following an effective, systematic approach to software testing, we no longer depend on very experienced software developers to write good tests. And if we find ways to automate most of the process, this frees us to focus on tests that do require creativity.

Who should read this book

This book was written for developers who want to learn more about testing or sharpen their testing skills. If you have years of experience in software engineering and have written lots of automated tests, but you always follow your intuition about what the next test case should be, this book will provide some structure for your thought process.

Developers with different levels of expertise will benefit from reading this book. Novice developers will be able to follow all the code examples and techniques I introduce. Senior developers will be introduced to techniques they may not be familiar with and will learn from the real-world, pragmatic discussions in every chapter.

The testing techniques I describe are meant to be applied by the developer writing the code. While this book can be read by dedicated software testers who see programs as black boxes, it is written from the standpoint of the developer who wrote the code that is being tested.

The examples in this book are written in Java, but I did my best to avoid fancy constructs that will be unfamiliar to developers using other programming languages. I also generalize the techniques so that even if the code does not translate directly to your context, the ideas do.

In chapter 7, I discuss designing testable systems. Those ideas make more sense for developers building object-oriented software systems than for systems built in a functional style. However, this is the only chapter that may not directly apply to functional programmers.

How this book is organized: A roadmap

This book is organized into 11 chapters. In chapter 1, I make my case for systematic and effective software testing. I present an example involving two developers—both implementing the same feature, one casually and the other systematically—and highlight the differences between their approaches. I then discuss the differences between unit, integration, and system tests and argue that developers should first focus on fast unit tests and integration tests (the well-known testing pyramid).

Chapter 2 introduces domain testing. This testing practice focuses on engineering test cases based on requirements. Software development teams use different practices when it comes to requirements—user stories, Unified Modeling Language (UML), or in-house formats—and domain testing uses this information. Every testing session should begin with the requirements of the feature being developed.

Chapter 3 shows how to use the program's source code and structure to augment the tests we engineer via domain testing. We can run code coverage tools and use the results to reflect on parts of code that our initial test suite did not cover. Some developers do not think code coverage is a useful metric, but in this chapter I hope to convince you that, when applied correctly, code coverage should be part of the testing process.

In chapter 4, I discuss the idea that quality goes beyond testing: it also depends on how you model your code and the certainties your methods and classes give to the system's other classes and methods. Design by contract makes the code's pre- and post-conditions explicit. This way, if something goes wrong, the program will halt without causing other problems.

Chapter 5 introduces property-based testing. Instead of writing tests based on a single concrete example, we test all the program's properties. The testing framework is responsible for generating input data that matches the properties. Mastering this technique can be tricky: it is not easy to express properties, and doing so requires practice. Property-based testing is also more appropriate for some pieces of code than others. This chapter is full of examples that demonstrate this concept.

Chapter 6 discusses practicalities that go beyond engineering good test cases. In more complex systems, classes depend on other classes, and writing tests can become a burden. I introduce mocks and stubs, which let us ignore some dependencies during testing. We also discuss a significant trade-off: although mocks simplify testing, they make our tests more coupled with the production code, which may result in tests that do not evolve gracefully. The chapter discusses the pros and cons of mocks as well as when to use (or not use) them.

In chapter 7, I explain the difference between systems that are designed with testability in mind and systems that are not. We discuss several simple patterns that will help you write code that is easy to control and easy to observe (the dream of any developer when it comes to testing). This chapter is about software design as well as testing—as you will see, they have a strong relationship.

Chapter 8 discusses test-driven development (TDD): writing tests before production code. TDD is an extremely popular technique, especially among Agile practitioners. I recommend reading this chapter even if you are already familiar with TDD—I have a somewhat unusual view of how TDD should be applied and, in particular, cases where I think TDD does not make much difference.

In chapter 9, I go beyond unit tests and discuss integration and system tests. You will see how the techniques discussed in earlier chapters (such as domain and structural testing) can be directly applied to these tests. Writing integration and system tests requires much more code, so if we do not organize the code well, we can end up with a complex test suite. This chapter introduces several best practices for writing test suites that are solid and easy to maintain.

In chapter 10, I discuss test code best practices. Writing tests in an automated fashion is a fundamental part of our process. We also want to write code that is easy to understand and maintain. This chapter introduces best practices (what we want from our tests) and bad practices (what we do not want from our tests).

In chapter 11, I revisit some of the concepts covered in the book, reinforce important topics, and give you some final advice about where to go next.

What this book does not cover

This book does not cover software testing for specific technologies and environments, such as choosing a testing framework or how to test mobile applications, React applications, or distributed systems.

I am confident that all the practices and techniques I discuss will apply to any software system you are developing. This book can serve as the basis for any testing you need to do. However, each domain has its own testing practices and tools; so, after reading the book, you should look for additional resources that focus on the type of application you are building.

This book focuses on functional testing rather than non-functional testing (performance, scalability, and security). If your application requires that type of testing, as many do, I suggest that you look for specific resources on that topic.

About the code

This book uses Java to illustrate all the ideas and concepts. However, the code is written so that developers from other languages can follow it and understand the techniques.

Due to space constraints, the code listings do not include all the required imports and packages. However, you can find the complete source code on the book's website (www.manning.com/books/effective-software-testing) and on GitHub (https://github .com/effective-software-testing/code). The code was tested with Java 11, and I do not expect any trouble with newer versions.

I also have a dedicated website for this book at www.effective-software-testing.com, and I share fresh software testing content there. You can also subscribe to my free newsletter.

liveBook discussion forum

Purchase of *Effective Software Testing* includes free access to liveBook, Manning's online reading platform. Using liveBook's exclusive discussion features, you can attach comments to the book globally or to specific sections or paragraphs. It's a snap to make notes for yourself, ask and answer technical questions, and receive help from the author and other users. To access the forum, go to https://livebook.manning.com/ book/effective-software-testing/discussion. You can also learn more about Manning's forums and the rules of conduct at https://livebook.manning.com/discussion.

Manning's commitment to our readers is to provide a venue where a meaningful dialogue between individual readers and between readers and the author can take place. It is not a commitment to any specific amount of participation on the part of the author, whose contribution to the forum remains voluntary (and unpaid). We suggest you try asking the author some challenging questions lest his interest stray! The forum and the archives of previous discussions will be accessible from the publisher's website as long as the book is in print.

about the author

DR. MAURÍCIO ANICHE'S life's mission is to make software engineers better at what they do. He leads the Tech Academy of Adyen, a Dutch payment company that allows businesses to accept e-commerce, mobile, and point-of-sale payments.

Maurício is also an assistant professor of software engineering at Delft University of Technology in the Netherlands, where he conducts research on how to make developers more productive during testing and maintenance. His teaching efforts in software testing earned him the Computer Science Teacher of the Year 2021 award and the TU Delft Education Fellowship, a prestigious fellowship given to innovative lecturers.

Maurício holds MSc and PhD degrees in computer science from the University of São Paulo, Brazil. During his MSc, he co-founded Alura, one of the most popular e-learning platforms for software engineers in Brazil. He is the author of two Brazilian Portuguese books popular among Brazilian developers: *Test-Driven Development in the Real World* and *Object-Oriented Programming and SOLID for Ninjas*.

Maurício strongly believes that software engineering will soon become a more science-based field. One of his goals is to make sure that practitioners get to know what academics are up to and that academics understand the real challenges that practitioners face in their daily jobs.

about the cover illustration

The figure on the cover of *Effective Software Testing* is "Homme Mordwine," or "Mordwine Man," taken from a collection by Jacques Grasset de Saint-Sauveur, published in 1797. Each illustration is finely drawn and colored by hand.

In those days, it was easy to identify where people lived and what their trade or station in life was just by their dress. Manning celebrates the inventiveness and initiative of the computer business with book covers based on the rich diversity of regional culture centuries ago, brought back to life by pictures from collections such as this one.

Effective and systematic software testing

This chapter covers

- Understanding the importance of effective, systematic testing
- Recognizing why testing software is difficult and why bug-free systems do not exist
- Introducing the testing pyramid

The developer community no longer needs to argue about the importance of software testing. Every software developer understands that software failures may cause severe damage to businesses, people, or even society as a whole. And although software developers once were primarily responsible for building software systems, today they are also responsible for the quality of the software systems they produce.

Our community has produced several world-class tools to help developers test, including JUnit, AssertJ, Selenium, and jqwik. We have learned to use the process of writing tests to reflect on what programs need to do and get feedback about the code design (or class design, if you are using an object-oriented language). We have also learned that writing test code is challenging, and paying attention to test code quality is fundamental for the graceful evolution of the test suite. And finally, we know what the common bugs are and how to look for them.

But while developers have become very good at using testing tools, they rarely apply systematic testing techniques to explore and find bugs. Many practitioners argue that tests are a feedback tool and should be used mostly to help you develop. Although this is true (and I will show throughout this book how to listen to your test code), tests can also help you find bugs. After all, that is what software testing is all about: *finding bugs*!

Most developers do not enjoy writing tests. I have heard many reasons: writing production code is more fun and challenging, software testing is too time-consuming, we are paid to write production code, and so on. Developers also overestimate how much time they spend on testing, as Beller and colleagues found in a nice empirical study with hundreds of developers in 2019. My goal with this book is to convince you that (1) as a developer, it is *your* responsibility to ensure the quality of what you produce; (2) that tests are the only tools to help you with that responsibility; and (3) that if you follow a collection of techniques, you can test your code in an effective and systematic way.

Note the words I used: *effective* and *systematic*. Soon you will understand what I mean. But first, let me convince you of the necessity of tests.

1.1   Developers who test vs. developers who do not

It is late on Friday afternoon, and John is about to implement the last feature of the sprint. He is developing an agile software management system, and this final feature supports developers during planning poker.

> ### Planning poker
>
> *Planning poker* is a popular agile estimation technique. In a planning poker session, developers estimate the effort required to build a specific feature of the backlog. After the team discusses the feature, each developer gives an estimate: a number ranging from one to any number the team defines. Higher numbers mean more effort to implement the feature. For example, a developer who estimates that a feature is worth eight points expects it to take four times more effort than a developer who estimates the feature to be worth two points.
>
> The developer with the smallest estimate and the developer with the highest estimate explain their points of view to the other members of the team. After more discussion, the planning poker repeats until the team members agree about how much effort the feature will take. You can read more about the planning poker technique in *Kanban in Action* by Marcus Hammarberg and Joakim Sundén (2014).

John is about to implement the feature's core method. This method receives a list of estimates and produces, as output, the names of the two developers who should explain their points of view. This is what he plans to do:

Method: identifyExtremes

The method should receive a list of developers and their respective estimates and return the two developers with the most extreme estimates.

Input: A list of Estimates, each containing the name of the developer and their estimate

Output: A list of Strings containing the name of the developer with the lowest estimate and the name of the developer with the highest estimate

After a few minutes, John ends up with the code in the following listing.

Listing 1.1   The first PlanningPoker implementation

```java
public class PlanningPoker {
  public List<String> identifyExtremes(List<Estimate> estimates) {

    Estimate lowestEstimate = null;          Defines placeholder variables for
    Estimate highestEstimate = null;         the lowest and highest estimates

    for(Estimate estimate: estimates) {      If the current estimate is higher than the
                                             highest estimate seen so far, we replace the
      if(highestEstimate == null ||          previous highest estimate with the current one.
        estimate.getEstimate() > highestEstimate.getEstimate()) {
        highestEstimate = estimate;
      }
      else if(lowestEstimate == null ||
        estimate.getEstimate() < lowestEstimate.getEstimate()) {
        lowestEstimate = estimate;
      }
                                             If the current estimate is lower than the
                                             lowest estimate seen so far, we replace the
    }                                        previous lowest estimate with the current one.

    return Arrays.asList(                     Returns the developers
        lowestEstimate.getDeveloper(),        with the lowest and the
        highestEstimate.getDeveloper()        highest estimates
    );
  }
}
```

The logic is straightforward: the algorithm loops through all the developers in the list and keeps track of the highest and lowest estimates. It returns the names of the developers with the lowest and highest estimates. Both lowestEstimate and highestEstimate are initialized with null and later replaced by the first estimate within the for loop.

Generalizing from the code examples

Experienced developers may question some of my coding decisions. Maybe this Estimate class is not the best way to represent developers and their estimates. Maybe the logic to find the smallest and highest estimates is not the best. Maybe

> **(continued)**
>
> the `if` statements could be simpler. I agree. But my focus in this book is not object-oriented design or the best ways to write code: rather, I want to focus on how to test the code once it's written.
>
> The techniques I show you throughout this book will work regardless of how you implement your code. So, bear with me when you see a piece of code that you think you could do better. Try to generalize from my examples to your own code. In terms of complexity, I am sure you have encountered code like that in listing 1.1.

John is not a fan of (automated) software testing. As is commonly done by developers who do not automate their tests, John runs the finished application and tries a few inputs. You can see one of these trials in figure 1.1. John sees that given the input in the figure (the estimates of Ted, Barney, Lily, and Robin), the program produces the correct output.

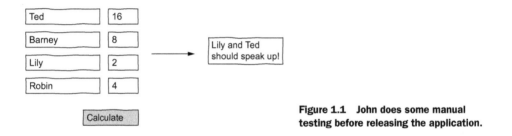

Figure 1.1   John does some manual testing before releasing the application.

John is happy with the results: his implementation worked from the beginning. He pushes his code, and the new feature is deployed automatically to customers. John goes home, ready for the weekend—but not even an hour later, the help desk starts to get e-mails from furious customers. The software is producing incorrect outputs!

John goes back to work, looks at the logs, and quickly identifies a case where the code fails. Can you find the input that makes the program crash? As illustrated in figure 1.2, if the developers' estimates are (by chance) in ascending order, the program throws a null pointer exception.

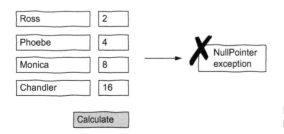

Figure 1.2   John finds a case where his implementation crashes.

It does not take John long to find the bug in his code: the extra `else` in listing 1.1. In the case of ascending estimates, that innocent `else` causes the program to never replace the `lowestEstimate` variable with the lowest estimate in the list, because the previous `if` is always evaluated to `true`.

John changes the `else if` to an `if`, as shown in listing 1.2. He then runs the program and tries it with the same inputs. Everything seems to work. The software is deployed again, and John returns home, finally ready to start the weekend.

Listing 1.2 The bug fix in the `PlanningPoker` implementation

```
if(highestEstimate == null ||
    estimate.getEstimate() > highestEstimate.getEstimate()) {
  highestEstimate = estimate;
}                                                         We fixed the bug here
                                                          by replacing the "else
if(lowestEstimate == null ||               ⊲─┘           if" with an "if".
    estimate.getEstimate() < lowestEstimate.getEstimate()) {
  lowestEstimate = estimate;
}
```

You may be thinking, "This was a very easy bug to spot! I would never make such a mistake!" That may be true. But in practice, it is hard to keep tabs on everything that may happen in our code. And, of course, it is even more difficult when the code is complex. Bugs happen not because we are bad programmers but because we program complicated things (and because computers are more precise than humans can be).

Let's generalize from John's case. John is a very good and experienced developer. But as a human, he makes mistakes. John performed some manual testing before releasing his code, but manual testing can only go so far, and it takes too long if we need to explore many cases. Also, John did not follow a systematic approach to testing—he just tried the first few inputs that came to mind. Ad hoc methods like "follow your instincts" may lead us to forget corner cases. John would greatly benefit from (1) a more *systematic* approach for deriving tests, to reduce the chances of forgetting a case; and (2) *test automation*, so he does not have to spend time running tests manually.

Now, let's replay the same story, but with Eleanor instead of John. Eleanor is also a very good and experienced software developer. She is highly skilled in software testing and only deploys once she has developed a strong test suite for all the code she writes.

Suppose Eleanor writes the same code as John (listing 1.1). She does not do test-driven development (TDD), but she does proper testing after writing her code.

NOTE In a nutshell, TDD means writing the tests before the implementation. Not using TDD is not a problem, as we discuss in chapter 8.

Eleanor thinks about what the `identifyExtremes` method does. Let's say her reasoning is the same as John's. She first focuses on the inputs of this method: a list of `Estimates`. She knows that whenever a method receives a list, there are several cases to try: a null list, an empty list, a list with one element, and a list with multiple elements. How does she know that? She read this book!

Eleanor reflects on the first three cases (null, empty, single element), considering how this method will fit in with the rest of the system. The current implementation would crash in these cases! So, she decides the method should reject such inputs. She goes back to the production code and adds some validation code as follows.

Listing 1.3 Adding validation to prevent invalid inputs

```java
public List<String> identifyExtremes(List<Estimate> estimates) {

  if(estimates == null) {                              ← The list of estimates cannot be null.
    throw new IllegalArgumentException("estimates cannot be null");
  }
  if(estimates.size() <= 1) {                          ←
    throw new IllegalArgumentException("there has to be more than 1
      estimate in the list");
  }                                                    The list of estimates should
                                                       contain more than one element.

  // continues here...
}
```

Although Eleanor is sure that the method now handles these invalid inputs correctly (it is clear in the code), she decides to write an automated test that formalizes the test case. This test will also prevent future regressions: later, if another developer does not understand why the assertions are in the code and removes them, the test will ensure that the mistake is noticed. The following listing shows the three test cases (note that, for now, I am making the tests verbose so they are easy to understand).

Listing 1.4 Test cases for null, an empty list, and a one-element list

```java
public class PlanningPokerTest {
  @Test                                   Asserts that an exception
  void rejectNullInput() {                happens when we call
    assertThatThrownBy(                   the method
      () -> new PlanningPoker().identifyExtremes(null)         Asserts that this
    ).isInstanceOf(IllegalArgumentException.class);    ←       assertion is an
  }                                                            IllegalArgumentException

  @Test                                                 Similar to the earlier
  void rejectEmptyList() {                              test, ensures that the
                                                        program throws an
    assertThatThrownBy(() -> {                          exception if an empty
      List<Estimate> emptyList = Collections.emptyList();   list of estimates is
      new PlanningPoker().identifyExtremes(emptyList);   passed as input
    }).isInstanceOf(IllegalArgumentException.class);
  }

  @Test
  void rejectSingleEstimate() {
```

```
  assertThatThrownBy(() -> {
    List<Estimate> list = Arrays.asList(new Estimate("Eleanor", 1));
    new PlanningPoker().identifyExtremes(list);
  }).isInstanceOf(IllegalArgumentException.class);
  }
}
```
**Ensures that the program throws an exception
if a list with a single estimate is passed**

The three test cases have the same structure. They all invoke the method under test with an invalid input and check that the method throws an `IllegalArgumentException`. This is common assertion behavior in Java. The `assertThatThrownBy` method provided by the AssertJ library (https://assertj.github.io/doc/) enables us to assert that the method throws an exception. Also note the `isInstanceOf` method, which allows us to assert that a specific type of exception is thrown.

If you are not familiar with Java, the lambda syntax `() ->` is basically an inline code block. This may be clearer in the second test, `rejectEmptyList()`, where `{` and `}` delimit the block. The testing framework will run this block of code and, if an exception happens, will check the type of the exception. If the exception type matches, the test will pass. Note that this test fails if the exception is not thrown—after all, having an exception is the behavior we expect in this case.

> **NOTE** If you are new to automated tests, this code may make you nervous. Testing exceptions involves some extra code, and it is also an "upside-down" test that passes if the exception is thrown! Don't worry—the more you see test methods, the better you will understand them.

With the invalid inputs handled, Eleanor now focuses on the *good weather* tests: that is, tests that exercise the valid behavior of the program. Looking back at Eleanor's test cases, this means passing lists of estimates with more than one element. Deciding how many elements to pass is always challenging, but Eleanor sees at least two cases: a list with exactly two elements and a list with more than two elements. Why two? A list with two elements is the smallest for which the method should work. There is a boundary between a list with one element (which does not work) and two elements (which does work). Eleanor knows that *bugs love boundaries*, so she decides to also have a dedicated test for it, illustrated in listing 1.5.

This resembles a more traditional test case. We define the input value we want to pass to the method under test (in this case, a list with two estimates); we invoke the method under test with that input; and, finally, we assert that the list returns the two developers we expect.

Listing 1.5　Test case for a list with two elements

```
@Test
void twoEstimates() {
  List<Estimate> list = Arrays.asList(          ⟵──┐  Declares a
      new Estimate("Mauricio", 10),                 │  list with two
      new Estimate("Frank", 5)                      │  estimates
  );
```

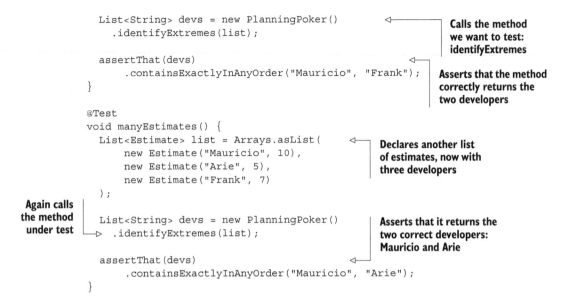

```
          List<String> devs = new PlanningPoker()
            .identifyExtremes(list);
```
Calls the method
we want to test:
identifyExtremes

```
          assertThat(devs)
            .containsExactlyInAnyOrder("Mauricio", "Frank");
       }
```
Asserts that the method
correctly returns the
two developers

```
       @Test
       void manyEstimates() {
          List<Estimate> list = Arrays.asList(
              new Estimate("Mauricio", 10),
              new Estimate("Arie", 5),
              new Estimate("Frank", 7)
          );
```
Declares another list
of estimates, now with
three developers

Again calls
the method
under test
```
          List<String> devs = new PlanningPoker()
            .identifyExtremes(list);
```
Asserts that it returns the
two correct developers:
Mauricio and Arie

```
          assertThat(devs)
            .containsExactlyInAnyOrder("Mauricio", "Arie");
       }
```

Before we continue, I want to highlight that Eleanor has five passing tests, but the else if bug is still there. Eleanor does not know about it yet (or, rather, has not found it). However, she knows that whenever lists are given as input, the order of the elements may affect the algorithm. Therefore, she decides to write a test that provides the method with estimates in random order. For this test, Eleanor does not use example-based testing (tests that pick one specific input out of many possible inputs). Rather, she goes for a property-based test, as shown in the following listing.

Listing 1.6 Property-based testing for multiple estimates

Makes this method a property-based
test instead of a traditional JUnit test

The list that the framework provides will contain
randomly generated estimates. This list is generated
by the method with the name that matches the
string "estimates" (declared later in the code).

```
       @Property
       void inAnyOrder(@ForAll("estimates") List<Estimate> estimates) {
```

Shuffles
the list to
ensure that
the order
does not
matter
```
          estimates.add(new Estimate("MrLowEstimate", 1));
          estimates.add(new Estimate("MsHighEstimate", 100));

          Collections.shuffle(estimates);

          List<String> dev = new PlanningPoker().identifyExtremes(estimates);
```
Ensures that the
generated list contains
the known lowest and
highest estimates

```
          assertThat(dev)
            .containsExactlyInAnyOrder("MrLowEstimate", "MsHighEstimate");
       }
```
Method that provides a random list of
estimates for the property-based test
```
       @Provide
       Arbitrary<List<Estimate>> estimates() {
```

Asserts that regardless of the list of estimates, the
outcome is always MrLowEstimate and MsHighEstimate

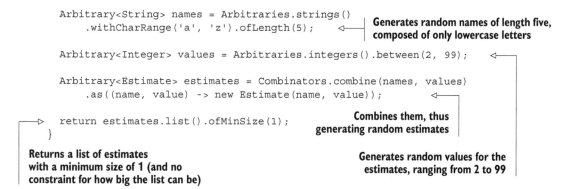

```
Arbitrary<String> names = Arbitraries.strings()
    .withCharRange('a', 'z').ofLength(5);
```
← Generates random names of length five, composed of only lowercase letters

```
Arbitrary<Integer> values = Arbitraries.integers().between(2, 99);
```
←

```
Arbitrary<Estimate> estimates = Combinators.combine(names, values)
    .as((name, value) -> new Estimate(name, value));
```
←

Combines them, thus generating random estimates

```
    return estimates.list().ofMinSize(1);
}
```

Returns a list of estimates with a minimum size of 1 (and no constraint for how big the list can be)

Generates random values for the estimates, ranging from 2 to 99

In property-based testing, our goal is to assert a specific property. We discuss this in more detail later in chapter 5, but here is a short explanation. The `estimates()` method returns random `Estimates`. We define that an estimate has a random name (for simplicity, of length five) and a random estimate that varies from 2 to 99. The method feeds lists of `Estimates` back to the test method. The lists all have at least one element. The test method then adds two more estimates: the lowest and the highest. Since our list only has values between 2 and 99, we ensure the lowest and highest by using the values 1 and 100, respectively. We then shuffle the list so order does not matter. Finally, we assert that no matter what the list of estimates contains, `MrLowEstimate` and `MsHighEstimate` are always returned.

The property-based testing framework runs the same test 100 times, each time with a different combination of estimates. If the test fails for one of the random inputs, the framework stops the test and reports the input that broke the code. In this book, we use the jqwik library (https://jqwik.net), but you can easily find a property-based testing framework for your language.

To Eleanor's surprise, when she runs this property-based test, it fails! Based on the example provided by the test, she finds that the `else if` is wrong and replaces it with a simple `if`. The test now passes.

Eleanor decides to delete the `manyEstimates` test, as the new property-based testing replaces it. Whether to delete a duplicate test is a personal decision; you could argue that the simple example-based test is easier to understand than the property-based test. And having simple tests that quickly explain the behavior of the production code is always beneficial, even if it means having a little duplication in your test suite.

Next, Eleanor remembers that in lists, duplicate elements can also break the code. In this case, this would mean developers with the same estimate. She did not consider this case in her implementation. She reflects on how this will affect the method, consults with the product owner, and decides that the program should return the duplicate developer who appears first in the list.

Eleanor notices that the program already has this behavior. Still, she decides to formalize it in the test shown in listing 1.7. The test is straightforward: it creates a list of estimates in which two developers give the same lowest estimate and two other developers give the same highest estimate. The test then calls the method under test and ensures that the two developers who appear earlier in the list are returned.

Listing 1.7 Ensuring that the first duplicate developer is returned

```
@Test
void developersWithSameEstimates() {
  List<Estimate> list = Arrays.asList(        ⬅  Declares a list of estimates
      new Estimate("Mauricio", 10),              with repeated estimate
      new Estimate("Arie", 5),                   values
      new Estimate("Andy", 10),
      new Estimate("Frank", 7),
      new Estimate("Annibale", 5)
  );
  List<String> devs = new PlanningPoker().identifyExtremes(list);

  assertThat(devs)                            ⬅  Asserts that whenever there are
    .containsExactlyInAnyOrder("Mauricio", "Arie");   repeated estimates, the developer
}                                                     who appears earlier in the list is
                                                      returned by the method
```

But, Eleanor thinks, what if the list only contains developers with the same estimates? This is another corner case that emerges when we systematically reflect on inputs that are lists. Lists with zero elements, one element, many elements, different values, and identical values are all common test cases to engineer whenever lists are used as inputs.

She talks to the product owner again. They are surprised that they did not see this corner case coming, and they request that in this case, the code should return an empty list. Eleanor changes the implementation to reflect the new expected behavior by adding an `if` statement near the end of the method, as in the following listing.

Listing 1.8 Returning an empty list if all estimates are the same

```
public List<String> identifyExtremes(List<Estimate> estimates) {

  if(estimates == null) {
    throw new IllegalArgumentException("Estimates
    ⮡ cannot be null");
  }
  if(estimates.size() <= 1) {
    throw new IllegalArgumentException("There has to be
    ⮡ more than 1 estimate in the list");
  }

  Estimate lowestEstimate = null;
  Estimate highestEstimate = null;

  for(Estimate estimate: estimates) {
    if(highestEstimate == null ||
        estimate.getEstimate() > highestEstimate.getEstimate()) {
      highestEstimate = estimate;
    }
```

```
        if (lowestEstimate == null ||
            estimate.getEstimate() < lowestEstimate.getEstimate()) {
            lowestEstimate = estimate;
        }
    }

    if (lowestEstimate.equals(highestEstimate))
        return Collections.emptyList();

    return Arrays.asList(
        lowestEstimate.getDeveloper(),
        highestEstimate.getDeveloper()
    );
}
```

◁─── **If the lowest and highest estimate objects are the same, all developers have the same estimate, and therefore we return an empty list.**

Eleanor then writes a test to ensure that her implementation is correct.

Listing 1.9 Testing for an empty list if the estimates are all the same

```
@Test
void allDevelopersWithTheSameEstimate() {
    List<Estimate> list = Arrays.asList(
        new Estimate("Mauricio", 10),
        new Estimate("Arie", 10),
        new Estimate("Andy", 10),
        new Estimate("Frank", 10),
        new Estimate("Annibale", 10)
    );
    List<String> devs = new PlanningPoker().identifyExtremes(list);

    assertThat(devs).isEmpty();
}
```

◁─── **Declares a list of estimates, this time with all the developers having the same estimate**

◁─── **Asserts that the resulting list is empty**

Eleanor is now satisfied with the test suite she has engineered from the requirements. As a next step, she decides to focus on the code itself. Maybe there is something that no tests are exercising. To help her in this analysis, she runs the code coverage tool that comes with her IDE (figure 1.3).

All the lines and branches of the code are covered. Eleanor knows that tools are not perfect, so she examines the code for other cases. She cannot find any, so she concludes that the code is tested enough. She pushes the code and goes home for the weekend. The code goes directly to the customers. On Monday morning, Eleanor is happy to see that monitoring does not report a single crash.

1.2 *Effective software testing for developers*

I hope the difference is clear between the two developers in the previous section. Eleanor used automated tests and systematically and effectively engineered test cases. She broke down the requirements into small parts and used them to derive test cases, applying a technique called *domain testing*. When she was done with the specification,

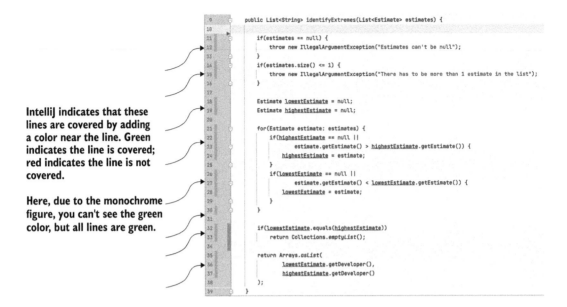

```
 9       public List<String> identifyExtremes(List<Estimate> estimates) {
10
11           if(estimates == null) {
12               throw new IllegalArgumentException("Estimates can't be null");
13           }
14           if(estimates.size() <= 1) {
15               throw new IllegalArgumentException("There has to be more than 1 estimate in the list");
16           }
17
18           Estimate lowestEstimate = null;
19           Estimate highestEstimate = null;
20
21           for(Estimate estimate: estimates) {
22               if(highestEstimate == null ||
23                       estimate.getEstimate() > highestEstimate.getEstimate()) {
24                   highestEstimate = estimate;
25               }
26               if(lowestEstimate == null ||
27                       estimate.getEstimate() < lowestEstimate.getEstimate()) {
28                   lowestEstimate = estimate;
29               }
30           }
31
32           if(lowestEstimate.equals(highestEstimate))
33               return Collections.emptyList();
34
35           return Arrays.asList(
36                   lowestEstimate.getDeveloper(),
37                   highestEstimate.getDeveloper()
38           );
39       }
```

IntelliJ indicates that these lines are covered by adding a color near the line. Green indicates the line is covered; red indicates the line is not covered.

Here, due to the monochrome figure, you can't see the green color, but all lines are green.

Figure 1.3   The result of the code coverage analysis done by my IDE, IntelliJ. All lines are covered.

she focused on the code; and through *structural testing* (or code coverage), she evaluated whether the current test cases were sufficient. For some test cases, Eleanor wrote *example-based tests* (that is, she picked a single data point for a test). For one specific case, she used *property-based testing*, as it helped her better explore possible bugs in the code. Finally, she reflected frequently about the *contracts* and *pre-* and *post-conditions* of the method she was devising (although in the end, she implemented a set of validation checks and not pre-conditions per se; we discuss the differences between contracts and validation in chapter 4).

This is what I call *effective and systematic software testing for developers*. In the remainder of this chapter, I explain how software developers can perform effective testing together with their development activities. Before we dive into the specific techniques, I describe effective testing within the development processes and how testing techniques complement each other. I discuss the different types of tests and which ones you should focus on. Finally, I illustrate why software testing is so difficult.

1.2.1   *Effective testing in the development process*

In this book, I propose a straightforward flow for developers who apply effective and systematic testing. First, we implement a feature, using tests to facilitate and guide development. Once we are reasonably happy with the feature or small unit we've coded, we dive into effective and systematic testing to ensure that it works as expected (that is, we test to find bugs). Figure 1.4 illustrates the development workflow in more detail; let's walk through it:

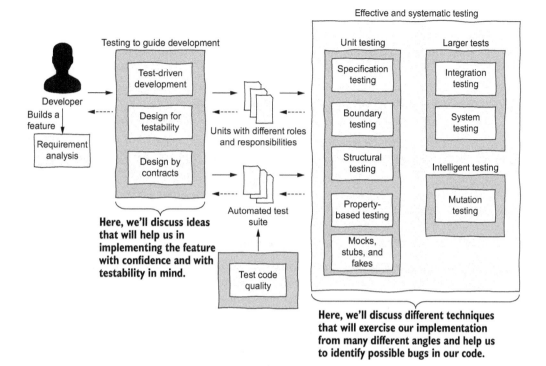

Figure 1.4 The workflow of a developer who applies effective and systematic testing. The arrows indicate the iterative nature of the process; developers may go back and forth between the different techniques as they learn more about the program under development and test.

1 Feature development often starts with a developer receiving some sort of *requirement*. Requirements are often in the form of natural language and may follow a specific format, such as Unified Modeling Language (UML) use cases or agile user stories. After building up some understanding (that is, *requirement analysis*), the developer starts writing code.

2 To guide the development of the feature, the developer performs short *test-driven development* (TDD) cycles. These cycles give the developer rapid feedback about whether the code they just wrote makes sense. They also support the developer through the many refactorings that occur when a new feature is being implemented.

3 Requirements are often large and complex and are rarely implemented by a single class or method. The developer creates several *units* (classes and methods) with different *contracts*, and they collaborate and together form the required functionality. Writing classes such that they're easy to test is challenging, and the developer must design with *testability* in mind.

4 Once the developer is satisfied with the units they've created and believes the requirement is complete, they shift to testing. The first step is to exercise each

new unit. *Domain testing, boundary testing,* and *structural testing* are the go-to techniques.

5 Some parts of the system may require the developer to write *larger tests* (integration or system tests). To devise larger test cases, the developer uses the same three techniques—domain testing, boundary testing, and structural testing—but looking at larger parts of the software system.

6 When the developer has engineered test cases using the various techniques, they apply automated, *intelligent testing* tools to look for tests that humans are not good at spotting. Popular techniques include *test case generation, mutation testing,* and *static analysis.* In this book, we cover *mutation testing.*

7 Finally, after this rigorous testing, the developer feels comfortable releasing the feature.

1.2.2 Effective testing as an iterative process

While the previous description may sound like a sequential/waterfall process, it is more iterative. A developer may be rigorously testing a class and suddenly notice that a coding decision they made a few hours ago was not ideal. They then go back and redesign the code. They may be performing TDD cycles and realize the requirement is unclear about something. The developer then goes back to the requirement analysis to better grasp the expectations. Quite commonly, while testing, the developer finds a bug. They go back to the code, fix it, and continue testing. Or the developer may have implemented only half of the feature, but they feel it would be more productive to rigorously test it now than to continue the implementation.

The development workflow I propose throughout this book is not meant to restrain you. Feel free to go back and forth between techniques or change the order in which you apply them. In practice, you have to find what works best for you and makes you the most productive.

1.2.3 Focusing on development and then on testing

I find it liberating to focus separately on developing and testing. When I am coding a feature, I do not want to be distracted by obscure corner cases. If I think of one, I take notes so I do not forget to test it later. However, I prefer to focus all my energy on the business rules I am implementing and, at the same time, ensure that the code is easy for future developers to maintain.

Once I am finished with the coding decisions, I focus on testing. First I follow the different techniques as if I were working my way down a systematic checklist. As you saw in the example with Eleanor, she did not have to think much about what to exercise when the method received a list: she responded as if she had a checklist that said "null, empty list, one element, many elements." Only then do I use my creativity and domain knowledge to exercise other cases I find relevant.

1.2.4 The myth of "correctness by design"

Now that you have a clearer picture of what I mean by effective and systematic software testing, let me debunk a myth. There is a perception among software developers that if you design code in a simple way, it will not have bugs, as if the secret of bug-free code is simplicity.

Empirical research in software engineering has repeatedly shown that simple, non-smelly code is less prone to defects than complex code (see, for example, the 2006 paper by Shatnawi and Li). However, simplicity is far from enough. It is naive to believe that testing can be fully replaced by simplicity. The same is true for "correctness by design": designing your code well does not mean you avoid all possible bugs.

1.2.5 The cost of testing

You may be thinking that forcing developers to apply rigorous testing may be too costly. Figure 1.4 shows the many techniques developers have to apply if they follow the flow I am proposing. It is true: testing software properly is more work than not doing so. Let me convince you why it is worth it:

- The cost of bugs that happen in production often outweighs the cost of prevention (as shown by Boehm and Papaccio, 1988). Think of a popular web shop and how much it would cost the shop if the payment application goes down for 30 minutes due to a bug that could have been easily prevented via testing.
- Teams that produce many bugs tend to waste time in an eternal loop where developers write bugs, customers (or dedicated QAs) find the bugs, developers fix the bugs, customers find a different set of bugs, and so on.
- Practice is key. Once developers are used to engineering test cases, they can do it much faster.

1.2.6 The meaning of effective and systematic

I have been using two words to describe how I expect a developer to test: *effectively* and *systematically*. Being *effective* means we focus on writing the right tests. Software testing is all about trade-offs. Testers want to maximize the number of bugs they find while minimizing the effort required to find the bugs. How do we achieve this? By knowing what to test.

All the techniques I present in this book have a clear beginning (what to test) and a clear end (when to stop). Of course, I do not mean your systems will be bug-free if you follow these techniques. As a community, we still do not know how to build bug-free systems. But I can confidently say that the number of bugs will be reduced, hopefully to tolerable levels.

Being *systematic* means that for a given piece of code, any developer should come up with the same test suite. Testing often happens in an ad hoc manner. Developers engineer the test cases that come to mind. It is common to see two developers developing different test suites for the same program. We should be able to systematize our processes to reduce the dependency on the developer who is doing the job.

I understand and agree with the argument that software development is a creative process that cannot be executed by robots. I believe that humans will always be in the loop when it comes to building software; but why not let developers focus on what requires creativity? A lot of software testing can be systematized, and that is what you will see throughout this book.

1.2.7   *The role of test automation*

Automation is key for an effective testing process. Every test case we devise here is later automated via a testing framework such as JUnit. Let me clearly distinguish between test case *design* and test case *execution*. Once a test case is written, a framework runs it and shows reports, failures, and so on. This is all that these frameworks do. Their role is very important, but the real challenge in software testing is not writing JUnit code but designing decent test cases that may reveal bugs. Designing test cases is mostly a human activity and is what this book primarily focuses on.

> **NOTE**   If you are not familiar with JUnit, it should not be a problem, because the examples in the book are easy to read. But as I mention throughout the book, the more familiar you are with the testing framework, the better.

In the chapters where I discuss testing techniques, we first engineer the test cases and only later automate them with JUnit code. In real life, you may mingle both activities; but in this book, I decided to keep them separate so you can see the difference. This also means the book does not talk much about tooling. JUnit and other testing frameworks are powerful tools, and I recommend reading the manuals and books that focus on them.

1.3   *Principles of software testing (or, why testing is so difficult)*

A simplistic view of software testing is that if we want our systems to be well tested, we must keep adding tests until we have enough. I wish it were that simple. Ensuring that programs have no bugs is virtually impossible, and developers should understand why that is the case.

In this section, I discuss some principles that make our lives as software testers more difficult and what we can do to mitigate them. These principles were inspired by those presented in the International Software Testing Qualifications Board (ISTQB) book by Black, Veenendaal, and Graham (2012).

1.3.1   *Exhaustive testing is impossible*

We do not have the resources to completely test our programs. Testing all possible situations in a software system might be impossible even if we had unlimited resources. Imagine a software system with "only" 300 different flags or configuration settings (such as the Linux operating system). Each flag can be set to true or false (Boolean) and can be set independently from the others. The software system behaves differently according to the configured combination of flags. Having two possible values for each of the 300 flags gives 2^{300} combinations that need to be tested. For comparison, the number of atoms in the universe is estimated to be 10^{80}. In other words, this software system has more possible combinations to be tested than the universe has atoms.

Knowing that testing everything is not possible, we have to choose (or prioritize) what to test. This is why I emphasize the need for *effective tests*. The book discusses techniques that will help you identify the relevant test cases.

1.3.2   *Knowing when to stop testing*

Prioritizing which tests to engineer is difficult. Creating too few tests may leave us with a software system that does not behave as intended (that is, it's full of bugs). On the other hand, creating test after test without proper consideration can lead to ineffective tests (and cost time and money). As I said before, our goal should always be to maximize the number of bugs found while minimizing the resources we spend on finding those bugs. To that aim, I will discuss different adequacy criteria that will help you decide when to stop testing.

1.3.3   *Variability is important (the pesticide paradox)*

There is no silver bullet in software testing. In other words, there is no single testing technique that you can always apply to find all possible bugs. Different testing techniques help reveal different bugs. If you use only a single technique, you may find all the bugs you can with that technique and no more.

A more concrete example is a team that relies solely on unit testing techniques. The team may find all the bugs that can be captured at the unit test level, but they may miss bugs that only occur at the integration level.

This is known as the *pesticide paradox*: every method you use to prevent or find bugs leaves a residue of subtler bugs against which those methods are ineffectual. Testers must use different testing strategies to minimize the number of bugs left in the software. When studying the various testing strategies presented in this book, keep in mind that combining them all is probably a wise decision.

1.3.4   *Bugs happen in some places more than others*

As I said earlier, given that exhaustive testing is impossible, software testers have to prioritize the tests they perform. When prioritizing test cases, note that bugs are not uniformly distributed. Empirically, our community has observed that some components present more bugs than others. For example, a `Payment` module may require more rigorous testing than a `Marketing` module.

As a real-world example, take Schröter and colleagues (2006), who studied bugs in the Eclipse projects. They observed that 71% of files that imported compiler packages had to be fixed later. In other words, such files were more prone to defects than the other files in the system. As a software developer, you may have to watch and learn from your software system. Data other than the source code may help you prioritize your testing efforts.

1.3.5   *No matter what testing you do, it will never be perfect or enough*

As Dijkstra used to say, "Program testing can be used to show the presence of bugs, but never to show their absence." In other words, while we may find more bugs by simply testing more, our test suites, however large they may be, will never ensure that the software system is 100% bug-free. They will only ensure that the cases we test for behave as expected.

This is an important principle to understand, as it will help you set your (and your customers') expectations. Bugs will still happen, but (hopefully) the money you pay for testing and prevention will pay off by allowing only the less impactful bugs to go through. "You cannot test everything" is something we must accept.

> **NOTE**   Although monitoring is not a major topic in this book, I recommend investing in monitoring systems. Bugs will happen, and you need to be sure you find them the second they manifest in production. That is why tools such as the ELK stack (Elasticsearch, Logstash, and Kibana; www.elastic.co) are becoming so popular. This approach is sometimes called *testing in production* (Wilsenach, 2017).

1.3.6   *Context is king*

The context plays an important role in how we devise test cases. For example, devising test cases for a mobile app is very different from devising test cases for a web application or software used in a rocket. In other words, testing is context-dependent.

Most of this book tries to be agnostic about context. The techniques I discuss (domain testing, structural testing, property-based testing, and so on) can be applied in any type of software system. Nevertheless, if you are working on a mobile app, I recommend reading a book dedicated to mobile testing after you read this one. I give some context-specific tips in chapter 9, where I discuss larger tests.

1.3.7   *Verification is not validation*

Finally, note that a software system that works flawlessly but is of no use to its users is not a good software system. As a reviewer of this book said to me, "Coverage of code is easy to measure; coverage of requirements is another matter." Software testers face this *absence-of-errors fallacy* when they focus solely on verification and not on validation.

A popular saying that may help you remember the difference is, "Verification is about having the system right; validation is about having the right system." This book primarily covers verification techniques. In other words, I do not focus on techniques to, for example, collaborate with customers to understand their real needs; rather, I present techniques to ensure that, given a specific requirement, the software system implements it correctly.

Verification and validation can walk hand in hand. In this chapter's example about the planning poker algorithm, this was what happened when Eleanor imagined all the developers estimating the same effort. The product owner did not think of this case. A systematic testing approach can help you identify corner cases that even the product experts did not envision.

1.4 The testing pyramid, and where we should focus

Whenever we talk about pragmatic testing, one of the first decisions we need to make is the level at which to test the code. By a test *level*, I mean the *unit, integration*, or *system* level. Let's quickly look at each of them.

1.4.1 Unit testing

In some situations, the tester's goal is to test a single feature of the software, purposefully ignoring the other units of the system. This is basically what we saw in the planning poker example. The goal was to test the `identifyExtremes()` method and nothing else. Of course, we cared about how this method would interact with the rest of the system, and that is why we tested its contracts. However, we did not test it together with the other pieces of the system.

When we test units in isolation, we are doing *unit testing*. This test level offers the following advantages:

- *Unit tests are fast.* A unit test usually takes just a couple of milliseconds to execute. Fast tests allow us to test huge portions of the system in a small amount of time. Fast, automated test suites give us constant feedback. This fast safety net makes us feel more comfortable and confident in performing evolutionary changes to the software system we are working on.
- *Unit tests are easy to control.* A unit test tests the software by giving certain parameters to a method and then comparing the return value of this method to the expected result. These input values and the expected result value are easy to adapt or modify in the test. Again, look at the `identifyExtremes()` example and how easy it was to provide different inputs and assert its output.
- *Unit tests are easy to write.* They do not require a complicated setup or additional work. A single unit is also often cohesive and small, making the tester's job easier. Tests become much more complicated when we have databases, frontends, and web services all together.

As for disadvantages, the following should be considered:

- *Unit tests lack reality.* A software system is rarely composed of a single class. The large number of classes in a system and their interaction can cause the system to behave differently in its real application than in the unit tests. Therefore, unit tests do not perfectly represent the real execution of a software system.
- *Some types of bugs are not caught.* Some types of bugs cannot be caught at the unit test level; they only happen in the integration of the different components

(which are not exercised in a pure unit test). Think of a web application that has a complex UI: you may have tested the backend and the frontend thoroughly, but a bug may only reveal itself when the backend and frontend are put together. Or imagine multithreaded code: everything may work at the unit level, but bugs may appear once threads are running together.

Interestingly, one of the hardest challenges in unit testing is to define what constitutes a unit. A unit can be one method or multiple classes. Here is a definition for unit testing that I like, given by Roy Osherove (2009): "A unit test is an automated piece of code that invokes a unit of work in the system. And a unit of work can span a single method, a whole class or multiple classes working together to achieve one single logical purpose that can be verified."

For me, unit testing means testing a (small) set of classes that have no dependency on external systems (such as databases or web services) or anything else I do not fully control. When I unit-test a set of classes together, the number of classes tends to be small. This is primarily because testing many classes together may be too difficult, not because this isn't a unit test.

But what if a class I want to test depends on another class that talks to, for example, a database (figure 1.5)? This is where unit testing becomes more complicated. Here is a short answer: if I want to test a class, and this class depends on another class that depends on a database, I will simulate the database class. In other words, I will create a stub that acts like the original class but is much simpler and easier to use during testing. We will dive into this specific problem in chapter 6, where we discuss mocks.

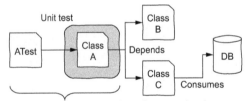

When unit testing class A, our focus is on testing A, as isolated as possible from the rest! If A depends on other classes, we have to decide whether to simulate them or to make our unit test a bit bigger.

Figure 1.5   Unit testing. Our goal is to test one unit of the system that is as isolated as possible from the rest of the system.

1.4.2   Integration testing

Unit tests focus on the smallest parts of the system. However, testing components in isolation sometimes is not enough. This is especially true when the code under test goes beyond the system's borders and uses other (often external) components. Integration testing is the test level we use to test the integration between our code and external parties.

Let's consider a real-world example. Software systems commonly rely on database systems. To communicate with the database, developers often create a class whose only responsibility is to interact with this external component (think of Data Access Object [DAO] classes). These DAOs may contain complicated SQL code. Thus, a tester feels the need to test the SQL queries. The tester does not want to test the entire system, only the integration between the DAO class and the database. The tester also does not want to test the DAO class in complete isolation. After all, the best way to know whether a SQL query works is to submit it to the database and see what the database returns.

This is an example of an integration test. Integration testing aims to test multiple components of a system together, focusing on the interactions between them instead of testing the system as a whole (see figure 1.6). Are they communicating correctly? What happens if component A sends message X to component B? Do they still present correct behavior?

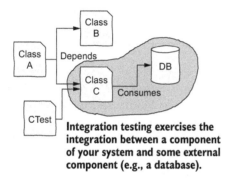
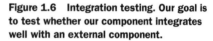

Integration testing exercises the integration between a component of your system and some external component (e.g., a database).

Figure 1.6   Integration testing. Our goal is to test whether our component integrates well with an external component.

Integration testing focuses on two parts: our component and the external component. Writing such a test is less complicated than writing a test that goes through the entire system and includes components we do not care about.

Compared to unit testing, integration tests are more difficult to write. In the example, setting up a database for the test requires effort. Tests that involve databases generally need to use an isolated instance of the database just for testing purposes, update the database schema, put the database into a state expected by the test by adding or removing rows, and clean everything afterward. The same effort is involved in other types of integration tests: web services, file reads and writes, and so on. We will discuss writing integration tests effectively in chapter 9.

1.4.3   System testing

To get a more realistic view of the software and thus perform more realistic tests, we should run the entire software system with all its databases, frontend apps, and other components. When we test the system in its entirety, instead of testing small parts of the system in isolation, we are doing system testing (see figure 1.7). We do not care how the system works from the inside; we do not care if it was developed in Java or

Ruby, or whether it uses a relational database. We only care that, given input X, the system will provide output Y.

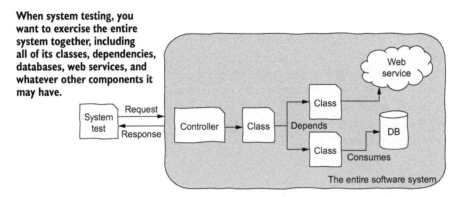

When system testing, you want to exercise the entire system together, including all of its classes, dependencies, databases, web services, and whatever other components it may have.

Figure 1.7 System testing. Our goal is to test the entire system and its components.

The obvious advantage of system testing is *how realistic the tests are.* Our final customers will not run the identifyExtremes() method in isolation. Rather, they will visit a web page, submit a form, and see the results. System tests exercise the system in that precise manner. The more realistic the tests are (that is, when the tests perform actions similar to the final user), the more confident we can be about the whole system.

System testing does, however, have its downsides:

- System tests are often *slow* compared to unit tests. Imagine everything a system test has to do, including starting and running the entire system with all its components. The test also has to interact with the real application, and actions may take a few seconds. Imagine a test that starts a container with a web application and another container with a database. It then submits an HTTP request to a web service exposed by this web app. This web service retrieves data from the database and writes a JSON response to the test. This obviously takes more time than running a simple unit test, which has virtually no dependencies.

- System tests are also *harder to write.* Some of the components (such as databases) may require a complex setup before they can be used in a testing scenario. Think of connecting, authenticating, and making sure the database has all the data required by that test case. Additional code is required just to automate the tests.

- System tests are more *prone to flakiness.* A *flaky* test presents erratic behavior: if you run it, it may pass or fail for the same configuration. Flaky tests are an important problem for software development teams, and we discuss this issue in chapter 10. Imagine a system test that exercises a web app. After the tester clicks a button, the HTTP POST request to the web app takes half a second longer than usual (due to small variations we often do not control in real-life scenarios). The test does not expect this and thus fails. The test is executed again, the web app takes the usual time to respond, and the test passes. Many uncertainties in a system test can lead to unexpected behavior.

1.4.4   *When to use each test level*

With a clear understanding of the different test levels and their benefits, we have to decide whether to invest more in unit testing or system testing and determine which components should be tested via unit testing and which components should be tested via system testing. A wrong decision may have a considerable impact on the system's quality: a wrong level may cost too many resources and may not find sufficient bugs. As you may have guessed, the best answer here is, "It depends."

Some developers—including me—favor unit testing over other test levels. This does not mean such developers do not do integration or system testing; but whenever possible, they push testing toward the unit test level. A pyramid is often used to illustrate this idea, as shown in figure 1.8. The size of the slice in the pyramid represents the relative number of tests to carry out at each test level.

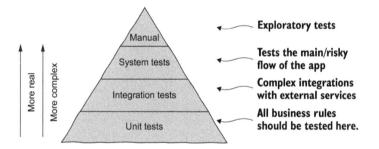

Figure 1.8   **My version of the testing pyramid. The closer a test is to the top, the more real and complex the test becomes. At the right part you see what I test at each test level.**

Unit testing is at the bottom of the pyramid and has the largest area. This means developers who follow this scheme favor unit testing (that is, write more unit tests). Climbing up in the diagram, the next level is integration testing. The area is smaller, indicating that, in practice, these developers write fewer integration tests than unit tests. Given the extra effort that integration tests require, the developers write tests only for the integrations they need. The diagram shows that these developers favor system tests less than integration tests and have even fewer manual tests.

1.4.5   *Why do I favor unit tests?*

As I said, I tend to favor unit testing. I appreciate the advantages that unit tests give me. They are easy to write, they are fast, I can write them intertwined with production code, and so on. I also believe that unit testing fits very well with the way software developers work. When developers implement a new feature, they write separate units that will eventually work together to deliver larger functionality. While developing each unit, it is easy to ensure that it works as expected. Testing small units rigorously and effectively is much easier than testing a larger piece of functionality.

Because I am also aware of the disadvantages of unit testing, I think carefully about how the unit under development will be used by the other units of the system. Enforcing clear contracts and systematically testing them gives me more certainty that things will work out when they are put together.

Finally, given the intensity with which I test my code using (simple and cheap) unit tests, I can use integration and system tests for the parts that really matter. I do not have to retest all the functionalities again at these levels. I use integration or system testing to test specific parts of the code that I believe may cause problems during integration.

1.4.6   *What do I test at the different levels?*

I use unit tests for units that are concerned with an algorithm or a single piece of business logic of the software system. Most enterprise/business systems are used to transform data. Such business logic is often expressed by using entity classes (for example, an `Invoice` class and an `Order` class) to exchange messages. Business logic often does not depend on external services, so it can easily be tested and fully controlled through unit tests. Unit tests give us full control over the input data as well as full observability in terms of asserting that the behavior is as expected.

> **NOTE** If a piece of code deals with specific business logic but cannot be tested via unit tests (for example, the business logic can only be tested with the full system running), previous design or architectural decisions are probably preventing you from writing unit tests. How you design your classes has a significant impact on how easy it is to write unit tests for your code. We discuss design for testability in chapter 7.

I use integration tests whenever the component under test interacts with an external component (such as a database or web service). A DAO, whose sole responsibility is to communicate with a database, is better tested at the integration level: you want to ensure that communication with the database works, the SQL query returns what you want it to, and transactions are committed to the database. Again, note that integration tests are more expensive and harder to set up than unit tests, and I use them only because they are the only way to test a particular part of the system. Chapter 7 discusses how having a clear separation between business rules and infrastructure code will help you test business rules with unit tests and integration code with integration tests.

As we know already, system tests are very costly (they are difficult to write and slow to run) and, thus, at the top of the pyramid. It is impossible to retest the entire system at the system level. Therefore, I have to prioritize what to test at this level, and I perform a simple risk analysis to decide. What are the critical parts of the software system under test? In other words, what parts of the system would be significantly affected by a bug? These are the areas where I do some system testing.

Remember the *pesticide paradox*: a single technique usually is not enough to identify all the bugs. Let me give you a real-world example from one of my previous projects. In developing an e-learning platform, one of our most important functionalities was payment. The worst type of bug would prevent users from buying our product. Therefore, we were rigorous in testing all the code related to payment. We used unit tests for business rules related to what the user bought being converted into the right product, access and permissions, and so on. Integration with the two payment gateways we supported was tested via integration testing: the integration tests made real HTTP calls to a sandbox web service provided by the payment gateways, and we tested different types of users buying products with various credit cards. Finally, our system tests represented the entire user journey in buying our product. These tests started a Firefox browser, clicked HTML elements, submitted forms, and checked that the right product was available after confirming payment.

Figure 1.8 also includes manual testing. I've said that every test should be automated, but I see some value in manual testing when these tests focus on exploration and validation. As a developer, it is nice to use and explore the software system you are building from time to time, both for real and via a test script. Open the browser or the app, and play with it—you may gain better insight into what else to test.

1.4.7 What if you disagree with the testing pyramid?

Many people disagree about the idea of a testing pyramid and whether we should favor unit testing. These developers argue for the *testing trophy*: a thinner bottom level with unit tests, a bigger middle slice with integration tests, and a thinner top with system tests. Clearly, these developers see the most value in writing integration tests.

While I disagree, I see their point. In many software systems, most of the complexity is in integrating components. Think of a highly distributed microservices architecture: in such a scenario, the developer may feel more comfortable if the automated tests make actual calls to other microservices instead of relying on stubs or mocks that simulate them. Why write unit tests for something you have to test anyway via integration tests?

In this particular case, as someone who favors unit testing, I would prefer to tackle the microservices testing problem by first writing lots and lots of unit tests in each microservice to ensure that they all behaved correctly, investing heavily in contract design to ensure that the microservices had clear pre- and post-conditions. Then, I would use many integration tests to ensure that communication worked as expected and that the normal variations in the distributed system did not break the system—yes, lots of them, because their benefits would outweigh their costs in this scenario. I might even invest in some smart (maybe AI-driven) tests to explore corner cases I could not see.

Another common case I see in favor of integration testing rather than unit testing involves database-centric information systems: that is, systems where the main responsibility is to store, retrieve, and display information. In such systems, the complexity relies on ensuring that the flow of information successfully travels through the UI to the database and back. Such applications often are not composed of complex algorithms or business rules. In that case, integration tests to ensure that SQL queries (which are often complex) work as expected and system tests to ensure that the overall application behaves as expected may be the way to go. As I said before and will say many times in this book, context is king.

I've written most of this section in the first person because it reflects my point of view and is based on my experience as a developer. Favoring one approach over another is largely a matter of personal taste, experience, and context. You should do the type of testing you believe will benefit your software. I am not aware of any scientific evidence that argues in favor of or against the testing pyramid. And in 2020, Trautsch and colleagues analyzed the fault detection capability of 30,000 tests (some unit tests, some integration tests) and could not find any evidence that certain defect types are more effectively detected by either test level. All the approaches have pros and cons, and you will have to find what works best for you and your development team.

I suggest that you read the opinions of others, both in favor of unit testing and in favor of integration testing:

- In *Software Engineering at Google* (Winters, Manshreck, and Wright, 2020), the authors mention that Google often opts for unit tests, as they tend to be cheaper and execute more quickly. Integration and system tests also happen, but to a lesser extent. According to the authors, around 80% of their tests are unit tests.
- Ham Vocke (2018) defends the testing pyramid in Martin Fowler's wiki.
- Fowler himself (2021) discusses the different test shapes (testing pyramid and testing trophy).
- André Schaffer (2018) discusses how Spotify prefers integration testing over unit testing.
- Julia Zarechneva and Picnic, a scale-up Dutch company (2021), reason about the testing pyramid.

TEST SIZES RATHER THAN THEIR SCOPE

Google also has an interesting definition of test *sizes*, which engineers consider when designing test cases. A *small test* is a test that can be executed in a single process. Such tests do not have access to main sources of test slowness or determinism. In other words, they are fast and not flaky. A *medium test* can span multiple processes, use threads, and make external calls (like network calls) to localhost. Medium tests tend to be slower and flakier than small ones. Finally, *large tests* remove the localhost restriction and can thus require and make calls to multiple machines. Google reserves large tests for full end-to-end tests.

The idea of classifying tests not in terms of their boundaries (unit, integration, system) but in terms of how fast they run is also popular among many developers. Again, what matters is that for each part of the system, your goal is to maximize the effectiveness of the test. You want your test to be as cheap as possible to write and as fast as possible to run and to give you as much feedback as possible about the system's quality.

Most of the code examples in the remainder of this book are about methods, classes, and unit testing, but the techniques can easily be generalized to coarse-grained components. For example, whenever I show a method, you can think of it as a web service. The reasoning will be the same, but you will probably have more test cases to consider, as your component will do more things.

1.4.8 Will this book help you find all the bugs?

I hope the answer to this question is clear from the preceding discussion: *no*! Nevertheless, the techniques discussed in this book will help you discover many bugs— hopefully, all the important ones.

In practice, many bugs are very complex. We do not even have the right tools to search for some of them. But we know a lot about testing and how to find different classes of bugs, and those are the ones we focus on in this book.

Exercises

1.1 In your own words, explain what systematic testing is and how it is different from non-systematic testing.

1.2 Kelly, a very experienced software tester, visits Books!, a social network focused on matching people based on the books they read. Users do not report bugs often, as the Books! developers have strong testing practices in place. However, users say that the software is not delivering what it promises. What testing principle applies here?

1.3 Suzanne, a junior software tester, has just joined a very large online payment company in the Netherlands. As her first task, Suzanne analyzes the past two years' worth of bug reports. She observes that more than 50% of the bugs happen in the international payments module. Suzanne promises her manager that she will design test cases that completely cover the international payments module and thus find all the bugs.

Which of the following testing principles may explain why this is not possible?

   A Pesticide paradox

   B Exhaustive testing

   C Test early

   D Defect clustering

1.4 John strongly believes in unit testing. In fact, this is the only type of testing he does for any project he's part of. Which of the following testing principles will *not* help convince John that he should move away from his "only unit testing" approach?

   A Pesticide paradox

   B Tests are context-dependent

    c Absence-of-errors fallacy

    d Test early

1.5 Sally just started some consultancy for a company that develops a mobile app to help people keep up with their daily exercises. The development team members are fans of automated software testing and, more specifically, unit tests. They have high unit test code coverage (>95% branch coverage), but users still report a significant number of bugs.

Sally, who is well versed in software testing, explains a testing principle to the team. Which of the following principles did she talk about?

    A Pesticide paradox

    B Exhaustive testing

    c Test early

    D Defect clustering

1.6 Consider this requirement: "A web shop runs a batch job, once a day, to deliver all orders that have been paid. It also sets the delivery date according to whether the order is from an international customer. Orders are retrieved from an external database. Orders that have been paid are then sent to an external web service."

As a tester, you have to decide which test level (unit, integration, or system) to apply. Which of the following statements is true?

    A Integration tests, although more complicated (in terms of automation) than unit tests, would provide more help in finding bugs in the communication with the web service and/or the communication with the database.

    B Given that unit tests could be easily written (by using mocks) and would cover as much as integration tests would, unit tests are the best option for any situation.

    c The most effective way to find bugs in this code is through system tests. In this case, the tester should run the entire system and exercise the batch process. Because this code can easily be mocked, system tests would also be cheap.

    D While all the test levels can be used for this problem, testers are more likely to find more bugs if they choose one level and explore all the possibilities and corner cases there.

1.7 Delft University of Technology (TU Delft) has built in-house software to handle employee payroll. The application uses Java web technologies and stores data in a Postgres database. The application frequently retrieves, modifies, and inserts large amounts of data. All this communication is done by Java classes that send (complex) SQL queries to the database.

As testers, we know that a bug can be anywhere, including in the SQL queries. We also know that there are many ways to exercise our system. Which one of the following is *not* a good option to detect bugs in SQL queries?

    A Unit testing

    B Integration testing

    C System testing

    D Stress testing

1.8 Choosing the level of a test involves a trade-off, because each test level has advantages and disadvantages. Which one of the following is the main advantage of a test at the system level?

    A The interaction with the system is much closer to reality.

    B In a continuous integration environment, system tests provide real feedback to developers.

    C Because system tests are never flaky, they provide developers with more stable feedback.

    D A system test is written by product owners, making it closer to reality.

1.9 What is the main reason the number of recommended system tests in the testing pyramid is smaller than the number of unit tests?

    A Unit tests are as good as system tests.

    B System tests tend to be slow and are difficult to make deterministic.

    C There are no good tools for system tests.

    D System tests do not provide developers with enough quality feedback.

Summary

- Testing and test code can guide you through software development. But software testing is about finding bugs, and that is what this book is primarily about.
- Systematic and effective software testing helps you design test cases that exercise all the corners of your code and (hopefully) leaves no space for unexpected behavior.
- Although being systematic helps, you can never be certain that a program does not have bugs.
- Exhaustive testing is impossible. The life of a tester involves making trade-offs about how much testing is needed.
- You can test programs on different levels, ranging from testing small methods to testing entire systems with databases and web services. Each level has advantages and disadvantages.

Specification-based testing

Software requirements are undoubtedly the most valuable artifact of software testing. By *requirements*, I mean any textual document that describes what a functionality should do. Requirements tell us precisely what the software needs to do and what it should not do. They describe the intricacies of the business rules that the software has to implement and we need to validate. Therefore, requirements should be the first artifact you go for when it comes to testing!

In this chapter, we explore *specification-based testing*. These techniques use the program requirements—such as agile user stories or UML use cases—as testing input. We will discuss how to use all the information available in a requirement to systematically derive a set of tests that exercise that requirement extensively.

Where does specification-based testing fit into the entire testing process? Imagine that a software developer receives a new feature to implement. The developer writes the implementation code, guided by test-driven development (TDD) cycles, and always ensures that the code is testable. With all the classes ready, the developer switches to "testing mode." It is time to systematically look for bugs. This is where specification testing fits in: it is the first testing technique I recommend using once you're in testing mode.

As I mentioned, the idea of specification-based testing is to derive tests from the requirements themselves. The specific implementation is less important. Of course, we use source code to test, too—this *structural testing* is the next technique in the workflow. Once you have a complete picture of all the techniques, you will be able to use them iteratively and go back and forth between them.

2.1 *The requirements say it all*

Let's start with an example. A new set of requirements comes in for you to develop. As soon as you begin to analyze the requirements, you identify a particular method you need to implement: a method that searches for substrings between two tags in a given string and returns all the matching substrings. Let's call this method `substrings-Between()`, inspired by the Apache Commons Lang library (http://mng.bz/nYR5). You are about to test a real-world open source method.

After some thinking, you end up with the following requirements for the `substringsBetween()` method:

Method: `substringsBetween()`

Searches a string for substrings delimited by a start and end tag, returning all matching substrings in an array.

- `str`—The string containing the substrings. Null returns `null`; an empty string returns another empty string.
- `open`—The string identifying the start of the substring. An empty string returns null.
- `close`—The string identifying the end of the substring. An empty string returns null.

The program returns a string array of substrings, or `null` if there is no match.

Example: if `str` = "a**x**ca**y**ca**z**c", `open` = "a", and `close` = "c", the output will be an array containing ["x", "y", "z"]. This is the case because the "a<*something*>c" substring appears three times in the original string: the first contains "x" in the middle, the second "y," and the last "z."

With these requirements in mind, you write the implementation shown in listing 2.1. You may or may not use TDD (discussed in chapter 8) to help you develop this feature. You are somewhat confident that the program works. Slightly, but not completely.

Listing 2.1   Implementing the `substringsBetween()` method

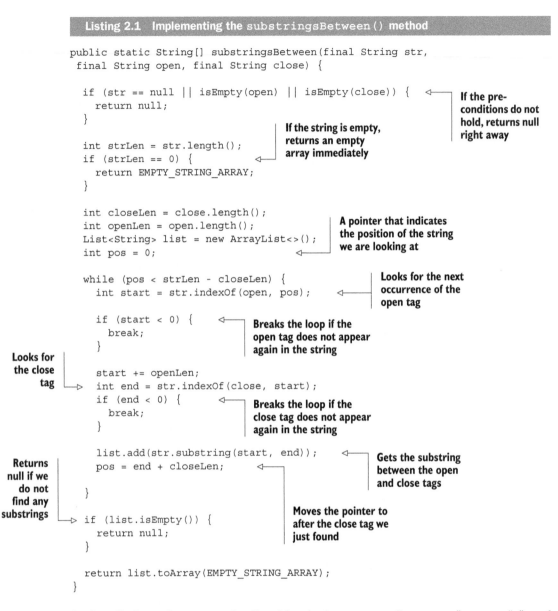

```
public static String[] substringsBetween(final String str,
 final String open, final String close) {

    if (str == null || isEmpty(open) || isEmpty(close)) {          ◄───  If the pre-
      return null;                                                       conditions do not
    }                                                                    hold, returns null
                                                                         right away
                                            If the string is empty,
    int strLen = str.length();              returns an empty
    if (strLen == 0) {                ◄──   array immediately
      return EMPTY_STRING_ARRAY;
    }

    int closeLen = close.length();
    int openLen = open.length();             A pointer that indicates
    List<String> list = new ArrayList<>();   the position of the string
    int pos = 0;                       ◄──   we are looking at

    while (pos < strLen - closeLen) {           Looks for the next
      int start = str.indexOf(open, pos);  ◄─── occurrence of the
                                                open tag
      if (start < 0) {       ◄───  Breaks the loop if the
        break;                     open tag does not appear
      }                            again in the string

      start += openLen;
      int end = str.indexOf(close, start);
      if (end < 0) {         ◄───  Breaks the loop if the
        break;                     close tag does not appear
      }                            again in the string

      list.add(str.substring(start, end));   ◄───  Gets the substring
      pos = end + closeLen;            ◄──         between the open
                                                   and close tags
    }
                                         Moves the pointer to
    if (list.isEmpty()) {                after the close tag we
      return null;                       just found
    }

    return list.toArray(EMPTY_STRING_ARRAY);
}
```

Looks for the close tag

Returns null if we do not find any substrings

Let's walk through an example. Consider the inputs str = "axcaycazc", open = "a", and close = "c". None of the three strings are empty, so the method goes straight to the openLen and closeLen variables. These two variables store the length of the open and close strings, respectively. In this case, both are equal to 1, as "a" and "c" are strings with a single character.

The program then goes into its main loop. This loop runs while there still may be substrings in the string to check. In the first iteration, pos equals zero (the beginning of the string). We call indexOf, looking for a possible occurrence of the open tag. We pass the open tag and the position to start the search, which at this point is 0. indexOf returns 0, which means we found an open tag. (The first element of the string is already the open tag.)

The program then looks for the end of the substring by calling the indexOf method again, this time on the close tag. Note that we increase the start position by the length of the open tag because we want to look for the close tag after the end of the entire open tag. Remember that the open tag has a length of one but can have any length. If we find a close tag, this means there is a substring to return to the user. We get this substring by calling the substring method with the start and end positions as parameters. We then reposition our pos pointer, and the loop iterates again. Figure 2.1 shows the three iterations of the loop as well as the locations to which the main pointers (start, end, and pos) are pointing.

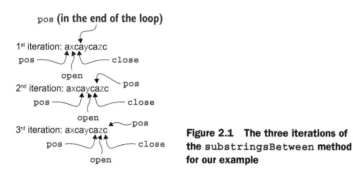

Figure 2.1   The three iterations of the substringsBetween method for our example

Now that you have finished the first implementation, you flip your mind to testing mode. It is time for specification and boundary testing. As an exercise, before we work on this problem together, look at the requirements one more time and write down all the test cases you can come up with. The format does not matter—it can be something like "all parameters null." When you are finished with this chapter, compare your initial test suite with the one we are about to derive together.

The best way to ensure that this method works properly would be to test all the possible combinations of inputs and outputs. Given that substringsBetween() receives three string parameters as an input, we would need to pass all possible valid strings to the three parameters, combined in all imaginable ways. As we discussed in chapter 1, exhaustive testing is rarely possible. We have to be pragmatic.

2.1.1   Step 1: Understanding the requirements, inputs, and outputs

Regardless of how your requirements are written (or even if they are only in your mind), they include three parts. First is what the program/method must do: its business rules. Second, the program receives data as inputs. Inputs are a fundamental part of our reasoning, as it is through them that we can test the different cases. Third, reasoning about the output will help us better understand what the program does and how the inputs are converted to the expected output.

For the `substringsBetween()` method, my reasoning would be

1 The *goal* of this method is to collect all substrings in a string that are delimited by an `open` tag and a `close` tag (the user provides these).
2 The program receives three *parameters*:
   a `str`, which represents the string from which the program will extract substrings
   b The `open` tag, which indicates the start of a substring
   c The `close` tag, which indicates the end of the substring
3 The program *returns* an array composed of all the substrings found by the program.

Such reflection is useful to think about what you want from the method.

2.1.2 *Step 2: Explore what the program does for various inputs*

An ad hoc exploration of what the method does may increase your understanding of it. I have noticed this when observing professional software developers writing test cases for methods they have never seen before (Aniche, Treude, and Zaidman, 2021). This step is more relevant when you did not write the code—if you wrote it, this exploration phase may not be needed.

To illustrate this step, suppose you did not write this code (which, in this case, is true). My process would be as follows (see the JUnit code in listing 2.2):

Let's see the program working on a happy case. I will pass the string "abcd" with the open tag "a" and the `close` tag "d". I expect it to return an array with a single element: `["bc"]`. I try that (in a unit test), and the program returns what I expect.

Next, let's see what happens if there are multiple substrings in the main string. I will pass the string "abcdabcdab" with the same `open` and `close` tags. I expect it to return an array with two strings: `["bc", "bc"]`. The program returns what I expect.

I expect the program to behave the same with `open` and `close` tags larger than a single character. I will repeat the second test, doubling the "a"s and the "d"s in all the parameters. I will also change one of the "bc"s to "bf", so it is easier to check that the method returns two different substrings: `["bc", "bf"]`. The program returns what I expect.

Listing 2.2 Exploratory tests for `substringsBetween()`

```
@Test
void simpleCase() {          ←——|  We write these test cases based on our feelings.
  assertThat(                     What do we want to explore next?
    StringUtils.substringsBetween("abcd", "a", "d")
  ).isEqualTo(new String[] { "bc" });
}

@Test                              I don't care if they are good
void manySubstrings() {      ←——  tests, as long as they teach me
  assertThat(                      something about the code.
```

```
      StringUtils.substringsBetween("abcdabcdab", "a", "d")
    ).isEqualTo(new String[] { "bc", "bc" });
}

@Test
void openAndCloseTagsThatAreLongerThan1Char() {
  assertThat(
    StringUtils.substringsBetween("aabcddaabfddaab", "aa", "dd")
  ).isEqualTo(new String[] { "bc", "bf" });
}
```

> **I wrote all the test code in a single line, although you cannot see that in the printed book. Feel free to write it any way you prefer.**

I stop this exploration phase when I have a clear mental model of how the program should work. Note that I do not expect you to perform the same exploration I did—it is personal and guided by my hypothesis about the program. Also note that I did not explore any corner cases; that comes later. At this moment, I am only interested in better understanding the program.

2.1.3 Step 3: Explore possible inputs and outputs, and identify partitions

We should find a way to prioritize and select a subset of inputs and outputs that will give us sufficient certainty about the correctness of the program. Although the number of possible program inputs and outputs is nearly infinite, some sets of inputs make the program behave the same way, regardless of the precise input value.

In the case of our example, for testing purposes, the input "abcd" with open tag "a" and close tag "d", which makes the program return "bc", is the same as the input "xyzw" with open tag "x" and close tag "w". You change the letters, but you expect the program to do the same thing for both inputs. Given your resource constraints, you will test just one of these inputs (it does not matter which), and you will trust that this single case represents that entire class of inputs. In testing terminology, we say that these two inputs are *equivalent.*

Once you have identified this class (or partition), you repeat the process and look for another class that will make the program behave in a different way that you have not yet tested. If you keep dividing the domain, you will eventually identify all the different possible classes (or partitions) of inputs.

A systematic way to do such an exploration is to think of the following:

1 Each input individually: "What are the possible classes of inputs I can provide?"
2 Each input in combination with other inputs: "What combinations can I try between the open and close tags?"
3 The different classes of output expected from this program: "Does it return arrays? Can it return an empty array? Can it return nulls?"

I find it easiest to start with individual inputs. Follow me:

- str *parameter*—The string can be any string. The specification mentions the null and empty cases; I would have tested those anyway, because they are always good exceptional test cases. Given that this is a string (which is basically a list of characters), I will also test what happens if the string has length 1.

- a Null string
- b Empty string
- c String of length 1
- d String of length > 1 (any string)

- open *parameter*—This can also be anything. I will try it with null and empty, as I learned from the `str` parameter that those cases are special in this program. I will also try strings with length 1 and greater than 1:

- a Null string
- b Empty string
- c String of length 1
- d String of length > 1

- close *parameter*—This parameter is like the previous one:

- a Null string
- b Empty string
- c String of length 1
- d String of length > 1

Once the input variables are analyzed in detail, we explore possible *combinations* of variables. A program's input variables may be related to each other. In the example, it is clear that the three variables have a dependency relationship. Follow me again:

- (str, open, close) *parameters*—open and close may or may not be in the string. Also, open may be there, but not close (and vice versa).

- a str contains neither the open nor the close tag.
- b str contains the open tag but not the close tag.
- c str contains the close tag but not the open tag.
- d str contains both the open and close tags.
- e str contains both the open and close tags multiple times.

Note that this thought process depended on my experience as a tester. The documentation does not explicitly mention tags not being in the string, nor does it mention the open tag being present but the close tag not. I saw this case because of my experience as a tester.

Finally, we reflect on the possible outputs. The method returns an array of substrings. I can see a set of possible different outputs, both for the array itself and for the strings within the array:

- *Array of strings* (output)

- a Null array
- b Empty array

    c Single item

    d Multiple items

- *Each individual string* (output)

    a Empty

    b Single character

    c Multiple characters

You may think that reflecting on the outputs is not necessary. After all, if you reasoned correctly about the inputs, you are probably exercising all the possible kinds of outputs. This is a valid argument. Nevertheless, for more complex programs, reflecting on the outputs may help you see an input case that you did not identify before.

2.1.4 *Step 4: Analyze the boundaries*

Bugs in the boundaries of the input domain are common in software systems. As developers, we have all made mistakes such as using a "greater than" operator (>) where it should have been a "greater than or equal to" operator (>=). Programs with such bugs tend to work well for most provided inputs, but they fail when the input is near the boundary. Boundaries are everywhere, and our goal in this section is to learn how to identify them.

When we devise partitions, they have *close boundaries* with the other partitions. Imagine a simple program that prints "hiphip" if the given input is a number smaller than 10 or "hooray" if the given input is greater than or equal to 10. A tester can divide the input domain into two partitions: (1) the set of inputs that make the program print "hiphip" and (2) the set of inputs that make the program print "hooray". Figure 2.2 illustrates this program's inputs and partitions. Note that the input value 9 belongs to the "hiphip" partition, while the input value 10 belongs to the "hooray" partition.

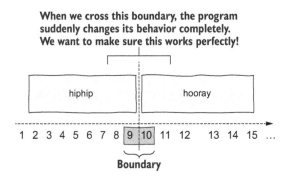

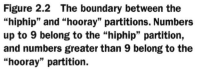

Figure 2.2 The boundary between the "hiphip" and "hooray" partitions. Numbers up to 9 belong to the "hiphip" partition, and numbers greater than 9 belong to the "hooray" partition.

The odds of a programmer writing a bug near the boundary (in this case, near the input values 9 and 10) are greater than for other input values. This is what boundary testing is about: making the program behave correctly when inputs are near a boundary. And this is what this fourth step is about: boundary testing.

Whenever a boundary is identified, I suggest that you test what happens to the program when inputs go from one boundary to the other. In the previous example, this would mean having a test with 9 as input and another test with 10 as input. This idea is similar to what Jeng and Weyuker proposed in their 1994 paper: testing two points whenever there is a boundary. One test is for the *on point*, which is the point that is *on* the boundary; and the other test is for the *off point*, which is the point closest to the boundary that belongs to the partition the on point does not belong to (that is, the other partition).

In the hiphip-hooray example, the on point is 10. Note that 10 is the number that appears in the specification of the program (input >= 10) and is likely to also be the number the developer uses in the `if` statement. The value 10 makes the program print "hooray". The off point is the point closest to the boundary that belongs to the other partition. In this case, the off point is 9. The number 9 is the closest number to 10, and it belongs to the "hiphip" partition.

Let's discuss two more common terms: *in point* and *out point*. In points are points that make the condition true. You may have an infinite number of them. In the hiphip-hooray example, 11, 12, 25, and 42 are all examples of in points. Out points, on the other hand, are points that make the condition false. 8, 7, 2, and –42 are all examples of out points. In equalities, the in point is the one in the condition, and all others are out points. For example, in `a == 10`, 10 is the (only) in point and the on point; 12 is an out point and an off point; and 56 is an out point. Whenever you find a boundary, two tests (for the on and off points) are usually enough, although, as I will discuss later, I do not mind throwing in some interesting in and out points to have a more complete test suite.

Another common situation in boundary testing is finding boundaries that deal with equalities. In the previous example, suppose that instead of input >= 10, the specification says that the program prints "hooray" whenever the input is 10 or "hiphip" otherwise. Given that this is an equality, we now have one on point (10) but two off points (9 and 11), because the boundary applies to both sides. In this case, as a tester, you would write three test cases.

My trick to explore boundaries is to look at all the partitions and think of inputs between them. Whenever you find one that is worth testing, you test it.

In our example, a straightforward boundary happens when the string passes from empty to non-empty, as you know that the program stops returning empty and will (possibly) start to return something. You already covered this boundary, as you have partitions for both cases. As you examine each partition and how it makes boundaries with others, you analyze the partitions in the (`str, open, close`) category. The program can have no substrings, one substring, or multiple substrings. And the `open` and `close` tags may not be in the string; or, more importantly, they may be in the string, but with no substring between them. This is a boundary you should exercise! See figure 2.3.

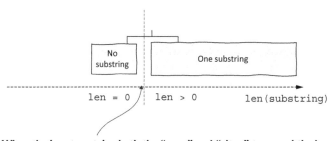

When the input contains both the "open" and "close" tags, and the length
of the substring changes from 0 to greater than 0, the program starts to
return this substring. It's a boundary, and we should exercise it!

Figure 2.3   Some of the boundaries in the `substringsBetween()` **problem.**

Whenever we identify a boundary, we devise two tests for it, one for each side of the
boundary. For the "no substring"/"one substring" boundary, the two tests are as follows:

- `str` contains both `open` and `close` tags, with *no* characters between them.
- `str` contains both `open` and `close` tags, with characters between them.

The second test is not necessary in this case, as other tests already exercise this situation. Therefore, we can discard it.

2.1.5   *Step 5: Devise test cases*

With the inputs, outputs, and boundaries properly dissected, we can generate concrete test cases. Ideally, we would combine all the partitions we've devised for each of
the inputs. The example has four categories, each with four or five partitions: the `str`
category with four partitions (*null string, empty string, string of length 1*, and *string of
length > 1*), the `open` category with four partitions (the same as `str`), the `close` category with four partitions (also the same as `str`), and the (`str`, `open`, `close`) category
with five partitions (*string does not contain either the* `open` *or* `close` *tags, string contains the*
`open` *tag but does not contain the* `close` *tag, string contains the* `close` *tag but does not contain*
the `open` *tag, string contains both the* `open` *and* `close` *tags, string contains both the* `open` *and*
`close` *tags multiple times*). This means you would start with the `str` null partition and
combine it with the partitions of the `open`, `close`, and (`str`, `open`, `close`) categories.
You would end up with $4 \times 4 \times 4 \times 5 = 320$ tests. Writing 320 tests may be an effort that
will not pay off.

In such situations, we pragmatically decide which partitions should be combined
with others and which should not. A first idea to reduce the number of tests is to test
exceptional cases only once and not combine them. For example, the *null string* partition may be tested only once and not more than that. What would we gain from combining *null string* with `open` being null, empty, length = 1, and length > 1 as well as
with `close` being null, empty, length = 1, length > 1, and so on? It would not be
worth the effort. The same goes for *empty string*: one test may be good enough. If we

apply the same logic to the other two parameters and test them as null and empty just once, we already drastically reduce the number of test cases.

There may be other partitions that do not need to be combined fully. In this problem, I see two:

- For the *string of length 1* case, given that the string has length 1, two tests may be enough: one where the single character in the string matches open and close, and one where it does not.
- Unless we have a good reason to believe that the program handles open and close tags of different lengths in different ways, we do not need the four combinations of (*open length = 1, close length = 1*), (*open length > 1, close length = 1*), (*open length = 1, close length > 1*), and (*open length > 1, close length > 1*). Just (*open length = 1, close length = 1*) and (*open length > 1, close length > 1*) are enough.

In other words, do not blindly combine partitions, as doing so may lead to less relevant test cases. Looking at the implementation can also help you reduce the number of combinations. We discuss using the source code to design test cases in chapter 3.

In the following list, I've marked with an [x] partitions we will not test multiple times:

- str—Null string [x], empty string [x], length = 1 [x], length > 1
- open—Null string [x], empty string [x], length = 1, length > 1
- close—Null string [x], empty string [x], length = 1, length > 1
- str—Null string [x], empty string [x], length = 1, length > 1
- (str, open, close)—String does not contain either the open or the close tag, string contains the open tag but does not contain the close tag, string contains the close tag but does not contain the open tag, string contains both the open and close tags, string contains both the open and close tags multiple times

With a clear understanding of which partitions need to be extensively tested and which ones do not, we can derive the test cases by performing the combination. First, the exceptional cases:

- T1: str is null.
- T2: str is empty.
- T3: open is null.
- T4: open is empty.
- T5: close is null.
- T6: close is empty.

Then, *str length = 1*:

- T7: The single character in str matches the open tag.
- T8: The single character in str matches the close tag.
- T9: The single character in str does not match either the open or the close tag.
- T10: The single character in str matches both the open and close tags.

Now, *str length > 1, open length = 1,* close *= 1*:

- T11: str does not contain either the open or the close tag.
- T12: str contains the open tag but does not contain the close tag.
- T13: str contains the close tag but does not contain the open tag.
- T14: str contains both the open and close tags.
- T15: str contains both the open and close tags multiple times.

Next, *str length > 1, open length > 1,* close *> 1*:

- T16: str does not contain either the open or the close tag.
- T17: str contains the open tag but does not contain the close tag.
- T18: str contains the close tag but does not contain the open tag.
- T19: str contains both the open and close tags.
- T20: str contains both the open and close tags multiple times.

Finally, here is the test for the boundary:

- T21: str contains both the open and close tags with no characters between them.

We end up with 21 tests. Note that deriving them did not require much creativity: the process we followed was systematic. This is the idea!

2.1.6 Step 6: Automate the test cases

It is now time to transform the test cases into automated JUnit tests. Writing those tests is mostly a mechanical task. The creative part is coming up with inputs to exercise the specific partition and understanding the correct program output for that partition.

The automated test suite is shown in listings 2.3 through 2.7. They are long but easy to understand. Each call to the substringsBetween method is one of our test cases. The 21 calls to it are spread over the test methods, each matching the test cases we devised earlier.

First are the tests related to the string being null or empty.

Listing 2.3 Tests for substringsBetween, **part 1**

```
import org.junit.jupiter.api.Test;
import static ch2.StringUtils.substringsBetween;
import static org.assertj.core.api.Assertions.assertThat;

public class StringUtilsTest {

  @Test
  void strIsNullOrEmpty() {
    assertThat(substringsBetween(null, "a", "b"))      ⟵  This first call to
      .isEqualTo(null);                                       substringsBetween
                                                              is our test T1.
```

```
    assertThat(substringsBetween("", "a", "b"))        ⟵──┐  Test T2
      .isEqualTo(new String[]{});
  }

}
```

Next are all the tests related to open or close being null or empty.

Listing 2.4 Tests for `substringsBetween`, part 2

```java
@Test
void openIsNullOrEmpty() {
  assertThat(substringsBetween("abc", null, "b")).isEqualTo(null);
  assertThat(substringsBetween("abc", "", "b")).isEqualTo(null);
}

@Test
void closeIsNullOrEmpty() {
  assertThat(substringsBetween("abc", "a", null)).isEqualTo(null);
  assertThat(substringsBetween("abc", "a", "")).isEqualTo(null);
}
```

Now come all the tests related to string and open and close tags with length 1.

Listing 2.5 Tests for `substringsBetween`, part 3

```java
@Test
void strOfLength1() {
  assertThat(substringsBetween("a", "a", "b")).isEqualTo(null);
  assertThat(substringsBetween("a", "b", "a")).isEqualTo(null);
  assertThat(substringsBetween("a", "b", "b")).isEqualTo(null);
  assertThat(substringsBetween("a", "a", "a")).isEqualTo(null);
}

@Test
void openAndCloseOfLength1() {
  assertThat(substringsBetween("abc", "x", "y")).isEqualTo(null);
  assertThat(substringsBetween("abc", "a", "y")).isEqualTo(null);
  assertThat(substringsBetween("abc", "x", "c")).isEqualTo(null);
  assertThat(substringsBetween("abc", "a", "c"))
    .isEqualTo(new String[] {"b"});
  assertThat(substringsBetween("abcabc", "a", "c"))
    .isEqualTo(new String[] {"b", "b"});
}
```

Then we have the tests for the open and close tags of varying sizes.

Listing 2.6 Tests for `substringsBetween`, part 4

```java
@Test
void openAndCloseTagsOfDifferentSizes() {
  assertThat(substringsBetween("aabcc", "xx", "yy")).isEqualTo(null);
  assertThat(substringsBetween("aabcc", "aa", "yy")).isEqualTo(null);
```

```
assertThat(substringsBetween("aabcc", "xx", "cc")).isEqualTo(null);
assertThat(substringsBetween("aabbcc", "aa", "cc"))
  .isEqualTo(new String[] {"bb"});
assertThat(substringsBetween("aabbccaaeecc", "aa", "cc"))
  .isEqualTo(new String[] {"bb", "ee"});
}
```

Finally, here is the test for when there is no substring between the open and close tags.

Listing 2.7 Tests for `substringsBetween`, part 5

```
@Test
void noSubstringBetweenOpenAndCloseTags() {
  assertThat(substringsBetween("aabb", "aa", "bb"))
    .isEqualTo(new String[] {""});
  }
}
```

I decided to group the assertions in five different methods. They almost match my groups when engineering the test cases in step 5. The only difference is that I broke the exceptional cases into three test methods: `strIsNullOrEmpty`, `openIsNullOrEmpty`, and `closeIsNullOrEmpty`.

Some developers would vouch for a single method per test case, which would mean 21 test methods, each containing one method call and one assertion. The advantage would be that the test method's name would clearly describe the test case. JUnit also offers the `ParameterizedTest` feature (http://mng.bz/voKp), which could be used in this case.

I prefer simple test methods that focus on one test case, especially when implementing complex business rules in enterprise systems. But in this case, there are lots of inputs to test, and many of them are variants of a larger partition, so it made more sense to me to code the way I did.

Deciding whether to put all tests in a single method or in multiple methods is highly subjective. We discuss test code quality and how to write tests that are easy to understand and debug in chapter 10.

Also note that sometimes there are values we do not care about. For example, consider test case 1: `str` is null. We do not care about the values we pass to the open and close tags here. My usual approach is to select reasonable values for the inputs I do not care about—that is, values that will not interfere with the test.

2.1.7 *Step 7: Augment the test suite with creativity and experience*

Being systematic is good, but we should never discard our experience. In this step, we look at the partitions we've devised and see if we can develop interesting variations. Variation is always a good thing to have in testing.

In the example, when revisiting the tests, I noticed that we never tried strings with spaces. I decided to engineer two extra tests based on T15 and T20, both about "`str` contains both open and close tags multiple times": one for open and close tags with lengths 1, another for `open` and `close` tags with larger lengths. These check whether the implementation works if there are whitespaces in the string. You see them in listing 2.8.

> **NOTE** It's possible we don't need to test for this extra case. Maybe the implementation handles strings in a generic way. For now, we are only looking at the requirements, and testing special characters is always a good idea. If you have access to the implementation (as we discuss in the next chapter), the code can help you decide whether a test is relevant.

Listing 2.8 Tests for `substringsBetween` using parameterized tests, part 6

```
@Test
void openAndCloseOfLength1() {
  // ... previous assertions here
  assertThat(substringsBetween("abcabyt byrc", "a", "c"))
    .isEqualTo(new String[] {"b", "byt byr"});
}

@Test
void openAndCloseTagsOfDifferentSizes() {
  // ... previous assertions here
  assertThat(substringsBetween("a abb ddc ca abbcc", "a a", "c c")).
  ⇨ isEqualTo(new String[] {"bb dd"});
}
```

We end up with 23 test cases. Take time to revisit all the steps we have worked through, and then consider this question: are we finished?

We are finished with specification testing. However, we are not done testing. After specification testing, the next step is to bring the implementation into play and augment our test suite with what we see in the code. That is the topic of chapter 3.

Four eyes are better than two

A reviewer of this book had an interesting question: what about a test case where the input is **aabcddaabeddaab**, open is **aa**, and `close` is **d**? "bc" and "be" are the substrings between the provided open and the `close` tags (aa**bc**>ddaa**be**>ddaab), but "bcddaabed" could also be considered a substring (aa**bcddaabed**>daab).

At first, I thought I had missed this test case. But in fact, it is the same as T15 and T20.

Different people approach problems in different ways. My thought process was, "Let's see if the program breaks if we have multiple open and close tags in the string." The reviewer may have thought, "Let's see if the program will incorrectly go for the longer substring."

We want to make testing as systematic as possible, but a lot depends on how the developer models the problem. Sometimes you will not see all the test cases. When you do come up with a new test, add it to the test suite!

2.2 Specification-based testing in a nutshell

I propose a seven-step approach to derive systematic tests based on a specification. This approach is a mix of the *category-partition method* proposed by Ostrand and Balcer in their seminal 1988 work, and Kaner et al.'s *Domain Testing Workbook* (2013), with my own twist: see figure 2.4.

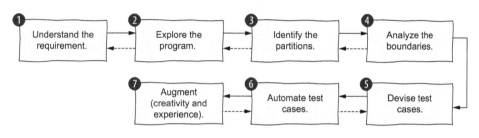

Figure 2.4 **The seven steps I propose to derive test cases based on specifications. The solid arrows indicate the standard path to follow. The dashed arrows indicate that, as always, the process should be iterative, so in practice you'll go back and forth until you are confident about the test suite you've created.**

The steps are as follows:

1 *Understand the requirement, inputs, and outputs.* We need an overall idea of what we are about to test. Read the requirements carefully. What should the program do? What should it not do? Does it handle specific corner cases? Identify the input and output variables in play, their types (integers, strings, and so on), and their input domain (for example, is the variable a number that must be between 5 and 10?). Some of these characteristics can be found in the program's specification; others may not be stated explicitly. Try to understand the nitty-gritty details of the requirements.

2 *Explore the program.* If you did not write the program yourself, a very good way to determine what it does (besides reading the documentation) is to play with it. Call the program under test with different inputs and see what it produces as output. Continue until you are sure your mental model matches what the program does. This exploration does not have to be (and should not be) systematic. Rather, focus on increasing your understanding. Remember that you are still not testing the program.

3 *Judiciously explore the possible inputs and outputs, and identify the partitions.* Identifying the correct partitions is the hardest part of testing. If you miss one, you may let a bug slip through. I propose three steps to identify the partitions:

   a Look at each input variable individually. Explore its type (is it an integer? is it a string?) and the range of values it can receive (can it be null? is it a number ranging from 0 to 100? does it allow negative numbers?).

   b Look at how each variable may interact with another. Variables often have dependencies or put constraints on each other, and those should be tested.

c Explore the possible types of outputs, and make sure you are testing them all. While exploring the inputs and outputs, pay attention to any implicit (business) rules, logic, or expected behavior.

4 *Identify the boundaries.* Bugs love boundaries, so be extra thorough here. Analyze the boundaries of all the partitions you devised in the previous step. Identify the relevant ones, and add them to the list.

5 *Devise test cases based on the partitions and boundaries.* The basic idea is to combine all the partitions in the different categories to test all possible combinations of inputs. However, combining them all may be too expensive, so part of the task is to reduce the number of combinations. The common strategy is to test exceptional behavior only once and not combine it with the other partitions.

6 *Automate the test cases.* A test is only a test when it is automated. Therefore, the goal is to write (JUnit) automated tests for all the test cases you just devised. This means identifying concrete input values for them and having a clear expectation of what the program should do (the output). Remember that test code is code, so reduce duplication and ensure that the code is easy to read and that the different test cases are easily identifiable in case one fails.

7 *Augment the test suite with creativity and experience.* Perform some final checks. Revisit all the tests you created, using your experience and creativity. Did you miss something? Does your gut feeling tell you that the program may fail in a specific case? If so, add a new test case.

2.3 *Finding bugs with specification testing*

The developers of the Apache Commons Lang framework (the framework where I extracted the implementation of the substringsBetween method) are just too good. We did not find any bugs there. Let's look at another example: one implemented by me, an average developer who makes mistakes from time to time. This example will show you the value of specification testing. Try to spot the bug before I reveal it!

Some friends and I have participated in many coding challenges, primarily for fun. A couple of years ago we worked on the following problem inspired by LeetCode (https://leetcode.com/problems/add-two-numbers):

The method receives two numbers, left and right (each represented as a list of digits), adds them, and returns the result as a list of digits.

Each element in the left and right lists of digits should be a number from [0–9]. An IllegalArgumentException is thrown if this pre-condition does not hold.

- left—A list containing the left number. Null returns null; empty means 0.
- right—A list containing the right number. Null returns null; empty means 0.

The program returns the sum of left and right as a list of digits.

For example, adding the numbers 23 and 42 means a (left) list with two elements [2,3], a (right) list with two elements [4,2] and, as an output, a list with two elements [6,5] (since 23 + 42 = 65).

My initial implementation was as follows.

Listing 2.9 Initial implementation of the `add()` method

```
public List<Integer> add(List<Integer> left, List<Integer> right) {
    if (left == null || right == null)          ←  Returns null if left
        return null;                               or right is null

    Collections.reverse(left);          ←  Reverses the numbers so the least
    Collections.reverse(right);            significant digit is on the left

    LinkedList<Integer> result = new LinkedList<>();

    int carry = 0;
                                                          While there
    for (int i = 0; i < max(left.size(), right.size()); i++) {  ←  is a digit, keeps
                                                          summing, taking
        int leftDigit = left.size() > i ? left.get(i) : 0;   carries into
        int rightDigit = right.size() > i ? right.get(i) : 0;  consideration

        if (leftDigit < 0 || leftDigit > 9 ||         Throws an exception
          rightDigit < 0 || rightDigit > 9)      ←   if the pre-condition
            throw new IllegalArgumentException();      does not hold

        int sum = leftDigit + rightDigit + carry;   ←  Sums the left digit with
                                                        the right digit with the
        result.addFirst(sum % 10);          ←           possible carry

        carry = sum / 10;          ←
    }                              The digit should be a number between 0 and
    return result;                 9. We calculate it by taking the rest of the
}                                  division (the % operator) of the sum by 10.
```
If the sum is greater than 10, carries the rest of the division to the next digit

The algorithm works as follows. First it reverses both lists of digits, so the least significant digit is on the left. This makes it easier for us to loop through the list. Then, for each digit in both the left and right numbers, the algorithm gets the next relevant digits and sums them. If the resulting sum is greater than 10, +1 needs to be carried to the next most significant digit. In the end, the algorithm returns the list.

I was just having fun with coding, so I did not write systematic tests. I tried a couple of inputs and observed that the output was correct. If you already understand the concept of code coverage, these four tests achieve 100% branch coverage if we discard the ifs related to checking null and pre-conditions (if you are not familiar with code coverage, don't worry; we discuss it in the next chapter):

- T1 = [1] + [1] = [2]
- T2 = [1,5] + [1,0] = [2,5]

- T3 = [1,5] + [1,5] = [3,0]
- T4 = [5,0,0] + [2,5,0] = [7,5,0]

The program worked fine for these inputs. I submitted it to the coding challenge platform, and, to my surprise, the implementation was rejected! There was a bug in my code. Before I show you where it is, here is how specification testing would have caught it.

First we analyze each parameter in isolation:

- left *parameter*—It is a list, so we should first exercise basic inputs such as null, empty, a single digit, and multiple digits. Given that this list represents a number, we should also try a number with many zeroes on the left. Such zeroes are useless, but it is good to see whether the implementation can handle them. Thus we have the following partitions:
  - Empty
  - Null
  - Single digit
  - Multiple digits
  - Zeroes on the left
- right *parameter*—We have the same list of partitions as for the left parameter:
  - Empty
  - Null
  - Single digit
  - Multiple digits
  - Zeroes on the left

left and right have a relationship. Let's explore that:

- (left, right) *parameters*—They can be different sizes, and the program should be able to handle it:
  - length(left list) > length(right list)
  - length(left list) < length(right list)
  - length(left list) = length(right list)

While not explicit in the documentation, we know that the sum of two numbers should be the same regardless of whether the highest number is on the left or right side of the equation. We also know that some sums require carrying. For example, suppose we're summing 18 + 15: 8 + 5 = 13, which means we have a 3, and we carry +1 to the next digit. We then add 1 + 1 + 1: the first 1 from the left number, the second 1 from the right number, and the third 1 carried from the previous sum. The final result is 33. Figure 2.5 illustrates this process.

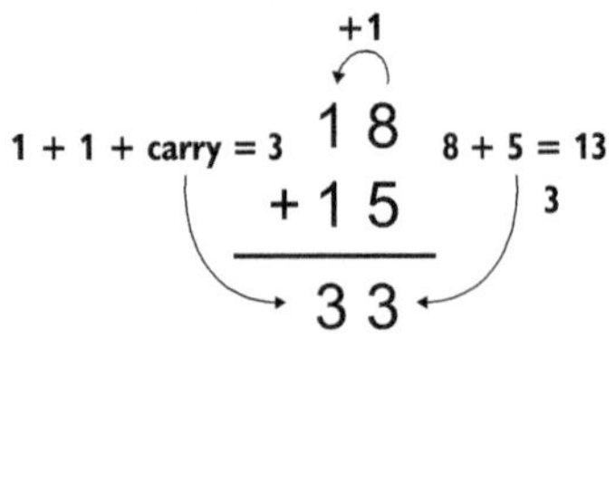

Figure 2.5   Illustrating the carry when summing 18 + 15

The carry is such an important concept in this program that it deserves testing. This is what I meant in listing 2.9 when I said to pay extra attention to specific (business) rules and logic:

- *Carry*—Let's try sums that require carrying in many different ways. These are good places to start:
  - Sum without a carry
  - Sum with a carry: one carry at the beginning
  - Sum with a carry: one carry in the middle
  - Sum with a carry: many carries
  - Sum with a carry: many carries, not in a row
  - Sum with a carry: carry propagated to a new (most significant) digit

---

Domain knowledge is still fundamental to engineer good test cases

Up to this point, this chapter may have given you the impression that if you analyze every parameter of the method, you can derive all the test cases you need. Life would be much easier if that were true!

Analyzing parameters, even without much domain knowledge, will help you uncover many bugs. However, having a deep understanding of the requirements is still key in devising good test cases. In the current example, the requirements do not discuss the carry. We devised many tests around the carry because we have a deep knowledge of the problem. We build up knowledge over time; so although the systematic approaches I discuss will help you uncover many common bugs, it is your job to learn about the domain of the software system you're working on. (And if you wrote the code, you have an advantage: you know it deeply!)

The only boundary worth testing is the following: ensuring that cases such as 99 + 1 (where the final number is carried to a new, most significant digit) are covered. This comes from the last partition derived when analyzing the *carry*: "Sum with a carry: carry propagated to a new (most significant) digit."

With all the inputs and outputs analyzed, it is time to derive concrete test cases. Let's apply the following strategy:

1. Test nulls and empties just once.
2. Test numbers with single digits just once.
3. Test numbers with multiple digits, with `left` and `right` having the same and different lengths. We will be thorough and have the same set of tests for both equal and different lengths, and we will duplicate the test suite to ensure that everything works if `left` is longer than `right` or vice versa.
4. We will exercise the zeroes on the left, but a few test cases are enough.
5. Test the boundary.

Let's look at the specific test cases:

- Nulls and empties
  - T1: left null
  - T2: left empty
  - T3: right null
  - T4: right empty
- Single digits
  - T5: single digit, no carry
  - T6: single digit, carry
- Multiple digits
  - T7: no carry
  - T8: carry in the least significant digit
  - T9: carry in the middle
  - T10: many carries
  - T11: many carries, not in a row
  - T12: carry propagated to a new (now most significant) digit
- Multiple digits with different lengths (one for `left` longer than `right`, and one for `right` longer than `left`)
  - T13: no carry
  - T14: carry in the least significant digit
  - T15: carry in the middle
  - T16: many carries
  - T17: many carries, not in a row
  - T18: carry propagated to a new (now most significant) digit
- Zeroes on the left
  - T19: no carry
  - T20: carry
- Boundaries
  - T21: carry to a new most significant digit, by one (such as 99 +1).

Now we transform them into automated test cases, as shown in listing 2.10. A few remarks about this listing:

- This test uses the `ParameterizedTest` feature from JUnit. The idea is that we write a single generic test method that works like a skeleton. Instead of having hard-coded values, it uses variables. The concrete values are passed to the test method later. The `testCases()` method provides inputs to the `shouldReturn-CorrectResult` test method. The link between the test method and the method source is done through the `@MethodSource` annotation. JUnit offers other ways to provide inputs to methods, such as inline comma-separated values (see the `@CsvSource` annotation in the documentation).

- The `numbers()` helper method receives a list of integers and converts it to a `List<Integer>`, which the method under test receives. This helper method increases the legibility of the test methods. (For the Java experts, the `Arrays.asList()` native method would have yielded the same result.)

Listing 2.10 Tests for the `add` method

```java
import org.junit.jupiter.params.ParameterizedTest;
import org.junit.jupiter.params.provider.Arguments;
import org.junit.jupiter.params.provider.MethodSource;

import java.util.ArrayList;
import java.util.List;
import java.util.stream.Stream;

import static org.assertj.core.api.Assertions.assertThat;
import static org.assertj.core.api.Assertions.assertThatThrownBy;
import static org.junit.jupiter.params.provider.Arguments.of;

public class NumberUtilsTest {                    // A parameterized test is
                                                  // a perfect fit for these
                                                  // kinds of tests!
    @ParameterizedTest
    @MethodSource("testCases")                    // Indicates the name of
    void shouldReturnCorrectResult(List<Integer> left,  // the method that will
      List<Integer> right, List<Integer> expected) {    // provide the inputs
      assertThat(new NumberUtils().add(left, right))     // Calls the method
          .isEqualTo(expected);                          // under test, using the
    }                                                    // parameterized values

    static Stream<Arguments> testCases() {        // One argument per test case

      return Stream.of(
        of(null, numbers(7,2), null), // T1
        of(numbers(), numbers(7,2), numbers(7,2)), // T2       Tests with nulls
        of(numbers(9,8), null, null), // T3                    and empties
        of(numbers(9,8), numbers(), numbers(9,8 )), // T4

        of(numbers(1), numbers(2), numbers(3)), // T5          Tests with
        of(numbers(9), numbers(2), numbers(1,1)), // T6        single digits

        of(numbers(2,2), numbers(3,3), numbers(5,5)), // T7
        of(numbers(2,9), numbers(2,3), numbers(5,2)), // T8
        of(numbers(2,9,3), numbers(1,8,3), numbers(4,7,6)), // T9    Tests with
        of(numbers(1,7,9), numbers(2,6,8), numbers(4,4,7)), // T10   multiple
        of(numbers(1,9,1,7,1), numbers(1,8,1,6,1),                   digits
          numbers(3,7,3,3,2)), // T11
        of(numbers(9,9,8), numbers(1,7,2), numbers(1,1,7,0)), // T12

        of(numbers(2,2), numbers(3), numbers(2,5)), // T13.1
        of(numbers(3), numbers(2,2), numbers(2,5)), // T13.2
        of(numbers(2,2), numbers(9), numbers(3,1)), // T14.1
        of(numbers(9), numbers(2,2), numbers(3,1)), // T14.2
        of(numbers(1,7,3), numbers(9,2), numbers(2,6,5)), // T15.1
        of(numbers(9,2), numbers(1,7,3), numbers(2,6,5)), // T15.2
```

Tests with multiple digits, different length, with and without carry (from both sides)

Tests with multiple digits, different length, with and without carry (from both sides)

```
  of(numbers(3,1,7,9), numbers(2,6,8), numbers(3,4,4,7)), // T16.1
  of(numbers(2,6,8), numbers(3,1,7,9), numbers(3,4,4,7)), // T16.2
  of(numbers(1,9,1,7,1), numbers(2,1,8,1,6,1),
    numbers(2,3,7,3,3,2)), // T17.1
  of(numbers(2,1,8,1,6,1), numbers(1,9,1,7,1),
    numbers(2,3,7,3,3,2)), // T17.2
  of(numbers(9,9,8), numbers(9,1,7,2), numbers(1,0,1,7,0)), // T18.1
  of(numbers(9,1,7,2), numbers(9,9,8), numbers(1,0,1,7,0)), // T18.2
```

Tests with zeroes on the left

```
  of(numbers(0,0,0,1,2), numbers(0,2,3), numbers(3,5)), // T19
  of(numbers(0,0,0,1,2), numbers(0,2,9), numbers(4,1)), // T20

  of(numbers(9,9), numbers(1), numbers(1,0,0)) // T21    ◁─────  The boundary
  );                                                             test
}

private static List<Integer> numbers(int... nums) {   ◁─────┐
  List<Integer> list = new ArrayList<>();                    Auxiliary method
  for(int n : nums)                                          that produces a list of
    list.add(n);                                             integers. Auxiliary methods
  return list;                                               are common in test suites to
}                                                            help developers write more
                                                             maintainable test code.
}
```

Interestingly, a lot of these test cases break! See the JUnit report in figure 2.6. For example, take the first failing test, T6 (single digit with a carry). Given left = [9] and right = [2], we expect the output to be [1,1]. But the program outputs [1]! T12 ("carry propagated to a new (now most significant) digit") also fails: given left = [9,9,8] and right = [1,7,2], we expect the output to be [1,1,7,0], but it is [1,7,0]. The program cannot handle the carry when the carry needs to become a new leftmost digit.

What a tricky bug! Did you see it when we wrote the method implementation?

There is a simple fix: all we need to do is add the carry at the end, if necessary. Here's the implementation.

Listing 2.11   First bug fix in the add program

```
// ... all the code here ...
if (carry > 0)
    result.addFirst(carry);
return result;
```

With these tests passing, we see that the program does not handle zeroes to the left. When left = [0,0,0,1,2] and right = [0,2,3], we expect the output to be [3,5], but the program returns [0,0,0,3,5]. The fix is also straightforward: remove the zeroes on the left before returning the result (listing 2.12).

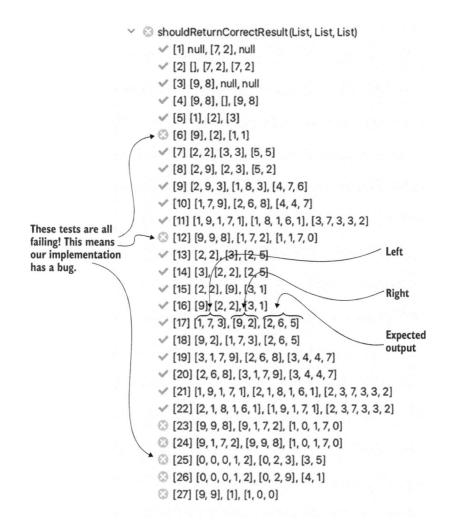

∨ ⊗ shouldReturnCorrectResult(List, List, List)
  ✔ [1] null, [7, 2], null
  ✔ [2] [], [7, 2], [7, 2]
  ✔ [3] [9, 8], null, null
  ✔ [4] [9, 8], [], [9, 8]
  ✔ [5] [1], [2], [3]
  ⊗ [6] [9], [2], [1, 1]
  ✔ [7] [2, 2], [3, 3], [5, 5]
  ✔ [8] [2, 9], [2, 3], [5, 2]
  ✔ [9] [2, 9, 3], [1, 8, 3], [4, 7, 6]
  ✔ [10] [1, 7, 9], [2, 6, 8], [4, 4, 7]
  ✔ [11] [1, 9, 1, 7, 1], [1, 8, 1, 6, 1], [3, 7, 3, 3, 2]

These tests are all failing! This means our implementation has a bug.

  ⊗ [12] [9, 9, 8], [1, 7, 2], [1, 1, 7, 0]
  ✔ [13] [2, 2], [3], [2, 5]   **Left**
  ✔ [14] [3], [2, 2], [2, 5]
  ✔ [15] [2, 2], [9], [3, 1]   **Right**
  ✔ [16] [9], [2, 2], [3, 1]
  ✔ [17] [1, 7, 3], [9, 2], [2, 6, 5]   **Expected output**
  ✔ [18] [9, 2], [1, 7, 3], [2, 6, 5]
  ✔ [19] [3, 1, 7, 9], [2, 6, 8], [3, 4, 4, 7]
  ✔ [20] [2, 6, 8], [3, 1, 7, 9], [3, 4, 4, 7]
  ✔ [21] [1, 9, 1, 7, 1], [2, 1, 8, 1, 6, 1], [2, 3, 7, 3, 3, 2]
  ✔ [22] [2, 1, 8, 1, 6, 1], [1, 9, 1, 7, 1], [2, 3, 7, 3, 3, 2]
  ⊗ [23] [9, 9, 8], [9, 1, 7, 2], [1, 0, 1, 7, 0]
  ⊗ [24] [9, 1, 7, 2], [9, 9, 8], [1, 0, 1, 7, 0]
  ⊗ [25] [0, 0, 0, 1, 2], [0, 2, 3], [3, 5]
  ⊗ [26] [0, 0, 0, 1, 2], [0, 2, 9], [4, 1]
  ⊗ [27] [9, 9], [1], [1, 0, 0]

Figure 2.6   The results of the test cases we just created. A lot of them fail, indicating that the program has a bug!

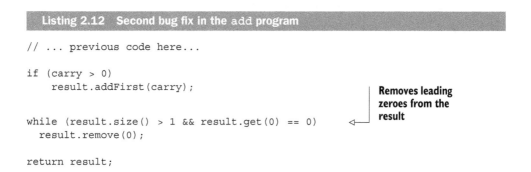

Listing 2.12   Second bug fix in the `add` program

```
// ... previous code here...

if (carry > 0)
    result.addFirst(carry);

while (result.size() > 1 && result.get(0) == 0)     ⟵ Removes leading
  result.remove(0);                                     zeroes from the
                                                        result
return result;
```

We're only missing test cases to ensure that the pre-condition holds that each digit is a number between 0 and 9. All we need to do is pass various invalid digits. Let's do it directly in the JUnit test as follows.

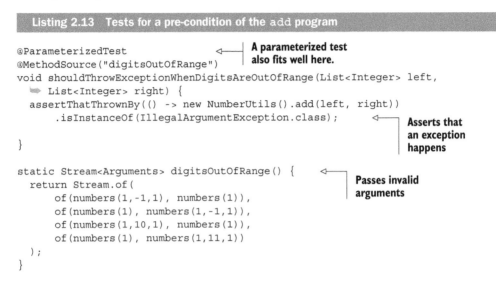

Listing 2.13   Tests for a pre-condition of the add program

```
@ParameterizedTest                          ←—  A parameterized test
@MethodSource("digitsOutOfRange")               also fits well here.
void shouldThrowExceptionWhenDigitsAreOutOfRange(List<Integer> left,
  ➥ List<Integer> right) {
    assertThatThrownBy(() -> new NumberUtils().add(left, right))
        .isInstanceOf(IllegalArgumentException.class);     ←—┐  Asserts that
                                                              an exception
}                                                             happens

static Stream<Arguments> digitsOutOfRange() {   ←—┐
    return Stream.of(                               Passes invalid
        of(numbers(1,-1,1), numbers(1)),            arguments
        of(numbers(1), numbers(1,-1,1)),
        of(numbers(1,10,1), numbers(1)),
        of(numbers(1), numbers(1,11,1))
    );
}
```

All tests are now passing. Given the thoroughness of our test suite, I feel confident enough to move on.

> **NOTE** Interestingly, the bugs we found in this example were caused not by buggy code but by a lack of code. This is a common type of bug, and it can be caught by specification testing. When in doubt, write a test! Writing automated (unit) test cases is so quick that they let you easily see what happens. Having too many useless tests is a problem, but a couple will not hurt.

2.4   Specification-based testing in the real world

Now that you have a clear understanding of how to systematically devise test cases based on specifications, here are a few pragmatic tips I have learned over the years.

2.4.1   The process should be iterative, not sequential

Describing iterative processes in writing is challenging. My explanation may have given you the impression that this process is fully sequential and that you move to the next step only when you have completed the previous one. However, the entire process is meant to be iterative. In practice, I go back and forth between the different steps. Often, when I'm writing test cases, I notice that I missed a partition or boundary, and I go back and improve my test suite.

2.4.2 *How far should specification testing go?*

The pragmatic answer to this question is to understand the risks of a failure. What would be the cost of a failure in that part of the program? If the cost is high, it may be wise to invest more in testing, explore more corner cases, and try different techniques to ensure quality. But if the cost is low, being less thorough may be good enough. Personally, I stop testing when I have been through all the steps a couple of times and cannot see a case I am not testing.

2.4.3 *Partition or boundary? It does not matter!*

When you are exploring inputs and outputs, identifying partitions, and devising test cases, you may end up considering a boundary to be an exclusive partition and not a boundary between two partitions. It does not matter if a specific case emerges when you are identifying partitions or in the boundaries step. Each developer may interpret the specification differently, and minor variations may result. The important thing is that the test case emerges and the bug will not slip into the program.

2.4.4 *On and off points are enough, but feel free to add in and out points*

On and off points belong to specific partitions, so they also serve as concrete test cases for the partitions. This means testing all the boundaries of your input domain is enough. Nevertheless, I often try some in and out points in my tests. They are redundant, because the on and off points exercise the same partition as the in and out points; but these extra points give me a better understanding of the program and may better represent real-life inputs. Striving for the leanest test suite is always a good idea, but a few extra points are fine.

2.4.5 *Use variations of the same input to facilitate understanding*

You can simplify your understanding of the different test cases by using the same input seed for all of them, as we noticed in an observational study with professional developers described in my paper with Treude and Zaidman (2021). For each partition, you then make small modifications to the input seed: just enough to meet the criteria of that partition. In the chapter example, all the test cases are based on the string "abc"; as soon as one test case fails, it is easy to compare it to similar inputs from other test cases that pass.

Note that this trick goes against the common testing idea of varying inputs as much as possible. Varying inputs is essential, as it allows us to explore the input space and identify corner cases. However, when doing specification-based testing, I prefer to focus on rigorously identifying and testing partitions. Later in the book, we will write test cases that explore the input domain in an automated fashion via property-based testing in chapter 5.

2.4.6   *When the number of combinations explodes, be pragmatic*

If we had combined all the partitions we derived from the substringsBetween program, we would have ended up with 320 tests. This number is even larger for more complex problems. Combinatorial testing is an entire area of research in software testing; I will not dive into the techniques that have been proposed for such situations, but I will provide you with two pragmatic suggestions.

First, reduce the number of combinations as much as possible. Testing exceptional behavior isolated from other behaviors (as we did in the example) is one way to do so. You may also be able to leverage your domain knowledge to further reduce the number of combinations.

Second, if you are facing many combinations at the method level, consider breaking the method in two. Two smaller methods have fewer things to test and, therefore, fewer combinations to test. Such a solution works well if you carefully craft the method contracts and the way they should pass information. You also reduce the chances of bugs when the two simple methods are combined into a larger, more complex one.

2.4.7   *When in doubt, go for the simplest input*

Picking concrete input for test cases is tricky. You want to choose a value that is realistic but, at the same time, simple enough to facilitate debugging if the test fails.

I recommend that you avoid choosing complex inputs unless you have a good reason to use them. Do not pick a large integer value if you can choose a small integer value. Do not pick a 100-character string if you can select a 5-character string. Simplicity matters.

2.4.8   *Pick reasonable values for inputs you do not care about*

Sometimes, your goal is to exercise a specific part of the functionality, and that part does not use one of the input values. You can pass any value to that "useless" input variable. In such scenarios, my recommendation is to pass realistic values for these inputs.

2.4.9   *Test for nulls and exceptional cases, but only when it makes sense*

Testing nulls and exceptional cases is always important because developers often forget to handle such cases in their code. But remember that you do not want to write tests that never catch a bug. Before writing such tests, you should understand the overall picture of the software system (and its architecture). The architecture may ensure that the pre-conditions of the method are satisfied before calling it.

If the piece of code you are testing is very close to the UI, exercise more corner cases such as null, empty strings, uncommon integer values, and so on. If the code is far from the UI and you are sure the data is sanitized before it reaches the component under test, you may be able to skip such tests. Context is king. Only write tests that will eventually catch a bug.

2.4.10 Go for parameterized tests when tests have the same skeleton

A little duplication is never a problem, but a lot of duplication is. We created 21 different tests for the substringsBetween program. The test code was lean because we grouped some of the test cases into single test methods. Imagine writing 21 almost-identical test cases. If each method took 5 lines of code, we would have a test class with 21 methods and 105 lines. This is much longer than the test suite with the parameterized test that we wrote.

Some developers argue that parameterized tests are confusing. Deciding whether to use JUnit test cases or parameterized tests is, most of all, a matter of taste. I use parameterized tests when the amount of duplication in my test suite is too large. In this chapter, I leaned more toward JUnit test cases: lots of test cases logically grouped in a small set of test methods. We discuss test code quality further in chapter 10.

2.4.11 Requirements can be of any granularity

The seven-step approach I propose in this chapter works for requirements of any granularity. Here, we applied it in a specification that could be implemented by a single method. However, nothing prevents you from using it with larger requirements that involve many classes. Traditionally, specification-based testing techniques focus on black-box testing: that is, testing an entire program or feature, rather than unit-testing specific components. I argue that these ideas also make sense at the unit level.

When we discuss larger tests (integration testing), we will also look at how to devise test cases for sets of classes or components. The approach is the same: reflect on the inputs and their expected outputs, divide the domain space, and create test cases. You can generalize the technique discussed here to tests at any level.

2.4.12 How does this work with classes and state?

The two methods we tested in this chapter have no state, so all we had to do was think of inputs and outputs. In object-oriented systems, classes have state. Imagine a Shop-pingCart class and a behavior totalPrice() that requires some CartItems to be inserted before the method can do its job. How do we apply specification-based testing in this case? See the following listing.

Listing 2.14 ShoppingCart and CartItem classes

```
public class ShoppingCart {

  private List<CartItem> items = new ArrayList<CartItem>();

  public void add(CartItem item) {          ◁──┐ Adds items
    this.items.add(item);                       │ to the cart
  }

  public double totalPrice() {        ◁──┐ Loops through all the items
    double totalPrice = 0;                │ and sums up the final price
    for (CartItem item : items) {
```

```
        totalPrice += item.getUnitPrice() * item.getQuantity();
    }
    return totalPrice;
    }
}

public class CartItem {

    private final String product;
    private final int quantity;
    private final double unitPrice;

    public CartItem(String product, int quantity,
      double unitPrice) {
        this.product = product;
        this.quantity = quantity;
        this.unitPrice = unitPrice;
    }

    // getters
}
```

A simple class that represents an item in the cart

Nothing changes in the way we approach specification-based testing. The only difference is that when we reflect about the method under test, we must consider not only the possible input parameters, but also the state the class should be in. For this specific example, looking at the expected behavior of the totalPrice method, I can imagine tests exercising the behavior of the method when the cart has zero items, a single item, multiple items, and various quantities (plus corner cases such as nulls). All we do differently is to set up the class's state (by adding multiple items to the cart) before calling the method we want to test, as in the following listing.

Listing 2.15 Tests for the ShoppingCart class

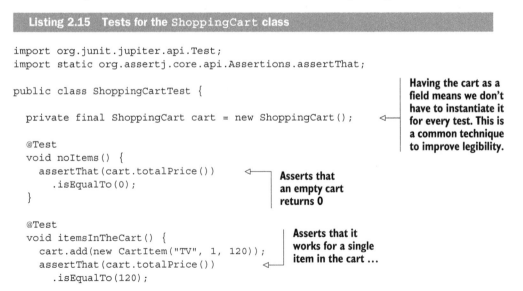

```
import org.junit.jupiter.api.Test;
import static org.assertj.core.api.Assertions.assertThat;

public class ShoppingCartTest {

    private final ShoppingCart cart = new ShoppingCart();

    @Test
    void noItems() {
        assertThat(cart.totalPrice())
          .isEqualTo(0);
    }

    @Test
    void itemsInTheCart() {
        cart.add(new CartItem("TV", 1, 120));
        assertThat(cart.totalPrice())
          .isEqualTo(120);
```

Having the cart as a field means we don't have to instantiate it for every test. This is a common technique to improve legibility.

Asserts that an empty cart returns 0

Asserts that it works for a single item in the cart ...

```
      cart.add(new CartItem("Chocolate", 2, 2.5));
      assertThat(cart.totalPrice())          ◁─────┐  ... as well as for
        .isEqualTo(120 + 2.5*2);                    │  many items in
  }                                                 │  the cart.
}
```

Again, the mechanics are the same. We just have to take more into consideration when engineering the test cases.

2.4.13 *The role of experience and creativity*

If two testers performed the specification-based testing technique I described earlier in the same program, would they develop the same set of tests? Ideally, but possibly not. In the substringsBetween() example, I would expect most developers to come up with similar test cases. But it is not uncommon for developers to approach a problem from completely different yet correct angles.

I am trying to reduce the role of experience and creativity by giving developers a process that everybody can follow, but in practice, experience and creativity make a difference in testing. We observed that in a small controlled experiment (Yu, Treude, and Aniche, 2019).

In the substringsBetween() example, experienced testers may see more complicated test cases, but a novice tester may have difficulty spotting those. A more experienced tester may realize that spaces in the string play no role and skip this test, whereas a novice developer may be in doubt and write an extra "useless" test. This is why I like the specification-based testing systematic approach I described in this chapter: it will help you remember what to think about. But it is still up to you to do the thinking!

Exercises

2.1 Which statement is false about applying the specification-based testing method on the following Java method?

```
/**
 * Puts the supplied value into the Map,
 * mapped by the supplied key.
 * If the key is already in the map, its
 * value will be replaced by the new value.
 *
 * NOTE: Nulls are not accepted as keys;
 *   a RuntimeException is thrown when key is null.
 *
 * @param key the key used to locate the value
 * @param value the value to be stored in the HashMap
 * @return the prior mapping of the key,
 *   or null if there was none.
 */
public V put(K key, V value) {
  // implementation here
}
```

A The specification does not specify any details about the value input parameter, and thus, experience should be used to partition it (for example, value being null or not null).

B The number of tests generated by the category/partition method can grow quickly, as the chosen partitions for each category are later combined one by one. This is not a practical problem for the put() method because the number of categories and partitions is small.

C In an object-oriented language, in addition to using the method's input parameters to explore partitions, we should also consider the object's internal state (the class's attributes), as it can also affect the method's behavior.

D With the available information, it is not possible to perform the category/partition method, as the source code is required for the last step (adding constraints).

2.2 Consider a find program that finds occurrences of a pattern in a file. The program has the following syntax:

```
find <pattern> <file>
```

After reading the specification and following specification-based testing, a tester devised the following partitions:

A Pattern size: empty, single character, many characters, longer than any line in the file

B Quoting: pattern is quoted, pattern is not quoted, pattern is improperly quoted

C Filename: good filename, no filename with this name, omitted

D Occurrences in the file: none, exactly one, more than one

E Occurrences in a single line, assuming the line contains the pattern: one, more than one

Now the number of combinations is too high. What actions could we take to reduce the number of combinations?

2.3 Postal codes in some imaginary country are always composed of four numbers and two letters: for example, 2628CD. Numbers are in the range [1000, 4000]. Letters are in the range [C, M].

Consider a program that receives two inputs—an integer (for the four numbers) and a string (for the two letters)—and returns true (valid postal code) or false (invalid postal code). The boundaries for this program appear to be straightforward:

A Anything below 1000: invalid

B [1000, 4000]: valid

C Anything above 4000: invalid

     D [A, B]: invalid

     E [C, M]: valid

     F [N, Z]: invalid

Based on what you as a tester assume about the program, what other corner or boundary cases can you come up with? Describe these invalid cases and how they may exercise the program based on your assumptions.

2.4 A program called FizzBuzz does the following: given an integer n, return the string formed from the number followed by "!". If the number is divisible by 3, use "Fizz" instead of the number; and if the number is divisible by 5, use "Buzz" instead of the number, and if the number is divisible by both 3 and 5, use "Fizz-Buzz" instead of the number.

    Examples:

    A The integer 3 yields "Fizz!"

    B The integer 4 yields "4!"

    C The integer 5 yields "Buzz!"

    D The integer 15 yields "FizzBuzz!"

    A novice tester is trying to devise as many tests as possible for the FizzBuzz method and comes up with the following:

    A T1 = 15

    B T2 = 30

    C T3 = 8

    D T4 = 6

    E T5 = 25

    Which of these tests can be removed while maintaining a good test suite? Which concept can we use to determine the test(s) that can be removed?

2.5 A game has the following condition: numberOfPoints <= 570. Perform boundary analysis on the condition. What are the on and off points?

    A On point = 570, off point = 571

    B On point = 571, off point = 570

    C On point = 570, off point = 569

    D On point = 569, off point = 570

2.6 Perform boundary analysis on the following equality: x == 10. What are the on and off points?

Summary

- Requirements are the most important artifact we can use to generate tests.
- Specification-based testing techniques help us explore the requirements in a systematic way. For example, they help us examine the domain space of the different input variables and how they interact with each other.

- I propose a seven-step approach for specification testing: (1) understand the requirements, (2) explore the program if you do not know much about it, (3) judiciously analyze the properties of the inputs and outputs and identify the partitions, (4) analyze the boundaries, (5) devise concrete test cases, (6) implement the concrete test cases as automated (JUnit) tests, and (7) use creativity and experience to augment the test suite.
- Bugs love boundaries. However, identifying the boundaries may be the most challenging part of specification testing.
- The number of test cases may be too large, even in simpler programs. This means you must decide what should be tested and what should not be tested.

Structural testing and code coverage

This chapter covers

- Creating test cases based on the code structure
- Combining structural testing and specification-based testing
- Using code coverage properly
- Why some developers (wrongly) dislike code coverage

In the previous chapter, we discussed using software requirements as the main element to guide the testing. Once specification-based testing is done, the next step is to *augment the test suite with the help of the source code*. There are several reasons to do so.

First, you may have forgotten a partition or two when analyzing the requirements, and you may notice that while looking at the source code. Second, when implementing code, you take advantage of language constructs, algorithms, and data structures that are not explicit in the documentation. Implementation-specific details should also be exercised to increase the likelihood of ensuring the program's full correctness.

In this chapter, we learn how to systematically reflect on the source code, see what is being exercised by the test suite we derived with the help of the specification, and what remains to be tested. Using the structure of the source code to guide testing is also known as *structural testing*. Understanding structural testing techniques means understanding the *coverage criteria*. The remainder of this chapter explores using code coverage information to gain more confidence that the program works as expected.

3.1   Code coverage, the right way

Consider the following requirement for a small program that counts the number of words in a string that end with either "r" or "s" (inspired by a CodingBat problem, https://codingbat.com/prob/p199171):

> Given a sentence, the program should count the number of words that end with either "s" or "r". A word ends when a non-letter appears. The program returns the number of words.

A developer implements this requirement as shown in the following listing.

Listing 3.1   Implementing the `CountWords` program

```java
public class CountWords {
  public int count(String str) {
    int words = 0;
    char last = ' ';                          Loops through
                                              each character
    for (int i = 0; i < str.length(); i++) {  in the string

      if (!isLetter(str.charAt(i)) &&         If the current character is a non-
        (last == 's' || last == 'r')) {       letter and the previous character
          words++;                            was "s" or "r", we have a word!
      }

      last = str.charAt(i);          Stores the current
    }                                character as the
                                     "last" one

    if (last == 'r' || last == 's') {      Counts one more
      words++;                             word if the string
    }                                      ends in "r" or "s"

    return words;
  }
}
```

Now, consider a developer who does not know much about specification-based testing techniques and writes the following two JUnit tests for the implementation.

Listing 3.2   Initial (incomplete) tests for `CountWords`

```
@Test
void twoWordsEndingWithS() {
    int words = new CountLetters().count("dogs cats");
    assertThat(words).isEqualTo(2);
}

@Test
void noWordsAtAll() {
    int words = new CountLetters().count("dog cat");
    assertThat(words).isEqualTo(0);
}
```

Two words ending in "s" (dogs and cats): we expect the program to return 2.

No words ending in "s" or "r" in the string: the program returns 0.

This test suite is far from complete—for example, it does not exercise words ending in "r". Structural testing shows its value in such situations: we can identify parts of the test code that our test suite does not exercise, determine why this is the case, and create new test cases.

Identifying which parts of the code our tests exercise is straightforward today, thanks to the many production-ready code coverage tools on the market for all programming languages and environments. For example, figure 3.1 shows the report generated by JaCoCo (www.jacoco.org/jacoco), a very popular code coverage tool for Java, after running the two tests in listing 3.2.

Diamonds indicate that this is a branching instruction and there may be many cases to cover.

```
public class CountWords {
    public int count(String str) {
        int words = 0;
        char last = ' ';
        for (int i = 0; i < str.length(); i++) {
            if (!Character.isLetter(str.charAt(i)) && (last == 's' || last == 'r')) {
                words++;
            }
            last = str.charAt(i);
        }
        if (last == 'r' || last == 's')
            words++;
        return words;
    }
}
```

The color indicates whether the line is covered.

Figure 3.1   Code coverage achieved by the two tests in the `CountWords` implementation. The two `if` lines are only partially covered.

The background color of each line indicates its coverage (the colors appear as shades of gray in the printed book):

- A green background indicates that a line is completely covered by the test suite. In the figure, all lines with the exception of the two `if`s are green.
- A yellow background means the line is partially covered by the test suite. For example, in the figure, the two `if` statement lines are only partially covered.

- A red background means the line is not covered. In the figure, there are no red lines, which means all lines are exercised by at least one test.
- Lines with no background color (such as }) are lines the coverage tool does not see. Behind the scenes, coverage tools are instrumenting the compiled byte-code of the program. Things like closing brackets and method declaration lines are not really counted.

JaCoCo also uses a diamond to identify a line that may branch the program, including the for and if statements in figure 3.1, as well as while, for, do-while, ternary ifs, lambda expressions, and so on. Hovering your mouse over the diamond shows the details.

As previously mentioned, the first if statement has a yellow background, indicating that although the line is covered, not all of its branches are. When I look at the details of the report, the tool says that one out of six combinations (three conditions in the if statement times two options, true and false) is not covered. See figure 3.2.

```
1.  package book;
2.
3.  public class CountWords {
4.      public int count(String str) {
5.          int words = 0;
6.          char last = ' ';
7.  ◆       for (int i = 0; i < str.length(); i++) {
8.  ◆           if (!Character.isLetter(str.charAt(i)) && (last == 's' || last == 'r')) {
9.                  words++;
10.             }
11.             last = str.charAt(i);
12.         }
13. ◆       if (last == 'r' || last == 's')
14.             words++;
15.         return words;
16.     }
17. }
```

Figure 3.2 JaCoCo shows how many branches we are missing.

The current test suite does not fully exercise the last == 'r' condition. This is useful information; thanks to structural testing, the tester can now figure out why this test case did not emerge before.

Reasons to miss a test case

Here are some pragmatic reasons a developer may miss a test case:

- The developer made a mistake. The specification was clear about the requirement.
- The specification did not mention the case, and it is unclear whether the behavior is expected. The developer must decide whether to bring it to the requirements engineer. Is it a mistake in the implementation?

- The specification did not mention the case, but the code has a reason to exist. For example, implementation details such as performance and persistence often force developers to write code that is not reflected in the (functional) requirement. The developer should add a new test to the test suite, which will exercise the implementation-specific behavior that may cause bugs.

Moving on with the example, we write a test case that exercises the "words that end in 'r'" partition as follows.

Listing 3.3 Testing for words that end in "r"

```
@Test
void wordsThatEndInR() {
  int words = new CountWords().count("car bar");
  assertThat(words).isEqualTo(2);
}
```

> Words that end in "r" should be counted.

With the newly added test case in the test suite, we rerun the coverage tool. Figure 3.3 shows the new JaCoCo report. Every line is now fully covered: we have covered all the lines and conditions of the code under test. If parts of the code were still not covered, we would repeat the process: identify uncovered parts, understand why they are not covered, and write a test that exercises that piece of code.

> All lines are green, which means all lines and branches of the method are covered by at least one test case.

```
public class CountWords {
    public int count(String str) {
        int words = 0;
        char last = ' ';
        for (int i = 0; i < str.length(); i++) {
            if (!Character.isLetter(str.charAt(i)) && (last == 's' || last == 'r')) {
                words++;
            }
            last = str.charAt(i);
        }
        if (last == 'r' || last == 's')
            words++;
        return words;
    }
}
```

Figure 3.3 Code coverage of the three tests for the CountWords implementation. The test suite now achieves full coverage of branches and conditions.

3.2   *Structural testing in a nutshell*

Based on what we just did, let me define a simple approach that any developer can follow (see figure 3.4):

1 Perform *specification-based testing,* as discussed in the previous chapter.
2 *Read the implementation,* and understand the main coding decisions made by the developer.
3 Run the devised test suite with a *code coverage tool.*
4 For each piece of code that is *not* covered:

    a *Understand* why that piece of code was not tested. Why didn't you see this test case during specification-based testing? Consult with the requirements engineer if you need more clarity.

    b *Decide* whether the piece of code deserves a test. Testing or not testing that piece of code is now a conscious decision on your part.

    c If a test is needed, *implement an automated test case* that covers the missing piece.

5 Go back to the source code and *look for other interesting tests you can devise* based on the code. For each identified piece of the code, perform the substeps of step 4.

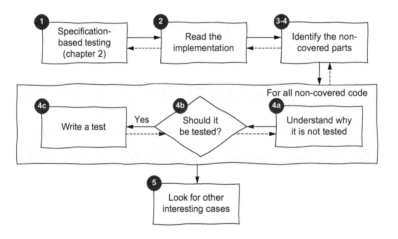

Figure 3.4   Applying structural testing in a nutshell. Arrows indicate the iterative nature of the process. The diamond represents the moment where the developer decides whether to write the test case.

The most important thing about this approach is that *structural testing complements the test suite previously devised via specification-based testing.* The code coverage tool is an automated way to identify parts that are not covered.

    Just like the approach I proposed in chapter 2, this one is meant to be iterative and not to restrain you to a single way of working. It is not uncommon to go back to the specification and devise additional interesting test cases.

Before I show another running example of structural testing and discuss how to pragmatically use it in our daily lives, the next section introduces the coverage criteria we use with this approach.

3.3 *Code coverage criteria*

Whenever we identify a line of code that is not covered, we have to decide how thorough (or rigorous) we want to be when covering that line. Let's revisit an `if` statement from the `CountWords` program.

Listing 3.4 An `if` expression from the `CountWords` program

```
if (!Character.isLetter(str.charAt(i)) &&
  (last == 's' || last == 'r'))
```

A developer may decide to only *cover the line*—in other words, if a test passes through that `if` line, the developer will consider it covered. A single test case can do this. A slightly more thorough developer may cover the `if` being evaluated to `true` and `false`; doing so requires two test cases. A third developer may explore each condition in the `if` statement. This particular `if` has three conditions requiring at least two tests each, for a total of six tests. Finally, a very thorough tester may decide to cover every possible execution path of this statement. Given that it has three different conditions, doing so requires $2 \times 2 \times 2 = 8$ test cases.

Let's formalize this discussion. Note that you've already seen some of these terms.

3.3.1 *Line coverage*

A developer who aims to achieve line coverage wants at least one test case that covers the line under test. It does not matter if that line contains a complex `if` statement full of conditions. If a test touches that line in any way, the developer can count the line as covered.

3.3.2 *Branch coverage*

Branch coverage takes into consideration the fact that branching instructions (`if`s, `for`s, `while`s, and so on) make the program behave in different ways, depending how the instruction is evaluated. For a simple `if(a && b)` statement, having a test case T1 that makes the `if` statement `true` and another test case T2 that makes the statement `false` is enough to consider the branch covered.

Figure 3.5 illustrates a control-flow graph (CFG) of the `CountWords` program. You can see that for each `if` instruction, two edges come out of the node: one representing where the flow goes if the statement is evaluated to `true` and another representing where the program goes if the statement is evaluated to `false`. Covering all the edges in the graph means achieving 100% branch coverage.

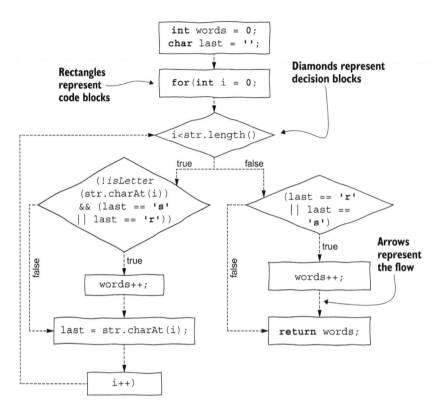

Figure 3.5   A control-flow graph of the CountWords **program**

3.3.3   *Condition + branch coverage*

Condition + branch coverage considers not only possible branches but also each condition of each branch statement. For example, the first if statement in the Count-Words program contains three conditions: !Character.isLetter(str.charAt(i)), last == 's', and last == 'r'. Therefore, a developer aiming for condition + branch coverage should create a test suite that exercises each of those individual conditions being evaluated to true and false at least once *and* the entire branch statement being true and false at least once.

Note that blindly looking only at the conditions (and ignoring how they are combined) may result in test suites that do not cover everything. Imagine a simple if (A || B). A test suite composed of two tests (T1 that makes A true and B false and T2 that makes A false and B true) covers the two conditions, as each condition is exercised as true and false. However, the test suite does not fully cover the branch, as in both tests, the evaluation of the entire if statement is always true. This is why we use condition + branch coverage, and not only (basic) condition coverage.

In the extended CFG in figure 3.6, branch nodes contain only a single condition. The complicated if is broken into three nodes.

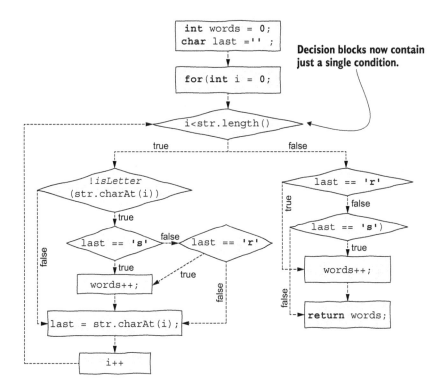

Figure 3.6   The extended control-flow graph of the CountWords **program. Each condition is in its own node. Covering all the edges in the graph means achieving 100% condition + branch coverage.**

3.3.4   Path coverage

A developer aiming for path coverage covers *all* the possible paths of execution of the program. While ideally this is the strongest criterion, it is often impossible or too expensive to achieve. In a single program with three conditions, where each condition could be independently evaluated to true or false, we would have $2^3 = 8$ paths to cover. In a program with 10 conditions, the total number of combinations would be $2^{10} = 1024$. In other words, we would need to devise more than a thousand tests!

Path coverage also gets more complicated for programs with loops. In a program with an unbounded loop, the loop might iterate hundreds of times. A rigorous tester aiming for path coverage would have to try the program with the loop executing one time, two times, three times, and so on.

3.4   *Complex conditions and the MC/DC coverage criterion*

Devising test suites that maximize the number of bugs they can identify while minimizing the effort/cost of building the test suite is part of any tester's job. The question is, what can we do about complex, lengthy `if` statements? Modified condition/decision coverage (MC/DC) is a good answer.

The MC/DC criterion looks at combinations of conditions, as path coverage does. However, instead of testing *all* possible combinations, we identify the *important* combinations that need to be tested. MC/DC exercises each of these conditions so that it can, independently of the other conditions, affect the outcome of the entire decision. Every possible condition of each parameter must influence the outcome at least once. (For details, read Kelly Hayhurst's 2001 paper.)

3.4.1   *An abstract example*

Let's take a simple abstract example: `if(A && (B || C))`, where A, B, and C all evaluate to booleans. MC/DC dictates the following:

- For condition A:
  - There must be one test case where A = true (say, T1).
  - There must be one test case where A = false (say, T2).
  - T1 and T2 (which we call *independence pairs*) must have different outcomes (for example, T1 makes the entire decision evaluate to true, and T2 makes the entire decision evaluate to false).
  - Variables B and C in T1 must be equivalent (either both evaluate to true or both evaluate to false) to B and C in T2. In other words, B and C must have the same truth values in T1 and T2.
- For condition B:
  - There must be one test case where B = true (say, T3).
  - There must be one test case where B = false (say, T4).
  - T3 and T4 must have different outcomes.
  - Variables A and C in T3 must be equivalent to A and C in T4.
- For condition C:
  - There must be one test case where C = true (say, T5).
  - There must be one test case where C = false (say, T6).
  - T5 and T6 have different outcomes.
  - Variables A and B in T5 must be equivalent to A and B in T6.

If conditions have only binary outcomes (that is, true or false), the number of tests required to achieve 100% MC/DC coverage is N + 1, where N is the number of conditions in the decision (as shown by Chilenski [2001]). Note that N + 1 is smaller than the total number of possible combinations (2^N). So, to devise a test suite that achieves 100% MC/DC, we must create N + 1 test cases that, when combined, exercise all the combinations independently from the others.

3.4.2   Creating a test suite that achieves MC/DC

The question is how to (mechanically) select such test cases. Let's continue using the same if statement from the CountWords program (from listing 3.4). The statement takes three booleans as input: (1) whether the current character is a letter and whether this letter is (2) "s" or (3) "r". Generically, this is the same as the A && (B || C) example we just discussed.

To test this program, we first use a truth table to see all the combinations and their outcomes. In this case, we have three decisions, and $2^3 = 8$. Therefore, we have tests T1 to T8, as listed in table 3.1.

Table 3.1   Truth table for the if expression from the CountWords program

Test case	isLetter	last == s	last == r	decision
T1	true	true	true	true
T2	true	true	false	true
T3	true	false	true	true
T4	true	false	false	false
T5	false	true	true	false
T6	false	true	false	false
T7	false	false	true	false
T8	false	false	false	false

Our goal is to apply the MC/DC criterion to these test cases and select N + 1 tests, which in this case means 3 + 1 = 4. To determine which four tests satisfy MC/DC, we need to go condition by condition, beginning by selecting the pairs of combinations (or tests) for the isLetter part of the condition:

- For T1, isLetter, last == s, and last == r are all true, and decision (that is, the outcome of the entire boolean expression) is also true. We now look for another test in the table where the value of isLetter is the opposite of the value in T1 but the other values (last == s and last == r) are the same. This means look for a test where isLetter is false, last == s is true, last == r is true, and decision is false. This combination appears in T5.

  Thus, we have found a pair of tests, T1 and T5 (an independence pair), where isLetter is the only parameter that is different and the outcome (decision) changes. In other words, for this pair of tests, isLetter *independently* influences the outcome (decision). Let's keep the pair {T1, T5} in our list of test cases.

- We could stop here and move to the next variable. But finding all independence pairs for isLetter may help us reduce the final number of test cases, as you will see. So let's continue and look at the next test. In T2, isLetter is true, `last == s` is true, `last == r` is false, and `decision` is true. We repeat the process and search for a test where `isLetter` is the opposite of the value in T2 but `last == s` and `last == r` remain the same. We find this combination in T6.

We have found another pair of tests, T2 and T6, where `isLetter` is the only parameter that is different and the outcome (`decision`) also changes, which we also add to our list of test cases.

- We repeat the process for T3 (`isLetter` is true, `last == s` is false, `last == r` is true) and find that the `isLetter` parameter in T7 (`isLetter` is false, `last == s` is false, `last == r` is true) is the opposite of the value in T3 and changes the outcome (`decision`).
- The pair for T4 (`isLetter` is true, `last == s` is false, `last == r` is false) is T8 (`isLetter` is false, `last == s` is false, `last == r` is false). The outcome of both tests is the same (`decision` is false), which means the pair {T4, T8} does *not* show how `isLetter` can independently affect the overall outcome.

We do not find another new or suitable pair when repeating the process for T5, T6, T7, and T8, so we move on from the `isLetter` parameter to the `last == s` parameter. We repeat the same process, but now we search for the opposite value of parameter `last == s`, while `isLetter` and `last == r` stay the same:

- For T1 (`isLetter` is true, `last == s` is true, `last == r` is true), we search for a test where `isLetter` is true, `last == s` is false, `last == r` is true). This appears to be the case in T3. However, the outcome is the same for both test cases. Therefore, {T1, T3} does *not* show how the `last == s` parameter independently affects the outcome.
- After repeating all the steps for the other tests, we find that only {T2, T4} have different values for the `last == s` parameter where the outcome also changes.

Finally, we move to the `last == r` parameter. As with the `last == s` parameter, one pair of combinations works: {T3, T4}. I highly recommend carrying out the entire process yourself to get a feel for how it works.

We now have all the pairs for each parameter:

- `isLetter`: {1, 5}, {2, 6}, {3, 7}
- `last == s`: {2, 4}
- `last == r`: {3, 4}

Having a single independence pair per variable (`isLetter`, `last == s`, and `last == r`) is enough. We want to minimize the total number of tests, and we know we can achieve this with N + 1 tests. We do not have any choices with conditions `last == s` and `last == r`, as we found only one pair of tests for each parameter. This means we need tests T2, T3, and T4. Finally, we need to find the appropriate pair of tests for `isLetter`. Note that any of the test pairs (T1-T5, T2-T6, or T3-T7) would work. However, we want to reduce the total number of tests in the test suite (and again, we know we only need four in this case).

If we were to pick T1 or T5, we would have to include the other as well, as they are opposites. Therefore, they are unnecessarily increasing the number of tests. To ensure that our test suite contains at most four test cases, we can add either T6 or T7, as their opposites (T2 and T3) are already included in our test cases. I picked T6 randomly. (You can have more than one set of tests that achieves 100% MC/DC, and all solutions are equally acceptable.)

Therefore, the tests we need for 100% MC/DC coverage are {T2, T3, T4, T6}. These are the only four tests we need—certainly cheaper than the eight tests we would need for path coverage. Now that we know which tests we need to implement, we can automate them.

> **NOTE** I have a video on YouTube that explains MC/DC visually: www.youtube .com/watch?v=HzmnCVaICQ4.

3.5   *Handling loops and similar constructs*

You may wonder what to do in the case of loops, such as `for` and `while`. The code block inside the loop may be executed different numbers of times, making testing more complicated.

Think of a `while(true)` loop, which can be non-terminating. To be rigorous, we would have to test the program with the loop block executed one time, two times, three times, and so on. Or imagine a `for(i = 0; i < 10; i++)` loop with a `break` inside the body. We would have to test what happened if the loop body executed up to 10 times. How can we handle a long-lasting loop (that runs for many iterations) or an unbounded loop (that is executed an unknown number of times)?

Given that exhaustive testing is impossible, testers often rely on the *loop boundary adequacy criterion* to decide when to stop testing a loop. A test suite satisfies this criterion if and only if for every loop

- There is a test case that exercises the loop zero times.
- There is a test case that exercises the loop once.
- There is a test case that exercises the loop multiple times.

Pragmatically speaking, my experience shows that the main challenge comes when devising the test case for the loop being executed multiple times. Should the test case force the loop to iterate 2, 5, or 10 times? This decision requires a good understanding of the program and its requirement. With optimal understanding of the specs, you should be able to devise good tests for the loop. Do not be afraid to create two or more tests for the "multiple times" case. Do whatever you need to do to ensure that the loop works as expected.

3.6   *Criteria subsumption, and choosing a criterion*

You may have noticed that some of the criteria we have discussed are more rigorous than others. For example, a single test is enough to achieve 100% line coverage, but two tests are needed for 100% branch coverage. Some strategies *subsume* other strategies.

Formally, a strategy X subsumes strategy Y if all elements that Y exercises are also exercised by X. Figure 3.7 illustrates the relationships among the coverage criteria.

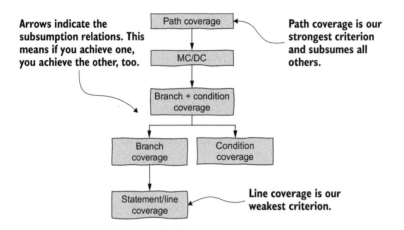

Figure 3.7   The different coverage criteria and their subsumption relations

Branch coverage subsumes line coverage, which means 100% branch coverage always implies 100% line coverage. However, 100% line coverage does not imply 100% branch coverage. Moreover, 100% condition + branch coverage always implies 100% branch coverage and 100% line coverage. Following this train of thought, we see that path coverage subsumes all other criteria. This is logical as path coverage covers all possible paths of the program. Next, we see that MC/DC is stronger than condition + branch coverage, as MC/DC ensures the independence of each condition. And condition + branch coverage subsumes both branch and condition coverage independently. Finally, all other criteria, except basic condition coverage, subsume line coverage, which is the weakest criterion in the figure.

   You now understand the trade-offs of choosing one criterion over another. A weaker criterion may be cheaper and faster to achieve but leave many parts of the code uncovered. On the other hand, a stronger criterion may cover the code more rigorously at a higher cost. It is up to you, the developer, to decide which criterion to use.

> **NOTE**   Basic condition coverage does not necessarily subsume line coverage, for the same reason we always use condition + branch coverage together. We can achieve 100% basic condition coverage in a simple `if(A || B)` by having two tests, T1={true, false} and T2={false, true}. But both tests make the decision block `true`, so the `false` branch and its lines are not exercised.

3.7 Specification-based and structural testing: A running example

Let's try specification-based testing and structural testing together on a real-world example: the leftPad() function from Apache Commons Lang (http://mng.bz/zQ2g):

Left-pad a string with a specified string. Pad to a size of size.

- str—The string to pad out; may be null.
- size—The size to pad to.
- padStr—The string to pad with. Null or empty is treated as a single space.

The method returns a left-padded string, the original string if no padding is necessary, or null if a null string is input.

For example, if we give "abc" as the string input, a dash "-" as the pad string, and 5 as the size, the program will output "--abc".

A developer on your team comes up with the implementation in listing 3.5. For now, suppose you are testing code written by others, so you need to build an understanding of the code before you can test it properly. Specification-based testing and structural testing are applied the same way, regardless of whether you wrote the code. In later chapters, we discuss test-driven development and how you can use tests to guide you through implementation.

Listing 3.5 `leftPad` **implementation from the Apache Commons**

```
public static String leftPad(final String str, final int size,
  String padStr) {

  if (str == null) {            ⟵─┤ If the string to pad is
    return null;                     │ null, we return null
  }                                  │ right away.


  if (padStr==null || padStr.isEmpty()) {    ⟵   If the pad string is
    padStr = SPACE;                                 null or empty, we
  }                                                  make it a space.
  final int padLen = padStr.length();
  final int strLen = str.length();
  final int pads = size - strLen;    ┌─ There is no
                                      │ need to pad
                                      │ this string.
  if (pads <= 0) {            ⟵─┘
    // returns original String when possible
    return str;
  }                                         If the number of characters to
                                            pad matches the size of the
                                            pad string, we concatenate it.
  if (pads == padLen) {         ⟵────────
    return padStr.concat(str);
  } else if (pads < padLen) {      ⟵──────── If we cannot fit the entire
    return padStr.substring(0, pads).concat(str);      pad string, we add only
                                                        the part that fits.
```

```
  } else {
    final char[] padding = new char[pads];
    final char[] padChars = padStr.toCharArray();

    for (int i = 0; i < pads; i++) {
      padding[i] = padChars[i % padLen];
    }

    return new String(padding).concat(str);
  }
}
```

◁──┐ **We have to add the pad string more than once. We go character by character until the string is fully padded.**

Now it is time for some systematic testing. As we know, the first step is to apply specification-based testing. Let's follow the process discussed in chapter 2 (I suggest you try to do it yourself and compare your solution to mine):

1 We read the requirements. We understand that the program adds a given character/string to the beginning (left) of the string, up to a specific size. The program has three input parameters: str, representing the original string to be padded; size, representing the desired size of the returned string; and padStr, representing the string used to pad. The program returns a String. The program has specific behavior if any of the inputs is null. (If we had implemented the feature ourselves, we would probably skip this step, as we would already have a complete understanding of the requirements.)

2 Based on all the observations in step 1, we derive the following list of partitions:
   – str parameter
     ▪ Null
     ▪ Empty string
     ▪ Non-empty string
   – size parameter
     ▪ Negative number
     ▪ Positive number
   – padStr parameter
     ▪ Null
     ▪ Empty
     ▪ Non-empty
   – str, size parameters
     ▪ size < len(str)
     ▪ size > len(str)

3 There are several boundaries:
   – size being precisely 0
   – str having length 1
   – padStr having length 1
   – size being precisely the length of str

4 We can devise single tests for exceptional cases such as null, empty, and negative size. We also have a boundary related to padStr: we can exercise padStr with a single character only once and have all other tests use a pad with a single character (otherwise, the number of combinations would be too large). We obtain the following tests:

- T1: str is null.
- T2: str is empty.
- T3: negative size.
- T4: padStr is null.
- T5: padStr is empty.
- T6: padStr has a single character.
- T7: size is equal to the length of str.
- T8: size is equal to 0.
- T9: size is smaller than the length of str.

Now we automate the tests. I used a parameterized test, but it is fine if you prefer nine traditional JUnit tests.

Listing 3.6   Tests for LeftPad after specification-based testing

```
public class LeftPadTest {

    @ParameterizedTest
    @MethodSource("generator")
    void test(String originalStr, int size, String padString,
      String expectedStr) {                              ◁─────  The parameterized
        assertThat(leftPad(originalStr, size, padString))        test, similar to the
            .isEqualTo(expectedStr);                             ones we have written
    }                                                            before

    static Stream<Arguments> generator() {          ◁─────  The nine tests we created
        return Stream.of(                                   are provided by the
T1 └──▷     of(null, 10, "-", null),                         method source.
T2 ┌──▷     of("", 5, "-", "-----"),
           of("abc", -1, "-", "abc"),     ◁───  T3
T4 ───▷    of("abc", 5, null, " abc"),
           of("abc", 5, "", " abc"),      ◁───  T5
T6 ───▷    of("abc", 5, "-", "--abc"),
           of("abc", 3, "-", "abc"),      ◁───  T7
T8 ───▷    of("abc", 0, "-", "abc"),
           of("abc", 2, "-", "abc")       ◁───  T9
        );
    }
}
```

It is time to augment the test suite through structural testing. Let's use a code coverage tool to tell us what we have already covered (see figure 3.8). The report shows that we are missing some branches: the if (pads == padLen) and else if (pads < padLen) expressions.

```java
public static String leftPad(final String str, final int size, String padStr) {
    if (str == null) {
        return null;
    }
    if (isEmpty(padStr)) {
        padStr = SPACE;
    }
    final int padLen = padStr.length();
    final int strLen = str.length();
    final int pads = size - strLen;
    if (pads <= 0) {
        return str; // returns original String when possible
    }

    if (pads == padLen) {
        return padStr.concat(str);
    } else if (pads < padLen) {
        return padStr.substring(0, pads).concat(str);
    } else {
        final char[] padding = new char[pads];
        final char[] padChars = padStr.toCharArray();
        for (int i = 0; i < pads; i++) {
            padding[i] = padChars[i % padLen];
        }
        return new String(padding).concat(str);
    }
}
```

**The red lines indicate parts of the
code that are still not covered!**

Figure 3.8   Code coverage achieved by the specification-based tests for the `leftPad` method. The
two `return` lines near the arrow are not covered; the `if` and `else if`, also near the arrow, are
only partially covered. The remaining lines are fully covered.

This is useful information. Why didn't we cover these lines? What did we miss? As a
developer, you should triangulate what you see in the source with the specification
and your mental model of the program. In this case, we conclude that we did not
exercise padStr being smaller, greater, or equal to the remaining space in str. What a
tricky boundary! This is why structural testing is essential: it helps identify partitions
and boundaries we may have missed.

With that information in mind, we derive three more test cases:

- T10: the length of padStr is equal to the remaining spaces in str.
- T11: the length of padStr is greater than the remaining spaces in str.
- T12: the length of padStr is smaller than the remaining spaces in str (this test
  may be similar to T6).

We add these three extra test cases to our parameterized test, as shown in listing 3.7.
When we run the coverage tool again, we get a report similar to the one in figure 3.9.
We now cover all the branches.

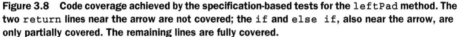

Listing 3.7   Three new test cases for `leftPad`

```java
static Stream<Arguments> generator() {
  return Stream.of(
    // ... others here
```

```
    of("abc", 5, "--", "--abc"), // T10
    of("abc", 5, "---", "--abc"), // T11
    of("abc", 5, "-", "--abc") // T12
  );
}
```

**All lines are green.
Everything is
covered!**

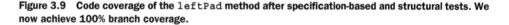

```
public static String leftPad(final String str, final int size, String padStr) {
    if (str == null) {
        return null;
    }
    if (isEmpty(padStr)) {
        padStr = SPACE;
    }
    final int padLen = padStr.length();
    final int strLen = str.length();
    final int pads = size - strLen;
    if (pads <= 0) {
        return str; // returns original String when possible
    }

    if (pads == padLen) {
        return padStr.concat(str);
    } else if (pads < padLen) {
        return padStr.substring(0, pads).concat(str);
    } else {
        final char[] padding = new char[pads];
        final char[] padChars = padStr.toCharArray();
        for (int i = 0; i < pads; i++) {
            padding[i] = padChars[i % padLen];
        }
        return new String(padding).concat(str);
    }
}
```

Figure 3.9   Code coverage of the `leftPad` method after specification-based and structural tests. We now achieve 100% branch coverage.

NOTE   Interestingly, if you look at the entire class, JaCoCo does not give 100% coverage, but only 96%. The report highlights the first line of the file: the declaration of the class, `public class LeftPadUtils {`. The `leftPad` method is static, so none of our tests instantiate this class. Given that we know the context, we can ignore the fact that this line is not covered. This is a good example of why only looking at the numbers makes no sense. We discuss this further, later in the chapter.

With all the branches covered, we now look for other interesting cases to test. The implementation contains interesting decisions that we may decide to test. In particular, we observe an `if (pads <= 0)` block with the code comment "returns original String when possible". As a tester, you may decide to test this specific behavior: "If the string is not padded, the program should return the same `String` instance." That can be written as a JUnit test as follows.

Listing 3.8   Another extra test for `leftPad`

```
@Test
void sameInstance() {
  String str = "sometext";
  assertThat(leftPad(str, 5, "-")).isSameAs(str);
}
```

We are now much more confident that our test suite covers all the critical behavior of the program. Structural testing and code coverage helped us identify parts of the code that we did not test (or partitions we missed) during our specification-based testing—and that is what structural testing is all about.

3.8   Boundary testing and structural testing

The most challenging part of specification-based testing is identifying boundaries. They are tricky to find, given the way we write specifications. Luckily, they are much easier to find in source code, given how precise code has to be. All the boundary testing ideas we discussed in the previous chapter apply here.

The idea of identifying and testing on and off points fits nicely in structural testing. For example, we can analyze the `if` statements in the `leftPad` program:

- `if (pads <= 0)`—The on point is 0 and evaluates the expression to `true`. The off point is the nearest point to the on point that makes the expression evaluate to `false`. In this case, given that `pads` is an integer, the nearest point is 1.
- `if (pads == padLen)`—The on point is `padLen`. Given the equality and that `padLen` is an integer, we have two off points: one that happens when `pads == padLen - 1` and another that happens when `pads = padLen + 1`.
- `if (pads < padLen)`—The on point is again `padLen`. The on point evaluates the expression to `false`. The off point is, therefore, `pads == padLen - 1`.

As a tester, you may want to use this information to see whether you can augment your test suite.

We discussed the loop boundary criterion earlier, which helps us try different possible boundaries. If a loop has a less conventional, more complicated expression, consider applying on and off analysis there as well.

3.9   Structural testing alone often is not enough

If code is the source of all truth, why can't we just do structural testing? This is a very interesting question. Test suites derived only with structural testing can be reasonably effective, but they may not be strong enough. Let's look at an example (see the "counting clumps" problem, inspired by a CodingBat assignment: https://codingbat .com/prob/p193817):

The program should count the number of clumps in an array. A clump is a sequence of the same element with a length of at least 2.

- nums—The array for which to count the clumps. The array must be non-null and length > 0; the program returns 0 if any pre-condition is violated.

The program returns the number of clumps in the array.

The following listing shows an implementation.

Listing 3.9 Implementing the code clumps requirement

```
public static int countClumps(int[] nums) {
  if (nums == null || nums.length == 0) {       ◄─┐ If null or empty
    return 0;                                        (pre-condition),
  }                                                  return 0 right away.
  int count = 0;
  int prev = nums[0];
  boolean inClump = false;
  for (int i = 1; i < nums.length; i++) {
    if (nums[i] == prev && !inClump) {    ◄─┐ If the current number is the
      inClump = true;                          same as the previous number,
      count += 1;                              we have identified a clump.
    }
    if (nums[i] != prev) {    ◄─┐ If the current number
      prev = nums[i];              differs from the previous
      inClump = false;             one, we are not in a clump.
    }
  }
  return count;
}
```

Suppose we decide not to look at the requirements. We want to achieve, say, 100% branch coverage. Three tests are enough to do that (T1–T3). Maybe we also want to do some extra boundary testing and decide to exercise the loop, iterating a single time (T4):

- T1: an empty array
- T2: a null array
- T3: an array with a single clump of three elements in the middle (for example, [1,2,2,2,1])
- T4: an array with a single element

To check that for yourself, write down these three tests as (JUnit) automated test cases and run your favorite code coverage tool as in the following.

Listing 3.10 100% branch coverage for the clump-counting problem

```
@ParameterizedTest
@MethodSource("generator")
void testClumps(int[] nums, int expectedNoOfClumps) {
  assertThat(Clumps.countClumps(nums))
```

```
      .isEqualTo(expectedNoOfClumps);
}

static Stream<Arguments> generator() {        ⟵——┤  The four test
  return Stream.of(                                 │  cases we defined
    of(new int[]{}, 0), // empty
    of(null, 0), // null
    of(new int[]{1,2,2,2,1}, 1), // one clump
    of(new int[]{1}, 0) // one element
  );
}
```

This test suite is reasonable and exercises the main behavior of the program, but note how weak it is. It achieves 100% branch coverage, but it misses many interesting test cases. Even without performing systematic specification testing, in a program that counts clumps, it is natural to try the program with multiple clumps instead of just one. We could try it with the last clump happening at the last item of the array or with an array that has a clump starting in the first position. Such specific cases cannot be captured by pure structural testing guided mainly by coverage. This is yet another reason not to rely blindly on coverage. Structural testing shows its value when combined with knowledge of the specification.

3.10   *Structural testing in the real world*

Now that you have a clear picture of structural testing, the coverage criteria you can use for guidance, and how to use structural testing in combination with specification-based testing, let me discuss a few interesting points.

3.10.1   *Why do some people hate code coverage?*

I find it interesting that some people rage against code coverage. A prevalent opinion is, "If I write a test case with no assertions, I achieve 100% coverage, but I am not testing anything!" This is true. If your tests have no assertions, they do not test anything, but the production code is exercised. However, I consider that a flawed argument. It assumes the very worst (unrealistic) scenario possible. If you are writing test suites with no assertions, you have bigger problems to take care of before you can enjoy the benefits of structural testing.

Between the lines, people use such an argument to explain that you should not look at the coverage number blindly, because it can mislead you. That I fully agree with. Here, the misconception is how people see code coverage. If code coverage is only a number you should achieve, you may end up writing less useful test cases and gaming the metric (something that Bouwers, Visser, and Van Deursen have argued in 2012).

I hope this chapter has clarified how structural testing and code coverage should be used: to augment specification-based testing, quickly identify parts of the code that are not currently exercised by the test suite, and identify partitions you missed when doing specification-based testing. Achieving a high coverage number may be a consequence of you doing that, but the purpose is different. If you leave a line uncovered, it is because you thought about it and decided not to cover it.

EMPIRICAL EVIDENCE IN FAVOR OF CODE COVERAGE

Understanding whether structural coverage helps and whether high coverage numbers lead to better-tested software has been the goal of many empirical software engineering researchers. Interestingly, while researchers have not yet found a magical coverage number that we should aim for, some evidence points toward the benefits of structural testing. I quote four of these studies:

- *Hutchins et al. (1994)*—"Within the limited domain of our experiments, test sets achieving coverage levels over 90% usually showed significantly better fault detection than randomly chosen test sets of the same size. In addition, significant improvements in the effectiveness of coverage-based tests usually occurred as coverage increased from 90% to 100%. However, the results also indicate that 100% code coverage alone is not a reliable indicator of the effectiveness of a test set."
- *Namin and Andrews (2009)*—"Our experiments indicate that coverage is sometimes correlated with effectiveness when test suite size is controlled for, and that using both size and coverage yields a more accurate prediction of effectiveness than test suite size alone. This, in turn, suggests that both size and coverage are important to test suite effectiveness."
- *Inozemtseva and Holmes (2014)*—"We found that there is a low to moderate correlation between coverage and effectiveness when the number of test cases in the suite is controlled for. In addition, we found that stronger forms of coverage do not provide greater insight into the effectiveness of the suite. Our results suggest that coverage, while useful for identifying under-tested parts of a program, should not be used as a quality target because it is not a good indicator of test suite effectiveness."
- *Gopinath et al. (2020)*—"This paper finds a correlation between lightweight, widely available coverage criteria (statement, block, branch, and path coverage) and mutation kills for hundreds of Java programs (…). For both original and generated suites, statement coverage is the best predictor for mutation kills, and in fact does a relatively good job of predicting suite quality."

Although developing sound experiments to show whether coverage helps is difficult, and we are not quite there yet (see Chen et al.'s 2020 paper for a good statistical explanation of why it is hard), the current results make sense to me. Even with the small code examples we have been exploring, we can see a relationship between covering all the partitions via specification-based testing and covering the entire source code. The opposite is also true: if you cover a significant part of the source code, you also cover most of the partitions. Therefore, high coverage implies more partitions being tested.

The empirical results also show that coverage alone is not always a strong indicator of how good a test suite is. We also noticed that in the test cases we derived for the CountWords problem at the beginning of this chapter. We purposefully did bad specification-based testing and then augmented the test suite with structural testing. We ended up with three test cases that achieve 100% condition + branch coverage. But is the test suite strong enough? I don't think so. I can think of many extra test cases that would touch the same lines and branches again but would nonetheless make the test suite much more effective against possible bugs.

On the other hand, although 100% coverage does not necessarily mean the system is properly tested, having very low coverage *does* mean your system is *not* properly tested. Having a system with, say, 10% coverage means there is much to be done as far as testing.

I suggest reading Google's code coverage best practices (Arguelles, Ivankovic, and Bender, 2020). Their perceptions are in line with everything we have discussed here.

3.10.2   *What does it mean to achieve 100% coverage?*

I have purposefully skipped talking much about achieving 100% line coverage or branch coverage or other coverage. I do not believe that achieving a number should be the goal. Nevertheless, given how prevalent those numbers are in practice, it is important to understand them. First, let's talk about the metrics themselves.

> **NOTE**   Formulas vary among the tools on the market. Check your tool's manual to better understand the precise numbers you get.

If the entire test suite covers all the lines in the program (or in the class or method under test), that suite achieves *100% line coverage*. A simple formula to calculate the line coverage of a given program or method is to divide the number of lines covered by the total number of lines:

$$\text{line coverage} = \frac{\text{lines covered}}{\text{total number of lines}} \times 100\%$$

You can calculate this number at the method level, class level, package level, system level, or whatever level you are interested in.

Similar to line coverage, a formula to calculate the achieved *branch coverage* of a program or method is the number of branches covered divided by the total number of branches:

$$\text{branch coverage} = \frac{\text{branches covered}}{\text{total number of branches}} \times 100\%$$

In a simple program such as if(x) { do A } else { do B }, the total number of branches is two (the single if statement branches the program in two ways). Therefore, if one test in your test suite covers, say x = true, your test suite achieves $1/2 \times 100\% = 50\%$ branch coverage. Note that due to criteria subsumption, which we discussed earlier, if you cover all the branches of the program, you also cover all the lines.

Finally, a formula to calculate the *condition + branch coverage* of a given program or method is the sum of all branches and conditions covered, divided by the total number of branches and conditions:

$$\text{c+b coverage} = \frac{\text{branches covered} + \text{conditions covered}}{\text{number of branches} + \text{number of conditions}} \times 100\%$$

In a simple program such as if(x || y) { do A } else { do B }, the total number of branches is two (the single if statement branches the program in two ways) and the total number of conditions is four (two conditions for x and two conditions for y). Therefore, if you have two tests in your test suite—T1: (true, true) and T2: (false, true)—the test suite achieves $(1 + 3)/(2 + 4) \times 100\% = 66.6\%$ condition + branch coverage. The test suite covers only one branch of the program (the true branch, as both T1 and T2 make the if expression evaluate to true), and three of the four conditions (x is exercised as true and false, but y is only exercised as true).

Figure 3.10 shows a simple illustration of line coverage, branch coverage, and condition + branch coverage. When someone says, "My test suite achieves 80% condition + branch coverage," you now understand that 80% of the branches and conditions are covered by at least one test case. And when someone says, "My test suite achieves 100% line coverage," you know that 100% of the lines are covered by at least one test case.

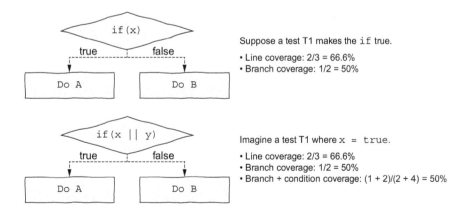

Figure 3.10 Two control-flow graphs of simple programs and how the different coverage criteria are calculated

3.10.3 *What coverage criterion to use*

This is a popular question among practitioners and researchers. If we settle for a less-rigorous criterion, such as line coverage instead of branch coverage, we might miss something. Plus this question brings the focus back to the metric, which we do not want.

Which criterion to use depends on the context: what you are testing at that moment and how rigorous you want the testing to be. Structural testing is meant to complement specification-based testing. When you dive into the source code and look for uncovered parts, you may decide to use branch coverage for a specific if expression but MC/DC for another if expression. This makes the approach less systematic (and, therefore, more prone to errors and different developers using different criteria), but it is the most pragmatic approach I know. You may want to perform some risk assessment to determine how important it is to be thorough.

My rule of thumb is branch coverage: I always try to at least reach all the branches of the program. Whenever I see a more complicated expression, I evaluate the need for condition + branch coverage. If I see an even more complex expression, I consider MC/DC.

3.10.4 *MC/DC when expressions are too complex and cannot be simplified*

MC/DC is increasingly valuable as expressions become more complicated. Listing 3.11 shows an example of a complex expression that I extracted from Chilenski's 2001 paper. It is an anonymized version of a condition found in a level A flight simulation program and contains an impressive 76 conditions. Achieving path coverage in such a complex expression is impossible (2^{76} = 7.5 × 10^{22} test cases), so smart approaches such as MC/DC come in handy.

Listing 3.11   Complex expression from flight simulation software

```
Bv or (Ev != El) or Bv2 or Bv3 or Bv4 or Bv5 or Bv6 or Bv7 or Bv8 or Bv9 or
Bv10 or Bv11 or Bv12 or Bv13 or Bv14 or Bv15 or Bv16 or Bv17 or Bv18 or
Bv19 or Bv20 or Bv21 or Bv22 or Bv23 or Bv24 or Bv25 or Bv26 or Bv27 or
Bv28 or Bv29 or Bv30 or Bv31 or Bv32 or Bv33 or Bv34 or Bv35 or Bv36 or
Bv37 or Bv38 or Bv39 or Bv40 or Bv41 or Bv42 or Bv43 or Bv44 or Bv45 or
Bv46 or Bv47 or Bv48 or Bv49 or Bv50 or Bv51 or (Ev2 = El2) or
((Ev3 = El2) and (Sav != Sac)) or Bv52 or Bv53 or Bv54 or Bv55 or Bv56
or Bv57 or Bv58 or Bv59 or Bv60 or Bv61 or Bv62 or Bv63 or Bv64 or Bv65
or Ev4 != El3 or Ev5 = El4 or Ev6 = El4 or Ev7 = El4 or Ev8 = El4 or
Ev9 = El4 or Ev10 = El4
```

Pragmatically speaking, testing such a complex expression, with or without MC/DC, is a challenge, and you should avoid doing so when possible. Sometimes you can break an expression into smaller bits that you can then test. But in cases where breaking complex expressions is not possible, MC/DC shines.

MC/DC in SQLite

A nice story of the benefits of MC/DC was told by Richard Hipp, the creator and primary developer of SQLite, the most popular embedded database. In the Corecursive #066 podcast, Richard says, "I had this idea, I'm going to write tests to bring SQLite up to the quality of 100% MC/DC, and that took a year of 60-hour weeks. That was hard, hard work. I was putting in 12-hour days every single day. I was getting so tired of this because with this sort of thing, it's the old joke of, you get 95% of the functionality with the first 95% of your budget, and the last 5% on the second 95% of your budget. It's kind of the same thing. It's pretty easy to get up to 90 or 95% test coverage. Getting that last 5% is really, really hard, and it took about a year for me to get there, but once we got to that point, we stopped getting bug reports from Android." What a powerful success story of MC/DC.

For completeness, here are some final remarks about MC/DC. First, in the example in section 3.1, we apply *unique-cause MC/DC criteria*: we identify an independence pair (T1, T2) where only a single condition and the final outcome change between T1 and T2. That may not be possible in all cases. For example, consider (A && B) || (A && C). Ideally, we would demonstrate the independence of the first A, B, the second A, and C. But it is impossible to change the first A and not change the second A. Thus, we cannot demonstrate the independence of each A in the expression. In such cases, we allow A to vary, but we fix all other variables (this is called *masked MC/DC*).

Second, note that it may not be possible to achieve MC/DC in some expressions, such as (A and B) or (A and not B). While the independence pairs (TT, FT) would show the independence of A, there are no pairs that show the independence of B. In such cases, revisit the expression, as it may have been poorly designed. In this example, the expression could be reformulated to simply A.

Finally, mathematically speaking, N + 1 is the theoretical lower bound for the number of tests you may need when applying MC/DC. In other words, you may need more than N + 1 test cases to achieve MC/DC in some expressions. However, the empirical study by Chilenski (2001) shows that the majority of expressions in practice require N + 1 tests. This has been my observation, too: N + 1 is most of the times the number of required test cases.

3.10.5 *Other coverage criteria*

Throughout this chapter, we have used the program's control flow as a way to derive different tests. Another way of approaching structural testing is to look at the *data flow*: examining how the data flows to different parts of the program.

For example, imagine that a variable is defined, then modified one, two, or three times in other parts of the program, and then used again later. You may want to ensure that you exercise all the possible ways this variable is touched. Trying to summarize data-flow coverage in one sentence is unfair, and a lot of energy has been spent coming up with criteria, but this should give you some intuition about it.

I do not discuss data-flow coverage in this book, but I suggest you read more about it. Pezzè and Young (2008) give a nice explanation.

3.10.6   *What should not be covered?*

We have talked a lot about what to test and cover. Let's quickly discuss what *not* to cover. Achieving 100% coverage may be impossible or not even desirable. For example, the code snippet in listing 3.12 returns the full path of a specific directory. The code may throw a URISyntaxException, which we catch and wrap around a Runtime-Exception. (For the Java experts, we are converting a checked exception to an unchecked exception.)

Listing 3.12   **A method that does not deserve full coverage**

```
public static String resourceFolder(String path) {
  try {
    return Paths.get(ResourceUtils.class
      .getResource("/").toURI()).toString() + path;
  } catch (URISyntaxException e) {
    throw new RuntimeException(e);
  }
}
```

To achieve 100% line coverage, we would need to exercise the catch block. For that to happen, we would have to somehow force the toURI method to throw the exception. We could use mocks (discussed later in this book), but I cannot see any advantage in doing that. It is more important to test what would happen to the rest of the system if resourceFolder threw a RuntimeException. That is much easier to do, as we have more control over the resourceFolder method than the Java toURI() method. Therefore, this piece of code it is not worth covering and shows why blindly aiming for 100% coverage makes no sense.

In Java, in particular, I tend not to write dedicated tests for equals and hashCode methods or straightforward getters and setters. These are tested implicitly by the tests that exercise the other methods that use them.

To close this discussion, I want to reinforce that, for me, *all code should be covered until proven otherwise.* I start from the idea that I should have 100% coverage. Then, if I see that a piece of code does not need to be covered, I make an exception. But be careful—experience shows that bugs tend to appear in areas you do not cover well.

3.11   *Mutation testing*

All the coverage criteria discussed in this chapter consider how much of the production code is exercised by a test. What they all miss is whether the assertions that these tests make are good and strong enough to capture bugs. If we introduce a bug in the code, even in a line covered by a test, will the test break?

As mentioned earlier, coverage alone is not enough to determine whether a test suite is good. We have been thinking about how far our test suite goes to evaluate the strength of our test suite. Now let's think of the test suite's *fault detection capability*. How many bugs can it reveal?

This is the idea behind *mutation testing*. In a nutshell, we purposefully insert a bug in the existing code and check whether the test suite breaks. If it does, that's a point for the test suite. If it does not (all tests are green even with the bug in the code), we have found something to improve in our test suite. We then repeat the process: we create another buggy version of the problem by changing something else in the code, and we check whether the test suite captures that bug.

These buggy versions are *mutants* of the original, supposedly correct, version of the program. If the test suite breaks when executed against a mutant, we say that the test suite *kills* that mutant. If it does not break, we say that the mutant *survives*. A test suite achieves 100% mutation coverage if it kills all possible mutants.

Mutation testing makes two interesting assumptions. First, the *competent programmer hypothesis* assumes that the program is written by a competent programmer and that the implemented version is either correct or differs from the correct program by a combination of simple errors. Second, the *coupling effect* says that a complex bug is caused by a combination of many small bugs. Therefore, if your test suite can catch simple bugs, it will also catch the more complex ones.

Pitest is the most popular open source tool for mutation testing in Java (https://pitest.org/quickstart/mutators). Here are a few examples of mutators from its manual:

- *Conditionals boundary*—Relational operators such as `<` and `<=` are replaced by other relational operators.
- *Increment*—It replaces `i++` with `i--` and vice versa.
- *Invert negatives*—It negates variables: for example, `i` becomes `-i`.
- *Math operators*—It replaces mathematical operators: for example, a plus becomes a minus.
- *True returns*—It replaces entire boolean variables with `true`.
- *Remove conditionals*—It replaces entire `if` statements with a simple `if(true) {…}`.

Running Pitest is simple, as it comes with plugins for Maven and Gradle. For example, I ran it against the `LeftPad` implementation and tests we wrote earlier; figure 3.11 shows the resulting report. As in a code coverage report, a line's background color indicates whether all the mutants were killed by the test suite.

The next step is to evaluate the surviving mutants. It is very important to analyze each surviving mutant, as some may not be useful.

Remember that mutation testing tools do not know your code—they simply mutate it. This sometimes means they create mutants that are not useful. For example, in the line that contains `int pads = size - strLen`, Pitest mutated the `size` variable to `size++`. Our test suite does not catch this bug, but this is not a useful mutant: the `size` variable is not used after this line, so incrementing it has no effect on the program.

You should view mutation testing in the same way as coverage tools: it can augment the test suite engineered based on the program's requirements.

```
22          public static String leftPad(final String str, final int size, String padStr) {
23 4            if (str == null) {
24 2                return null;
25              }
26 9            if (isEmpty(padStr)) {
27                padStr = SPACE;
28              }
29 1            final int padLen = padStr.length();
30 1            final int strLen = str.length();
31 17           final int pads = size - strLen;
32 14           if (pads <= 0) {
33 2                return str; // returns original String when possible
34              }
35
36 18           if (pads == padLen) {
37 5                return padStr.concat(str);
38 19           } else if (pads < padLen) {
39 17               return padStr.substring(0, pads).concat(str);
40              } else {
41 5                final char[] padding = new char[pads];
42 1                final char[] padChars = padStr.toCharArray();
43 25               for (int i = 0; i < pads; i++) {
44 22                   padding[i] = padChars[i % padLen];
45                  }
46 6                return new String(padding).concat(str);
47              }
48          }
49
50      }
```

Figure 3.11   Part of a report generated by Pitest. Lines 26, 31, 32, 36, 38, 39, 43, and 44 have surviving mutants.

Mutation testing faces various challenges in practice, including the cost. To use mutation testing, we must generate many mutants and execute the whole test suite with each one. This makes mutation testing quite expensive. Considerable research is dedicated to lowering the cost of mutation testing, such as reducing the number of mutants to try, detecting equivalent mutants (mutants that are identical to the original program in terms of behavior), and reducing the number of test cases or test case executions (see the work of Ferrari, Pizzoleto, and Offutt, 2018). As a community, we are taking steps toward a solution, but we are not there yet.

Despite the cost, mutation testing is highly beneficial. In a very recent paper by Parsai and Demeyer (2020), the authors demonstrate that mutation coverage reveals additional weaknesses in the test suite compared to branch coverage and that it can do so with an acceptable performance overhead during project build. Even large companies like Google are investing in mutation testing in their systems, as reported by Petrović and Ivanković (2018).

Researchers are also exploring mutation testing in areas other than Java backend code. Yandrapally and Mesbah (2021) propose mutations for the Document Object Model (DOM) in HTML pages to assess whether web tests (which we discuss in chapter 9) are strong enough. In addition, Tuya and colleagues (2006) proposed the use of mutation in SQL queries.

I suggest that you try to apply mutation testing, especially in more sensitive parts of your system. While running mutation testing for the entire system can be expensive, running it for a smaller set of classes is feasible and may give you valuable insights about what else to test.

Exercises

3.1 Consider the following piece of code, which plays a game of Blackjack:

```
01. public int play(int left, int right) {
02.     int ln = left;
03.     int rn = right;
04.     if (ln > 21)
05.         ln = 0;
06.     if (rn > 21)
07.         rn = 0;
08.     if (ln > rn)
09.         return ln;
10.     else
11.         return rn;
12. }
```

What is the line coverage of a test where `left=22` and `right=21`? In the calculation, disregard the lines with the function signature and the last curly bracket (lines 1 and 12).

  A 60%

  B 80%

  c 70%

  D 100%

3.2 Consider the following remove method:

```
public boolean remove(Object o) {
  if (o == null) {
    for (Node<E> x = first; x != null; x = x.next) {
      if (x.item == null) {
        unlink(x);
        return true;
      }
    }
  } else {
    for (Node<E> x = first; x != null; x = x.next) {
      if (o.equals(x.item)) {
        unlink(x);
        return true;
      }
    }
  }
  return false;
}
```

This is the implementation of the Java Platform, Standard Edition 8 Development Kit (JDK 8) `LinkedList` remove method.

Create a test suite (a set of tests) that achieves 100% line coverage. Use as few tests as possible. Feel free to write them as JUnit tests or as a set of inputs and expected outputs.

3.3 Following is Java's implementation of the `LinkedList`'s `computeIfPresent()` method:

```java
public V computeIfPresent(K key,
    BiFunction<? super K, ? super V, ? extends V> rf) {
  if (rf == null) {
    throw new NullPointerException();
  }

  Node<K,V> e;
  V oldValue;
  int hash = hash(key);
  e = getNode(hash, key);
  oldValue = e.value;

  if (e != null && oldValue != null) {

    V v = rf.apply(key, oldValue);

    if (v != null) {
      e.value = v;
      afterNodeAccess(e);
      return v;
    } else {
      removeNode(hash, key, null, false, true);
    }
  }
  return null;
}
```

What is the minimum number of tests required to achieve 100% branch coverage?

   A 2
   B 3
   C 4
   D 6

3.4 Consider the expression `(A & B) | C` with the following truth table:

Test case	A	B	C	(A & B) | C
1	T	T	T	T
2	T	T	F	T
3	T	F	T	T

Test case	A	B	C	(A & B) | C
4	T	F	F	F
5	F	T	T	T
6	F	T	F	F
7	F	F	T	T
8	F	F	F	F

What test suite(s) achieve 100% MC/DC? The numbers correspond to the test case column in the truth table. Select all that apply.

- **A** {2, 3, 4, 6}
- **B** {2, 4, 5, 6}
- **C** {1, 3, 4, 6}
- **D** {3, 4, 5, 8}

3.5 Draw the truth table for the expression A && (A || B).

Is it possible to achieve MC/DC coverage for this expression? Why or why not? What would you tell the developer who wrote this expression?

3.6 Consider the following method:

```
public String sameEnds(String string) {
  int length = string.length();
  int half = length / 2;

  String left = "";
  String right = "";

  int size = 0;
  for (int i = 0; i < half; i++) {
    left = left + string.charAt(i);
    right = string.charAt(length - 1 - i) + right;

    if (left.equals(right)) {
      size = left.length();
    }
  }

  return string.substring(0, size);
}
```

Which of the following statements is *not* correct?

- **A** It is possible to devise a single test case that achieves 100% line coverage and 100% decision coverage.
- **B** It is possible to devise a single test case that achieves 100% line coverage and 100% (basic) condition coverage.

    c It is possible to devise a single test case that achieves 100% line coverage and 100% decision + condition coverage.

    D It is possible to devise a single test case that achieves 100% line coverage and 100% path coverage.

3.7 Which of the following statements concerning the subsumption relations between test adequacy criteria is true?

    A MC/DC subsumes statement coverage.

    B Statement coverage subsumes branch coverage.

    c Branch coverage subsumes path coverage.

    D Basic condition coverage subsumes branch coverage.

3.8 A test suite satisfies the loop boundary adequacy criterion if for every loop L:

    A Test cases iterate L zero times, once, and more than once.

    B Test cases iterate L once and more than once.

    c Test cases iterate L zero times and one time.

    D Test cases iterate L zero times, once, more than once, and N, where N is the maximum number of iterations.

3.9 Which of the following statements is *correct* about the relationship between specification-based testing and structural testing?

    A A testing process should prioritize structural testing because it's cheaper yet highly effective (maybe even more effective than specification-based testing).

    B Specification-based testing can only be effectively performed when we have proper models of the program under test. A simple user story is not enough.

    c Boundary analysis can only be done if testers have access to the source code, and thus it should be considered a structural testing technique.

    D None of the other answers is true.

Summary

- Structural testing uses the source code to augment the test suite engineered via specification-based testing.
- The overall idea of structural testing is to analyze which parts of the code are not yet covered and reflect on whether they should be covered or not.
- Some coverage criteria are less rigorous and therefore less expensive (for example, line coverage). Others are more rigorous but also more expensive (such as MC/DC coverage). As a developer, you have to decide which criteria to use.
- Code coverage should not be used as a number to be achieved. Rather, coverage tools should be used to support developers in performing structural testing (that is, understanding what parts are not covered and why).
- Mutation testing ensures that our test suite is strong enough: in other words, that it can catch as many bugs as possible.

Designing contracts

4

This chapter covers

- Designing pre-conditions, post-conditions, and invariants
- Understanding the differences between contracts and validation

Imagine a piece of software that handles a very complex financial process. For that big routine to happen, the software system chains calls to several subroutines (or classes) in a complex flow of information: that is, the results of one class are passed to the next class, whose results are again passed to the next class, and so on. As usual, the data comes from different sources, such as databases, external web services, and users. At some point in the routine, the class TaxCalculator (which handles calculating a specific tax) is called. From the requirements of this class, the calculation only makes sense for positive numbers.

We need to think about how we want to model such a restriction. I see three options when facing such a restriction:

- Ensure that classes never call other classes with invalid inputs. In our example, any other classes called TaxCalculator will ensure that they will never pass a negative number. While this simplifies the code of the class under development, since it does not need to deal with the special cases, it adds complexity to the caller classes that need to be sure they never make a bad call.

- Program in a more defensive manner, ensuring that if an invalid input happens, the system halts and returns an error message to the user. This adds a little complexity to every class in the system, as they all have to know how to handle invalid inputs. At the same time, it makes the system more resilient. However, coding defensively in an ad hoc manner is not productive. You may end up adding unnecessary code, such as restrictions that were already checked.
- My favorite approach, and the goal of this chapter, is to define clear contracts for each class we develop. These contracts clearly establish what the class requires as pre-conditions, what the class provides as post-conditions, and what invariants always hold for the class. This is a major modeling activity for which the *design-by-contract* idea will inspire us (originally proposed by Bertrand Meyer).

Such contract decisions happen while the developer is implementing the functionality. That is why design-by-contract appears on the "testing to guide development" side of the development flow I propose (see figure 1.4).

4.1   *Pre-conditions and post-conditions*

Going back to the tax calculation example, we need to reflect on *pre-conditions* that the method needs to function properly, as well as its *post-conditions*: what the method guarantees as outcomes. We already mentioned a pre-condition: the method *does not* accept negative numbers. A possible post-condition of this method is that it also does not return negative numbers.

Once the method's pre- and post-conditions are established, it is time to add them to the source code. Doing so can be as simple as an `if` instruction, as shown in the following listing.

Listing 4.1   `TaxCalculator` with pre- and post-conditions

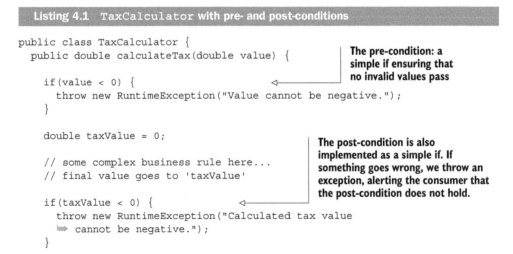

```
public class TaxCalculator {
  public double calculateTax(double value) {

    if(value < 0) {                                    ← The pre-condition: a
      throw new RuntimeException("Value cannot be negative.");    simple if ensuring that
    }                                                              no invalid values pass

    double taxValue = 0;

    // some complex business rule here...              The post-condition is also
    // final value goes to 'taxValue'                  implemented as a simple if. If
                                                       something goes wrong, we throw an
    if(taxValue < 0) {                     ←           exception, alerting the consumer that
      throw new RuntimeException("Calculated tax value the post-condition does not hold.
      ⮑ cannot be negative.");
    }
```

```
        return taxValue;
    }
}
```

> **NOTE** You may be wondering what `value`, the input parameter of the `calculateTax` method, represents. Also, how is the tax rate set? In real life, the requirements and implementation of a tax calculator would be much more complex—this simple code lets you focus on the technique. Bear with me!

Note that the pre- and post-conditions ensure different things. Pre-conditions (in this case, a single pre-condition) ensure that the input values received by a method adhere to what it requires. Post-conditions ensure that the method returns what it promises to other methods.

You may be wondering, "How can I have a value that breaks the post-condition if I am coding the implementation of this method?" In this example, you hope that your implementation will never return a negative number. But in very complex implementations, a bug may slip in! If bugs did not exist, there would be no reason for this book. The post-condition check ensures that if there is a bug in the implementation, the method will throw an exception instead of returning an invalid value. An exception will make your program halt—and halting is often much better than continuing with an incorrect value.

Making your pre- and post-conditions clear in the documentation is also fundamental and very much recommended. Let's do that in the next listing.

Listing 4.2 Javadoc of the `calculateTax` method describing its contract

```
/**
 * Calculates the tax according to (some
 * explanation here...)
 *
 * @param value the base value for tax calculation. Value has
 *              to be a positive number.
 * @return the calculated tax. The tax is always a positive number.
 */
public double calculateTax(double value) { ... }
```

4.1.1 The assert keyword

The Java language offers the keyword `assert`, which is a native way of writing assertions. In the previous example, instead of throwing an exception, we could write `assert value >= 0 : "Value cannot be negative."`. If `value` is not greater than or equal to 0, the Java Virtual Machine (JVM) will throw an `AssertionError`. In the following listing, I show a version of the `TaxCalculator` using asserts.

Listing 4.3 `TaxCalculator` with pre- and post-conditions implemented via asserts

```
public class TaxCalculator {
  public double calculateTax(double value) {
```

```
    assert value >= 0 : "Value cannot be negative";

    double taxValue = 0;

    // some complex business rule here...
    // final value goes to 'taxValue'

    assert taxValue >= 0 : "Calculated tax value
➡ cannot be negative.";

    return taxValue;
  }
}
```

The same pre-condition, now as an assert statement

The same post-condition, now as an assert statement

Deciding whether to use `assert` instructions or simple `if` statements that throw exceptions is something to discuss with your team members. I'll give you my opinion about it later in section 4.5.3.

The `assert` instruction can be disabled via a parameter to the JVM, so it does not have to be executed at all times. If you disable it in production, for example, the pre-conditions will not be checked while running the system. If you do not have full control of your production environment, you may want to opt for exceptions so you can be sure your pre-conditions will be checked.

An argument against the use of `asserts` is that they always throw `AssertionError`, which is a generic error. Sometimes you may want to throw a more specific exception that the caller can handle. For simplicity, I make use of `assert` in the remainder of this chapter.

Later in this chapter, we differentiate between pre-conditions and validations. This may also be taken into account when deciding between asserts and exceptions.

4.1.2 Strong and weak pre- and post-conditions

When defining pre- and post-conditions, an important decision is how weak or strong you want them to be. In the previous example, we handle the pre-condition very strongly: if a negative value comes in, it violates the pre-condition of the method, so we halt the program.

One way to avoid halting the program due to negative numbers would be to weaken the pre-condition. In other words, instead of accepting only values that are greater than zero, the method could accept any value, positive or negative. We could do this by removing the `if` statement, as shown in the following listing (the developer would have to find a way to take negative numbers into account and handle them).

Listing 4.4 `TaxCalculator` with a weaker pre-condition

```
public double calculateTax(double value) {

    // method continues ...
}
```

No pre-conditions check; any value is valid.

Weaker pre-conditions make it easier for other classes to invoke the method. After all, regardless of the value you pass to `calculateTax`, the program will return something. This is in contrast to the previous version, where a negative number throws an error.

There is no single answer for whether to use weaker or stronger pre-conditions. It depends on the type of system you are developing as well as what you expect from the consumers of the class you are modeling. I prefer stronger conditions, as I believe they reduce the range of mistakes that may happen in the code. However, this means I spend more time encoding these conditions as assertions, so my code becomes more complex.

> **Can you apply the same reasoning to post-conditions?**
>
> You may find a reason to return a value instead of throwing an exception. To be honest, I cannot recall a single time I've done that. In the `TaxCalculator` example, a negative number would mean there was a bug in the implementation, and you probably do not want someone to pay zero taxes.

In some cases, you cannot weaken the pre-condition. For the tax calculation, there is no way to accept negative values, and the pre-condition should be strong. Pragmatically speaking, another way of handling such a case is to return an error value. For example, if a negative number comes in, the program can return 0 instead of halting, as in the following listing.

Listing 4.5 `TaxCalculator` **returning an error code instead of an exception**

```
public double calculateTax(double value) {
  // pre-condition check
  if(value < 0) {          ◄┐  If the pre-condition does not hold,
    return 0;                │  the method returns 0. The client of
  }                          │  this method does not need to worry
                             │  about exceptions.
  // method continues ...
}
```

While this approach simplifies the clients' lives, they now have to be aware that if they receive a 0, it might be because of invalid input. Perhaps the method could return –1 to differentiate from zero taxes. Deciding between a weaker pre-condition or an error value is another decision to make after considering all the possibilities.

For those that know the original theory of design-by-contracts: we do not weaken the pre-condition here to make it easier for clients to handle the outcomes of the method. We decided to return an error code instead of throwing an exception. In the remainder of this chapter, you see that my perspective on contracts is more pragmatic than that in the original design-by-contract paper by Meyer in 1992. What matters to me is reflecting on what classes and methods can and cannot handle and what they should do in case a violation happens.

4.2   *Invariants*

We have seen that pre-conditions should hold before a method's execution, and post-conditions should hold after a method's execution. Now we move on to conditions that must always hold before *and* after a method's execution. These conditions are called *invariants*. An invariant is thus a condition that holds throughout the entire lifetime of an object or a data structure.

Imagine a `Basket` class that stores the products the user is buying from an online shop. The class offers methods such as add(Product p, int quantity), which adds a product p a quantity number of times, and remove(Product p), which removes the product completely from the cart. Here is a skeleton of the class.

Listing 4.6   The Basket class

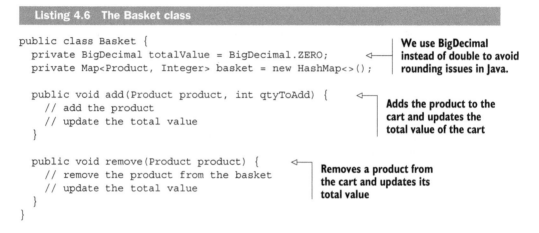

```
public class Basket {
    private BigDecimal totalValue = BigDecimal.ZERO;        ◁─┤ We use BigDecimal
    private Map<Product, Integer> basket = new HashMap<>();      instead of double to avoid
                                                                  rounding issues in Java.

    public void add(Product product, int qtyToAdd) {     ◁─┐
        // add the product                                   Adds the product to the
        // update the total value                            cart and updates the
    }                                                        total value of the cart

    public void remove(Product product) {     ◁─┐
        // remove the product from the basket      Removes a product from
        // update the total value                  the cart and updates its
    }                                              total value
}
```

Before we talk about invariants, let's focus on the method's pre- and post-conditions. For the add() method, we can ensure that the product is not null (you cannot add a null product to the cart) and that the quantity is greater than 0 (you cannot buy a product 0 or fewer times). In addition, a clear post-condition is that the product is now in the basket. Listing 4.7 shows the implementation. Note that I am using Java's assert method to express the pre-condition, which means I must have assertions enabled in my JVM when I run the system. You could also use a simple if statement, as I showed earlier.

Listing 4.7   Basket's add method with its pre-conditions

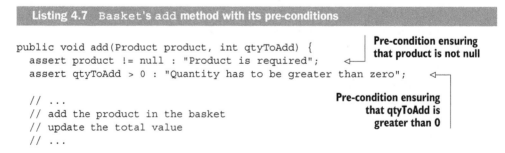

```
public void add(Product product, int qtyToAdd) {                  Pre-condition ensuring
    assert product != null : "Product is required";           that product is not null
    assert qtyToAdd > 0 : "Quantity has to be greater than zero";   ◁─┐

    // ...                                                  Pre-condition ensuring
    // add the product in the basket                        that qtyToAdd is
    // update the total value                               greater than 0
    // ...
```

```
    assert basket.containsKey(product) :
      "Product was not inserted in the basket";
}
```

Post-condition ensuring that the product was added to the cart

You could model other post-conditions here, such as "the new total value should be greater than the previous total value." Java does not provide an easy way to do that, so we need extra code to keep the old total value, which we use in the post-condition check (see listing 4.8). Interestingly, in languages like Eiffel, doing so would not require an extra variable! Those languages provide old and new values of variables to facilitate the post-condition check.

Listing 4.8   Another post-condition for `Basket`'s add method

```
public void add(Product product, int qtyToAdd) {
  assert product != null : "Product is required";
  assert qtyToAdd > 0 : "Quantity has to be greater than zero";
  BigDecimal oldTotalValue = totalValue;

  // add the product in the basket
  // update the total value

  assert basket.containsKey(product) :
    "Product was not inserted in the basket";

  assert totalValue.compareTo(oldTotalValue) == 1 :
    "Total value should be greater than
  ⇒ previous total value";
}
```
For the post-condition to happen, we need to save the old total value.

The post-condition ensures that the total value is greater than before.

NOTE   We use the `BigDecimal` class here instead of a simple `double`. Big-Decimals are recommended whenever you want to avoid rounding issues that may happen when you use doubles. Check your programming language for how to do that. `BigDecimal` gives us precision, but it is verbose. In listing 4.8, for example, we have to use the `compareTo` method to compare two Big-Decimals, which is more complicated than a > b. Another trick is to represent money in cents and use `integer` or `long` as the types, but that is beyond the scope of this book.

Now for the pre-conditions of the `remove()` method. The product should not be null; moreover, the product to be removed needs to be in the basket. If the product is not in the basket, how can you remove it? As a post-condition, we can ensure that, after the removal, the product is no longer in the basket. See the implementation of both pre- and post-conditions in the following listing.

Listing 4.9   Pre- and post-conditions for the `remove` method

Pre-conditions: the product cannot be null, and it must exist in the basket.

```
public void remove(Product product) {
  assert product != null : "product can't be null";
  assert basket.containsKey(product) : "Product must already be in the
  ⇒ basket";
```

```
// ...
// remove the product from the basket
// update the total value
// ...

    assert !basket.containsKey(product) : "Product is still in the
➥ basket";
}
```

Post-condition: the product
is no longer in the basket.

We are finished with the pre- and post-conditions. It is time to model the class invariants. Regardless of products being added to and removed from the basket, the total value of the basket should never be negative. This is not a pre-condition nor a post-condition: this is an *invariant*, and the class is responsible for maintaining it. For the implementation, you can use assertions or `if`s or whatever your programming language offers. Whenever a method that manipulates the `totalValue` field is called, we ensure that `totalValue` is still a positive number at the end of the method. See the implementation of the invariants in the following listing.

Listing 4.10 Invariants of the `Basket` class

```
public class Basket {
  private BigDecimal totalValue = BigDecimal.ZERO;
  private Map<Product, Integer> basket = new HashMap<>();

  public void add(Product product, int qtyToAdd) {
    assert product != null : "Product is required";
    assert qtyToAdd > 0 : "Quantity has to be greater than zero";
    BigDecimal oldTotalValue = totalValue;

    // add the product in the basket
    // update the total value

    assert basket.containsKey(product) : "Product was not inserted in
➥ the basket";
    assert totalValue.compareTo(oldTotalValue) == 1 : "Total value should
➥ be greater than previous total value";

    assert totalValue.compareTo(BigDecimal.ZERO) >= 0 :
      "Total value can't be negative."
  }
```

The invariant ensures that the total
value is greater than or equal to 0.

```
  public void remove(Product product) {
    assert product != null : "product can't be null";
    assert basket.containsKey(product) : "Product must already be in the
     basket";
➥
    // remove the product from the basket
    // update the total value

    assert !basket.containsKey(product) : "Product is still in the basket";

    assert totalValue.compareTo(BigDecimal.ZERO) >= 0 :
      "Total value can't be negative."
  }
}
```

The same invariant
check for the remove

Because the invariant checking may happen at the end of all the methods of a class, you may want to reduce duplication and create a method for such checks, such as the `invariant()` method in listing 4.11. We call `invariant()` at the end of every public method: after each method does its business (and changes the object's state), we want to ensure that the invariants hold.

Listing 4.11 `invariant()` **method for the invariant check**

```
public class Basket {

  public void add(Product product, int qtyToAdd) {
    // ... method here ...
    assert invariant() : "Invariant does not hold";
  }

  public void remove(Product product) {
    // ... method here ...
    assert invariant() : "Invariant does not hold";
  }

  private boolean invariant() {
    return totalValue.compareTo(BigDecimal.ZERO) >= 0;
  }
}
```

Note that invariants may not hold, say, in the middle of the method execution. The method may break the invariants for a second, as part of its algorithm. However, the method needs to ensure that, in the end, the invariants hold.

> **NOTE** You might be curious about the concrete implementation of the Basket class and how we would test it. We cannot test all possible combinations of method calls (adds and removes, in any order). How would you tackle this? We get to property-based testing in chapter 5.

4.3 Changing contracts, and the Liskov substitution principle

What happens if we change the contract of a class or method? Suppose the `calculate-Tax` method we discussed earlier needs new pre-conditions. Instead of "value should be greater than or equal to 0," they are changed to "value should be greater than or equal to 100." What impact would this change have on the system and our test suites? Or suppose the `add` method from the previous section, which does not accept null as `product`, now accepts it. What is the impact of this decision? Do these two changes impact the system in the same way, or does one change have less impact than the other?

In an ideal world, we would not change the contract of a class or method after we define it. In the real world, we are sometimes forced to do so. While there may not be anything we can do to prevent the change, we can understand its impact. If you do not understand the impact of the change, your system may behave unexpectedly—and this is how contract changes are related to testing and quality.

The easiest way to understand the impact of a change is not to look at the change itself or at the class in which the change is happening, but at all the other classes (or *dependencies*) that may use the changing class. Figure 4.1 shows the calculateTax() method and three other (imaginary) classes that use it. When these classes were created, they knew the pre-conditions of the calculateTax() at that point: "value has to be greater than or equal to 0." They knew calculateTax() would throw an exception if they passed a negative number. So, these client classes currently ensure that they never pass a negative number to calculateTax().

The calculateTax() method is used by many other classes in the system. The TaxCalculator class doesn't know about them.

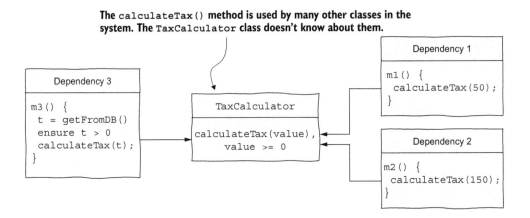

Figure 4.1 The calculateTax() method and all the classes that possibly depend on it

Notice that m1() passes 50 as value, m2() passes 150, and m3 passes a value from a database (after ensuring that the value is greater than 0). Now, suppose we change the pre-condition to value > 100. What will happen to these three dependencies? Nothing will happen to m2(): by pure luck, the new pre-condition holds for the value of 150. However, we cannot say the same for the other two methods: m1() will crash, and m3() will have erratic behavior, as some values from the database may be greater than 100, while others may be smaller than 100. What do we learn here? If we change our pre-conditions to something stronger and more restrictive, such as accepting a smaller set of values (100 to infinity instead of 0 to infinity), we may have a problem with classes that depend on the previously defined contract.

Now, suppose calculateTax() changes its pre-condition to accept negative numbers as inputs. In this case, the three existing dependencies would not break. The new pre-condition is more relaxed than the previous one: it accepts a larger set of inputs. What do we learn? If we change our pre-conditions to something weaker and less restrictive, we do not break the contracts with the clients of the changing class.

The same type of reasoning can be applied to the post-conditions. There, we observe the inverse relation. The clients know that `calculateTax` never returns negative numbers. Although this would make no business sense, let's suppose the method now also returns negative numbers. This is a breaking change: the clients of this class do not expect negative numbers to come back and probably are not ready to handle them. The system may behave erratically, depending on whether the returned tax is negative. We learn that if we change our post-condition to something weaker and less restrictive, our clients may break.

On the other hand, if the post-condition changes to "the returned value is always greater than 100," the clients will not break. They were already prepared for the returning value to be between 0 and infinity, and the range from 100 to infinity is a subset of the previous domain. We learn that changing post-conditions to something stronger and more restrictive prevents breaking changes in the dependencies.

4.3.1 Inheritance and contracts

We mostly use Java for the examples in this book, and Java is an object-oriented language, so I must discuss what happens when we use inheritance. Figure 4.2 shows that the `TaxCalculator` class has many children (`TaxCalculatorBrazil` which calculates taxes in Brazil, `TaxCalculatorNL`, which calculates taxes in the Netherlands, and so on). These child classes all override `calculateTax()` and change the pre- or post-conditions one way or another. Are these contract changes breaking changes?

We can apply the same reasoning as when we discussed changing contracts. Let's start by focusing on the client class rather than the child classes. Suppose the client

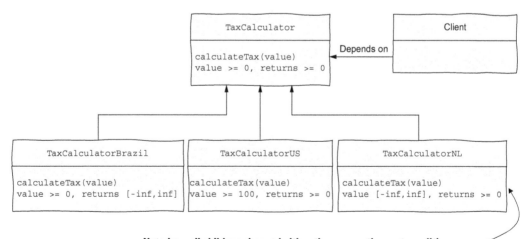

Note how all children changed either the pre- or the post-condition, in comparison to the base class. Are these breaking changes or not?

Figure 4.2 A base class and its child classes. The client depends on the base class, which means any of its children may be used at run time.

class receives a `TaxCalculator` in its constructor and later uses it in its methods. Due to polymorphism, we know that any of the child classes can also be passed to the client: for example, we can pass a `TaxCalculatorBrazil` or a `TaxCalculatorUS`, and it will be accepted because they are all children of the base class.

Since the client class does not know which tax calculator was given to it, it can only assume that whatever class it received will respect the pre- and post-conditions of the base class (the only class the client knows). In this case, `value` must be greater than or equal to 0 and should return a value greater than or equal to 0. Let's explore what will happen if each of the child classes is given to the client class:

- `TaxCalculatorBrazil` has the same pre-conditions as the base class. This means there is no way the client class will observe strange behavior regarding the pre-conditions if it is given `TaxCalculatorBrazil`. On the other hand, the `TaxCalculatorBrazil` class has a post-condition that the returned value is any number. This is bad. The client class expects only values that are greater than or equal to zero; it does not expect negative numbers. So if `TaxCalculatorBrazil` returns a negative number to the client, this may surprise the client and lead to a failure.
- `TaxCalculatorUS` has the following pre-condition: "`value` greater than or equal to 100." This pre-condition is stronger than the pre-condition of the base class (`value >= 0`), and the client class does not know that. Thus the client may call the tax calculator with a value that is acceptable for the base class but not acceptable for `TaxCalculatorUS`. We can expect a failure to happen. The post-condition of `TaxCalculatorUS` is the same as that of the base class, so we do not expect problems there.
- `TaxCalculatorNL` has a different pre-condition from the base class: it accepts any value. In other words, the pre-condition is weaker than that of the base class. So although the client is not aware of this pre-condition, we do not expect failures, as `TaxCalculatorNL` can handle all of the client's inputs.

If we generalize what we observe in this example, we arrive at the following rules whenever a subclass `S` (for example, `TaxCalculatorBrazil`) inherits from a base class `B` (for example, `TaxCalculator`):

1 The pre-conditions of subclass `S` should be the same as or weaker (accept more values) than the pre-conditions of base class `B`.
2 The post-conditions of subclass `S` should be the same as or stronger (return fewer values) than the post-conditions of base class `B`.

This idea that a subclass may be used as a substitution for a base class without breaking the expected behavior of the system is known as the *Liskov substitution principle* (LSP). This principle was introduced by Barbara Liskov in a 1987 keynote and later refined by her and Jeannette Wing in the famous "A behavioral notion of subtyping" paper (1994). The LSP became even more popular among software developers when Robert Martin popularized the SOLID principles, where the "L" stands for LSP.

NOTE A well-known best practice is to avoid inheritance whenever possible (see Effective Java's item 16, "favor compostion over inheritance"). If you avoid inheritance, you naturally avoid all the problems just discussed. But it is not the goal of this book to discuss best practices in object-oriented design. If you ever need to use inheritance, you now know what to pay attention to.

4.4   *How is design-by-contract related to testing?*

Defining clear pre-conditions, post-conditions, and invariants (and automating them in your code via, for example, assertions) helps developers in many ways. First, assertions ensure that bugs are detected early in the production environment. As soon as a contract is violated, the program halts instead of continuing its execution, which is usually a good idea. The error you get from an assertion violation is very specific, and you know precisely what to debug for. This may not be the case without assertions. Imagine a program that performs calculations. The method that does the heavy calculation does not work well with negative numbers. However, instead of defining such a restriction as an explicit pre-condition, the method returns an invalid output if a negative number comes in. This invalid number is then passed to other parts of the system, which may incur other unexpected behavior. Given that the program does not crash per se, it may be hard for the developer to know that the root cause of the problem was a violation of the pre-condition.

Second, pre-conditions, post-conditions, and invariants provide developers with ideas about what to test. As soon as we see the `qty > 0` pre-condition, we know this is something to exercise via unit, integration, or system tests. Therefore, contracts do not replace (unit) testing: they complement it. In chapter 5, you will see how to use such contracts and write test cases that automatically generate random input data, looking for possible violations.

Third, such explicit contracts make the lives of consumers much easier. The class (or server, if you think of it as a client-server application) does its job as long as its methods are used properly by the consumer (or client). If the client uses the server's methods so that their pre-conditions hold, the server guarantees that the post-conditions will hold after the method call. In other words, the server makes sure the method delivers what it promises. Suppose a method expects only positive numbers (as a pre-condition) and promises to return only positive numbers (as a post-condition). As a client, if you pass a positive number, you are sure the server will return a positive number and never a negative number. The client, therefore, does not need to check if the return is negative, simplifying its code.

I do not see design-by-contract as a testing practice per se. I see it as more of a design technique. That is also why I include it in the development part of the developer testing workflow (figure 1.4).

NOTE Another benefit of assertions is that they serve as oracles during fuzzing or other intelligent testing. These tools reason about the pre-conditions, post-conditions, and invariants that are clearly expressed in the code and look for ways to break them. If you want to read more about fuzzing, I suggest *The Fuzzing Book* (https://fuzzingbook.org).

4.5   *Design-by-contract in the real world*

Let me close this chapter with some pragmatic tips on how to use design-by-contract in practice.

4.5.1 *Weak or strong pre-conditions?*

A very important design decision when modeling contracts is whether to use strong or weak contracts. This is a matter of trade-offs.

Consider a method with a weak pre-condition. For example, the method accepts any input value, including null. This method is easy for clients to use for the clients: any call to it will work, and the method will never throw an exception related to a pre-condition being violated (as there are no pre-conditions to be violated). However, this puts an extra burden on the method, as it has to handle any invalid inputs.

On the other hand, consider a strong contract: the method only accepts positive numbers and does not accept null values. The extra burden is now on the side of the client. The client must make sure it does not violate the pre-conditions of the method. This may require extra code.

There is no clear way to go, and the decision should be made considering the whole context. For example, many methods of the Apache Commons library have weak pre-conditions, making it much easier for clients to use the API. Library developers often prefer to design weaker pre-conditions and simplify the clients' lives.

4.5.2 *Input validation, contracts, or both?*

Developers are aware of how important input validation is. A mistake in the validation may lead to security vulnerabilities. Therefore, developers often handle input validation whenever data comes from the end user.

Consider a web application that stores products for an online store. To add a new product, a user must pass a name, a description, and a value. Before saving the new product to the database, the developer performs checks to ensure that the input values are as expected. Here is the greatly simplified pseudo-code.

Listing 4.12 Pseudo-code for input validation

These parameters come directly from the end user, and they need to be validated before being used.

We use the made-up sanitize() method to sanitize (remove invalid characters from) the inputs.

```
class ProductController {
    // more code here ...

    public void add(String productName, String productDescription,
        double price) {

        String sanitizedProductName = sanitize(productName);
        String sanitizedProductDescription = sanitize(productDescription);
```

Ensures that values are within the expected format, range, and so on

```
if(!isValidProductName(sanitizedProductName)) {
    errorMessages.add("Invalid product name");
}
if(!isValidProductDescription(sanitizedProductDescription)) {
    errorMessages.add("Invalid product description");
}
if(!isValidPriceRange(price)) {
    errorMessages.add("Invalid price");
}

if(errorMessages.empty()) {
    Product newProduct = new Product(sanitizedProductName,
        productDescription, price);
    database.save(newProduct);

    redirectTo("productPage", newProduct.getId());
} else {
    redirectTo("addProduct", errorMessages.getErrors());
}
}
}
```

Only when the parameters are valid do we create objects. Is this a replacement for design-by-contract?

Otherwise, we return to the Add Product page and display the error messages.

Given all this validation *before* the objects are even created, you may be thinking, "Do I need to model pre-conditions and post-conditions in the classes and methods? I already know the values are valid!" Let me give you a pragmatic perspective.

First, let's focus on the difference between *validation* and *contracts*. Validation ensures that bad or invalid data that may come from users does not infiltrate our systems. For example, if the user types a string in the Quantity field on the Add Product page, we should return a friendly message saying "Quantity should be a numeric value." This is what validation is about: it validates that the data coming from the user is correct and, if not, returns a message.

On the other hand, contracts ensure that communication between classes happens without a problem. We do not expect problems to occur—the data is already validated. However, if a violation occurs, the program halts, since something unexpected happened. The application also returns an error message to the user. Figure 4.3 illustrates the difference between validation and code contracts.

Both validation and contracts should happen, as they are different. The question is how to avoid repetition. Maybe the validation and pre-condition are the same, which means either there is code repetition or the check is happening twice.

I tend to be pragmatic. As a rule of thumb, I prefer to avoid repetition. If the input validation already checked for, say, the length of the product description being greater than 10 characters, I don't re-check it as a pre-condition in the constructor of the `Product` class. This implies that no instances of `Product` are instantiated without input validation first. Your architecture must ensure that some zones of the code are safe and that data has been already cleaned up.

On the other hand, if a contract is very important and should never be broken (the impact could be significant), I do not mind using a little repetition and extra

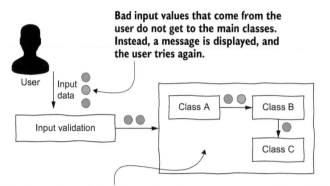

Bad input values that come from the
user do not get to the main classes.
Instead, a message is displayed, and
the user tries again.

If a class makes a bad call to another class, e.g., a pre-condition violation,
the program halts, as this should not happen. The user may also be informed
about the problem, although commonly with a more generic message.

Figure 4.3   The difference between validation and code contracts. Each
circle represents one input coming to the system.

computational power to check it at both input-validation time and contract-checking
time. Again, consider the context to decide what works best for each situation.

NOTE   Arie van Deursen offers a clear answer on Stack Overflow about the
differences between design-by-contract and validation, and I strongly recommend that you check it out: https://stackoverflow.com/a/5452329.

4.5.3   *Asserts and exceptions: When to use one or the other*

Java does not offer a clear mechanism for expressing code contracts. Only a few
popular programming languages do, such as F#. The `assert` keyword in Java is okay,
but if you forget to enable it in the runtime, the contracts may not be checked in
production. That is why many developers prefer to use (checked or unchecked)
exceptions.

Here is my rule of thumb:

- If I am modeling the contracts of a library or utility class, I favor exceptions, following the wisdom of the most popular libraries.
- If I am modeling business classes and their interactions and I know that the
  data was cleaned up in previous layers (say, in the controller of a Model-View-
  Controller [MVC] architecture), I favor assertions. The data was already validated, and I am sure they start their work with valid data. I do not expect pre-
  conditions or post-conditions to be violated, so I prefer to use the `assert`
  instruction. It will throw an `AssertionError`, which will halt execution. I also
  ensure that my final user does not see an exception stack trace but instead is
  shown a more elegant error page.
- If I am modeling business classes but I am not sure whether the data was already
  cleaned up, I go for exceptions.

When it comes to validation, I tend not to use either assertions or exceptions. I prefer to model validations in more elegant ways. First, you rarely want to stop the validation when the first check fails. Instead, it is more common to show a complete list of errors to the user. Therefore, you need a structure that allows you to build the error message as you go. Second, you may want to model complex validations, which may require lots of code. Having all the validations in a single class or method may lead to code that is very long, highly complex, and hard to reuse.

If you are curious, I suggest the Specification pattern proposed by Eric Evans in his seminal book, *Domain-Driven Design* (2004). Another nice resource is the article "Use of Assertions" by John Regehr (2014); it discusses the pros and cons of assertions, misconceptions, and limitations in a very pragmatic way.

Finally, in this chapter, I used native Java exceptions, such as `RuntimeException`. In practice, you may prefer to throw more specialized and semantic exceptions, such as `NegativeValueException`. That helps clients treat business exceptions differently from real one-in-a-million exceptional behavior.

> **NOTE** Formal semantics scholars do not favor the use of assertions over exceptions. I should not use the term *design-by-contract* for the snippets where I use an `if` statement and throw an exception—that is defensive programming. But, as I said before, I am using the term *design-by-contract* for the idea of reflecting about contracts and *somehow* making them explicit in the code.

4.5.4 *Exception or soft return values?*

We saw that a possible way to simplify clients' lives is to make your method return a "soft value" instead of throwing an exception. Go back to listing 4.5 for an example.

My rule of thumb is the following:

- If it is behavior that should not happen, and clients would not know what to do with it, I throw an exception. That would be the case with the `calculateTax` method. If a negative value comes in, that is unexpected behavior, and we should halt the program rather than let it make bad calculations. The monitoring systems will catch the exception, and we will debug the case.
- On the other hand, if I can see a soft return for the client method that would allow the client to keep working, I go for it. Imagine a utility method that trims a string. A pre-condition of this method could be that it does not accept null strings. But returning an empty string in case of a null is a soft return that clients can deal with.

4.5.5 *When not to use design-by-contract*

Understanding when not to use a practice is as important as knowing when to use it. In this case, I may disappoint you, as I cannot see a single good reason not to use the design-by-contract ideas presented in this chapter. The development of object-oriented systems is all about ensuring that objects can communicate and collaborate properly. Experience shows me that making the pre-conditions, post-conditions, and invariants explicit in the code is not expensive and does not take a lot of time. Therefore,

I recommend that you consider using this approach. (Note that I am not discussing input validation here, which is fundamental and has to be done whether or not you like design-by-contracts.)

I also want to highlight that design-by-contract does not replace the need for testing. Why? Because, to the best of my knowledge and experience, you cannot express all the expected behavior of a piece of code solely with pre-conditions, post-conditions, and invariants. In practice, I suggest that you design contracts to ensure that classes can communicate with each other without fear, and test to ensure that the behavior of the class is correct.

4.5.6   *Should we write tests for pre-conditions, post-conditions, and invariants?*

In a way, assertions, pre-conditions, post-conditions, and invariant checks test the production code from the inside. Do we also need to write (unit) tests for them?

To answer this question, let me again discuss the difference between validation and pre-conditions. Validation is what you do to ensure that the data is valid. Pre-conditions explicitly state under what conditions a method can be invoked.

I usually write automated tests for validation. We want to ensure that our validation mechanisms are in place and working as expected. On the other hand, I rarely write tests for assertions. They are naturally covered by tests that focus on other business rules. I suggest reading Arie van Deursen's answer on Stack Overflow about writing tests for assertions (https://stackoverflow.com/a/6486294/165292).

> **NOTE**   Some code coverage tools do not handle asserts well. JaCoCo, for example, cannot report full branch coverage in assertions. This is another great example of why you should not use coverage numbers blindly.

4.5.7   *Tooling support*

There is more and more support for pre- and post-condition checks, even in languages like Java. For instance, IntelliJ, a famous Java IDE, offers the `@Nullable` and `@NotNull` annotations (http://mng.bz/QWMe). You can annotate your methods, attributes, or return values with them, and IntelliJ will alert you about possible violations. IntelliJ can even transform those annotations into proper `assert` checks at compile time.

In addition, projects such as Bean Validation (https://beanvalidation.org) enable you to write more complex validations, such as "this string should be an email" or "this integer should be between 1 and 10." I appreciate such useful tools that help us ensure the quality of our products. The more, the merrier.

Exercises

4.1   Which of the following is a valid reason to use assertions in your code?

  A To verify expressions with side effects

  B To handle exceptional cases in the program

    c To conduct user input validation

    d To make debugging easier

4.2 Consider the following `squareAt` method:

```
public Square squareAt(int x, int y){
   assert x >= 0;
   assert x < board.length;
   assert y >= 0;
   assert y < board[x].length;
   assert board != null;

   Square result = board[x][y];

   assert result != null;
   return result;
}
```

Suppose we remove the last assertion (`assert result != null`), which states that the result can never be null. Are the existing pre-conditions of the `squareAt` method enough to ensure the property of the removed assertion? What can we add to the class (other than the just-removed post-condition) to guarantee this property?

4.3 See the `squareAt` method in exercise 4.3. Which assertion(s), if any, can be turned into class invariants? Choose all that apply.

    A `x >= 0` and `x < board.length`

    B `board != null`

    C `result != null`

    D `y >= 0` and `y < board[x].length`

4.4 You run your application with assertion checking enabled. Unfortunately, it reports an assertion failure, signaling a *class invariant violation* in one of the libraries your application uses. Assume that your application is following all the pre-conditions established by the library.

Which of the following statements *best characterizes* the situation and corresponding action to take?

    A Since you assume that the contract is correct, the safe action is to run the server with assertion checking disabled.

    B This indicates an integration fault and requires a redesign that involves the interface that is offered by the library and used by your application.

    C This indicates a problem in the implementation of that library and requires a fix in the library's code.

    D This indicates that you invoked one of the methods of the library in the wrong way and requires a fix in your application.

4.5 Can static methods have invariants? Explain your answer.

4.6 A method M belongs to a class C and has a pre-condition P and a post-condition Q. Suppose that a developer creates a class C' that extends C and creates a method M' that overrides M.

Which one of the following statements correctly explains the relative strength of the pre- (P') and post-conditions (Q') of the overridden method M'?

A P' should be equal to or weaker than P, and Q' should be equal to or stronger than Q.

B P' should be equal to or stronger than P, and Q' should be equal to or stronger than Q.

C P' should be equal to or weaker than P, and Q' should be equal to or weaker than Q.

D P' should be equal to or stronger than P, and Q' should be equal to or weaker than Q.

Summary

- Contracts ensure that classes can safely communicate with each other without surprises.
- In practice, designing contracts boils down to explicitly defining the pre-conditions, post-conditions, and invariants of our classes and methods.
- Deciding to go for a weaker or a stronger contract is a contextual decision. Both have advantages and disadvantages.
- Design-by-contract does not remove the need for validation. Validation and contract checking are different things with different objectives. Both should be done.
- Whenever changing a contract, we need to reflect on the impact of the change. Some contract changes might be breaking changes.

Property-based testing

5

This chapter covers
- Writing property-based tests
- Understanding when to write property-based tests or example-based tests

So far, we have been doing *example-based testing*. We judiciously divide the input space of a program (into partitions), pick one concrete example from all the possible ones, and write the test case. What if we did not have to pick one concrete example out of many? What if we could express the *property* we are trying to exercise and let the test framework choose several concrete examples for us? Our tests would be less dependent on a concrete example, and the test framework would be able to call the method under test multiple times with different input parameters—usually with zero effort from us.

This is what *property-based testing* is about. We do not pick a concrete example; rather, we define a property (or a set of properties) that the program should adhere to, and the test framework tries to find a counterexample that causes the program to break with these properties.

I have learned that the best way to teach how to write property-based tests is with multiple examples. So, this chapter presents five different examples with varying levels of complexity. I want you to focus on my way of thinking and notice how much creativity is required to write such tests.

5.1   *Example 1: The passing grade program*

Consider the following requirement, inspired by a similar problem in Kaner et al.'s book (2013):

> A student passes an exam if they get a grade >= 5.0. Grades below that are a fail. Grades fall in the range [1.0, 10.0].

A simple implementation for this program is shown in the following listing.

Listing 5.1   Implementation of the `PassingGrade` program

```
public class PassingGrade {
  public boolean passed(float grade) {
    if (grade < 1.0 || grade > 10.0)              Note the pre-condition
      throw new IllegalArgumentException();       check here.
    return grade >= 5.0;
  }
}
```

If we were to apply specification-based testing to this program, we would probably devise partitions such as "passing grade," "failing grade," and "grades outside the range." We would then devise a single test case per partition. With property-based testing, we want to formulate properties that the program should have. I see the following properties for this requirement:

- fail—For all numbers ranging from 1.0 (inclusive) to 5.0 (exclusive), the program should return `false`.
- pass—For all numbers ranging from 5.0 (inclusive) to 10.0 (inclusive), the program should return `true`.
- invalid—For all invalid grades (which we define as any number below 1.0 or greater than 10.0), the program must throw an exception.

Can you see the difference between what we do in specification-based testing and what we aim to do in property-based testing? Let's write a suite test by test, starting with the `fail` property. For that, we will use jqwik (https://jqwik.net), a popular property-based testing framework for Java.

> **NOTE**   Property-based testing frameworks are available in many different languages, although their APIs vary significantly (unlike unit testing frameworks like JUnit, which all look similar). If you are applying this knowledge to another language, your task is to study the framework that is available in your programming language. The way to think and reason is the same across different languages.

Before I show the concrete implementation, let me break down property-based testing step by step, using jqwik's lingo:

1. For each property we want to express, we create a method and annotate it with @Property. These methods look like JUnit tests, but instead of containing a single example, they contain an overall property.

2. Properties use randomly generated data. Jqwik includes several generators for various types (including Strings, Integers, Lists, Dates, and so on.). Jqwik allows you to define different sets of constraints and restrictions to these parameters: for example, to generate only positive Integers or only Strings with a length between 5 and 10 characters. The property method receives all the required data for that test as parameters.

3. The property method calls the method under test and asserts that the method's behavior is correct.

4. When the test runs, jqwik generates a large amount of random data (following the characteristics you defined) and calls the test for it, looking for an input that would break the property. If jqwik finds an input that makes your test fail, the tool reports this input back to the developer. The developer then has an example of an input that breaks their program.

The following listing shows the code for the fail property.

Listing 5.2   A property-based test for the fail property

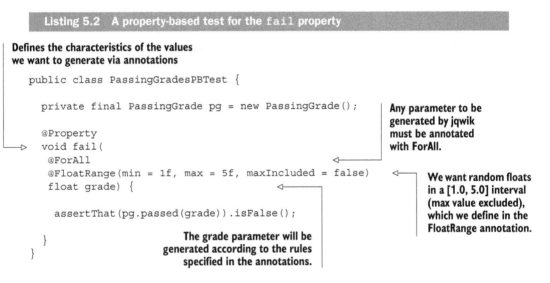

Defines the characteristics of the values we want to generate via annotations

```
public class PassingGradesPBTest {

    private final PassingGrade pg = new PassingGrade();

    @Property
    void fail(
      @ForAll
      @FloatRange(min = 1f, max = 5f, maxIncluded = false)
      float grade) {

        assertThat(pg.passed(grade)).isFalse();

    }
}
```

Any parameter to be generated by jqwik must be annotated with ForAll.

We want random floats in a [1.0, 5.0] interval (max value excluded), which we define in the FloatRange annotation.

The grade parameter will be generated according to the rules specified in the annotations.

We annotate the test method with @Property instead of @Test. The test method receives a grade parameter that jqwik will set, following the rules we give it. We then annotate the grade parameter with two properties. First, we say that this property should hold for all (@ForAll) grades. This is jqwik's terminology. If we left only the @ForAll annotation, jqwik would try any possible float as input. However, for this fail property, we want numbers varying from 1.0 to 5.0, which we specify using the @FloatRange annotation. The test then asserts that the program returns false for all the provided grades.

When we run the test, jqwik randomly provides values for the grade parameter, following the ranges we specified. With its default configuration, jqwik randomly generates 1,000 different inputs for this method. If this is your first time with property-based testing, I suggest that you write some print statements in the body of the test method to see the values generated by the framework. Note how random they are and how much they vary.

Correspondingly, we can test the pass property using a similar strategy, as shown next.

Listing 5.3   A property-based test for the `pass` property

```
@Property
void pass(
  @ForAll
  @FloatRange(min = 5f, max = 10f, maxIncluded = true)      ◁─┐ We want random
  float grade) {                                                floats in the range
  assertThat(pg.passed(grade)).isTrue();                        of [5.0, 10.0], max
}                                                               value included.
```

Finally, to make jqwik generate numbers that are outside of the valid range of grades, we need to use a smarter generator (as FloatRange does not allow us to express things like "grade < 1.0 or grade > 10.0"). See the invalidGrades() provider method in the following listing: methods annotated with @Provide are used to express more complex inputs that need to be generated.

Listing 5.4   A property-based test for the `invalidGrades` property

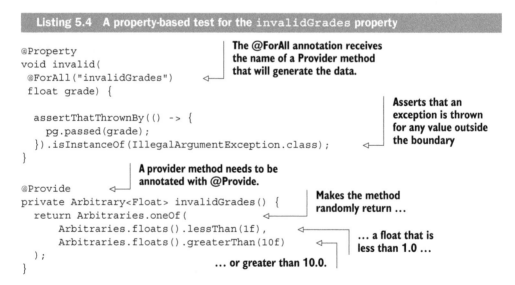

```
@Property                        The @ForAll annotation receives
void invalid(                    the name of a Provider method
 @ForAll("invalidGrades")        that will generate the data.
 float grade) {              ◁─┘

                                                    Asserts that an
  assertThatThrownBy(() -> {                         exception is thrown
    pg.passed(grade);                                for any value outside
  }).isInstanceOf(IllegalArgumentException.class);  ◁─┘ the boundary
}
                       A provider method needs to be
@Provide          ◁─┘  annotated with @Provide.
private Arbitrary<Float> invalidGrades() {    Makes the method
  return Arbitraries.oneOf(              ◁─┘  randomly return ...
      Arbitraries.floats().lessThan(1f),      ◁─── ... a float that is
      Arbitraries.floats().greaterThan(10f)   ◁─┐  less than 1.0 ...
  );                                             │
}                              ... or greater than 10.0.
```

The @Property test method is straightforward: for all grades generated, we assert that an exception is thrown. The challenge is generating random grades. We express this in the invalidGrades provider method, which should return either a grade smaller than 1 or a grade greater than 10. Also, note that the method returns an Arbitrary.

An `Arbitrary` is how jqwik handles arbitrary values that need to be generated. If you need, say, arbitrary floats, your provider method should return an `Arbitrary<Float>`.

To give the two options to jqwik, we use the `Arbitraries.oneOf()` method. The `Arbitraries` class contains dozens of methods that help build arbitrary data. The `oneOf()` method receives a list of arbitrary values it may return. Behind the scenes, this method ensures that the distribution of data points generated is fairly distributed: for example, it generates as many "smaller than 1" inputs as "greater than 10" inputs. Then, we use another helper, the `Arbitraries.floats()` method, to generate random floats. Finally, we use the `lessThan()` and `greaterThan()` methods to generate numbers less than 1 and greater than 10, respectively.

> **NOTE** I suggest exploring the methods that the `Arbitraries` class provides! Jqwik is a very extensive framework and contains lots of methods to help you build any property you need. I will not discuss every feature of the framework, as that would be an entire book by itself. Instead, I recommend that you dive into jqwik's excellent user guide: https://jqwik.net/docs/current/user-guide.html.

When we run the tests, all of them pass, since our implementation is correct. Now, let's introduce a bug in the code to see the jqwik output. For example, let's change `return grade >= 5.0` to `return grade > 5.0`, a simple off-by-one mistake. When we run our test suite again, the `pass` property test fails as expected! Jqwik also produces nice output to help us debug the problem.

Listing 5.5 An example of a jqwik test failure

```
|-------------------jqwik-------------------
tries = 11                      | \# of calls to property
checks = 11                     | \# of not rejected calls
generation = RANDOMIZED         | parameters are randomly generated
after-failure = PREVIOUS_SEED   | use the previous seed
when-fixed-seed = ALLOW         | fixing the random seed is allowed
edge-cases\#mode = MIXIN        | edge cases are mixed in
edge-cases\#total = 2           | \# of all combined edge cases
edge-cases\#tried = 1           | \# of edge cases tried in current run
seed = 7015333710778187630      | random seed to reproduce generated values

Sample
------
  arg0: 5.0
```

The output shows that jqwik found a counterexample in attempt number 11. Only 11 trials were enough to find the bug! Jqwik then shows a set of configuration parameters that may be useful when reproducing and debugging more complex cases. In particular, note the `seed` information: you can reuse that seed later to force jqwik to come up with the same sequence of inputs. Below the configuration, we see the sample that caused the bug: the value 5.0, as expected.

NOTE   If you are connecting the dots with previous chapters, you may be wondering about boundary testing. Jqwik is smart enough to also generate boundary values! If we ask jqwik to generate, say, floats smaller than 1.0, jqwik will generate 1.0 as a test. If we ask jqwik to generate any integer, jqwik will try the maximum and minimum possible integers as well as 0 and negative numbers.

5.2   *Example 2: Testing the unique method*

The Apache Commons Lang offers the `unique` method (http://mng.bz/XWGM). Following is its adapted Javadoc:

> Returns an array consisting of the unique values in data. The return array is sorted in descending order. Empty arrays are allowed, but null arrays result in a `NullPointerException`. Infinities are allowed.

Parameters:

- data: Array to scan

The method returns a descending list of values included in the input array. It throws a `NullPointerException` if data is null.

You can see its implementation next.

Listing 5.6   Implementation of the `unique` method

```
public static int[] unique(int[] data) {
  TreeSet<Integer> values = new TreeSet<Integer>();        ◁─┐ Uses a treeset to
  for (int i = 0; i < data.length; i++) {                     │ filter out repeated
    values.add(data[i]);                                      │ elements
  }

  final int count = values.size();                 ┌ Creates the new array
  final int[] out = new int[count];              ◁─┘ using the size of the tree

  Iterator<Integer> iterator = values.iterator();
  int i = 0;
  while (iterator.hasNext()) {                  ◁─┐ Visits the treeset and
    out[count - ++i] = iterator.next();           │ adds the elements to
  }                                               │ the new array
  return out;
}
```

Let's go straight to property-based testing. Here, we focus on the main property of the method: given an array of integers, the method returns a new array containing only the unique values of the original array, sorted in descending order. This is the property we will embed in a jqwik test.

   Our test works as follows. First we create a random list of integers. To ensure that the list has repeated numbers, we create a list of size 100 and limit the range of integers to [0,20]. We then call the `unique` method and assert that the array contains all the elements of the original array, does not have duplicates, and is sorted in descending order. Let's write that down in jqwik.

Listing 5.7 Property-based test for the `unique` method

```
public class MathArraysPBTest {

  @Property
  void unique(
    @ForAll
    @Size(value = 100)              An array of
    List<@IntRange(min = 1, max = 20) Integer>     size 100
    numbers) {

                                With values in [0, 20]. Given
                                the size of the array (100),
                                we know it will contain
                                repeated elements.

    int[] doubles = convertListToArray(numbers);
    int[] result = MathArrays.unique(doubles);

    assertThat(result)
      .contains(doubles)              Contains all the elements
      .doesNotHaveDuplicates()        No duplicates
      .isSortedAccordingTo(reverseOrder());    In descending order
  }

  private int[] convertListToArray(List<Integer> numbers) {
    int[] array = numbers
      .stream()                         Utility method
      .mapToInt(x -> x)              that converts a list of
      .toArray();                    integers to an array

    return array;
  }
}
```

> **TIP** Note how AssertJ simplifies our lives with its many ready-to-use assertions. Without it, the developer would have to write lots of extra code. When writing complex assertions, check the documentation to see whether something is available out of the box!

> **NOTE** One of my students noticed that even if we do not restrict the integer list to numbers in [0, 20], jqwik will produce lists with duplicated elements. In his exploration, he noticed that 11% of the produced arrays had a duplicated element. As a tester, you may want to consider whether 11% is a good rate. To measure this, my student used jqwik's statistics feature (http://mng.bz/y4gE), which enables you to measure the distribution of the input values.

Jqwik did not find any inputs that would break the program. So, our implementation seems to work. Let's move to the next example.

5.3   *Example 3: Testing the indexOf method*

The Apache Commons Lang has an interesting method called indexOf() (http://mng
.bz/M24m) with the following documentation, adapted from its Javadoc:

> Finds the index of the given value in the array starting at the given index. This
> method returns –1 for a null input array. A negative startIndex is treated as
> zero. A startIndex larger than the array length will return –1.
>
> *Input parameters*:
>
> - array: Array to search for the object. May be null.
> - valueToFind: Value to find.
> - startIndex: Index at which to start searching.
>
> The method returns the index of the value within the array, or –1 if not found
> or null.

Following is the implementation of this method.

Listing 5.8   Implementation of the `indexOf` method

```
class ArrayUtils {
  public static int indexOf(final int[] array, final int valueToFind,
      int startIndex) {
    if (array == null) {            ◁──┐  The method accepts a null array and returns -1 in such a
      return -1;                        │  case. Another option could be to throw an exception, but
    }                                   │  the developer decided to use a weaker pre-condition.

    if (startIndex < 0) {           ◁──┐  The same goes for startIndex:
      startIndex = 0;                   │  if the index is negative, the
    }                                   │  method assumes it is 0.

    for (int i = startIndex; i < array.length; i++) {
      if (valueToFind == array[i]) {
        return i;                   ◁──┐  If the value is found,
      }                                │  return the index.
    }
    return -1;                      ◁──┐  If the value is not in
  }                                    │  the array, return -1.
}
```

In this example, let's first apply the techniques we already know. Start by exploring the
input variables and how they interact with each other:

- array of integers:
  - Null
  - Single element
  - Multiple elements
- valueToFind:
  - Any integer

- `startIndex`:
    - Negative number
    - 0 [boundary]
    - Positive number
- `(array, startIndex)`:
    - `startIndex` in array
    - `startIndex` outside the boundaries of `array`
- `(array, valueToFind)`:
    - `valueToFind` not in array
    - `valueToFind` in array
    - `valueToFind` many times in array
- `(array, valueToFind, startIndex)`:
    - `valueToFind` in array, but before `startIndex`
    - `valueToFind` in array, but after `startIndex`
    - `valueToFind` in array, precisely in `startIndex` [boundary]
    - `valueToFind` in array multiple times after `startIndex`
    - `valueToFind` in array multiple times, one before and another after `startIndex`

We now create the test cases by combining the different partitions:

1. array is null
2. array with a single element, `valueToFind` in array
3. array with a single element, `valueToFind` not in array
4. `startIndex` negative, value in array
5. `startIndex` outside the boundaries of `array`
6. array with multiple elements, `valueToFind` in array, `startIndex` after value-ToFind
7. array with multiple elements, `valueToFind` in array, `startIndex` before valueToFind
8. array with multiple elements, `valueToFind` in array, `startIndex` precisely at valueToFind
9. array with multiple elements, `valueToFind` in array multiple times, start-Index before valueToFind
10. array with multiple elements, `valueToFind` in array multiple times, one before startIndex
11. array with multiple elements, `valueToFind` not in array

In JUnit, the test suite looks like the following listing.

Listing 5.9 First tests for the `indexOf()` method

```
import static org.junit.jupiter.params.provider.Arguments.of;

public class ArrayUtilsTest {
```

```
@ParameterizedTest
@MethodSource("testCases")
void testIndexOf(int[] array, int valueToFind, int startIndex,
    ➥ int expectedResult) {
  int result = ArrayUtils.indexOf(array, valueToFind, startIndex);
  assertThat(result).isEqualTo(expectedResult);
}

static Stream<Arguments> testCases() {      ◁─── All the test cases we engineered
                                                 are implemented here.
  int[] array = new int[] { 1, 2, 3, 4, 5, 4, 6, 7 };

  return Stream.of(
    of(null, 1, 1, -1),       ◁───── T1
    of(new int[] { 1 }, 1, 0, 0),                    ◁── T2
    of(new int[] { 1 }, 2, 0, -1),    ◁───── T3
    of(array, 1, 10, -1),              ◁── T4
    of(array, 2, -1, 1),     ◁───── T5
    of(array, 4, 6, -1),      ◁── T6
    of(array, 4, 1, 3),      ◁───── T7
    of(array, 4, 3, 3),       ◁── T8
    of(array, 4, 1, 3),      ◁───── T9
    of(array, 4, 4, 5),        ◁── T10
    of(array, 8, 0, -1)      ◁───── T11
  );
 }
}
```

Listing 5.10 shows the test suite developed for the library method itself (http://mng
.bz/aDAY). I added some comments, so you can see how their tests related to our
tests. This test suite contains our test cases T1, T4, T5, T6, T7, T8, T10, and T11. Interestingly, it is not testing the behavior of the array with a single element or the case in
which the element appears again after the first time it is found.

Listing 5.10   Original test suite of the `indexOf()` method

```
@Test
public void testIndexOfIntWithStartIndex() {
  int[] array = null;
  assertEquals(-1, ArrayUtils.indexOf(array, 0, 2));      ◁─── Similar to test case T1

  array = new int[]{0, 1, 2, 3, 0};
  assertEquals(4, ArrayUtils.indexOf(array, 0, 2));       ◁─── Similar to test case T10

  assertEquals(-1, ArrayUtils.indexOf(array, 1, 2));      ◁─── Similar to test case T6

  assertEquals(2, ArrayUtils.indexOf(array, 2, 2));       ◁─── Similar to test case T8

  assertEquals(3, ArrayUtils.indexOf(array, 3, 2));       ◁─── Similar to test case T7

  assertEquals(3, ArrayUtils.indexOf(array, 3, -1));      ◁─── Similar to test case T4

  assertEquals(-1, ArrayUtils.indexOf(array, 99, 0));     ◁─── Similar to test case T11
```

```
    assertEquals(-1, ArrayUtils.indexOf(array, 0, 6));    ⟵———  Similar to test case T5
}
```

> **NOTE** Parameterized tests seem to be less popular in open source systems. For methods with simple signatures, inputs, and outputs, like indexOf, we could argue that parameterized tests are overkill. When creating this example, I considered writing two different traditional JUnit test cases: one containing only the exceptional behavior and another containing the remaining test cases. In the end, organizing test cases is a matter of personal taste—talk to your team and see what approach they prefer. We talk more about test code quality and readability in chapter 10.

Both test suites look good and are quite strong. But now, let's express the main behavior of the method via property-based testing.

The overall idea of the test is to insert a random value in a random position of a random array. The indexOf() method will look for this random value. Finally, the test will assert that the method returns an index that matches the random position where we inserted the element.

The tricky part of writing such a test is ensuring that the random value we add in the array does not already exist in the random array. If the value is already there, this may break our test. Consider a randomly generated array containing [1, 2, 3, 4]: if we insert a random element 4 (which already exists in the array) on index 1 of the array, we will get a different response depending on whether startIndex is 0 or 3. To avoid such confusion, we generate random values that do not exist in the randomly generated array. This is easily achievable in jqwik. The property-based test needs at least four parameters:

- numbers—A list of random integers (we generate a list, as it is much easier to add an element at a random position in a list than in an array). This list will have a size of 100 and will contain values between –1000 and 1000.
- value—A random integer that is the value to be inserted into the list. We generate values ranging from 1001 to 2000, ensuring that whatever value is generated will not exist in the list.
- indexToAddElement—A random integer that represents a random index for where to add this element. The index ranges from 0 to 99 (the list has size 100).
- startIndex—A random integer that represents the index where we ask the method to start the search. This is also a random number ranging from 0 to 99.

With all the random values ready, the method adds the random value at the random position and calls indexOf with the random array, the random value to search, and the random index at which to start the search. We then assert that the method returns indexToAddElement if indexToAddElement >= startIndex (that is, the element was inserted after the start index) or –1 if the element was inserted before the start index. Figure 5.1 illustrates this process.

The concrete implementation of the jqwik test can be found in listing 5.11.

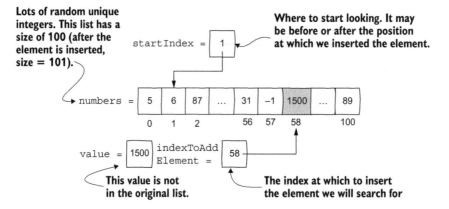

Lots of random unique integers. This list has a size of 100 (after the element is inserted, size = 101).

startIndex = 1

Where to start looking. It may be before or after the position at which we inserted the element.

numbers =

| 5 | 6 | 87 | ... | 31 | −1 | 1500 | ... | 89 |

0   1   2   56 57   58   100

value = 1500   indexToAddElement = 58

This value is not in the original list.

The index at which to insert the element we will search for

Figure 5.1 The data generation of the property-based test for the `indexOf` **method**

Listing 5.11 Property-based test for the `indexOf()` method

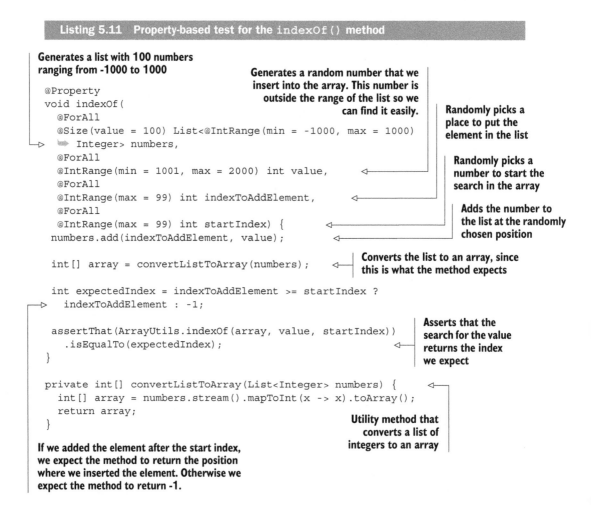

Generates a list with 100 numbers ranging from -1000 to 1000

Generates a random number that we insert into the array. This number is outside the range of the list so we can find it easily.

Randomly picks a place to put the element in the list

Randomly picks a number to start the search in the array

Adds the number to the list at the randomly chosen position

```java
@Property
void indexOf(
  @ForAll
  @Size(value = 100) List<@IntRange(min = -1000, max = 1000)
  Integer> numbers,
  @ForAll
  @IntRange(min = 1001, max = 2000) int value,
  @ForAll
  @IntRange(max = 99) int indexToAddElement,
  @ForAll
  @IntRange(max = 99) int startIndex) {
  numbers.add(indexToAddElement, value);

  int[] array = convertListToArray(numbers);

  int expectedIndex = indexToAddElement >= startIndex ?
    indexToAddElement : -1;

  assertThat(ArrayUtils.indexOf(array, value, startIndex))
    .isEqualTo(expectedIndex);
}

private int[] convertListToArray(List<Integer> numbers) {
  int[] array = numbers.stream().mapToInt(x -> x).toArray();
  return array;
}
```

Converts the list to an array, since this is what the method expects

Asserts that the search for the value returns the index we expect

Utility method that converts a list of integers to an array

If we added the element after the start index, we expect the method to return the position where we inserted the element. Otherwise we expect the method to return -1.

Jqwik will generate a large number of random inputs for this method, ensuring that regardless of where the value to find is, and regardless of the chosen start index, the method will always return the expected index. Notice how this property-based test better exercises the properties of the method than the testing method we used earlier.

I hope this example shows you that writing property-based tests requires creativity. Here, we had to come up with the idea of generating a random value that is never in the list so that the indexOf method could find it without ambiguity. We also had to be creative when doing the assertion, given that the randomly generated indexToAddElement could be larger or smaller than the startIndex (which would drastically change the output). Pay attention to these two points:

1 Ask yourself, "Am I exercising the property as closely as possible to the real world?" If you come up with input data that will be wildly different from what you expect in the real world, it may not be a good test.

2 Do all the partitions have the same likelihood of being exercised by your test? In the example, the element to be found is sometimes before and sometimes after the start index. If you write a test in which, say, 95% of the inputs have the element before the start index, you may be biasing your test too much. You want all the partitions to have the same likelihood of being exercised.

In the example code, given that both indexToAddElement and startIndex are random numbers between 0 and 99, we expect about a 50-50 split between the partitions. When you are unsure about the distribution, add some debugging instructions and see what inputs or partitions your test generates or exercises.

5.4 *Example 4: Testing the Basket class*

Let's explore one last example that revisits the Basket class from chapter 4. The class offers two methods: an add() method that receives a product and adds it a quantity of times to the basket, and a remove() method that removes a product completely from the cart. Let's start with the add method.

> **Listing 5.12 Implementation of Baskets add method**

**Stores the old value so we can check
the post-condition later**

```
import static java.math.BigDecimal.valueOf;

public class Basket {
    private BigDecimal totalValue = BigDecimal.ZERO;
    private Map<Product, Integer> basket = new HashMap<>();

    public void add(Product product, int qtyToAdd) {
        assert product != null : "Product is required";
        assert qtyToAdd > 0 : "Quantity has to be greater than zero";
        BigDecimal oldTotalValue = totalValue;
```

**Checks all the
pre-conditions**

```
                  int existingQuantity = basket.getOrDefault(product, 0);  ◁──┐ If the product
                  int newQuantity = existingQuantity + qtyToAdd;                │ is already in the
                  basket.put(product, newQuantity);                            │ cart, add to it.
```

Calculates the
previous and the
new value of the
product for the
relevant quantities
```
                  BigDecimal valueAlreadyInTheCart = product.getPrice()
                ▷ .multiply(valueOf(existingQuantity));
                  BigDecimal newFinalValueForTheProduct = product.getPrice()
                ▷ .multiply(valueOf(newQuantity));
```

Subtracts the previous value of the product from the total value of the basket and adds the new final value of the product to it

```
                  totalValue = totalValue
                    .subtract(valueAlreadyInTheCart)
                    .add(newFinalValueForTheProduct);   ◁──┘

              assert basket.containsKey(product) : "Product was not inserted in
              ➥ the basket";
              assert totalValue.compareTo(oldTotalValue) == 1 : "Total value should
              ➥ be greater than previous total value";
              assert invariant() : "Invariant does not hold";
          }
      }
```

Post-conditions and invariant checks

The implementation is straightforward. First it does the pre-condition checks we discussed in chapter 4. The product cannot be null, and the quantity of the product to be added to the cart has to be larger than zero. Then the method checks whether the basket already contains the product. If so, it adds the quantity on top of the quantity already in the cart. It then calculates the value to add to the total value of the basket. To do so, it calculates the value of that product based on the previous amount in the basket, subtracts that from the total value, and then adds the new total value for that product. Finally, it ensures that the invariant (the total value of the basket must be positive) still holds.

The remove method is simpler than the add method. It looks for the product in the basket, calculates the amount it needs to remove from the total value of the basket, subtracts it, and removes the product (listing 5.13). The method also ensures the same two pre-conditions we discussed before: the product cannot be null, and the product has to be in the basket.

Listing 5.13 Implementation of `Baskets remove` method

Pre-conditions check
```
public void remove(Product product) {
    assert product != null : "product can't be null";
    assert basket.containsKey(product) : "Product must already be in
    ➥ the basket";

    int qty = basket.get(product);

    BigDecimal productPrice = product.getPrice();         │ Calculates the
    BigDecimal productTimesQuantity = productPrice.multiply(│ amount that
    ➥ valueOf(qty));                                      │ should be removed
    totalValue = totalValue.subtract(productTimesQuantity);│ from the basket
```

```
basket.remove(product);          ◄─┐  Removes the product
                                   └  from the hashmap

assert !basket.containsKey(product) : "Product is still   ┐  Post-conditions
⇒ in the basket";                                         │  and invariant
assert invariant() : "Invariant does not hold";           ┘  check
}
```

A developer who did not read the chapters on specification-based testing and structural testing would come up with at least three tests: one to ensure that add() adds the product to the cart, another to ensure that the method behaves correctly when the same product is added twice, and one to ensure that remove() indeed removes the product from the basket. Then they would probably add a few tests for the exceptional cases (which in this class are clearly specified in the contracts). Here are the automated test cases.

Listing 5.14 Non-systematic tests for the Basket class

```java
import static java.math.BigDecimal.valueOf;

public class BasketTest {
  private Basket basket = new Basket();
                                              ┐  Ensures that
                                              │  products are added
  @Test                                       │  to the basket
  void addProducts() {            ◄───────────┘
    basket.add(new Product("TV", valueOf(10)), 2);
    basket.add(new Product("Playstation", valueOf(100)), 1);

    assertThat(basket.getTotalValue())
        .isEqualByComparingTo(valueOf(10*2 + 100*1));
  }
                                              ┐  If the same product is
                                              │  added twice, the basket
  @Test                                       │  sums up the quantities.
  void addSameProductTwice() {    ◄───────────┘
    Product p = new Product("TV", valueOf(10));
    basket.add(p, 2);
    basket.add(p, 3);

    assertThat(basket.getTotalValue())
        .isEqualByComparingTo(valueOf(10*5));
  }
                                       ┐  Ensures that products are
  @Test                                │  removed from the basket
  void removeProducts() {   ◄──────────┘
    basket.add(new Product("TV", valueOf(100)), 1);

    Product p = new Product("PlayStation", valueOf(10));
    basket.add(p, 2);
    basket.remove(p);
                                              ┐  Food for thought: is this
                                              │  assertion enough? You
    assertThat(basket.getTotalValue())        │  might also want to verify
        .isEqualByComparingTo(valueOf(100));  │  that PlayStation is not in
  }                                 ◄──────────┘  the basket.
```

```
    // tests for exceptional cases...
}
```

> **NOTE** I used the `isEqualByComparingTo` assert instruction. Remember that `BigDecimals` are instances of a strange class, and the correct way to compare one `BigDecimal` to another is with the `compareTo()` method. That is what the `isEqualByComparingTo` assertion does. Again, the `BigDecimal` class is not easy to handle.

The problem with these tests is that they do not exercise the feature extensively. If there is a bug in our implementation, it is probably hidden and will only appear after a long and unexpected sequence of adds and removes to and from the basket. Finding this specific sequence might be hard to see, even after proper domain and structural testing. However, we can express it as a property: given any arbitrary sequence of additions and removals, the basket still calculates the correct final amount. We have to customize jqwik so that it understands how to randomly call a sequence of add()s and remove()s, as shown in figure 5.2.

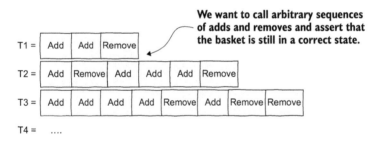

Figure 5.2   We want our test to call arbitrary sequences of add and remove actions.

Fasten your seatbelt, because this takes a lot of code. The first step is to create a bunch of jqwik `Actions` to represent the different actions that can happen with the basket. Actions are a way to explain to the framework how to execute a more complex action. In our case, two things can happen: we can add a product to the basket, or we can remove a product from the basket. We define how these two actions work so that later, jqwik can generate a random sequence of actions.

Let's start with the add action. It will receive a `Product` and a quantity and insert the `Product` into the `Basket`. The action will then ensure that the `Basket` behaved as expected by comparing its current total value against the expected value. Note that everything happens in the `run()` method: this method is defined by jqwik's `Action` interface, which our action implements. In practice, jqwik will call this method whenever it generates an add action and passes the current basket to the `run` method. The following listing shows the implementation of the `AddAction` class.

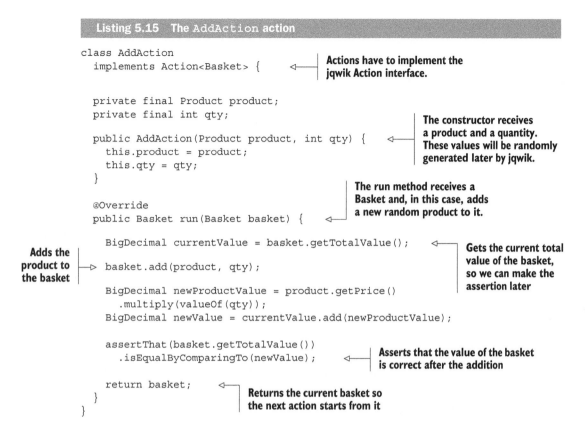

Listing 5.15 The `AddAction` action

```
class AddAction
  implements Action<Basket> {        ◁—— Actions have to implement the
                                          jqwik Action interface.

  private final Product product;
  private final int qty;

  public AddAction(Product product, int qty) {   ◁—— The constructor receives
    this.product = product;                            a product and a quantity.
    this.qty = qty;                                     These values will be randomly
  }                                                      generated later by jqwik.

  @Override                                  The run method receives a
  public Basket run(Basket basket) {    ◁—— Basket and, in this case, adds
                                             a new random product to it.

    BigDecimal currentValue = basket.getTotalValue();   ◁——┐ Gets the current total
                                                             value of the basket,
    basket.add(product, qty);                                so we can make the
                                                             assertion later
    BigDecimal newProductValue = product.getPrice()
      .multiply(valueOf(qty));
    BigDecimal newValue = currentValue.add(newProductValue);

    assertThat(basket.getTotalValue())
      .isEqualByComparingTo(newValue);   ◁—— Asserts that the value of the basket
                                              is correct after the addition

    return basket;   ◁——┐ Returns the current basket so
  }                        the next action starts from it
}
```

Adds the product to the basket (annotation pointing to `basket.add(product, qty);`)

Now let's implement the remove action. This is tricky: we need a way to get the set of products that are already in the basket and their quantities. Note that we do not have such a method in the Basket class. The simplest thing to do is add such a method to the class.

You might be thinking that adding more methods for the tests is a bad idea. It's a trade-off. I often favor anything that eases testing. An extra method will not hurt and will help our testing, so I'd do it, as shown next.

Listing 5.16 `Basket` class modified to support the test

```
class Basket {
  // ... the code of the class here ...           We only return the quantity if
                                                   the product is in the cart. Note
  public int quantityOf(Product product) {   ◁—— that here, we could have gone
    assert basket.containsKey(product);             for a weaker pre-condition: for
    return basket.get(product);                     example, if the product is not
  }                                                  in the basket, return 0.

  public Set<Product> products() {   ◁——┐ Returns a copy of
    return Collections.unmodifiableSet(basket.keySet());   the set, not the
  }                                                          original one!
}
```

The remove action picks a random product from the basket, removes it, and then ensures that the current total value is the total value minus the value of the product that was just removed. The `pickRandom()` method chooses a random product from the set of products; I do not show the code here, to save space, but you can find it in the book's code repository.

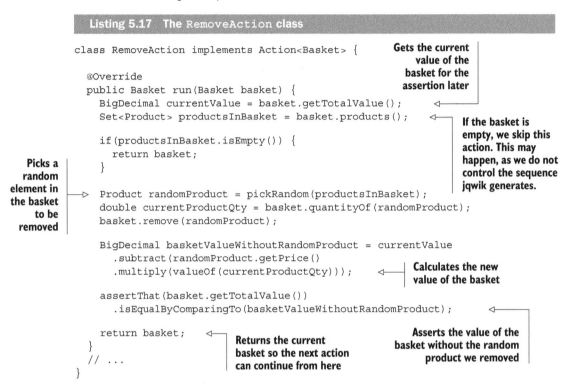

Listing 5.17 The `RemoveAction` class

```java
class RemoveAction implements Action<Basket> {          Gets the current
                                                        value of the
  @Override                                             basket for the
  public Basket run(Basket basket) {                    assertion later
    BigDecimal currentValue = basket.getTotalValue();   ◁
    Set<Product> productsInBasket = basket.products();  ◁          If the basket is
                                                                   empty, we skip this
    if(productsInBasket.isEmpty()) {                               action. This may
      return basket;                                               happen, as we do not
    }                                                              control the sequence
                                                                   jqwik generates.
    Product randomProduct = pickRandom(productsInBasket);
    double currentProductQty = basket.quantityOf(randomProduct);
    basket.remove(randomProduct);

    BigDecimal basketValueWithoutRandomProduct = currentValue
      .subtract(randomProduct.getPrice()
      .multiply(valueOf(currentProductQty)));           ◁    Calculates the new
                                                             value of the basket
    assertThat(basket.getTotalValue())
      .isEqualByComparingTo(basketValueWithoutRandomProduct);    ◁

    return basket;    ◁
  }                        Returns the current            Asserts the value of the
  // ...                   basket so the next action      basket without the random
}                          can continue from here         product we removed
```

`Picks a random element in the basket to be removed`

Jqwik now knows how to call `add()` (via `AddAction`) and `remove()` (via `RemoveAction`). The next step is to explain how to instantiate random products and sequences of actions. Let's start by explaining to jqwik how to instantiate an arbitrary `AddAction`. First we randomly pick a product from a predefined list of products. Then we generate a random quantity value. Finally, we add the random product in the random quantity to the basket.

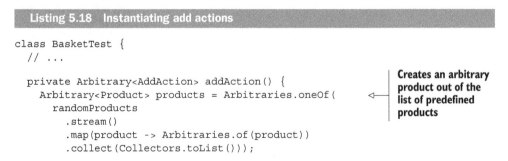

Listing 5.18 Instantiating add actions

```java
class BasketTest {
  // ...

  private Arbitrary<AddAction> addAction() {
    Arbitrary<Product> products = Arbitraries.oneOf(    ◁          Creates an arbitrary
      randomProducts                                               product out of the
        .stream()                                                  list of predefined
        .map(product -> Arbitraries.of(product))                  products
        .collect(Collectors.toList()));
```

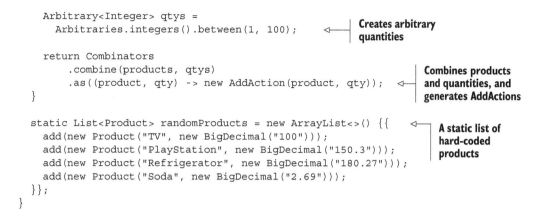

```
    Arbitrary<Integer> qtys =
      Arbitraries.integers().between(1, 100);        ◄─┤ Creates arbitrary
                                                          quantities

    return Combinators
        .combine(products, qtys)                         Combines products
        .as((product, qty) -> new AddAction(product, qty)); ◄─ and quantities, and
  }                                                        generates AddActions

  static List<Product> randomProducts = new ArrayList<>() {{  ◄─ A static list of
    add(new Product("TV", new BigDecimal("100")));            hard-coded
    add(new Product("PlayStation", new BigDecimal("150.3")));  products
    add(new Product("Refrigerator", new BigDecimal("180.27")));
    add(new Product("Soda", new BigDecimal("2.69")));
  }};
}
```

This is a complex piece of code, and it involves a lot of details about how jqwik works. Let's digest it step by step:

1 Our first goal is to randomly select an arbitrary `Product` from the list of products. To do so, we use jqwik's `Arbitraries.oneOf()` method, which randomly picks an arbitrary element of a given set of options. Given that the `oneOf` method needs a `List<Arbitrary<Product>>`, we have to convert our `randomProducts` (which is a `List<Product>`). This is easily done using Java's Stream API.

2 We generate a random integer that will serve as the quantity to pass to the `add()` method. We define an `Arbitrary<Integer>` with numbers between 1 and 100 (random choices that I made after exploring the method's source code).

3 We return an `AddAction` that is instantiated using a combination of arbitrary products and quantities.

We can now create our test. The property test should receive an `ActionSequence`, which we define as an arbitrary sequence of `AddActions` and `RemoveActions`. We do so with the `Arbitraries.sequences()` method. Let's define this in an `addsAndRemoves` method.

We also need arbitrary remove actions, as we did for add actions, but this is much simpler since the `RemoveAction` class does not receive anything in its constructor. So, we use `Arbitraries.of()`.

Listing 5.19 Adding remove actions to the test

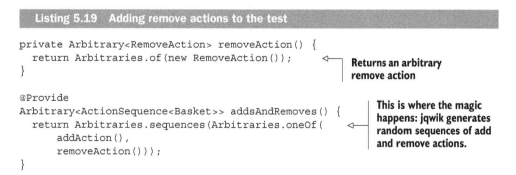

```
private Arbitrary<RemoveAction> removeAction() {
  return Arbitraries.of(new RemoveAction());        ◄─┐ Returns an arbitrary
}                                                        remove action

@Provide
Arbitrary<ActionSequence<Basket>> addsAndRemoves() {     This is where the magic
  return Arbitraries.sequences(Arbitraries.oneOf(        happens: jqwik generates
      addAction(),                                ◄─     random sequences of add
      removeAction()));                                  and remove actions.
}
```

We now only need a `@Property` test method that runs the different sequences of actions generated by the `addsAndRemoves` method.

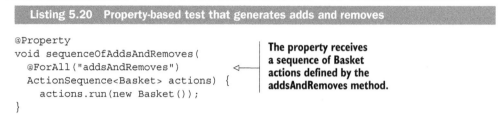

Listing 5.20 Property-based test that generates adds and removes

```
@Property
void sequenceOfAddsAndRemoves(
  @ForAll("addsAndRemoves")
  ActionSequence<Basket> actions) {
    actions.run(new Basket());
}
```

The property receives a sequence of Basket actions defined by the addsAndRemoves method.

And we are finished. As soon as we run the test, jqwik randomly invokes sequences of adds and removes, passing random `Products` and quantities and ensuring that the value of the basket is always correct.

This was a long, complex property-based test, and you may be wondering if it is worth the effort. For this specific `Basket` implementation, I would probably write thorough example-based tests. But I hope this example illustrates the power of property-based testing. Although they tend to be more complicated than traditional example-based tests, you will get used to it, and you will soon be writing them quickly.

5.5   *Example 5: Creating complex domain objects*

Building more complex objects may come in handy when testing business systems. This can be done using jqwik's `Combinators` feature, which we'll use in the following listing. Imagine that we have the following `Book` class, and we need to generate different books for a property-based test.

Listing 5.21 A simple Book class

```
public class Book {

  private final String title;
  private final String author;
  private final int qtyOfPages;

  public Book(String title, String author, int qtyOfPages) {
    this.title = title;
    this.author = author;
    this.qtyOfPages = qtyOfPages;
  }

  // getters...
}
```

One way to do this would be to have a property test that receives three parameters: a `String` for title, a `String` for author, and an `Integer` for quantity of pages. Inside the property test, we would instantiate the `Book` class. Jqwik offers a better way to do that, as shown in the next listing.

Listing 5.22 Using the `Combinators` API to generate complex objects

```
public class BookTest {

  @Property
  void differentBooks(@ForAll("books") Book book) {
    // different books!
    System.out.println(book);

    // write your test here!
  }

  @Provide
  Arbitrary<Book> books() {
    Arbitrary<String> titles = Arbitraries.strings().withCharRange(
      'a', 'z')
      .ofMinLength(10).ofMaxLength(100);
    Arbitrary<String> authors = Arbitraries.strings().withCharRange(
      'a', 'z')
      .ofMinLength(5).ofMaxLength(21);
    Arbitrary<Integer> qtyOfPages = Arbitraries.integers().between(
      0, 450);

    return Combinators.combine(titles, authors, qtyOfPages)
      .as((title, author, pages) -> new Book(title, author, pages));
  }
}
```

Instantiates one arbitrary for each of the Book's fields

Combines them to generate an instance of Book

The `Combinators` API lets us combine different generators to build a more complex object. All we have to do is to build specific `Arbitrarys` for each of the attributes of the complex class we want to build: in this case, one `Arbitrary<String>` for the title, another `Arbitrary<String>` for the author, and one `Arbitrary<Integer>` for the number of pages. After that, we use the `Combinators.combine()` method, which receives a series of `Arbitrarys` and returns an `Arbitrary` of the complex object. The magic happens in the `as()` method, which gives us the values we use to instantiate the object.

Note how flexible jqwik is. You can build virtually any object you want. Moreover, nothing prevents you from building even more realistic input values: for example, instead of building random author names, we could develop something that returns real people's names. Try implementing such an arbitrary yourself.

5.6 Property-based testing in the real world

Let me give you some tips on writing property-based tests.

5.6.1 Example-based testing vs. property-based testing

Property-based testing seems much fancier than example-based testing. It also explores the input domain much better. Should we only use property-based testing from now on?

In practice, I mix example-based testing and property-based testing. In the testing workflow I propose, I use example-based testing when doing specification-based and structural testing. Example-based tests are naturally simpler than property-based tests, and they require less creativity to automate. I like that: their simplicity allows me to focus on understanding the requirements and engineer better test cases. When I am done with both testing techniques and have a much better grasp of the program under test, I evaluate which test cases would be better as property-based tests.

Do I always write property-based tests for my programs? Honestly, no. In many of the problems I work on, I feel pretty confident with example-based testing. I use property-based testing when I do not feel entirely secure that my example-based tests were enough.

5.6.2   *Common issues in property-based tests*

I see three common issues in the property-based tests my students write when they learn this technique. The first is requiring jqwik to generate data that is very expensive or even impossible. If you ask jqwik to, say, generate an array of 100 elements in which the numbers have to be unique and multiples of 2, 3, 5, and 15, such an array can be difficult to find, given jqwik's random approach. Or if you want an array with 10 unique elements, but you give jqwik a range of 2 to 8, the array is impossible to generate. In general, if jqwik is taking too long to generate the data for you, maybe you can find a better way to generate the data or write the test.

Second, we saw in previous chapters that boundaries are a perfect place for bugs. So, we want to exercise those boundaries when writing property-based tests. Ensure that you are expressing the boundaries of the property correctly. When we wrote the tests for the passing-grade problem (section 5.1), we wrote arbitraries like `Arbitraries .floats().lessThan(1f)` and `Arbitraries.floats().greaterThan(10f)`. Jqwik will do its best to generate boundary values: for example, the closest possible number to `1f` or the smallest possible float. The default configuration for jqwik is to mix edge cases with random data points. Again, all of this will work well only if you express the properties and boundaries correctly.

The third caveat is ensuring that the input data you pass to the method under test is fairly distributed among all the possible options. Jqwik does its best to generate well-distributed inputs. For example, if you ask for an integer between 0 and 10, all the numbers in the interval will have the same probability of being generated. But I have seen tests that manipulate the generated data and then harm this property. For example, imagine testing a method that receives three integers, a, b, and c, and returns a boolean indicating whether these three sides can form a triangle. The implementation of this method is simple, as shown in the following listing.

Listing 5.23   Implementation of the `isTriangle` method

```
public class Triangle {
  public static boolean isTriangle(int a, int b, int c) {
    boolean hasABadSide = a >= (b + c) || c >= (b + a) || b >= (a + c);
    return !hasABadSide;
  }
}
```

To write a property-based test for this method, we need to express two properties: valid triangles and invalid triangles. If the developer generates three random integer values as shown next, there is a very low chance of them forming a valid triangle.

Listing 5.24 A bad property-based test for `isTriangle`

```
@Property
void triangleBadTest(                  ◁
  @ForAll @IntRange(max = 100) int a,
  @ForAll @IntRange(max = 100) int b,
  @ForAll @IntRange(max = 100) int c) {

  // ... test here ...

}
```

> Generates three different integers. The odds are that these a, b, and c will be an invalid triangle. We therefore do not exercise the valid triangle property as much as we wanted to.

The test exercises the invalid triangle property more than the valid triangle property. A good property-based test for this problem would ensure that jqwik generates the same number of valid and invalid triangles. The easiest way to do that would be to split it into two tests: one for valid triangles and one for invalid triangles. (The solution is available in the code repository.)

5.6.3 *Creativity is key*

Writing property-based tests requires a lot of creativity from the developer. Finding ways to express the property, generating random data, and being able to assert the expected behavior without knowing the concrete input is not easy. Property-based testing requires more practice than traditional example-based testing: get your hands dirty as soon as possible. I hope the examples have given you some ideas!

Exercises

5.1 What is the main difference between example-based testing and property-based testing?

5.2 Suppose we have a method that returns `true` if the passed string is a palindrome or `false` otherwise. (A palindrome is a word or sentence that reads the same backward and forward.) What properties do you see that could be tested via property-based tests? Also describe how you would implement such tests.

5.3 Find out what *fuzz testing* or *fuzzing* is. What is the difference between property-based testing and fuzzing?

Summary

- In property-based testing, instead of coming up with concrete examples, we express the property that should hold for that method. The framework then randomly generates hundreds of different inputs.

- Property-based testing does not replace specification-based testing and structural testing. It is one more tool to have in your belt. Sometimes traditional example-based testing is enough.
- Writing property-based tests is a tad more challenging than example-based testing. You have to be creative to express the properties. Practice is key.

Test doubles and mocks

6

This chapter covers

- Using stubs, fakes, and mocks to simplify testing
- Understanding what to mock, when to mock, and when not to mock
- How to mock the unmockable

Until now, we have been testing classes and methods that were isolated from each other. We passed the inputs to a single method call and asserted its output. Or, when a class was involved, we set up the state of the class, called the method under test, and asserted that the class was in the expected state.

But some classes depend on other classes to do their job. Exercising (or testing) many classes together may be desirable. We often break down complex behavior into multiple classes to improve maintainability, each with a small part of the business logic. We still want to ensure, however, that the whole thing works together; we will discuss this in chapter 9. This chapter focuses on testing that unit in an isolated fashion without caring too much about its dependencies. But why would we want that?

The answer is simple: because exercising the class under test together with its concrete dependencies might be too slow, too hard, or too much work. As an example, consider an application that handles invoices. This system has a class called

IssuedInvoices, which handles the database and contains lots of SQL queries. Other parts of the system (such as the InvoiceGenerationService class, which generates new invoices) depend on this IssuedInvoices class to persist the generated invoice in the database. This means that whenever we test InvoiceGenerationService, this class will consequently call IssuedInvoices, which will then communicate with a database.

In other words, the InvoiceGenerationService class indirectly depends on the database that stores the issued invoices. This means testing the InvoiceGeneration-Service requires setting up a database, making sure it contains all the right data, and so on. That is clearly much more work than writing tests that do not require a database. Figure 6.1 shows a more generic illustration of this problem. How do we test a class that depends on many other classes, some of which may involve databases and other complicated things?

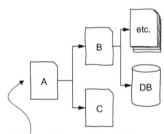

How do we write tests for A without depending on B, C, and all their transitive dependencies?

Figure 6.1   A simple illustration of the challenges we face when testing a class that depends on many other classes

But when systematically testing the InvoiceGenerationService class, maybe we do not want to test whether the SQL query in the IssuedInvoices class is correct. We only want to ensure that, for example, the invoice is generated correctly or contains all the right values. Testing whether the SQL query works will be the responsibility of the IssuedInvoicesTest test suite, not InvoiceGenerationServiceTest. We will write integration tests for SQL queries in chapter 9.

We must figure out how to test a class that depends on another class without using that dependency. This is where *test doubles* come in handy. We create an object to mimic the behavior of component B ("it looks like B, but it is not B"). Within the test, we have full control over what this fake component B does, so we can make it behave as B would *in the context of this test* and thus cut the dependency on the real object.

In the previous example, suppose A is a plain Java class that depends on Issued-Invoices to retrieve values from a database. We can implement a fake IssuedInvoices that returns a hard-coded list of values rather than retrieving them from an external database. This means we can control the environment around A so we can check how A behaves without dealing with complex dependencies. I show examples of how this works later in the chapter.

Using objects that simulate the behavior of other objects has the following advantages:

- *We have more control.* We can easily tell these fake objects what to do. If we want a method to throw an exception, we tell the mock method to throw it. There is no need for complicated setups to force the dependency to throw the exception. Think of how hard it is to force a class to throw an exception or return a fake date. This effort is close to zero when we simulate the dependencies with mock objects.
- *Simulations are faster.* Imagine a dependency that communicates with a web service or a database. A method in one of these classes might take a few seconds to process. On the other hand, if we simulate the dependency, it will no longer need to communicate with a database or web service and wait for a response. The simulation will return what it was configured to return, and it will cost nothing in terms of time.
- When used as a design technique, mocks enable developers to *reflect on how classes should interact with each other*, what their contracts should be, and the conceptual boundaries. Therefore, mocks can be used to make testing easier and support developers in designing code.

NOTE   While some of the schools of thought in testing prefer to see mocks as a design technique, in this book, I talk about stubs and mocks mostly from a testing perspective, as our goal is to use mocks to ease our lives when looking for bugs. If you are interested in mocking as a design technique, I strongly recommend Freeman and Pryce's 2009 book, which is the canonical reference for the subject.

I sorted mocks into the unit testing section of my testing flow (go back to figure 1.4 in chapter 1) because our goal is to focus on a single unit without caring much about the other units of the system. Note, however, that we still care about the contracts of the dependencies, as our simulations must follow and do the same things that the simulated class promises.

6.1   *Dummies, fakes, stubs, spies, and mocks*

Before we dive into how to simulate objects, let's first discuss the different types of simulations we can create. Meszaros, in his book (2007), defines five different types: dummy objects, fake objects, stubs, spies, and mocks. Each makes sense in a specific situation.

6.1.1   *Dummy objects*

Dummy objects are passed to the class under test but never used. This is common in business applications where you need to fill a long list of parameters, but the test exercises only a few of them. Think of a unit test for a `Customer` class. Maybe this class depends on several other classes like `Address`, `Email`, and so on. Maybe a specific test case A wants to exercise a behavior, and this behavior does not care which `Address` this `Customer` has. In this case, a tester can set up a dummy `Address` object and pass it to the `Customer` class.

6.1.2   *Fake objects*

Fake objects have real working implementations of the class they simulate. However, they usually do the same task in a much simpler way. Imagine a fake database class that uses an array list instead of a real database. This fake object is simpler to control than the real database. A common example in real life is to use a simpler database during testing.

In the Java world, developers like to use HSQLDB (HyperSQL database, http://hsqldb.org), an in-memory database that is much faster and easier to set up in the test code than a real database. We will talk more about in-memory databases when we discuss integration testing in chapter 9.

6.1.3   *Stubs*

Stubs provide hard-coded answers to the calls performed during the test. Unlike fake objects, stubs do not have a working implementation. If the code calls a stubbed method `getAllInvoices`, the stub will return a hard-coded list of invoices.

Stubs are the most popular type of simulation. In most cases, all you need from a dependency is for it to return a value so the method under test can continue its execution. If we were testing a method that depends on this `getAllInvoices` method, we could stub it to return an empty list, then return a list with one element, then return a list with many elements, and so on. This would enable us to assert how the method under test would work for lists of various lengths being returned from the database.

6.1.4   *Mocks*

Mock objects act like stubs in the sense that you can configure how they reply if a method is called: for example, to return a list of invoices when `getAllInvoices` is called. However, mocks go beyond that. They save all the interactions and allow you to make assertions afterward. For example, maybe we only want the `getAllInvoices` method to be called once. If the method is called twice by the class under test, this is a bug, and the test should fail. At the end of our test, we can write an assertion along the lines of "verify that `getAllInvoices` was called just once."

Mocking frameworks let you assert all sorts of interactions, such as "the method was never called with this specific parameter" or "the method was called twice with parameter A and once with parameter B." Mocks are also popular in industry since they can provide insight into how classes interact.

6.1.5   *Spies*

As the name suggests, spies spy on a dependency. They wrap themselves around the real object and observe its behavior. Strictly speaking, we are not simulating the object but rather recording all the interactions with the underlying object we are spying on.

Spies are used in very specific contexts, such as when it is much easier to use the real implementation than a mock but you still want to assert how the method under test interacts with the dependency. Spies are less common in the wild.

6.2   *An introduction to mocking frameworks*

Mocking frameworks are available for virtually all programming languages. While they may differ in their APIs, the underlying idea is the same. Here, I will use Mockito (https://site.mockito.org), one of the most popular stubbing and mocking libraries for Java. Mockito offers a simple API, enabling developers to set up stubs and define expectations in mock objects with just a few lines of code. (Mockito is an extensive framework, and we cover only part of it in this chapter. To learn more, take a look at its documentation.)

Mockito is so simple that knowing the following three methods is often enough:

- `mock(<class>)`—Creates a mock object/stub of a given class. The class can be specified by `<ClassName>.class`.
- `when(<mock>.<method>).thenReturn(<value>)`—A chain of method calls that defines the (stubbed) behavior of the method. In this case `<value>` is returned. For example, to make the `all` method of an `issuedInvoices` mock return a list of invoices, we write `when(issuedInvoices.all()).thenReturn(someList-Here)`.
- `verify(<mock>).<method>`—Asserts that the interactions with the mock object happened in the expected way. For example, if we want to ensure that the method `all` of an `issuedInvoices` mock was invoked, we use `verify(issued-Invoices).all()`.

Let's dive into concrete examples to illustrate Mockito's main features and show you how developers use mocking frameworks in practice. If you are already familiar with Mockito, you can skip this section.

6.2.1   *Stubbing dependencies*

Let's learn how to use Mockito and set up stubs with a practical example. Suppose we have the following requirement:

> The program must return all the issued invoices with values smaller than 100. The collection of invoices can be found in our database. The class `Issued-Invoices` already contains a method that retrieves all the invoices.

The code in listing 6.1 is a possible implementation of this requirement. Note that `IssuedInvoices` is a class responsible for retrieving all the invoices from a real database (for example, MySQL). For now, suppose it has a method `all()` (not shown) that returns all the invoices in the database. The class sends SQL queries to the database and returns invoices. You can check the (naive) implementation in the book's code repository.

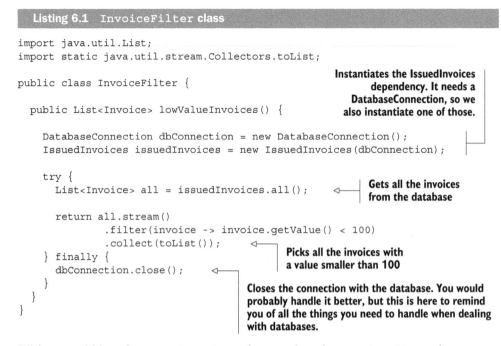

Listing 6.1 `InvoiceFilter` class

```
import java.util.List;
import static java.util.stream.Collectors.toList;

public class InvoiceFilter {

  public List<Invoice> lowValueInvoices() {

    DatabaseConnection dbConnection = new DatabaseConnection();
    IssuedInvoices issuedInvoices = new IssuedInvoices(dbConnection);

    try {
      List<Invoice> all = issuedInvoices.all();

      return all.stream()
              .filter(invoice -> invoice.getValue() < 100)
              .collect(toList());
    } finally {
      dbConnection.close();
    }
  }
}
```

Instantiates the IssuedInvoices dependency. It needs a DatabaseConnection, so we also instantiate one of those.

Gets all the invoices from the database

Picks all the invoices with a value smaller than 100

Closes the connection with the database. You would probably handle it better, but this is here to remind you of all the things you need to handle when dealing with databases.

Without stubbing the `IssuedInvoices` class, testing the `InvoiceFilter` class means having to set up a database. It also means having invoices in the database so the SQL query can return them. This is a lot of work, as you can see from the (simplified) test method in listing 6.2, which exercises `InvoiceFilter` together with the concrete `IssuedInvoices` class and the database. Because the tests need a populated database up and running, we first create a connection to the database and clean up any old data it may contain. Then, in the test method, we persist a set of invoices to the database. Finally, when the test is over, we close the connection with the database, as we do not want hanging connections.

Listing 6.2 Tests for `InvoiceFilter`

```
public class InvoiceFilterTest {
  private IssuedInvoices invoices;
  private DatabaseConnection dbConnection;

  @BeforeEach
  public void open() {
    dbConnection = new DatabaseConnection();
    invoices = new IssuedInvoices(dbConnection);

    dbConnection.resetDatabase();
  }

  @AfterEach
  public void close() {
    if (dbConnection != null)
```

BeforeEach methods are executed before every test method.

Cleans up the tables to make sure old data in the database does not interfere with the test

AfterEach methods are executed after every test method.

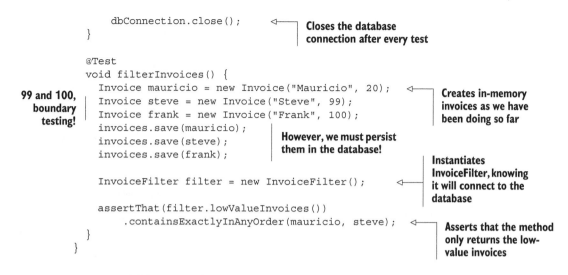

```
        dbConnection.close();                ◁─────┐  Closes the database
    }                                              │  connection after every test

    @Test
    void filterInvoices() {
        Invoice mauricio = new Invoice("Mauricio", 20);    ◁─────┐  Creates in-memory
        Invoice steve = new Invoice("Steve", 99);                │  invoices as we have
        Invoice frank = new Invoice("Frank", 100);               │  been doing so far
        invoices.save(mauricio);
        invoices.save(steve);           However, we must persist
        invoices.save(frank);           them in the database!
                                                             Instantiates
                                                             InvoiceFilter, knowing
        InvoiceFilter filter = new InvoiceFilter();    ◁──   it will connect to the
                                                             database
        assertThat(filter.lowValueInvoices())
            .containsExactlyInAnyOrder(mauricio, steve);    ◁─────┐  Asserts that the method
    }                                                            │  only returns the low-
}                                                               │  value invoices
```

99 and 100, boundary testing!

NOTE Did you notice the `assertThat…containsExactlyInAnyOrder` assertion? This ensures that the list contains exactly the objects we pass, in any order. Such assertions do not come with JUnit 5. Without AssertJ, we would have to write a lot of code for that assertion to happen. You should get familiar with AssertJ's assertions; they are handy.

This is a small example. Imagine a larger business class with a much more complex database structure. Imagine that instead of persisting a bunch of invoices, you need to persist invoices, customers, items, shopping carts, products, and so on. This can become tedious and expensive.

Let's rewrite the test. This time we will stub the `IssuedInvoices` class and avoid the hassle with the database. First, we need a way to inject the `InvoiceFilter` stub into the class under test. Its current implementation creates an instance of `Issued-Invoices` internally (see the first lines in the `lowValueInvoices` method). This means there is no way for this class to use the stub during the test: whenever this method is invoked, it instantiates the concrete database-dependent class.

We must change our production code to make testing easier (get used to the idea of changing the production code to facilitate testing). The most direct way to do this is to have `IssuedInvoices` passed in as an explicit dependency through the class constructor, as shown in listing 6.3. The class no longer instantiates the `Database-Connection` and `IssuedInvoices` classes. Rather, it receives `IssuedInvoices` via constructor. Note that there is no need for the `DatabaseConnection` class to be injected, as `InvoiceFilter` does not need it. This is good: the less we need to do in our test code, the better. The new implementation works for both our tests (because we can inject an `IssueInvoices` stub) and production (because we can inject the concrete `IssueInvoices`, which will go to the database, as we expect in production).

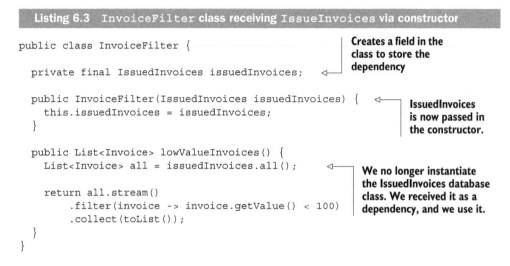

Listing 6.3 `InvoiceFilter` **class receiving** `IssueInvoices` **via constructor**

```
public class InvoiceFilter {                          Creates a field in the
                                                      class to store the
  private final IssuedInvoices issuedInvoices;   ◁──┘ dependency

  public InvoiceFilter(IssuedInvoices issuedInvoices) {  ◁──── IssuedInvoices
    this.issuedInvoices = issuedInvoices;                       is now passed in
  }                                                             the constructor.

  public List<Invoice> lowValueInvoices() {
    List<Invoice> all = issuedInvoices.all();      ◁──┐ We no longer instantiate
                                                       the IssuedInvoices database
    return all.stream()                                class. We received it as a
        .filter(invoice -> invoice.getValue() < 100)   dependency, and we use it.
        .collect(toList());
  }
}
```

Let's change our focus to the unit test of `InvoiceFilter`. The test is very similar to the one we wrote earlier, but now we do not handle the database. Instead, we configure the `IssuedInvoices` stub as shown in the next listing. Note how easy it is to write this test: full control over the stub enables us to try different cases (even exceptional ones) quickly.

Listing 6.4 **Tests for** `InvoiceFilter`, **stubbing** `IssuedInvoices`

```
public class InvoiceFilterTest {                   Instantiates a stub for the
                                                   IssuedInvoices class, using
  @Test                                              Mockito's mock method
  void filterInvoices() {
    IssuedInvoices issuedInvoices = mock(IssuedInvoices.class);   ◁──┘

    Invoice mauricio = new Invoice("Mauricio", 20);
    Invoice steve = new Invoice("Steve", 99);       Creates invoices as
    Invoice frank = new Invoice("Frank", 100);      we did before
    List<Invoice> listOfInvoices = Arrays.asList(mauricio, steve, frank);

    when(issuedInvoices.all()).thenReturn(listOfInvoices);

    InvoiceFilter filter = new InvoiceFilter(issuedInvoices);   ◁──┐

    assertThat(filter.lowValueInvoices())
        .containsExactlyInAnyOrder(mauricio, steve);
  }
}
```

Makes the stub return the predefined list of invoices if all() is called

Asserts that the behavior is as expected

Instantiates the class under test, and passes the stub as a dependency (instead of the concrete database class)

> **NOTE** This idea of classes not instantiating their dependencies by themselves but instead receiving them is a popular design technique. It allows us to inject mocks and also makes the production code more flexible. This idea is also

known as *dependency injection.* If you want to dive into the topic, I suggest *Dependency Injection: Principles, Practices, and Patterns* by Steven van Deursen and Mark Seemann (2019).

Note how we set up the stub using Mockito's `when()` method. In this example, we tell the stub to return a list containing `mauricio`, `frank`, and `steve`, the three invoices we instantiate as part of the test case. The test then invokes the method under test, `filter.lowValueInvoices()`. Consequently, the method under test invokes `issued-Invoices.all()`. However, at this point, `issuedInvoices` is a stub that returns the list with the three invoices. The method under test continues its execution and returns a new list with only the two invoices that are below 100, causing the assertion to pass.

Besides making the test easier to write, stubs also made the test class more cohesive and less prone to change if something other than `InvoiceFilter` changes. If `Issued-Invoices` changes—or, more specifically, if its contracts change—we may have to propagate it to the tests of `InvoiceFilter`, too. Our discussion of contracts in chapter 4 also makes sense when talking about mocks. Now `InvoiceFilterTest` only tests the `InvoiceFilter` class. It does not test the `IssuedInvoices` class. `IssuedInvoices` deserves to be tested, but in another place, using an integration test (which we'll discuss in chapter 9).

A cohesive test also has fewer chances of failing for another reason. In the old version, the `filterInvoices` test could fail because of a bug in the `InvoiceFilter` class or a bug in the `IssuedInvoices` class (imagine a bug in the SQL query that retrieves the invoices from the database). The new tests can only fail because of a bug in `InvoiceFilter`, never because of `IssuedInvoices`. This is handy, as a developer will spend less time debugging if this test fails. Our new approach for testing `Invoice-Filter` is faster, easier to write, and more cohesive.

> **NOTE** This part of the book does not focus on systematic testing. But that is what you should do, regardless of whether you are using mocks. Look at the `filterInvoices` test method. Its goal is to filter invoices that are below 100. In our (currently only) test case, we ensure that this works, and we even exercise the 100 boundary. You may want to exercise other cases, such as empty lists, or lists with a single element, or other test cases that emerge during specification-based and structural testing. I don't do that in this chapter, but you should remember all the techniques discussed in the previous chapters.

In a real software system, the business rule implemented by `InvoiceFilter` would probably be best executed in the database. A simple SQL query would do the job with a much better performance. Try to abstract away from this simple example: whenever you have a dependency that is expensive to use during testing, stubs may come in handy.

6.2.2   *Mocks and expectations*

Next, let's discuss mocks. Suppose our current system has a new requirement:

> All low-valued invoices should be sent to our SAP system (a software that manages business operations). SAP offers a `sendInvoice` web service that receives invoices.

You know you probably want to test the new class without depending on a real full-blown SAP web service. So, the `SAPInvoiceSender` class (which contains the main logic of the feature) receives, via its constructor, a class that communicates with SAP. For simplicity, suppose there is a `SAP` interface. The `SAPInvoiceSender`'s main method, `sendLowValuedInvoices`, gets all the low-valued invoices using the `InvoiceFilter` class discussed in the previous section and then passes the resulting invoices to SAP.

Listing 6.5   `SAPInvoiceSender` class

```
public interface SAP {                    ◄─┐   This interface encapsulates the communication
  void send(Invoice invoice);               │   with SAP. Note that it does not matter how the
}                                           │   concrete implementation will work.

public class SAPInvoiceSender {

  private final InvoiceFilter filter;          We have fields for both the
  private final SAP sap;                       required dependencies.

  public SAPInvoiceSender(InvoiceFilter filter, SAP sap) {
    this.filter = filter;                            The logic of the method is straightforward.
    this.sap = sap;                                  We first get the low-value invoices from
  }                                                  the InvoiceFilter. Then we pass each of
                                                     them to SAP.
  public void sendLowValuedInvoices() {     ◄─┘
    List<Invoice> lowValuedInvoices = filter.lowValueInvoices();
    for(Invoice invoice : lowValuedInvoices) {
      sap.send(invoice);
    }
  }
}
```

The two dependencies are required by the constructor of the class.

Let's test the `SAPInvoiceSender` class (see listing 6.6 for the implementation of the test suite). For this test, we stub the `InvoiceFilter` class. For `SAPInvoiceSender`, `InvoiceFilter` is a class that returns a list of invoices. It is not the goal of the current test to test `InvoiceFilter`, so we should stub this class to facilitate testing the method we do want to test. The stub returns a list of low-valued invoices.

The main purpose of this test is to ensure that every low-valued invoice is sent to SAP. How can we assert that this is happening without having the real SAP? It is simple: we ensure that the call to SAP's `send()` method happened. How do we do that?

Mockito, behind the scenes, records all the interactions with its mocks. This means if we mock the `SAP` interface and pass it to the class under test, at the end of the test, all we need to do is ask the mock whether the method is called. For that, we use Mockito's `verify` assertion (listing 6.6). Note the syntax: we repeat the method we expect to be called. We can even pass the specific parameters we expect. In the case of this test method, we expect the `send` method to be called for both the `mauricio` and `frank` invoices.

Listing 6.6 Tests for the `SAPInvoiceSender` class

```
public class SAPInvoiceSenderTest {

    private InvoiceFilter filter = mock(InvoiceFilter.class);
    private SAP sap = mock(SAP.class);

    private SAPInvoiceSender sender =
        new SAPInvoiceSender(filter, sap);

    @Test
    void sendToSap() {

        Invoice mauricio = new Invoice("Mauricio", 20);
        Invoice frank = new Invoice("Frank", 99);

        List<Invoice> invoices = Arrays.asList(mauricio, frank);

        when(filter.lowValueInvoices()).thenReturn(invoices);

        sender.sendLowValuedInvoices();

        verify(sap).send(mauricio);
        verify(sap).send(frank);
    }
}
```

Passes the mock and the stub to the class under test

Instantiates all the mocks as fields. Nothing changes in terms of behavior. JUnit instantiates a new class before running each of the test methods. This is a matter of taste, but I usually like to have my mocks as fields, so I do not need to instantiate them in every test method.

Sets up the InvoiceFilter stub. It will return two invoices whenever lowValueInvoices() is called.

Calls the method under test, knowing that these two invoices will be sent to SAP

Ensures that the send method was called for both invoices

Again, note how we define the expectations of the mock object. We know exactly how the `InvoiceFilter` class should interact with the mock. When the test is executed, Mockito checks whether these expectations were met and fails the test if they were not.

If you want to see Mockito in action, comment out the call to `sap.send()` in the `sendLowValuedInvoices` method to see the test fail. Mockito will say something like what you see in listing 6.7. Mockito expected the `send` method to be called to the "mauricio" invoice, but it was not. Mockito even complements the message and says that it did not see any interactions with this mock. This is an extra tip to help you debug the failing test.

Listing 6.7 Mockito's verify-failing message

```
Wanted but not invoked:
sap.send(
    Invoice{customer='Mauricio', value=20}
);

Actually, there were zero interactions with this mock.
```

send() was not invoked for this invoice!

This example illustrates the main difference between stubbing and mocking. Stubbing means returning hard-coded values for a given method call. Mocking means not only defining what methods do but also explicitly defining the interactions with the mock.

Mockito enables us to define even more specific expectations. For example, look at the following expectations.

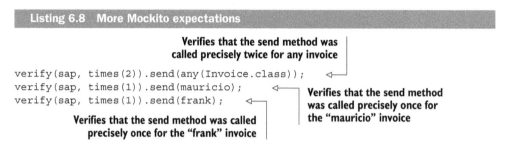

Listing 6.8   More Mockito expectations

Verifies that the send method was called precisely twice for any invoice

```
verify(sap, times(2)).send(any(Invoice.class));
verify(sap, times(1)).send(mauricio);
verify(sap, times(1)).send(frank);
```

Verifies that the send method was called precisely once for the "mauricio" invoice

Verifies that the send method was called precisely once for the "frank" invoice

These expectations are more restrictive than the earlier ones. We now expect the SAP mock to have its `send` method invoked precisely two times (for any given `Invoice`). We then expect the `send` method to be called once for the `mauricio` invoice and once for the `frank` invoice.

Let's write one more test so you become more familiar with Mockito. Let's exercise the case where there are no low-valued invoices. The code is basically the same as in the previous test, but we make our stub return an empty list when the `lowValue-Invoices()` method of `InvoiceFilter` is called. We then expect no interactions with the `SAP` mock. That can be accomplished through the `Mockito.never()` and `Mockito.any()` methods in combination with `verify()`.

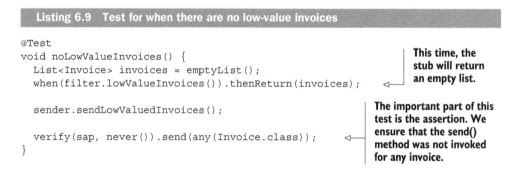

Listing 6.9   Test for when there are no low-value invoices

```
@Test
void noLowValueInvoices() {
  List<Invoice> invoices = emptyList();
  when(filter.lowValueInvoices()).thenReturn(invoices);

  sender.sendLowValuedInvoices();

  verify(sap, never()).send(any(Invoice.class));
}
```

This time, the stub will return an empty list.

The important part of this test is the assertion. We ensure that the send() method was not invoked for any invoice.

You may wonder why I did not put this new SAP sending functionality in the existing `InvoiceFilter` class. The `lowValueInvoices` method would then be both a command and a query. Mixing both concepts in a single method is not a good idea, as it may confuse developers who call this method. An advantage of separating commands from queries is that, from a mocking perspective, you know what to do. You should stub the queries, as you now know that queries return values and do not change the object's state; and you should mock commands, as you know they change the world outside the object under test.

> **NOTE** If you want to learn more, search for "command-query separation" (CQS) or read Fowler's wiki entry on CQS (2005). As you get used to testing and writing tests, you will see that the better the code, the easier it is to test it. In chapter 7, we will discuss code decisions you can make in your production code to facilitate testing.

To learn more about the differences between mocks and stubs, see the article "Mocks Aren't Stubs," by Martin Fowler (2007).

6.2.3 Capturing arguments

Imagine a tiny change in the requirements of sending the invoice to the SAP feature:

> Instead of receiving the Invoice entity directly, SAP now requires the data to be sent in a different format. SAP requires the customer's name, the value of the invoice, and a generated ID.
>
> The ID should have the following format: <date><customer code>.
>
> - The date should always be in the "MMddyyyy" format: <month><day><year with 4 digits>.
> - The customer code should be the first two characters of the customer's first name. If the customer's name has fewer than two characters, it should be "X".

Implementation-wise, we change the SAP interface to receive a new SapInvoice entity. This entity has three fields: customer, value, and id. We then modify the SAPInvoice-Sender so for each low-value invoice, it creates a new SapInvoice entity with the correct id and sends it to SAP. The next listing contains the new implementation.

Listing 6.10 Changing the SAP-related classes to support the new required format

```
public class SapInvoice {              ←─┐  A new entity to
  private final String customer;          │  represent the
  private final int value;                │  new format
  private final String id;

  public SapInvoice(String customer, int value, String id) {
    // constructor
  }

  // getters
}

public interface SAP {                 ←─┐  SAP receives this
  void send(SapInvoice invoice);          │  new SapInvoice
}                                         │  entity.
```

```
public class SAPInvoiceSender {

  private final InvoiceFilter filter;
  private final SAP sap;

  public SAPInvoiceSender(InvoiceFilter filter, SAP sap) {      ◁─── The constructor
    this.filter = filter;                                            is the same as
    this.sap = sap;                                                  before.
  }

  public void sendLowValuedInvoices() {
    List<Invoice> lowValuedInvoices = filter.lowValueInvoices();

    for(Invoice invoice : lowValuedInvoices) {
      String customer = invoice.getCustomer();
      int value = invoice.getValue();
      String sapId = generateId(invoice);             Instantiates the
      SapInvoice sapInvoice =                          new SAPInvoice
        new SapInvoice(customer, value, sapId);   ◁──  object

      sap.send(sapInvoice);        ◁──┐ Sends the new
    }                                 │ entity to SAP       Generates the
  }                                                         required ID as in
                                                            the requirements
  private String generateId(Invoice invoice) {    ◁──┘
    String date = LocalDate.now().format(
      ➥ DateTimeFormatter.ofPattern("MMddyyyy"));
    String customer = invoice.getCustomer();                    Returns the
                                                                date plus the
    return date +                                               customer's
      (customer.length()>=2 ? customer.substring(0,2) : "X");  ◁── code
  }
}
```

When it comes to testing, we know that we should stub the InvoiceFilter class. We can also mock the SAP class and ensure that the send() method was called, as shown next.

Listing 6.11 Test for the new implementation of SAPInvoiceSender

```
@Test
void sendSapInvoiceToSap() {
  Invoice mauricio = new Invoice("Mauricio", 20);


  List<Invoice> invoices = Arrays.asList(mauricio);          ┐ Again, we stub
  when(filter.lowValueInvoices()).thenReturn(invoices);  ◁── InvoiceFilter.

  sender.sendLowValuedInvoices();

  verify(sap).send(any(SapInvoice.class));   ◁──┐ Asserts that SAP received a SapInvoice.
}                                               │ But which SapInvoice? Any. That is not
                                                  good. We want to be more specific.
```

This test ensures that the send method of the SAP is called. But how do we assert that the generated SapInvoice is the correct one? For example, how do we ensure that the generated ID is correct?

One idea could be to extract the logic of converting an Invoice to a SapInvoice, as shown in listing 6.12. The convert() method receives an invoice, generates the new id, and returns a SapInvoice. A simple class like this could be tested via unit tests without any stubs or mocks. We can instantiate different Invoices, call the convert method, and assert that the returned SapInvoice is correct. I leave that as an exercise for you.

Listing 6.12   Class that converts from Invoice to SapInvoice

```
public class InvoiceToSapInvoiceConverter {

  public SapInvoice convert(Invoice invoice) {        ⟵   This method is straightforward.
    String customer = invoice.getCustomer();                It does not depend on any
    int value = invoice.getValue();                         complex classes, so we can
    String sapId = generateId(invoice);                     write unit tests for it as we
                                                            have done previously.

    SapInvoice sapInvoice = new SapInvoice(customer, value, sapId);
    return sapInvoice;
  }                                               The same generateId
                                                  method we saw
  private String generateId(Invoice invoice) {   ⟵  before
    String date = LocalDate.now()
      .format(DateTimeFormatter.ofPattern("MMddyyyy"));
    String customer = invoice.getCustomer();

    return date +
      (customer.length()>=2 ? customer.substring(0,2) : "X");
  }
}
```

In chapter 10, we further discuss refactorings you can apply to your code to facilitate testing. I strongly recommend doing so. But for the sake of argument, let's suppose this is not a possibility. How can we get the SapInvoice object generated in the current implementation of SAPInvoiceSender and assert it? This is our chance to use another of Mockito's features: the argument captor.

Mockito allows us to get the specific objects passed to its mocks. We then ask the SAP mock to give us the SapInvoice passed to it during the execution of the method, to make assertions on it (see listing 6.13). Instead of using any(SAPInvoice.class), we pass an instance of an ArgumentCaptor. We then capture its value, which in this case is an instance of SapInvoice. We make traditional assertions on the contents of this object.

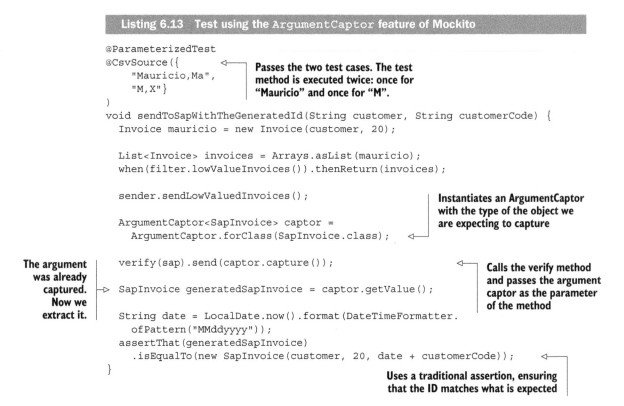

Listing 6.13   Test using the `ArgumentCaptor` feature of Mockito

```
@ParameterizedTest
@CsvSource({
    "Mauricio,Ma",
    "M,X"}
)
void sendToSapWithTheGeneratedId(String customer, String customerCode) {
    Invoice mauricio = new Invoice(customer, 20);

    List<Invoice> invoices = Arrays.asList(mauricio);
    when(filter.lowValueInvoices()).thenReturn(invoices);

    sender.sendLowValuedInvoices();

    ArgumentCaptor<SapInvoice> captor =
        ArgumentCaptor.forClass(SapInvoice.class);

    verify(sap).send(captor.capture());
    SapInvoice generatedSapInvoice = captor.getValue();

    String date = LocalDate.now().format(DateTimeFormatter.
        ofPattern("MMddyyyy"));
    assertThat(generatedSapInvoice)
        .isEqualTo(new SapInvoice(customer, 20, date + customerCode));
}
```

Passes the two test cases. The test method is executed twice: once for "Mauricio" and once for "M".

Instantiates an ArgumentCaptor with the type of the object we are expecting to capture

Calls the verify method and passes the argument captor as the parameter of the method

The argument was already captured. Now we extract it.

Uses a traditional assertion, ensuring that the ID matches what is expected

Note that we have at least two different test cases to ensure that the generated ID is correct: one where the customer's name is longer than two characters and another where it is shorter than two characters. Given that the structure of the test method would be the same for both methods, I decided to use a parameterized test. I also used the CsvSource to pass the different test cases to the test method. The CSV source enables us to pass the inputs via comma-separated values. I usually go for CSV sources whenever the inputs are simple and easily written, as in this case.

Interestingly, although my first option is always to try to refactor the code so I can write simple unit tests, I use argument captors often. In practice, it is common to have such classes, where most of what you do is coordinate the data flow between different components, and objects that need to be asserted may be created on the fly by the method but not returned to the caller.

> **NOTE** There is another test I find fundamental in the sendToSapWithThe-GeneratedId method: we are missing proper boundary testing. The length of the customer's name (two) is a boundary, so I would test with a customer name that is precisely of length two. Again, we are discussing mocks, but when it comes to designing test cases, all the techniques we have discussed apply.

6.2.4 Simulating exceptions

The developer realizes that SAP's send method may throw a SapException if a problem occurs. This leads to a new requirement:

> The system should return the list of invoices that failed to be sent to SAP. A failure should not make the program stop. Instead, the program should try to send all the invoices, even though some of them may fail.

One easy way to implement this is to try to catch any possible exceptions. If an exception happens, we store the failed invoice as shown in the following listing.

Listing 6.14 Catching a possible SAPException

```
public List<Invoice> sendLowValuedInvoices() {
  List<Invoice> failedInvoices = new ArrayList<>();

  List<Invoice> lowValuedInvoices = filter.lowValueInvoices();
  for(Invoice invoice : lowValuedInvoices) {
    String customer = invoice.getCustomer();
    int value = invoice.getValue();
    String sapId = generateId(invoice);

    SapInvoice sapInvoice = new SapInvoice(customer, value, sapId);

    try {                              ⟵┐  Catches the possible SAPException.
      sap.send(sapInvoice);               │  If that happens, we store the failed
    } catch(SAPException e) {             │  invoice in a list.
      failedInvoices.add(invoice);
    }
  }                                  ┐  Returns the
                                     │  list of failed
  return failedInvoices;         ⟵──┘  invoices
}
```

How do we test this? By now, you probably see that all we need to do is to force our sap mock to throw an exception for one of the invoices. We should use Mockito's doThrow() .when() chain of calls. This is similar to the when() API you already know, but now we want it to throw an exception (see listing 6.15). Note that we configure the mock to throw an exception for the frank invoice. Then we assert that the list of failed invoices returned by the new sendLowValuedInvoices contains that invoice and that SAP was called for both the mauricio and the frank invoices. Also, because the SAP interface receives a SapInvoice and not an Invoice, we must instantiate three invoices (Maurício's, Frank's, and Steve's) before asserting that the send method was called.

Listing 6.15 Mocks that throw exceptions

```
@Test
void returnFailedInvoices() {
  Invoice mauricio = new Invoice("Mauricio", 20);
  Invoice frank = new Invoice("Frank", 25);
  Invoice steve = new Invoice("Steve", 48);
```

```
    List<Invoice> invoices = Arrays.asList(mauricio, frank, steve);
    when(filter.lowValueInvoices()).thenReturn(invoices);

    String date = LocalDate.now()
      .format(DateTimeFormatter.ofPattern("MMddyyyy"));
    SapInvoice franksInvoice = new SapInvoice("Frank", 25, date + "Fr");
    doThrow(new SAPException())
      .when(sap).send(franksInvoice);

    List<Invoice> failedInvoices = sender.sendLowValuedInvoices();
    assertThat(failedInvoices).containsExactly(frank);

    SapInvoice mauriciosInvoice =
      new SapInvoice("Mauricio", 20, date + "Ma");
    verify(sap).send(mauriciosInvoice);

    SapInvoice stevesInvoice =
      new SapInvoice("Steve", 48, date + "St");
    verify(sap).send(stevesInvoice);
}
```

Configures the mock to throw an exception when it receives Frank's invoice. Note the call to doThrow().when(): this is the first time we use it.

Gets the returned list of failed invoices and ensures that it only has Frank's invoice

Asserts that we tried to send both Maurício's and Steve's invoices

NOTE Creating SapInvoices is becoming a pain, given that we always need to get the current date, put it in the MMddyyyy format, and concatenate it with the first two letters of the customer's name. You may want to extract all this logic to a helper method or a helper class. Helper methods are widespread in test code. Remember, test code is as important as production code. All the best practices you follow when implementing your production code should be applied to your test code, too. We will discuss test code quality in chapter 10.

Configuring mocks to throw exceptions enables us to test how our systems would behave in unexpected scenarios. This is perfect for many software systems that interact with external systems, which may not behave as expected. Think of a web service that is not available for a second: would your application behave correctly if this happened? How would you test the program behavior without using mocks or stubs? How would you force the web service API to throw you an exception? Doing so would be harder than telling the mock to throw an exception.

The requirement says one more thing: "A failure should not make the program stop; rather, the program should try to send all the invoices, even though some of them may fail." We also tested that in our test method. We ensured that steve's invoice—the one after frank's invoice, which throws the exception—is sent to SAP.

6.3   *Mocks in the real world*

Now that you know how to write mocks and stubs and how you can write powerful tests with them, it is time to discuss best practices. As you can imagine, some developers are big fans of mocking. Others believe mocks should not be used. It is a fact that mocks make your tests less real.

When should we mock? When is it best not to mock? What other best practices should I follow? I tackle those questions next.

6.3.1 *The disadvantages of mocking*

I have been talking a lot about the advantages of mocks. However, as I hinted before, a common (and heated) discussion among practitioners is whether to use mocks. Let's look at possible disadvantages.

Some developers strongly believe that using mocks may lead to test suites that *test the mock, not the code*. That can happen. When you use mocks, you are naturally making your test less realistic. In production, your code will use the concrete implementation of the class you mocked during the test. Something may go wrong in the way the classes communicate in production, for example, and you may miss it because you mocked them.

Consider a class A that depends on class B. Suppose class B offers a method sum() that always returns positive numbers (that is, the post-condition of sum()). When testing class A, the developer decides to mock B. Everything seems to work. Months later, a developer changes the post-conditions of B's sum(): now it also returns negative numbers. In a common development workflow, a developer would apply these changes in B and update B's tests to reflect the change. It is easy to forget to check whether A handles this new post-condition well. Even worse, A's test suite will still pass! A mocks B, and the mock does not know that B changed. In large-scale software, it can be easy to lose control of your mocks in the sense that mocks may not represent the real contract of the class.

For mock objects to work well on a large scale, developers must design careful (and hopefully stable) contracts. If contracts are well designed and stable, you do not need to be afraid of mocks. And although we use the example of a contract break as a disadvantage of mocks, it is part of the coder's job to find the dependencies of the contract change and check that the new contract is covered, mocks or not.

Another disadvantage is that tests that use mocks are naturally more coupled with the code they test than tests that do not use mocks. Think of all the tests we have written without mocks. They call a method, and they assert the output. They do not know anything about the actual implementation of the method. Now, think of all the tests we wrote in this chapter. The test methods know some things about the production code. The tests we wrote for SAPInvoiceSender know that the class uses Invoice-Filter's lowValueInvoices method and that SAP's send method must be called for all the invoices. This is a lot of information about the class under test.

What is the problem with the test knowing so much? It may be harder to change. If the developer changes how the SAPInvoiceSender class does its job and, say, stops using the InvoiceFilter class or uses the same filter differently, the developer may also have to change the tests. The mocks and their expectations may be completely different.

Therefore, although mocks simplify our tests, they increase the coupling between the test and the production code, which may force us to change the test whenever we change the production code. Spadini and colleagues, including me, observed this through empirical studies in open source systems (2019). *Can you avoid such coupling?* Not really, but at least now you are aware of it.

Interestingly, developers consider this coupling a major drawback of mocks. But I appreciate that my tests break when I change how a class interacts with other classes. The broken tests make me reflect on the changes I am making. Of course, my tests do not break as a result of every minor change I make in my production code. I also do not use mocks in every situation. I believe that when mocks are properly used, the coupling with the production code is not a big deal.

> ## Mocking as a design technique
> Whenever I say that mocks increase coupling with production code, I am talking about using mocks from a *testing* perspective: not using mocks as a way to design the code, but in the sense of "This is the code we have: let's test it." In this case, mocks are naturally coupled with the code under test, and changes in the code will impact the mocks.
>
> If you are using mocks as a design technique (as explained in Freeman and Pryce's 2009 book), you should look at it from a different angle. You want your mocks to be coupled with the code under test because you *care* about how the code does its job. If the code changes, you want your mocks to change.

6.3.2   *What to mock and what not to mock*

Mocks and stubs are useful tools for simplifying the process of writing unit tests. However, *mocking too much* might also be a problem. A test that uses the real dependencies is more real than a test that uses doubles and, consequently, is more prone to find real bugs. Therefore, we do not want to mock a dependency that should not be mocked. Imagine you are testing class A, which depends on class B. How do we know whether we should mock or stub B or whether it is better to use the real, concrete implementation?

Pragmatically, developers often mock or stub the following types of dependencies:

- *Dependencies that are too slow*—If the dependency is too slow for any reason, it might be a good idea to simulate it. We do not want slow test suites. Therefore, I mock classes that deal with databases or web services. Note that I still do integration tests to ensure that these classes work properly, but I use mocks for all the other classes that depend on these slow classes.
- *Dependencies that communicate with external infrastructure*—If the dependency talks to (external) infrastructure, it may be too slow or too complex to set up the required infrastructure. So, I apply the same principle: whenever testing a class that depends on a class that handles external infrastructure, I mock the dependency (as we mocked the `IssuedInvoices` class when testing the `Invoice-Filter` class). I then write integration tests for these classes.

- *Cases that are hard to simulate*—If we want to force the dependency to behave in a hard-to-simulate way, mocks or stubs can help. A common example is when we would like the dependency to throw an exception. Forcing an exception might be tricky when using the real dependency but is easy to do with a stub.

On the other hand, developers tend not to mock or stub the following dependencies:

- *Entities*—Entities are classes that represent business concepts. They consist primarily of data and methods that manipulate this data. Think of the Invoice class in this chapter or the ShoppingCart class from previous chapters. In business systems, entities commonly depend on other entities. This means, whenever testing an entity, we need to instantiate other entities.

  For example, to test a ShoppingCart, we may need to instantiate Products and Items. One possibility would be to mock the Product class when the focus is to test the ShoppingCart. However, this is not something I recommend. Entities are classes that are simple to manipulate. Mocking them may require more work. Therefore, I prefer to never mock them. If my test needs three entities, I instantiate them.

  I make exceptions for heavy entities. Some entities require dozens of other entities. Think of a complex Invoice class that depends on 10 other entities: Customer, Product, and so on. Mocking this complex Invoice class may be easier.

- *Native libraries and utility methods*—It is also not common to mock or stub libraries that come with our programming language and utility methods. For example, why would we mock ArrayList or a call to String.format? Unless you have a very good reason, avoid mocking them.

- *Things that are simple enough*—Simple classes may not be worth mocking. If you feel a class is too simple to be mocked, it probably is.

Interestingly, I always followed those rules, because they made sense to me. In 2018–2019, Spadini, myself, and colleagues performed a study to see how developers mock in the wild. Our findings were surprisingly similar to this list.

Let me illustrate with a code example. Consider a BookStore class with the following requirement:

Given a list of books and their respective quantities, the program should return the total price of the cart.

If the bookstore does not have all the requested copies of the book, it includes all the copies it has in stock in the final cart and lets the user know about the missing ones.

The implementation (listing 6.16) uses a BookRepository class to check whether the book is available in the store. If not enough copies are available, it keeps track of the unavailable ones in the Overview class. For the available books, the store notifies BuyBookProcess. In the end, it returns the Overview class containing the total amount to be paid and the list of unavailable copies.

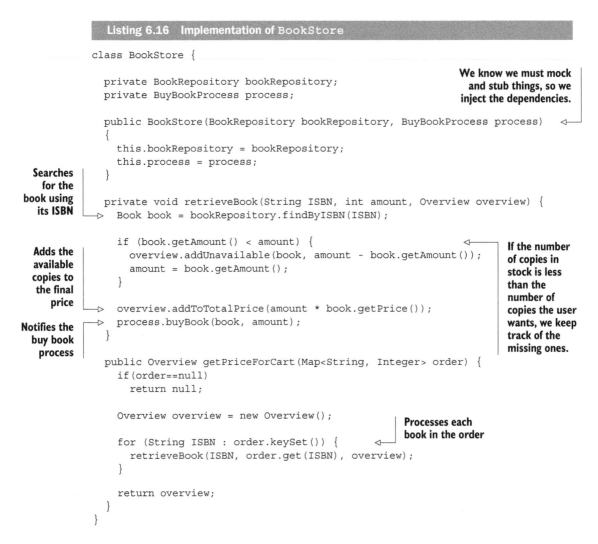

Listing 6.16 Implementation of `BookStore`

```
class BookStore {

  private BookRepository bookRepository;                          We know we must mock
  private BuyBookProcess process;                                  and stub things, so we
                                                                   inject the dependencies.
  public BookStore(BookRepository bookRepository, BuyBookProcess process)
  {
    this.bookRepository = bookRepository;
    this.process = process;
  }

  private void retrieveBook(String ISBN, int amount, Overview overview) {
    Book book = bookRepository.findByISBN(ISBN);

    if (book.getAmount() < amount) {                               If the number
      overview.addUnavailable(book, amount - book.getAmount());    of copies in
      amount = book.getAmount();                                   stock is less
    }                                                              than the
                                                                   number of
    overview.addToTotalPrice(amount * book.getPrice());           copies the user
    process.buyBook(book, amount);                                 wants, we keep
  }                                                                track of the
                                                                   missing ones.
  public Overview getPriceForCart(Map<String, Integer> order) {
    if(order==null)
      return null;

    Overview overview = new Overview();                   Processes each
                                                          book in the order
    for (String ISBN : order.keySet()) {
      retrieveBook(ISBN, order.get(ISBN), overview);
    }

    return overview;
  }
}
```

Searches for the book using its ISBN

Adds the available copies to the final price

Notifies the buy book process

Let's discuss the main dependencies of the `BookStore` class:

- The `BookRepository` class is responsible for, among other things, searching for books in the database. This means the concrete implementation of this class sends SQL queries to a database, parses the result, and transforms it into `Book` classes. Using the concrete `BookRepository` implementation in the test might be too painful: we would need to set up the database, ensure that it had the books we wanted persisted, clean the database afterward, and so on. This is a good dependency to mock.

- The `BuyBookProcess` class is responsible for the process of someone buying a book. We do not know exactly what it does, but it sounds complex. `BuyBookProcess` deserves its own test suite, and we do not want to mix that with the `BookStore` tests. This is another good dependency to mock.

- The Book class represents a book. The implementation of BookStore gets the books that are returned by BookRepository and uses that information to know the book's price and how many copies the bookstore has in stock. This is a simple class, and there is no need to mock it since it is easy to instantiate a concrete Book.

- The Overview class is also a simple, plain old Java object that stores the total price of the cart and the list of unavailable books. Again, there is no need to mock it.

- The Map<String, Integer> that the getPriceForCart receives as an input is a Map object. Map and its concrete implementation HashMap are part of the Java language. They are simple data structures that also do not need to be mocked.

Now that we have decided what should be mocked and what should not be mocked, we write the tests. The following test exercises the behavior of the program with a more complex order.

Listing 6.17   Test for `BookStore`, only mocking what needs to be mocked

```
@Test
void moreComplexOrder() {
    BookRepository bookRepo = mock(BookRepository.class);
    BuyBookProcess process = mock(BuyBookProcess.class);

    Map<String, Integer> orderMap = new HashMap<>();

    orderMap.put("PRODUCT-ENOUGH-QTY", 5);
    orderMap.put("PRODUCT-PRECISE-QTY", 10);
    orderMap.put("PRODUCT-NOT-ENOUGH", 22);

    Book book1 = new Book("PRODUCT-ENOUGH-QTY", 20, 11); // 11 > 5
    when(bookRepo.findByISBN("PRODUCT-ENOUGH-QTY"))
        .thenReturn(book1);

    Book book2 = new Book("PRODUCT-PRECISE-QTY", 25, 10); // 10 == 10
    when(bookRepo.findByISBN("PRODUCT-PRECISE-QTY"))
        .thenReturn(book2);

    Book book3 = new Book("PRODUCT-NOT-ENOUGH", 37, 21); // 21 < 22
    when(bookRepo.findByISBN("PRODUCT-NOT-ENOUGH"))
        .thenReturn(book3);

    BookStore bookStore = new BookStore(bookRepo, process);
    Overview overview = bookStore.getPriceForCart(orderMap);

    int expectedPrice =
        5*20 + // from the first product
            10*25 + // from the second product
            21*37; // from the third product

    assertThat(overview.getTotalPrice()).isEqualTo(expectedPrice);
```

No need to mock HashMap

As agreed, BookRepository and BuyBookProcess should be mocked.

The order has three books: one where there is enough quantity, one where the available quantity is precisely what is requested in the order, and one where there is not enough quantity.

Stubs the BookRepository to return the three books

Injects the mocks and stubs into BookStore

Ensures that the total price is correct

```
verify(process).buyBook(book1, 5);
verify(process).buyBook(book2, 10);
verify(process).buyBook(book3, 21);

assertThat(overview.getUnavailable())
    .containsExactly(entry(book3, 1));
}
```

Ensures that BuyBookProcess was called for three books with the right amounts

Ensures that the list of unavailable books contains the one missing book

Could we mock everything? Yes, we could—but doing so would not make sense. You should only stub and mock what is needed. But whenever you mock, you reduce the reality of the test. It is up to you to understand this trade-off.

6.3.3 *Date and time wrappers*

Software systems often use date and time information. For example, you might need the current date to add a special discount to the customer's shopping cart, or you might need the current time to start a batch processing job. To fully exercise some pieces of code, our tests need to provide different dates and times as input.

Given that date and time operations are common, a best practice is to wrap them into a dedicated class (often called Clock). Let's show that using an example:

> The program should give a 15% discount on the total amount of an order if the current date is Christmas. There is no discount on other dates.

A possible implementation for this requirement is shown next.

Listing 6.18 `ChristmasDiscount` implementation

```
public class ChristmasDiscount {

  public double applyDiscount(double amount) {
    LocalDate today = LocalDate.now();

    double discountPercentage = 0;
    boolean isChristmas = today.getMonth() == Month.DECEMBER
      && today.getDayOfMonth() == 25;

    if(isChristmas)
      discountPercentage = 0.15;

    return amount - (amount * discountPercentage);
  }
}
```

Gets the current date. Note the static call.

If it is Christmas, we apply the discount.

The implementation is straightforward; given the characteristics of the class, unit testing seems to be a perfect fit. The question is, how can we write unit tests for it? To test both cases (Christmas/not Christmas), we need to be able to control/stub the LocalDate class, so it returns the dates we want. Right now, this is not easy to do, given that the method makes explicit, direct calls to `LocalDate.now()`. The problem is analogous when `InvoiceFilter` instantiated the `IssuedInvoices` class directly: we could not stub it.

We can then ask a more specific question: how can we stub Java's Time API? In particular, how can we do so for the static method call to `LocalDate.now()`? Mockito allows developers to mock static methods (http://mng.bz/g48n), so we could use this Mockito feature.

Another solution (which is still popular in code bases) is to encapsulate all the date and time logic into a class. In other words, we create a class called `Clock`, and this class handles these operations. The rest of our system only uses this class when it needs dates and times. This new `Clock` class is passed as a dependency to all classes that need it and can therefore be stubbed. The new version of `ChristmasDiscount` is in the following listing.

Listing 6.19 The `Clock` abstraction

```
public class Clock {
  public LocalDate now() {        ◁──┐  Encapsulates the static call. This
    return LocalDate.now();            seems too simple, but think of other,
  }                                    more complex operations you will
                                       encapsulate in this class.

  // any other date and time operation here...
}

public class ChristmasDiscount {

  private final Clock clock;      ◁──┐  Clock is a plain old dependency
                                       that we store in a field and
  public ChristmasDiscount(Clock clock) {  ◁──┘  receive via the constructor.
    this.clock = clock;
  }

  public double applyDiscount(double rawAmount) {
    LocalDate today = clock.now();   ◁──┐  Calls the clock whenever we need,
                                           for example, the current date
    double discountPercentage = 0;
    boolean isChristmas = today.getMonth() == Month.DECEMBER
        && today.getDayOfMonth() == 25;

    if(isChristmas)
      discountPercentage = 0.15;

    return rawAmount - (rawAmount * discountPercentage);
  }
}
```

Testing it should be easy, given that we can stub the `Clock` class (see listing 6.20). We have two tests: one for when it is Christmas (where we set the clock to December 25 of any year) and another for when it is not Christmas (where we set the clock to any other date).

Listing 6.20   Testing the new `ChristmasDiscount`

```
public class ChristmasDiscountTest {
  private final Clock clock = mock(Clock.class);          ◁─┐  Clock is a stub.
  private final ChristmasDiscount cd = new ChristmasDiscount(clock);

  @Test
  public void christmas() {
    LocalDate christmas = LocalDate.of(2015, Month.DECEMBER, 25);
    when(clock.now()).thenReturn(christmas);              ◁─┐  Stubs the now()
                                                              method to return
    double finalValue = cd.applyDiscount(100.0);              the Christmas date
    assertThat(finalValue).isCloseTo(85.0, offset(0.001));
  }

  @Test
  public void notChristmas() {
    LocalDate notChristmas = LocalDate.of(2015, Month.DECEMBER, 26);
    when(clock.now()).thenReturn(notChristmas);          ◁─┐  Stubs the now()
                                                              method. It now
    double finalValue = cd.applyDiscount(100.0);              returns a date that
    assertThat(finalValue).isCloseTo(100.0, offset(0.001));   is not Christmas.
  }
}
```

As I said, creating an abstraction on top of date and time operations is common. The idea is that having a class that encapsulates these operations will facilitate the testing of the other classes in the system, because they are no longer handling date and time operations. And because these classes now receive this clock abstraction as a dependency, it can be easily stubbed. Martin Fowler's wiki even has an entry called `Clock-Wrapper`, which explains the same thing.

Is it a problem to use Mockito's ability to mock static methods? As always, there are no right and wrong answers. If your system does not have complex date and time operations, stubbing them using Mockito's `mockStatic()` API should be fine. Pragmatism always makes sense.

6.3.4   *Mocking types you do not own*

Mocking frameworks are powerful. They even allow you to mock classes you do not own. For example, we could stub the `LocalDate` class if we wanted to. We can mock any classes from any library our software system uses. The question is, do we want to?

When mocking, it is a best practice to avoid mocking types you do not own. Imagine that your software system uses a library. This library is costly, so you decide to mock it 100% of the time. In the long run, you may face the following complications:

- If this library ever changes (for example, a method stops doing what it was supposed to do), you will not have a breaking test. The entire behavior of that library was mocked. You will only notice it in production. Remember that you want your tests to break whenever something goes wrong.

- It may be difficult to mock external libraries. Think about the library you use to access a database such as Hibernate. Mocking all the API calls to Hibernate is too complex. Your tests will quickly become difficult to maintain.

What is the solution? When you need to mock a type you do not own, you create an abstraction on top of it that encapsulates all the interactions with that type of library. In a way, the Clock class we discussed is an example. We do not own the Time API, so we created an abstraction that encapsulates it. These abstractions will let you hide all the complexity of that type, offering a much simpler API to the rest of your software system (which is good for the production code). At the same time, we can easily stub these abstractions.

If the behavior of your class changes, you do not have any failing tests anyway, as your classes depend on the abstraction, not on the real thing. This is not a problem if you apply the right test levels. In all the classes of the system that depend on this abstraction, you can mock or stub the dependency. At this point, a change in the type you do not own will not be caught by the test suite. The abstraction depends on the contracts of the type before it changed. However, the abstraction itself needs to be tested using integration tests. These integration tests will break if the type changes.

Suppose you encapsulate all the behavior of a specific XML parser in an Xml-Writer class. The abstraction offers a single method: write(Invoice). All the classes of the system that depend on XmlWriter have write mocked in their unit tests. The XmlWriter class, which calls the XML parser, will not mock the library. Rather, it will make calls to the real library and see how it reacts. It will make sure the XML is written as expected. If the library changes, this one test will break. It will then be up to the developer to understand what to do, given the new behavior of the type. See figure 6.2 for an illustration.

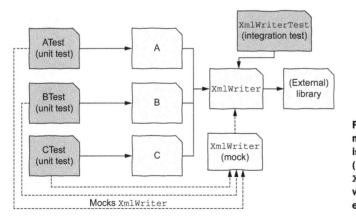

Figure 6.2 XmlWriter is mocked when the developer is testing classes that use it (A, B, and C, in the example). XmlWriter is then tested via integration tests, exercising the library.

In practice, unit tests are fast and easy to write and do not depend on external libraries. Integration tests ensure that the interaction with the library happens as expected, and they capture any changes in the behavior.

Creating abstractions on top of dependencies that you do not own, as a way to gain more control, is a common technique among developers. (The idea of only mocking types you own was suggested by Freeman et al. in the paper that introduced the concept of mock objects [2004] and by Mockito.) Doing so increases the overall complexity of the system and requires maintaining another abstraction. But does the ease in testing the system that we get from adding the abstraction compensate for the cost of the increased complexity? Often, the answer is yes: it does pay off.

6.3.5   *What do others say about mocking?*

As I said, some developers favor mocking, and others do not. *Software Engineering at Google*, edited by Winters, Manshreck, and Wright (2020), has an entire chapter dedicated to test doubles. Here's what I understood from it, along with my own point of view:

- *Using test doubles requires the system to be designed for testability.* Indeed, as we saw, if you use mocks, you need to make sure the class under test can receive the mock.
- *Building test doubles faithful to the real implementation is challenging. Test doubles must be as faithful as possible.* If your mocks do not offer the same contracts and expectations of the production class, your tests may all pass, but the software system will fail in production. Whenever you are mocking, make sure your mocks faithfully represent the class you are mocking.
- *Prefer realism over isolation. When possible, opt for the real implementation instead of fakes, stubs, or mocks.* I fully agree with this. Although I did my best to convince you about the usefulness of mocking (that was the point of this chapter), realism always wins over isolation. I am pragmatic about it, though. If it is getting too hard to test with the real dependency, I mock it.
- The following are trade-offs to consider when deciding whether to use a test double:
  - *The execution time of the real implementation*—I also take the execution time of the dependency into account when deciding to mock or not. I usually mock slow dependencies.
  - *How much non-determinism we would get from using the real implementation*— While I did not discuss non-deterministic behavior, dependencies that present such behavior may be good candidates for mocking.
- *When using the real implementation is not possible or too costly, prefer fakes over mocks.* I do not fully agree with this recommendation. In my opinion, you either use the real implementation or mock it. A fake implementation may end up having the same problems as a mock. How do you ensure that the fake implementation has the same behavior as the real implementation? I rarely use fakes.
- *Excessive mocking can be dangerous, as tests become unclear (hard to comprehend), brittle (may break too often), and less effective (reduced ability to detect faults).* I agree. If you are mocking too much or the class under test forces you to mock too much, that may be a sign that the production class is poorly designed.

- *When mocking, prefer state testing rather than interaction testing.* Google says you should make sure you are asserting a change of state and/or the consequence of the action under test, rather than the precise interaction that the action has with the mocked object. Google's point is similar to what we discussed about mocks and coupling. Interaction testing tends to be too coupled with the implementation of the system under test.

  While I agree with this point, properly written interaction tests are useful. They tell you when the interaction changed. This is my rule of thumb: if what matters in the class I am testing is the interaction between classes, I do interaction testing (my assertions check that the interactions are as expected). When what matters is the result of processing, I do state testing (my assertions check the return value or whether the state of the class is as expected).

- *Avoid over-specified interaction tests. Focus on the relevant arguments and functions.* This is a good suggestion and best practice. Make sure you only mock and stub what needs to be mocked and stubbed. Only verify the interactions that make sense for that test. Do not verify every single interaction that happens.

- *Good interaction testing requires strict guidelines when designing the system under test. Google engineers tend not to do this.* Using mocks properly is challenging even for senior developers. Focus on training and team education, and help your developer peers do better interaction testing.

Exercises

6.1 Mocks, stubs, and fakes. What are they, and how do they differ from each other?

6.2 The following `InvoiceFilter` class is responsible for returning the invoices for an amount smaller than 100.0. It uses the `IssuedInvoices` type, which is responsible for communication with the database.

```
public class InvoiceFilter {

  private IssuedInvoices invoices;

  public InvoiceFilter(IssuedInvoices invoices) {
    this.invoices = invoices;
  }

  public List<Invoice> filter() {
    return invoices.all().stream()
        .filter(invoice -> invoice.getValue() < 100.0)
        .collect(toList());
  }
}
```

Which of the following statements about this class is false?

A Integration testing is the only way to achieve 100% branch coverage.

B Its implementation allows for dependency injection, which enables mocking.

    c It is possible to write completely isolated unit tests by, for example, using mocks.

    D The `IssuedInvoices` type (a direct dependency of `InvoiceFilter`) should be tested using integration tests.

6.3 You are testing a system that triggers advanced events based on complex combinations of external, boolean conditions relating to the weather (outside temperature, amount of rain, wind, and so on). The system has been designed cleanly and consists of a set of cooperating classes, each of which has a single responsibility. You use specification-based testing for this logic and test it using mocks.

    Which of the following is a valid test strategy?

    A You use mocks to support observing the external conditions.

    B You create mock objects to represent each variant you need to test.

    c You use mocks to control the external conditions and to observe the event being triggered.

    D You use mocks to control the triggered events.

6.4 Class A depends on a static method in class B. If you want to test class A, which of the following two actions should you apply to do so properly?

    Approach 1: Mock class B to control the behavior of the methods in class B.

    Approach 2: Refactor class A, so the outcome of the method of class B is now used as a parameter.

    A Only approach 1

    B Neither

    c Only approach 2

    D Both

6.5 According to the guidelines provided in the book, what types of classes should you mock, and which should you not mock?

6.6 Now that you know the advantages and disadvantages of test doubles, what are your thoughts about them? Do you plan to use mocks and stubs, or do you prefer to focus on integration tests?

Summary

- Test doubles help us test classes that depend on slow, complex, or external components that are hard to control and observe.
- There are different types of test doubles. Stubs are doubles that return hard-coded values whenever methods are called. Mocks are like stubs, but we can define how we expect a mock to interact with other classes.
- Mocking can help us in testing, but it also has disadvantages. The mock may differ from the real implementation, and that would cause our tests to pass while the system would fail.

- Tests that use mocks are more coupled with the production code than tests that do not use mocks. When not carefully planned, such coupling can be problematic.
- Production classes should allow for the mock to be injected. One common approach is to require all dependencies via the constructor.
- You do not have to (and should not) mock everything, even when you decide to go for mocks. Only mock what is necessary.

Designing for testability

This chapter covers

- Designing testable code at the architectural, design, and implementation levels
- Understanding the Hexagonal Architecture, dependency injection, observability, and controllability
- Avoiding testability pitfalls

I usually say that every software system can be tested. However, *some systems are more testable than others.* Imagine that for a single test case, we need to set up three different web services, create five different files in different folders, and put the database in a specific state. After all that, we exercise the feature under test and, to assert the correct behavior, again need to see if the three web services were invoked, the five files were consumed correctly, and the database is now in a different state. All those steps are doable. But couldn't this process be simpler?

Software systems are sometimes not ready for or designed to be tested. In this chapter, we discuss some of the main ideas behind systems that have high testability. *Testability* is how easy it is to write automated tests for the system, class, or method under test. In chapter 6, we saw that by allowing dependencies to be injected, we could stub the dependency. This chapter is about other strategies you can use to make testing easier.

The topic of design for testability deserves an entire book. In this chapter, I cover several design principles that solve most of the problems I face. When presenting these principles, I will discuss the underlying ideas so you can apply them even if the code changes you must make differ from my examples.

Design for testability is fundamental if our goal is to achieve systematic testing—if your code is hard to test, you probably won't test it. When do I design for testability? What is the right moment to think about testability? *All the time.* Much of it happens while I am implementing a feature.

You should design for testability from the very beginning, which is why I put it in the "testing to guide development" part of the flow back in chapter 1, figure 1.4. Sometimes I cannot see the untestable part during the implementation phase, and it haunts me during the test phase. When that happens, I go back to my code and refactor it.

Some developers argue that designing for testability is harder and costs too many extra lines of code. This may be true. Writing spaghetti code is easier than developing cohesive classes that collaborate and are easily tested. One of the goals of this chapter is to convince you that the extra effort of designing for testability *will* pay off. Good, testable code costs more than bad code, but it is the only way to ensure quality.

7.1 Separating infrastructure code from domain code

I could spend pages discussing architectural patterns that enable testability. Instead, I will focus on what I consider the most important advice: *separate infrastructure code from domain code.*

The *domain* is where the core of the system lies: that is, where all the business rules, logic, entities, services, and similar elements reside. Entities like `Invoice` and services such as `ChristmasDiscount` are examples of domain classes. *Infrastructure* relates to all code that handles an external dependency: for example, pieces of code that handle database queries (in this case, the database is an external dependency) or web service calls or file reads and writes. In our previous examples, all of our data access objects (DAOs) are part of the *infrastructure* code.

In practice, when domain code and infrastructure code are mixed, the system becomes harder to test. You should separate them as much as possible so the infrastructure does not get in the way of testing. Let's start with `InvoiceFilter` example, now containing the SQL logic instead of depending on a DAO.

Listing 7.1 `InvoiceFilter` that mixes domain and infrastructure

```
public class InvoiceFilter {

  private List<Invoice> all() {
    try {
      Connection connection =
```

This method gets all the invoices directly from the database. Note that it resides in the InvoiceFilter class, unlike in previous examples.

```
      DriverManager.getConnection("db", "root", "");
  PreparedStatement ps =
    connection.prepareStatement("select * from invoice"));
  Result rs = ps.executeQuery();

  List<Invoice> allInvoices = new ArrayList<>();
  while (rs.next()) {
    allInvoices.add(new Invoice(
      rs.getString("name"), rs.getInt("value")));
  }

  ps.close();
  connection.close();

  return allInvoices;

  } catch(Exception e) {
  // handle the exception
  }
 }
}

public List<Invoice> lowValueInvoices() {
  List<Invoice> issuedInvoices = all();

  return issuedInvoices.all().stream()
    .filter(invoice -> invoice.value < 100)
    .collect(toList());
 }
}
```

JDBC code to execute a simple SELECT query. If you are not a Java developer, there is no need to know what PreparedStatement and Result are.

Database APIs often throw exceptions that we need to handle.

The same lowValueInvoices method we've seen before, but now it calls a method in the same class to get the invoices from the database.

We can make the following observations about this class:

- *Domain code and infrastructure code are mixed.* This means we will not be able to avoid database access when testing the low-value invoices rule. How would you stub the private method while exercising the public method? Because we cannot easily stub the database part, we must consider it when writing the tests. As we have seen many times already, this is more complex.
- *The more responsibilities, the more complexity, and the more chances for bugs.* Classes that are less cohesive contain more code. More code means more opportunities for bugs. This example class may have bugs related to SQL and the business logic, for example. Empirical research shows that longer methods and classes are more prone to defects (see the 2006 paper by Shatnawi and Li).

Infrastructure is not the only external influence our code may suffer from. User interfaces are often mixed with domain code, which is usually a bad idea for testability. You should not need the user interface to exercise your system's business rules.

Besides the hassle of handling infrastructure when writing tests, extra cognitive effort is often required to engineer the test cases. Speaking from experience, it is much easier to test a class that has a single responsibility and no infrastructure than it is to test a non-cohesive class that handles business rules and, for example, database access. Simpler code also has fewer possibilities and corner cases to see and explore. On the other hand, the more complex the code is, or the more responsibilities it has, the more we must think about test cases and possible interactions between features that are implemented in one place. In the example, the interaction between the infrastructure code and the business rule is simple: the method returns invoices from the database. But classes that do more complex things and handle more complex infrastructure can quickly become a nightmare during testing and maintenance.

The architecture of the software system under development needs to enforce a *clear separation of responsibilities*. The simplest way to describe it is by explaining the *Ports and Adapters* (or *Hexagonal Architecture*) pattern. As Alistair Cockburn proposed (2005), the domain (business logic) depends on *ports* rather than directly on the infrastructure. These ports are interfaces that define what the infrastructure can do and enable the application to get information from or send information to something else. They are completely separated from the implementation of the infrastructure. On the other hand, the *adapters* are very close to the infrastructure. They are the implementations of the ports that talk to the database, web service, and so on. They know how the infrastructure works and how to communicate with it.

Figure 7.1 illustrates a hexagonal architecture. The inside of the hexagon represents the application and all its business logic. The code is related to the application's business logic and functional requirements. It knows nothing about external systems or required infrastructure. However, the application will require information or interaction with the external world at some point. For that, the application does not interact directly with the external system: instead, it communicates with a port. The port should be agnostic of the technology and, from the application's perspective, abstract away details of how communication happens. Finally, the adapter is coupled to the external infrastructure. The

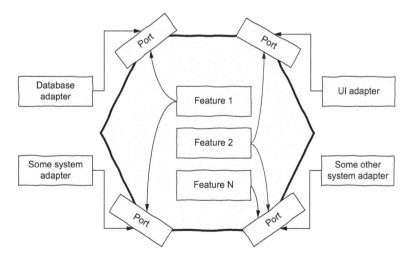

Figure 7.1   An illustration of the Hexagonal Architecture (or Ports and Adapters) pattern

adapter knows how to send or retrieve messages from the external infrastructure and sends them back to the application in the format defined by the port.

Let's cook up a simple example that illustrates these concepts in practice. Suppose an online web shop has the following requirements:

For all the shopping carts that were paid today, the system should

- Set the status of the shopping cart as ready for delivery, and persist its new state in the database.
- Notify the delivery center, and let them know they should send the goods to the customer.
- Notify the SAP system.
- Send an e-mail to the customer confirming that the payment was successful. The e-mail should contain an estimate of when delivery will happen. The information is available via the delivery center API.

The first step is identifying what belongs to the application (the hexagon) and what does not. It is clear that any business rule related to ShoppingCart, such as changing its state, as well as the entire workflow the shopping cart goes through once it's paid, belongs inside the hexagon. However, a service that provides e-mail capabilities, a service that communicates with the SAP, a service that communicates with the delivery center API (which is probably offered as a web service), and a service that can communicate with the database are all handled by external systems. For those, we need to devise a clear interface for the application to communicate with (the ports) together with a concrete implementation that can handle communication with the external system (the adapters). Figure 7.2 illustrates the concrete application of the Ports and Adapters pattern to this example.

A natural implementation for the PaidShoppingCartsBatch class would be the code in listing 7.2. It does not contain a single detail regarding infrastructure. This entire class could easily be unit-tested if we stubbed its dependencies. Does it need a list of paid shopping carts, normally returned by cartsPaidToday()? We stub it. Does it notify the SAP via the cartReadyForDelivery() method? We mock SAP and later assert the interaction with this method.

When we put everything together in production, the method will communicate with databases and web services. But at unit testing time, we do not care about that. The same testing philosophy we discussed in chapter 6 applies here: when (unit) testing the PaidShoppingCartsBatch class, we should focus on PaidShoppingCartsBatch and not its dependencies. This is possible here because (1) we receive its dependencies via the constructor (which enables us to pass mocks and stubs to the class), and (2) this class is only about business and has no lines of infrastructure code.

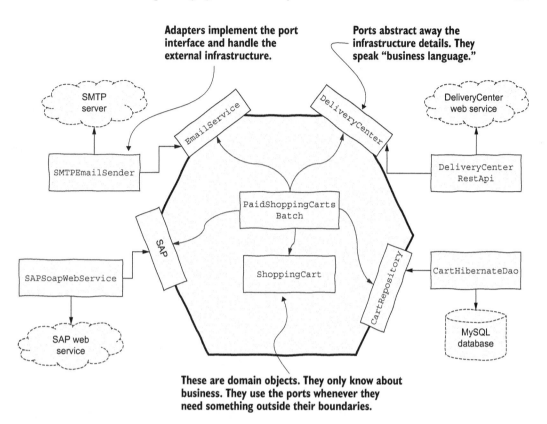

Adapters implement the port interface and handle the external infrastructure.

Ports abstract away the infrastructure details. They speak "business language."

These are domain objects. They only know about business. They use the ports whenever they need something outside their boundaries.

Figure 7.2 A concrete implementation of the Hexagonal Architecture (or Ports and Adapters) pattern for the shopping carts example

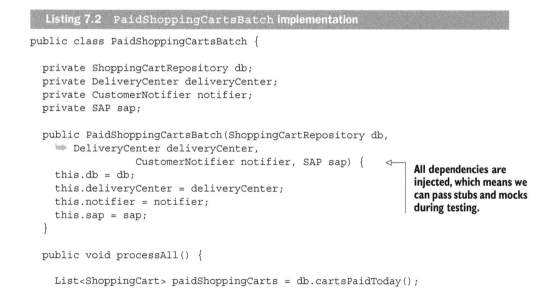

Listing 7.2 `PaidShoppingCartsBatch` **implementation**

```java
public class PaidShoppingCartsBatch {

  private ShoppingCartRepository db;
  private DeliveryCenter deliveryCenter;
  private CustomerNotifier notifier;
  private SAP sap;

  public PaidShoppingCartsBatch(ShoppingCartRepository db,
    ➥ DeliveryCenter deliveryCenter,
              CustomerNotifier notifier, SAP sap) {      ⟵
    this.db = db;
    this.deliveryCenter = deliveryCenter;
    this.notifier = notifier;
    this.sap = sap;
  }

  public void processAll() {

    List<ShoppingCart> paidShoppingCarts = db.cartsPaidToday();
```

All dependencies are injected, which means we can pass stubs and mocks during testing.

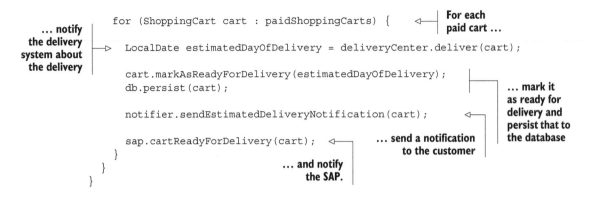

... notify the delivery system about the delivery

```
for (ShoppingCart cart : paidShoppingCarts) {        ⊲── For each
                                                          paid cart ...
    LocalDate estimatedDayOfDelivery = deliveryCenter.deliver(cart);

    cart.markAsReadyForDelivery(estimatedDayOfDelivery);
    db.persist(cart);

    notifier.sendEstimatedDeliveryNotification(cart);    ⊲──

    sap.cartReadyForDelivery(cart);   ⊲──
    }
  }
}
```

... mark it as ready for delivery and persist that to the database

... send a notification to the customer

... and notify the SAP.

Look at the class's four dependencies: ShoppingCartRepository, DeliveryCenter, CustomerNotifier, and SAP. These are interfaces and, in the Hexagonal Architecture, ports. They establish a protocol for communication between the application and the external world. These interfaces are completely agnostic of technology and infrastructure details. In other words, they abstract all the complexity of the infrastructure away from the domain code. As a result, the interfaces do not depend on anything strange, such as database or web service classes. They *do* depend on other domain classes, such as ShoppingCart, and that is fine. The following listing contains the interface declarations of all the ports.

Listing 7.3   Interface declarations of all the ports

```
public interface DeliveryCenter {          ⊲──
    LocalDate deliver(ShoppingCart cart);
}

public interface CustomerNotifier {
    void sendEstimatedDeliveryNotification(ShoppingCart cart);
}

public interface SAP {
    void cartReadyForDelivery(ShoppingCart cart);
}

public interface ShoppingCartRepository {   ⊲──
    List<ShoppingCart> cartsPaidToday();
    void persist(ShoppingCart cart);
}
```

The DeliveryCenter interface's concrete implementation will probably consume a very complex web service, but the port abstracts this away. Ports speak business language and do not let infrastructure details leak.

This one does not even have "database" in the name. "Repository" is a more business-like term.

The same thing happens for CustomerNotifier and all other interfaces/ports.

We are now only missing the implementation of the adapters. This code is out of the scope of this book, but in terms of implementation, these adapters are classes that implement the ports' interfaces. The next listing provides some skeleton code to give you an idea what the adapters will look like.

Listing 7.4 Simplified implementation of the adapters

```
public class DeliveryCenterRestApi implements DeliveryCenter {
  @Override
  public LocalDate deliver(ShoppingCart cart) {
    // all the code required to communicate
    // with the delivery API
    // and returns a LocalDate
  }
}

public class SMTPCustomerNotifier implements CustomerNotifier {
  @Override
  public void sendEstimatedDeliveryNotification(ShoppingCart cart) {
    // all the required code to
    // send an email via SMTP
  }
}

public class SAPSoapWebService implements SAP {
  @Override
  public void cartReadyForDelivery(ShoppingCart cart) {
    // all the code required to send the
    // cart to SAP's SOAP web service
  }
}

public class ShoppingCartHibernateDao
 implements ShoppingCartRepository {
  @Override
  public List<ShoppingCart> cartsPaidToday() {
    // a Hibernate query to get the list of all
    // invoices that were paid today
  }

  @Override
  public void persist(ShoppingCart cart) {
    // a hibernate code to persist the cart
    // in the database
  }
}
```

Why does this pattern improve testability? If our domain classes depend only on ports, we can easily exercise all the behavior of the domain logic by stubbing and mocking the ports. In the PaidShoppingCartsBatch example, we can stub and mock the ShoppingCartRepository, DeliveryCenter, CustomerNotifier, and SAP ports and focus on testing the main behavior of the PaidShoppingCartsBatch class. Again, we do not care if the DeliveryCenter adapter does its job properly. That one will be exercised in its own test suite.

Listing 7.5 shows an example test of PaidShoppingCartsBatch. This is a single test. As a developer, you should apply all the testing techniques and devise several test cases for any behavior and corner cases you see. Even exceptional behaviors can be easily exercised.

Listing 7.5   Test for `PaidShoppingCartsBatchTest`, mocking the ports

```
import static org.mockito.Mockito.*;

@ExtendWith(MockitoExtension.class)
public class PaidShoppingCartsBatchTest {

  @Mock ShoppingCartRepository db;
  @Mock private DeliveryCenter deliveryCenter;
  @Mock private CustomerNotifier notifier;
  @Mock private SAP sap;

  @Test
  void theWholeProcessHappens() {
    PaidShoppingCartsBatch batch = new PaidShoppingCartsBatch(db,
        deliveryCenter, notifier, sap);

    ShoppingCart someCart = spy(new ShoppingCart());
    LocalDate someDate = LocalDate.now();

    when(db.cartsPaidToday()).thenReturn(Arrays.asList(someCart));
    when(deliveryCenter.deliver(someCart)).thenReturn(someDate);

    batch.processAll();

    verify(deliveryCenter).deliver(someCart);
    verify(notifier).sendEstimatedDeliveryNotification(someCart);
    verify(db).persist(someCart);
    verify(sap).cartReadyForDelivery(someCart);
    verify(someCart).markAsReadyForDelivery(someDate);
  }
}
```

The @ExtendWith and @Mock annotations are extensions provided by Mockito. We do not even need to write Mockito.mock(...). The framework instantiates a mock for us in these fields.

Instantiates the class under test and passes the mocks as dependencies

Verifies that interactions with the dependencies happened as expected

The ShoppingCart is a simple entity, so we do not need to mock it. Nevertheless, let's spy on it to assert its interactions later.

Although we only tested the application code, the code from the adapters should also be tested. The real implementation of the `ShoppingCartRepository`—let's call it `ShoppingCartHibernateDao` (because it uses the Hibernate framework)—will contain SQL queries that are complex and prone to bugs, so it deserves a dedicated test suite. The real `SAPSoapWebService` class will have complex code to call the SOAP-like web service and should also be exercised. Those classes require integration testing, following our discussion of the testing pyramid in chapter 1. Later in this book, I show how to write some of those integration tests.

NOTE   Although I could also have mocked the `ShoppingCart` class, I followed the advice I gave in chapter 6: do not mock entities unless they are complex. I preferred to spy on them rather than mock them.

This idea of separating infrastructure from domain code appears not only in Cockburn's Hexagonal Architecture but also in many other interesting works on software design, such as the well-known *Domain-Driven Design* by Evans (2004) and Martin's *Clean Architecture* (2018). This principle is pervasive among those who talk about software design and testability. I agree with all these authors.

A common question for those new to the Hexagonal Architecture (or domain-driven design, or clean architecture) is, "Do I need to create interfaces for every port?" I hope to convince you that there are no rights and wrongs, that everything depends, and that being pragmatic is key. Of course you do not have to create interfaces for everything in your software system. I create interfaces for ports where I see more than one implementation. Even if I do not create an interface to represent an abstract behavior, I make sure the concrete implementation does not leak any of its implementation details. Context and pragmatism are kings.

To sum up, the main "design for testability" principle I follow at the architectural level is to separate infrastructure from business code. Do not be tempted to think, for instance, "This is a simple call to the database. Look how easy it is to implement here!" It is always easier to write untestable code, but doing so will bite you in the future.

7.2 Dependency injection and controllability

At the architectural level, we saw that an important concern is to ensure that application (or domain) code is fully separated from the infrastructure code. At the class level, the most important recommendation I can give you is to ensure that classes are fully *controllable* (that is, you can easily control what the class under test does) and *observable* (you can see what is going on with the class under test and inspect its outcome).

For controllability, the most common implementation strategy I apply is the one we used in chapter 6: if a class depends on another class, make it so the dependency can easily be replaced by a mock, fake, or stub. Look back at the `PaidShoppingCartsBatch` class (listing 7.2). It depends on four other classes. The `PaidShoppingCartsBatch` class receives all its dependencies via constructor, so we can easily inject mocks. The version of `PaidShoppingCartsBatch` in listing 7.6 does not receive its dependencies but instead instantiates them directly. How can we test this class without depending on databases, web services, and so on? It is almost the same implementation but much harder to test. It is that easy to write untestable code.

Listing 7.6 A badly implemented `PaidShoppingCartsBatch`

```
public class VeryBadPaidShoppingCartsBatch {

    public void processAll() {                          Instantiates the database
                                                        adapter. Bad for testability!
        ShoppingCartHibernateDao db = new ShoppingCartHibernateDao();
        List<ShoppingCart> paidShoppingCarts = db.cartsPaidToday();
        for (ShoppingCart cart : paidShoppingCarts) {
```

Notifies the delivery system about the delivery. But first, we need to instantiate its adapter. Bad for testability!

Notifies SAP using the adapter directly. Bad for testability!

Marks as ready for delivery and persist

Sends a notification using the adapter directly. Bad for testability!

```
DeliveryCenterRestApi deliveryCenter =
  new DeliveryCenterRestApi();
LocalDate estimatedDayOfDelivery = deliveryCenter.deliver(cart);

cart.markAsReadyForDelivery(estimatedDayOfDelivery);
db.persist(cart);

SMTPCustomerNotifier notifier = new SMTPCustomerNotifier();
notifier.sendEstimatedDeliveryNotification(cart);

SAPSoapWebService sap = new SAPSoapWebService();
sap.cartReadyForDelivery(cart);
    }
  }
}
```

Traditional code tends to be responsible for instantiating its dependencies. But this hinders our ability to control the internals of the class and use mocks to write unit tests. For our classes to be testable, we must allow their dependencies (especially the ones we plan to stub during testing) to be injected.

In the implementation, this can be as simple as receiving the dependencies via constructor or, in more complex cases, via setters. Making sure dependencies can be injected (the term *dependency injection* is commonly used to refer to this idea; I also describe it in chapter 6) improves our code in many ways:

- It enables us to mock or stub the dependencies during testing, increasing our productivity during the testing phase.
- It makes all the dependencies more explicit. They all need to be injected (via constructor, for example).
- It offers better separation of concerns: classes do not need to worry about how to build their dependencies, as the dependencies are injected into them.
- The class becomes more extensible. This point is not related to testing, but as a client of the class, you can pass any dependency via the constructor.

NOTE   A Java developer may recognize several frameworks and libraries connected to dependency injection, such as the well-known Spring framework and Google Guice. If your classes allow dependencies to be injected, Spring and Guice will automatically help you instantiate those classes and their tree of dependencies. While such frameworks are not needed at testing time (we usually pass the mocked dependencies manually to the classes under test), this approach is particularly useful to instantiate classes and their dependencies at production time. I suggest learning more about such frameworks!

By devising interfaces that represent the abstract interactions that domains and infrastructure classes will have with each other (the ports), we better separate the concerns, reduce the coupling between layers, and devise simpler flows of interactions between layers. In our example, the PaidShoppingCartsBatch domain class does not depend on the adapters directly. Rather, it depends on an interface that defines what the adapters should do abstractly. The SAP port interface knows nothing about how the real SAP works. It provides a cartReadyForDelivery method to the domain classes. This completely decouples the domain code from details of how the external infrastructure works.

The *dependency inversion* principle (note the word *inversion*, not *injection*) helps us formalize these concepts:

- High-level modules (such as our business classes) should not depend on low-level modules. Both should depend on abstractions (such as interfaces).
- Abstractions should not depend on details. Details (concrete implementations) should depend on abstractions.

Figure 7.3 illustrates the principle. The domain objects, which are considered high-level classes, do not depend on low-level details such as a database or web service communication. Instead, they depend on abstractions of those low-level details. In the figure, the abstractions are represented by the interfaces.

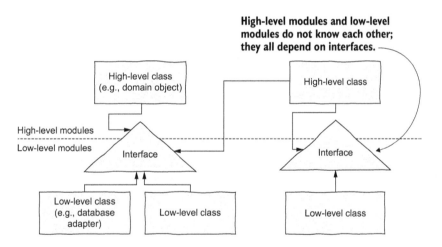

Figure 7.3 An illustration of the dependency inversion principle

Note the pattern: our code should always depend as much as possible on abstractions and as little as possible on details. The advantage of always depending on abstractions and not on low-level details is that abstractions are less fragile and less prone to change than low-level details. You probably do not want to change your code whenever a low-level detail changes.

Again, coming up with interfaces for everything is too much work. I prefer to make sure all of my classes offer a clear interface to their consumers—one that does not leak internal details. For those more familiar with object-oriented programming concepts, I am talking about proper encapsulation.

How does depending on an abstraction help with testing? When you unit-test a class, you probably mock and stub its dependencies. When you mock, you naturally depend on what the mocked class offers as a contract. The more complex the class you are mocking, the harder it is to write the test. When you have ports, adapters, and the dependency inversion principle in mind, the interface of a port is naturally simple. The methods that ports offer are usually cohesive and straight to the point.

In the example, the `ShoppingCartRepository` class has a `List<ShoppingCart>` `cartsPaidToday()` method. It is clear what this method does: it returns a list of shopping carts that were paid today. Mocking this method is trivial. Its concrete adapter implementation is probably complicated, full of database-related code and SQL queries. The interface removes all this complexity from testing the `PaidShoppingCarts-Batch` class. Therefore, designing the ports in a simple way also makes your code easier to test. Complex ports and interfaces require more work.

When things become more complicated, making sure dependencies are always injected may not be as straightforward as I have made it seem. It is much easier not to do this. But you must convince yourself that the extra effort will pay off later during testing.

> **NOTE**   This chapter is a quick introduction to the Hexagonal Architecture and to the Dependency Inversion Priniciple. I suggest you dive into the related literature, including the books by Martin (2014) and Freeman and Pryce (2009), for more details. I also recommend Schuchert's guest post on dependency inversion in the wild in Fowler's wiki (2013); he explains the difference between dependency inversion and dependency injection and gives lots of examples of how he applied the principle in real-world situations.

7.3   *Making your classes and methods observable*

Observability, at the class level, is about how easy it is to assert that the behavior of the functionality went as expected. My main advice is to ensure that your classes provide developers with simple and easy ways to assert their state. Does a class produce a list of objects you need to assert one by one? Create a `getListOfSomething` in that class, which the test can use to get the generated list of objects. Does a class make calls to other classes? Make sure these dependencies can be mocked and your test can assert their interaction. Does a class make internal changes in its attributes, but the class cannot or does not offer getters to each of them? Make the class offer a simple `isValid` method that returns whether the class is in a valid state.

It has to be easy for the test code to inspect the class behavior. Whenever it is difficult to observe whether the program behaves as expected, reflect on how observable the classes are. Do not be afraid to introduce simple getters or simple solutions to facilitate your testing. Behavior that is easy to observe will make the test code much easier! Let's look at two pragmatic changes I make in my code so it is more observable.

7.3.1   *Example 1: Introducing methods to facilitate assertions*

Take another look at the `processAll()` method and its test, in listings 7.2 and 7.5. Most of what its test asserts is the interaction with the ports. Such assertions are easily done, and we did not need much more than basic Mockito. Now, let's look closer at one specific assertion: `verify(someCart).markAsReadyForDelivery(someDate);`. The `someCart` instance of ShoppingCart is not a mock but a spy. To ensure that the cart was marked as ready for delivery, we had to spy on the object. Mockito's API enables us to spy objects with a single line of code. However, whenever we need a spy to assert the behavior, we must ask ourselves why we need a spy. Isn't there an easier way?

In this particular case, we need to check whether ShoppingCart is marked as ready for delivery after processing (listing 7.7). We can increase the observability of the ShoppingCart class (in other words, we can make it simpler to observe the expected behavior of the shopping cart) by making it provide a method that indicates whether it is ready for delivery: isReadyForDelivery.

Listing 7.7 Improving the observability of the ShoppingCart class

```
public class ShoppingCart {
    private boolean readyForDelivery = false;
    // more info about the shopping cart...

    public void markAsReadyForDelivery(Calendar estimatedDayOfDelivery) {
        this.readyForDelivery = true;
        // ...
    }

    public boolean isReadyForDelivery() {          ⊲──┐ The new isReadyForDelivery
        return readyForDelivery;                        │ method is here to improve
    }                                                   │ the observability of the class.
}
```

Because we can now easily ask ShoppingCart whether it is ready for delivery, our test no longer requires a spy. A vanilla assertion should do. Here is the new test.

Listing 7.8 Avoiding the spy when testing PaidShoppingCartsBatch

```
@Test
void theWholeProcessHappens() {
    PaidShoppingCartsBatch batch = new PaidShoppingCartsBatch(db,
        deliveryCenter, notifier, sap);
                                                         ┌─ No need for a spy
    ShoppingCart someCart = new ShoppingCart();    ⊲──┤  anymore, as it is now easy
    assertThat(someCart.isReadyForDelivery()).isFalse();│ to observe the behavior.

    Calendar someDate = Calendar.getInstance();
    when(db.cartsPaidToday()).thenReturn(Arrays.asList(someCart));
    when(deliveryCenter.deliver(someCart)).thenReturn(someDate);

    batch.processAll();

    verify(deliveryCenter).deliver(someCart);
    verify(notifier).sendEstimatedDeliveryNotification(someCart);
    verify(db).persist(someCart);
    verify(sap).cartReadyForDelivery(someCart);        ┌─ Uses a simple vanilla
                                                        │ assertion instead of a
    assertThat(someCart.isReadyForDelivery()).isTrue();⊲─┘ Mockito assertion
}
```

I urge you not to take this particular code change (the addition of a getter) as the solution for all observability issues. Rather, abstract away what we did here: we noticed that asserting that the shopping cart was marked as ready for delivery was not straightforward, as it required a spy. We then re-evaluated our code and looked for a simple way to let the test know that the shopping cart was marked as ready for delivery. In this case, a getter was the easy implementation.

7.3.2   *Example 2: Observing the behavior of void methods*

When a method returns an object, it is natural to think that assertions will check whether the returned object is as expected. However, this does not happen naturally in void methods. If your method does not return anything, what will you assert? It is even more complicated if what you need to assert stays within the method. As an example, the following method creates a set of Installments based on a Shopping-Cart.

Listing 7.9 `InstallmentGenerator`

```
public class InstallmentGenerator {

    private InstallmentRepository repository;        We can inject a stub of
                                                     InstallmentRepository.
    public InstallmentGenerator(InstallmentRepository repository) {
        this.repository = repository;
    }                                      Creates a variable to store the
                                           last installment date
    public void generateInstallments(ShoppingCart cart,
            int numberOfInstallments) {                          Calculates the
        LocalDate nextInstallmentDueDate = LocalDate.now();      amount per
                                                                 installment
        double amountPerInstallment = cart.getValue() / numberOfInstallments;

        for(int i = 1; i <= numberOfInstallments; i++) {      Creates a sequence
            nextInstallmentDueDate =                          of installments, one
              nextInstallmentDueDate.plusMonths(1);           month apart

            Installment newInstallment =
              new Installment(nextInstallmentDueDate, amountPerInstallment);
            repository.persist(newInstallment);        Creates and persists
        }                                              the installment
    }
}
```

Adds 1 to the month (annotation pointing to `nextInstallmentDueDate.plusMonths(1);`)

To test this method, we need to check whether the newly created Installments are set with the right value and date. The question is, how can we get the Installments easily? The Installment classes are instantiated within the method and sent to the repository for persistence, and that is it. If you know Mockito well, you know there is a way to get all the instances passed to a mock: an ArgumentCaptor. The overall idea is that we ask the mock, "Can you give me all the instances passed to you during the test?" We then make assertions about them. In this case, we can ask the repository mock whether all the Installments were passed to the persist method.

The test in listing 7.10 creates a shopping cart with value 100 and asks the generator for 10 installments. Therefore, it should create 10 installments of 10.0 each. That is what we want to assert. After the method under test is executed, we collect all the installments using an ArgumentCaptor. See the calls for capture() and getAllValues(). With the list available, we use traditional AssertJ assertions.

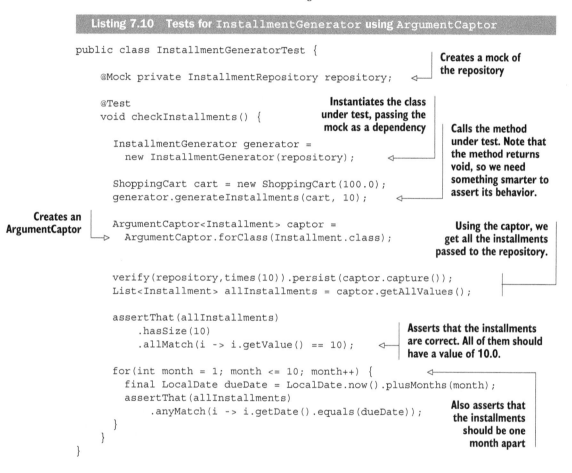

Listing 7.10 Tests for InstallmentGenerator using ArgumentCaptor

```
public class InstallmentGeneratorTest {

    @Mock private InstallmentRepository repository;    ← Creates a mock of
                                                          the repository

    @Test
    void checkInstallments() {              Instantiates the class
                                            under test, passing the
        InstallmentGenerator generator =    mock as a dependency
          new InstallmentGenerator(repository);    ← Calls the method
                                                      under test. Note that
        ShoppingCart cart = new ShoppingCart(100.0);  the method returns
        generator.generateInstallments(cart, 10);   ← void, so we need
                                                      something smarter to
                                                      assert its behavior.

        ArgumentCaptor<Installment> captor =          Using the captor, we
          ArgumentCaptor.forClass(Installment.class);  get all the installments
                                                        passed to the repository.

        verify(repository,times(10)).persist(captor.capture());
        List<Installment> allInstallments = captor.getAllValues();

        assertThat(allInstallments)
            .hasSize(10)                           Asserts that the installments
            .allMatch(i -> i.getValue() == 10);  ← are correct. All of them should
                                                    have a value of 10.0.
        for(int month = 1; month <= 10; month++) {
          final LocalDate dueDate = LocalDate.now().plusMonths(month);
          assertThat(allInstallments)
              .anyMatch(i -> i.getDate().equals(dueDate));   Also asserts that
        }                                                    the installments
      }                                                      should be one
    }                                                        month apart
}
```

(labels in margin) Creates an ArgumentCaptor

The ArgumentCaptor makes writing the test possible. ArgumentCaptors are handy whenever we test methods that return void.

If we apply the idea of simplicity, you may wonder if there is a way to avoid the ArgumentCaptor. It would be much simpler if there were a "get all generated installments" method. If we make the generateInstallments method return the list of all newly generated Installments, the test becomes even simpler. The change required in InstallmentGenerator is small: as all we need to do is keep track of the installments in a list. The following listing shows the new implementation.

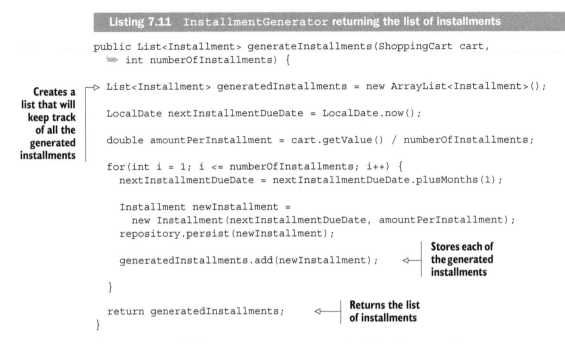

Listing 7.11   `InstallmentGenerator` returning the list of installments

```java
public List<Installment> generateInstallments(ShoppingCart cart,
    int numberOfInstallments) {

    List<Installment> generatedInstallments = new ArrayList<Installment>();

    LocalDate nextInstallmentDueDate = LocalDate.now();

    double amountPerInstallment = cart.getValue() / numberOfInstallments;

    for(int i = 1; i <= numberOfInstallments; i++) {
      nextInstallmentDueDate = nextInstallmentDueDate.plusMonths(1);

      Installment newInstallment =
        new Installment(nextInstallmentDueDate, amountPerInstallment);
      repository.persist(newInstallment);

      generatedInstallments.add(newInstallment);
    }

    return generatedInstallments;
}
```

Creates a list that will keep track of all the generated installments

Stores each of the generated installments

Returns the list of installments

Now we can avoid the `ArgumentCaptor` completely in the test code.

Listing 7.12   `InstallmentGeneratorTest` without the `ArgumentCaptor`

```java
public class InstallmentGeneratorTest {

    @Mock
    private InstallmentRepository repository;

    @Test
    void checkInstallments() {

      ShoppingCart cart = new ShoppingCart(100.0);
      InstallmentGenerator generator =
        new InstallmentGenerator(repository);

      List<Installment> allInstallments =
        generator.generateInstallments(cart, 10);

      assertThat(allInstallments)
          .hasSize(10)
          .allMatch(i -> i.getValue() == 10);

      for(int month = 1; month <= 10; month++) {
        final LocalDate dueDate = LocalDate.now().plusMonths(month);
        assertThat(allInstallments)
            .anyMatch(i -> i.getDate().equals(dueDate));
      }
    }
}
```

The method under test returns the list of installments. No need for ArgumentCaptor.

Same assertions as before

Again, do not take this example literally. Just remember that small design changes that improve your testability are fine. Sometimes it can be hard to tell whether a change will make the code design bad. Try it, and if you don't like it, discard it. Pragmatism is key.

7.4 Dependency via class constructor or value via method parameter?

A very common design decision is whether to pass a dependency to the class via constructor (so the class uses the dependency to get a required value) or pass that value directly to the method. As always, there is no right or wrong way. However, there is a trade-off you must understand to make the best decision.

Let's use the ChristmasDiscount example, as it fits this discussion perfectly. The following listing shows the code again.

Listing 7.13 ChristmasDiscount class, one more time

```
public class ChristmasDiscount {

  private final Clock clock;
                                              We can inject a stubbed
  public ChristmasDiscount(Clock clock) {  ◁  version of Clock here.
    this.clock = clock;
  }

  public double applyDiscount(double rawAmount) {
    LocalDate today = clock.now();         ◁   Calls the now() method
                                               to get the current date
    double discountPercentage = 0;
    boolean isChristmas = today.getMonth()== Month.DECEMBER
              && today.getDayOfMonth()==25;

    if(isChristmas)
      discountPercentage = 0.15;

    return rawAmount - (rawAmount * discountPercentage);
  }
}
```

The ChristmasDiscount class needs the current date so it knows whether it is Christmas and whether to apply the Christmas discount. To get the date, the class uses another dependency, which knows how to get the current date: the Clock class. Testing ChristmasDiscount is easy because we can stub Clock and simulate any date we want.

But having to stub one class is more complex than not having to stub one class. Another way to model this class and its expected behavior is to avoid the dependency on Clock and receive the data as a parameter of the method. This other implementation is shown in listing 7.14. Now the applyDiscount() method receives two parameters: rawAmount and today, which is today's date.

Listing 7.14   `ChristmasDiscount` without depending on `Clock`

```java
public class ChristmasDiscount {

  public double applyDiscount(double rawAmount, LocalDate today) {
    double discountPercentage = 0;
    boolean isChristmas = today.getMonth()== Month.DECEMBER
              && today.getDayOfMonth()==25;

    if(isChristmas)
      discountPercentage = 0.15;

    return rawAmount - (rawAmount * discountPercentage);
  }
}
```

The method receives one more parameter: a LocalDate.

This method is also easily testable. We do not even need mocks to test it, as we can pass any LocalDate object to this method. So, if it is easier to pass the value via method parameter rather than a dependency via its constructor, why do we do it?

First, let's explore the pros and cons of passing the value we want directly via a method parameter, avoiding all the dependencies. This is often the simplest solution in terms of both implementation (no need for dependencies via constructor) and testing (passing different values via method calls). But the downside is that all the callers of this class will need to provide this parameter. In this example, ChristmasDiscount expects today to be passed as a parameter. This means the clients of the applyDiscount() method must pass the current date. How do we get the current date in this code base? Using the Clock class. So, while ChristmasDiscount no longer depends on Clock, its callers will depend on it. In a way, we pushed the Clock dependency up one level. The question is, is this dependency better in the class we are modeling now or in its callers?

Now, let's explore the idea of passing a dependency that knows how to get the required parameter. We did this in the first implementation of the ChristmasDiscount class, which depends on Clock; the applyDiscount() method invokes clock.now() whenever it needs the current date. While this solution is more complicated than the previous one, it enables us to easily stub the dependency as we did in chapter 6.

It is also simple to write tests for the classes that depend on ChristmasDiscount. These classes will mock ChristmasDiscount's applyDiscount(double rawAmount) method without requiring the Clock. The next listing shows a generic consumer that receives the ChristmasDiscount class via the constructor, so you can stub it during testing.

Listing 7.15   Generic consumer of the `ChristmasDiscount` class

```java
public class SomeBusinessService {

  private final ChristmasDiscount discount;

  public SomeBusinessService(ChristmasDiscount discount) {
    this.discount = discount;
  }
```

We inject a ChristmasDiscount stub here.

```
public void doSomething() {
  // ... some business logic here ...

  discount.applyDiscount(100.0);

  // continue the logic here...
 }
}
```

Listing 7.16 shows the tests for this `SomeBusinessService` class. We stub the `Christmas-Discount` class. Note that this test does not need to handle `Clock`. Although `Clock` is a dependency of the concrete implementation of `ChristmasDiscount`, we do not care about that when stubbing. So, in a way, the `ChristmasDiscount` class gets more complicated, but we simplify testing its consumers.

Listing 7.16   Example of the test for the generic consumer class

```
@Test
void test() {
  ChristmasDiscount discount = Mockito.mock(ChristmasDiscount.class);   ⟵─┐
  SomeBusinessService service = new SomeBusinessService(discount);        │
                                                                          │
  service.doSomething();                         Mocks ChristmasDiscount. Note
                                                  that we do not need to mock
  // ... test continues ...                         or do anything with Clock.
}
```

Receiving a dependency via constructor adds a little complexity to the overall class and its tests but simplifies its client classes. Receiving the data via method parameter simplifies the class and its tests but adds a little complexity to the clients. Software engineering is all about trade-offs.

As a rule of thumb, I try to simplify the work of the callers of my class. If I must choose between simplifying the class I am testing now (such as making `Christmas-Discount` receive the date via parameter) but complicating the life of all its callers (they all must get the date of today themselves) or the other way around (`Christmas-Discount` gets more complicated and depends on `Clock`, but the callers do not need anything else), I always pick the latter.

7.5   *Designing for testability in the real world*

Writing tests offers a significant advantage during development: if you pay attention to them (or *listen* to them, as many developers say), they may give you hints about the design of the code you are testing. Achieving good class design is a challenge in complex object-oriented systems. The more help we get, the better.

The buzz about tests giving feedback about the design of the code comes from the fact that all your test code does is exercise the production class:

1   It instantiates the class under test. It can be as simple as a `new A()` or as complicated as `A(dependency1, dependency2, …)`. If a class needs dependencies, the test should also instantiate them.

2   It invokes the method under test. It can be as simple as `a.method()` or as complicated as `a.precall1(); a.precall2(); a.method(param1, param2, ...);`. If a method has pre-conditions before being invoked and/or receiving parameters, the test should also be responsible for those.

3   It asserts that the method behaves as expected. It can be as simple as `assert-That(return).isEqualTo(42);` or as complicated as dozens of lines to observe what has happened in the system. Again, your test code is responsible for all the assertions.

You should constantly monitor how hard it is to perform each of these steps. Is it difficult to instantiate the class under test? Maybe there is a way to design it with fewer dependencies. Is it hard to invoke the method under test? Maybe there is a way to design it so its pre-conditions are easier to handle. Is it difficult to assert the outcome of the method? Maybe there is a way to design it so it is easier to observe what the method does.

Next, I will describe some things I pay attention to when writing tests. They give me feedback about the design and testability of the class I am testing.

7.5.1 *The cohesion of the class under test*

Cohesion is about a module, a class, a method, or any element in your architecture having only a single responsibility. Classes with multiple responsibilities are naturally more complex and harder to comprehend than classes with fewer responsibilities. So, strive for classes and methods that do one thing. Defining what a single responsibility means is tricky and highly context-dependent. Nevertheless, sometimes it can be easy to detect multiple responsibilities in a single element, such as a method that calculates a specific tax and updates the values of all its invoices.

Let's give you some ideas about what you can observe in a test. Note that these tips are symptoms or indications that something *may* be wrong with the production code. It is up to you to make the final decision. Also, note that these tips are solely based on my experience as a developer and are not scientifically validated:

- *Non-cohesive classes have very large test suites.* They contain a lot of behavior that needs to be tested. Pay attention to the number of tests you write for a single class and/or method. If the number of tests grows beyond what you consider reasonable, maybe it is time to re-evaluate the responsibilities of that class or method. A common refactoring strategy is to break the class in two.
- *Non-cohesive classes have test suites that never stop growing.* You expect the class to reach a more stable status at some point. However, if you notice that you are always going back to the same test class and adding new tests, this may be a bad design. It is usually related to the lack of a decent abstraction.
  - A class that never stops growing breaks both the Single Responsibility (SRP) and the Open Closed (OCP) principles from the SOLID guidelines. A common refactoring strategy is to create an abstraction to represent the different

roles and move each calculation rule to its own class. Google the Strategy design pattern to see code examples.

7.5.2 The coupling of the class under test

In a world of cohesive classes, we combine different classes to build large behaviors. But doing so may lead to a highly coupled design. Excessive coupling may harm evolution, as changes in one class may propagate to other classes in ways that are not clear. Therefore, we should strive for classes that are coupled as little as possible.

Your test code can help you detect highly coupled classes:

- If the production class requires you to instantiate many dependencies in your test code, this may be a sign. Consider redesigning the class. There are different refactoring strategies you can employ. Maybe the large behavior that the class implements can be broken into two steps.
  - Sometimes coupling is unavoidable, and the best we can do is manage it better. Breaking a class enables developers to test it more easily. I will give more concrete examples of such cases in the following chapters.
- Another sign is if you observe a test failing in class `ATest` (supposedly testing the behavior of class `A`), but when you debug it, you find the problem in class `B`. This is a clear issue with dependencies: a problem in class `B` somehow leaked to class `A`. It is time to re-evaluate how these classes are coupled and how they interact and see if such leakages can be prevented in future versions of the system.

7.5.3 Complex conditions and testability

We have seen in previous chapters that very complex conditions (such as an `if` statement composed of multiple boolean operations) require considerable effort from testers. For example, we may devise too many tests after applying boundary testing or condition + branch coverage criteria. Reducing the complexity of such conditions by, for example, breaking them into multiple smaller conditions will not reduce the overall complexity of the problem but will at least spread it out.

7.5.4 Private methods and testability

A common question among developers is whether to test private methods. In principle, testers should test private methods only through their public methods. However, testers often feel the urge to test a particular private method in isolation.

A common reason for this feeling is the lack of cohesion or the complexity of the private method. In other words, this method does something so different from the public method, and/or its task is so complicated, that it must be tested separately. This is a good example of the test speaking to us. In terms of design, this may mean the private method does not belong in its current place. A common refactoring is to extract the method, perhaps to a brand new class. There, the former private method, now a public method, can be tested normally. The original class, where the private method used to be, should now depend on this new class.

7.5.5   Static methods, singletons, and testability

As we have seen, static methods adversely affect testability. Therefore, a good rule of thumb is to avoid creating static methods whenever possible. Exceptions to this rule are utility methods, which are often not mocked. If your system has to depend on a specific static method, perhaps because it comes with the framework your software depends on, adding an abstraction on top of it—similar to what we did with the `LocalDate` class in the previous chapter—may be a good decision to facilitate testability.

The same recommendation applies when your system needs code from others or external dependencies. Again, creating layers and classes that abstract away the dependency may help you increase testability. Don't be afraid to create these extra layers: although it may seem that they will increase the overall complexity of the design, the increased testability pays off.

Using the Singleton design pattern also harms testability. This approach ensures that there is only one instance of a class throughout the entire system. Whenever you need an instance of that class, you ask the singleton, and the singleton returns the same one. A singleton makes testing difficult because it is like having a global variable that is persistent throughout the program's life cycle. When testing software systems that use singletons, we often have to write extra code in the test suite to reset or replace the singleton in the different test cases. Singletons also bring other disadvantages to maintainability in general. If you are not familiar with this pattern, I suggest reading about it.

7.5.6   The Hexagonal Architecture and mocks as a design technique

Now that you know about the Hexagonal Architecture and the idea of ports and adapters, we can talk about mocks as a design technique. In a nutshell, whenever mockists develop a feature (or a domain object) and notice that they need something from another place, they let a port emerge. As we saw, the port is an interface that allows the mockist to develop the remainder of the feature without being bothered by the concrete implementation of the adapter. The mockist takes this as a design activity: they reflect on the contract that the port should offer to the core of the application and model the best interface possible.

Whenever I am coding a class (or set of classes) and notice that I need something else, I let an interface emerge that represents this "something else." I reflect on what the class under development needs from it, model the best interface, and continue developing the class. Only later do I implement the concrete adapter. I enjoy this approach as it lets me focus on the class I am implementing by giving me a way to abstract things that I do not care about right now, like the implementation of adapters.

7.5.7   *Further reading about designing for testability*

Entire books can be written about this topic. In fact, entire books *have* been written about it:

- Michael Feathers's *Working Effectively with Legacy Code* (2004) is about working with legacy systems, but a huge part of it is about untestable code (common in legacy) and how to make it testable. Feathers also has a nice talk on YouTube about the "deep synergy between well-designed production code and testability," as he calls it (2013).
- Steve Freeman and Nat Pryce's book *Growing-Object Oriented Systems Guided by Tests* (2009) is also a primer for writing classes that are easy to test.
- Robert Martin's *Clean Architecture* ideas (2018) align with the ideas discussed here.

Exercises

7.1   Observability and controllability are two important concepts of software testing. Three developers could benefit from improving either the observability or the controllability of the system/class they are testing, but each developer encounters a problem.

State whether each of the problems relates to observability or controllability.

- **A** Developer 1: "I can't assert whether the method under test worked well."
- **B** Developer 2: "I need to make sure this class starts with a boolean set to false, but I can't do it."
- **C** Developer 3: "I instantiated the mock object, but there's no way to inject it into the class."

7.2   Sarah has joined a mobile app team that has been trying to write automated tests for a while. The team wants to write unit tests for part of their code, but they tell Sarah, "It's hard." After some code review, the developers list the following problems in their code base:

- **A** Many classes mix infrastructure and business rules.
- **B** The database has large tables and no indexes.
- **C** There are lots of calls to libraries and external APIs.
- **D** Some classes have too many attributes/fields.

To increase testability, the team has a budget to work on two of these four issues. Which items should Sarah recommend that they tackle first?

Note: All four issues should be fixed, but try to prioritize the two most important ones. Which influences testability the most?

7.3   How can you improve the testability of the following `OrderDeliveryBatch` class?

```
public class OrderDeliveryBatch {

    public void runBatch() {
```

```
OrderDao dao = new OrderDao();
DeliveryStartProcess delivery = new DeliveryStartProcess();

List<Order> orders = dao.paidButNotDelivered();

for (Order order : orders) {
  delivery.start(order);

  if (order.isInternational()) {
    order.setDeliveryDate("5 days from now");
  } else {
    order.setDeliveryDate("2 days from now");
  }
}
}
}

class OrderDao {
  // accesses a database
}

class DeliveryStartProcess {
  // communicates with a third-party web service
}
```

7.4 Consider the `KingsDayDiscount` class below:

```
public class KingsDayDiscount {

  public double discount(double value) {

    Calendar today = Calendar.getInstance();

    boolean isKingsDay = today.get(MONTH) == Calendar.APRIL
        && today.get(DAY_OF_MONTH) == 27;

    return isKingsDay ? value * 0.15 : 0;

  }
}
```

What would you do to make this class more testable?

7.5 Think about your current project. Are parts of it hard to test? Can you explain why? What can you do to make it more testable?

Summary

- Writing tests can be easy or hard. Untestable code makes our lives harder. Strive for code that is easy (or at least easier) to test.
- Separate infrastructure from domain code. Infrastructure makes it harder to write tests. Separating domain from infrastructure enables us to write unit tests for the domain logic much more cheaply.

- Ensure that classes are easily controllable and observable. Controllability is usually achieved by ensuring that we can control the dependencies of the class under test. Observability is achieved by ensuring that the class provides easy ways for the test to assert expected behavior.
- While you should not change your code in ways you do not believe in, you should also be pragmatic. I am all in favor of changing the production code to facilitate testing.

Test-driven development 8

This chapter covers

- Understanding test-driven development
- Being productive with TDD
- When not to use TDD

Software developers are pretty used to the traditional development process. First, they implement. Then, and only then, they test. But why not do it the other way around? In other words, why not write a test first and then implement the production code?

In this chapter, we discuss this well-known approach: *test-driven development* (TDD). In a nutshell, TDD challenges our traditional way of coding, which has always been "write some code and then test it." With TDD, we start by writing a test representing the next small feature we want to implement. This test naturally fails, as the feature has not yet been implemented! We then make the test pass by writing some code. With the test now green, and knowing that the feature has been implemented, we go back to the code we wrote and refactor it.

TDD is a popular practice, especially among Agile practitioners. Before I dive into the advantages of TDD and pragmatic questions about working this way, let's look at a small example.

8.1 *Our first TDD session*

For this example, we will create a program that converts Roman numerals to integers. Roman numerals represent numbers with seven symbols:

- I, *unus*, 1, (one)
- V, *quinque*, 5 (five)
- X, *decem*, 10 (ten)
- L, *quinquaginta*, 50 (fifty)
- C, *centum*, 100 (one hundred)
- D, *quingenti*, 500 (five hundred)
- M, *mille*, 1,000 (one thousand)

To represent all possible numbers, the Romans combined the symbols, following these two rules:

- Digits of lower or equal value on the right are added to the higher-value digit.
- Digits of lower value on the left are subtracted from the higher-value digit.

For instance, the number XV represents 15 (10 + 5), and the number XXIV represents 24 (10 + 10 − 1 + 5).

The goal of our TDD session is to implement the following requirement:

Implement a program that receives a Roman numeral (as a string) and returns its representation in the Arabic numeral system (as an integer).

Coming up with examples is part of TDD. So, think about different inputs you can give the program, and their expected outputs. For example, if we input "I" to the program, we expect it to return 1. If we input "XII" to the program, we expect it to return 12. Here are the cases I can think of:

- Simple cases, such as numbers with single characters:
  - If we input "I", the program must return 1.
  - If we input "V", the program must return 5.
  - If we input "X", the program must return 10.
- Numbers composed of more than one character (without using the subtractive notation):
  - If we input "II", the program must return 2.
  - If we input "III", the program must return 3.
  - If we input "VI", the program must return 6.
  - If we input "XVII", the program must return 17.
- Numbers that use simple subtractive notation:
  - If we input "IV", the program must return 4.
  - If we input "IX", the program must return 9.

- Numbers that are composed of many characters and use subtractive notation:
  - If we input "XIV", the program must return 14.
  - If we input "XXIX", the program must return 29.

NOTE   You may wonder about corner cases: What about an empty string? or null? Those cases are worth testing. However, when doing TDD, I first focus on the happy path and the business rules; I consider corners and boundaries later.

Remember, we are not in testing mode. We are in development mode, coming up with inputs and outputs (or test cases) that will guide us through the implementation. In the development flow I introduced in figure 1.4, TDD is part of "testing to guide development." When we are finished with the implementation, we can dive into rigorous testing using all the techniques we have discussed.

Now that we have a (short) list of examples, we can write some code. Let's do it this way:

1. Select the simplest example from our list of examples.
2. Write an automated test case that exercises the program with the given input and asserts its expected output. The code may not even compile at this point. And if it does, the test will fail, as the functionality is not implemented.
3. Write as much production code as needed to make that test pass.
4. Stop and reflect on what we have done so far. We may improve the production code. We may improve the test code. We may add more examples to our list.
5. Repeat the cycle.

The first iteration of the cycle focuses on ensuring that if we give "I" as input, the output is 1. The RomanNumeralConverterTest class contains our first test case.

Listing 8.1   Our first test method

```java
public class RomanNumberConverterTest {
  @Test
  void shouldUnderstandSymbolI() {
    RomanNumeralConverter roman = new RomanNumeralConverter();
    int number = roman.convert("I");
    assertThat(number).isEqualTo(1);
  }
}
```

We will get compilation errors here, as the RomanNumeralConverter class does not exist!

At this moment, the test code does not compile, because the RomanNumberConverter class and its convert() method do not exist. To solve the compilation error, let's create some skeleton code with no real implementation.

Listing 8.2   Skeleton implementation of the class

```java
public class RomanNumeralConverter {
  public int convert(String numberInRoman) {
```

```
    return 0;
  }
}
```
⟵ We do not want to return 0, but
   this makes the test code compile.

The test code now compiles. When we run it, it fails: the test expected 1, but the program returned 0. This is not a problem, as we expected it to fail. Steps 1 and 2 of our cycle are finished. It is now time to write as much code as needed to make the test pass—and it looks weird.

Listing 8.3 Making the test pass

```
public class RomanNumeralConverter {
  public int convert(String numberInRoman) {
    return 1;
  }
}
```
⟵ Returning 1 makes the
   test pass. But is this the
   implementation we want?

The test passes, but it only works in a single case. Again, this is not a problem: we are still working on the implementation. We are taking baby steps.

  Let's move on to the next iteration of the cycle. The next-simplest example in the list is "If we input "V", the program must return 5." Let's again begin with the test.

Listing 8.4 Our second test

```
@Test
void shouldUnderstandSymbolV() {
  RomanNumeralConverter roman = new RomanNumeralConverter();
  int number = roman.convert("V");
  assertThat(number).isEqualTo(5);
}
```

The new test code compiles and fails. Now let's make it pass. In the implementation, we can, for example, make the method convert() verify the content of the number to be converted. If the value is "I", the method returns 1. If the value is "V", it returns 5.

Listing 8.5 Making the tests pass

```
public int convert(String numberInRoman) {
  if(numberInRoman.equals("I")) return 1;
  if(numberInRoman.equals("V")) return 5;
  return 0;
}
```
⟵ Hard-coded ifs are the easiest
   way to make both tests pass.

The two tests pass. We could repeat the cycle for X, L, C, M, and so on, but we already have a good idea about the first thing our implementation needs to generalize: when the Roman numeral has only one symbol, return the integer associated with it. How can we implement such an algorithm?

- Write a set of if statements. The number of characters we need to handle is not excessive.

- Write a `switch` statement, similar to the `if` implementation.
- Use a map that is initialized with all the symbols and their respective integer values.

The choice is a matter of taste. I will use the third option because I like it best.

Listing 8.6   `RomanNumeralConverter` for single-character numbers

```
public class RomanNumeralConverter {

  private static Map<String, Integer> table =
      new HashMap<>() {{
        put("I", 1);
        put("V", 5);
        put("X", 10);
        put("L", 50);
        put("C", 100);
        put("D", 500);
        put("M", 1000);
      }};
  public int convert(String numberInRoman) {
    return table.get(numberInRoman);
  }
}
```

Declares a conversion table that contains the Roman numerals and their corresponding decimal numbers

Gets the number from the table

How do we make sure our implementation works? We have our (two) tests, and we can run them. Both pass. The production code is already general enough to work for single-character Roman numbers. But our test code is not: we have a test called `shouldUnderstandSymbolI` and another called `shouldUnderstandSymbolV`. This specific case would be better represented in a parameterized test called `shouldUnderstandOne-CharNumbers`.

Listing 8.7   Generalizing our first test

```
public class RomanNumeralConverterTest {

  @ParameterizedTest
  @CsvSource({"I,1","V,5", "X,10","L,50",
  "C, 100", "D, 500", "M, 1000"})
  void shouldUnderstandOneCharNumbers(String romanNumeral,
      int expectedNumberAfterConversion) {
    RomanNumeralConverter roman = new RomanNumeralConverter();
    int convertedNumber = roman.convert(romanNumeral);
    assertThat(convertedNumber).isEqualTo(expectedNumberAfterConversion);
  }
}
```

Passes the inputs as a comma-separated value to the parameterized test. JUnit then runs the test method for each of the inputs.

NOTE   The test code now has some duplicate code compared to the production code. The test inputs and outputs somewhat match the map in the production code. This is a common phenomenon when doing testing by example, and it will be mitigated when we write more complex tests.

We are finished with the first set of examples. Let's consider the second scenario: two or more characters in a row, such as II or XX. Again, we start with the test code.

Listing 8.8 Tests for Roman numerals with multiple characters

```
@Test
void shouldUnderstandMultipleCharNumbers() {
  RomanNumeralConverter roman = new RomanNumeralConverter();
  int convertedNumber = roman.convert("II");
  assertThat(convertedNumber).isEqualTo(2);
}
```

To make the test pass in a simple way, we could add the string "II" to the map.

Listing 8.9 Map with all the Roman numerals

```
private static Map<String, Integer> table =
  new HashMap<>() {{
    put("I", 1);

    put("II", 2);        ◁──┐  Adds II. But that means
                            │  we would need to add III,
    put("V", 5);            │  IV, and so on—not a
    put("X", 10);           │  good idea!
    put("L", 50);
    put("C", 100);
    put("D", 500);
    put("M", 1000);
}};
```

If we did this, the test would succeed. But it does not seem like a good idea for implementation, because we would have to include all possible symbols in the map. It is time to generalize our implementation again. The first idea that comes to mind is to iterate over each symbol in the Roman numeral we're converting, accumulate the value, and return the total value. A simple loop should do.

Listing 8.10 Looping through each character in the Roman numeral

```
public class RomanNumeralConverter {
  private static Map<Character, Integer> table =
    new HashMap<>() {{         ◁──┐  The conversion table
      put('I', 1);                │  only contains the
      put('V', 5);                │  unique Roman
      put('X', 10);               │  numeral.
      put('L', 50);
      put('C', 100);
      put('D', 500);
      put('M', 1000);
  }};
                                       Variable that aggregates
                                       the value of each Roman
  public int convert(String numberInRoman) {    numeral
    int finalNumber = 0;         ◁──────┘
```

```
    for(int i = 0; i < numberInRoman.length(); i++) {
      finalNumber += table.get(numberInRoman.charAt(i));
    }

    return finalNumber;
  }
}
```

Gets each
character's
corresponding
decimal value
and adds it to
the total sum

Note that the type of key in the map has changed from String to Character. The algorithm iterates over each character of the string numberInRoman using the charAt() method, which returns a char type. We could convert the char to String, but doing so would add an extra, unnecessary step.

The three tests continue passing. It is important to realize that our focus in this cycle was to make our algorithm work with Roman numerals with more than one character—we were not thinking about the previous examples. This is one of the main advantages of having the tests: we are sure that each step we take is sound. Any bugs we introduce to previously working behavior (*regression bugs*) will be captured by our tests.

We can now generalize the test code and exercise other examples that are similar to the previous one. We again use parameterized tests, as they work well for the purpose.

Listing 8.11 Parameterizing the test for multiple characters

```
@ParameterizedTest
@CsvSource({"II,2","III,3", "VI, 6", "XVIII, 18",
"XXIII, 23", "DCCLXVI, 766"})
void shouldUnderstandMultipleCharNumbers(String romanNumeral,
    int expectedNumberAfterConversion) {
  RomanNumeralConverter roman = new RomanNumeralConverter();
  int convertedNumber = roman.convert(romanNumeral);
  assertThat(convertedNumber).isEqualTo(expectedNumberAfterConversion);
}
```

Tries many inputs
with multiple
characters. Again,
CSVSource is the
simplest way to
do this.

NOTE I chose the examples I passed to the test at random. Our goal is not to be fully systematic when coming up with examples but only to use the test cases as a safety net for developing the feature. When we're finished, we will perform systematic testing.

A single test method or many?
This test method is very similar to the previous one. We could combine them into a single test method, as shown here:

```
@ParameterizedTest
@CsvSource({
  // single character numbers
  "I,1","V,5", "X,10","L,50", "C, 100", "D, 500", "M, 1000",
  // multiple character numbers
  "II,2","III,3", "V,5","VI, 6", "XVIII, 18", "XXIII, 23", "DCCLXVI, 766"
})
```

All the inputs from the different tests
are combined into a single method.

```
void convertRomanNumerals(String romanNumeral,
    int expectedNumberAfterConversion) {
  RomanNumeralConverter roman = new RomanNumeralConverter();
  int convertedNumber = roman.convert(romanNumeral);
  assertThat(convertedNumber).isEqualTo(expectedNumberAfterConversion);
}
```

This is a matter of taste and your team's preference. For the remainder of the chapter, I keep the test methods separated.

Our next step is to make the subtractive notation work: for example, IV should return 4. As always, let's start with the test. This time, we add multiple examples: we understand the problem and can take a bigger step. If things go wrong, we can take a step back.

Listing 8.12   Test for the subtractive notation

```
@ParameterizedTest
@CsvSource({"IV,4","XIV,14", "XL, 40",          ┐ Provides many inputs that exercise
"XLI,41", "CCXCIV, 294"})                       ┘ the subtractive notation rule
void shouldUnderstandSubtractiveNotation(String romanNumeral,
    int expectedNumberAfterConversion) {
  RomanNumeralConverter roman = new RomanNumeralConverter();
  int convertedNumber = roman.convert(romanNumeral);
  assertThat(convertedNumber).isEqualTo(expectedNumberAfterConversion);
}
```

Implementing this part of the algorithm requires more thought. The characters in a Roman numeral, from right to left, increase in terms of value. However, when a numeral is smaller than its neighbor on the right, it must be subtracted from instead of added to the accumulator. Listing 8.13 uses a trick to accomplish this: the `multiplier` variable becomes -1 if the current numeral (that is, the current character we are looking at) is smaller than the last neighbor (that is, the character we looked at previously). We then multiply the current digit by `multiplier` to make the digit negative.

Listing 8.13   Implementation for the subtractive notation

```
public int convert(String numberInRoman) {
    int finalNumber = 0;
    int lastNeighbor = 0;        ┐ Keeps the last          ┌ Loops through the
                                 ┘ visited digit            │ characters, but now
                                                            │ from right to left
    for(int i = numberInRoman.length() - 1; i >= 0; i--) {  ◄──┘

      int current = table.get(numberInRoman.charAt(i));  ◄── Gets the decimal value of
                                                              the current Roman digit
      int multiplier = 1;
      if(current < lastNeighbor) multiplier = -1;  ◄── If the previous digit was
                                                       higher than the current one,
                                                       multiplies the current digit
                                                       by -1 to make it negative
```

```
    finalNumber +=
        table.get(numberInRoman.charAt(i)) * multiplier;
```
⟵ **Adds the current digit to the finalNumber variable. The current digit is positive or negative depending on whether we should add or subtract it, respectively.**

```
    lastNeighbor = current;
    }
```
⟵ **Updates lastNeighbor to be the current digit**

```
    return finalNumber;
}
```

The tests pass. Is there anything we want to improve in the production code? We use `numberInRoman.charAt(i)` when summing the final number, but this value is already stored in the `current` variable, so we can reuse it. Also, extracting a variable to store the current digit after it is multiplied by 1 or -1 will help developers understand the algorithm. We can refactor the code, as shown in the following listing, and run the tests again.

Listing 8.14   Refactored version

```
public int convert(String numberInRoman) {
    int finalNumber = 0;
    int lastNeighbor = 0;              ⟵ Keeps the last
                                          digit visited

    for(int i = numberInRoman.length() - 1; i >= 0; i--) {

        int current = table.get(numberInRoman.charAt(i));

        int multiplier = 1;
        if(current < lastNeighbor) multiplier = -1;

        int currentNumeralToBeAdded = current * multiplier;    ⟵
        finalNumber += currentNumeralToBeAdded;

        lastNeighbor = current;            Uses the current
    }                                      variable and introduces the
                                           currentNumeralToBeAdded variable

    return finalNumber;
}
```

Now that we have implemented all the examples in our initial list, we can think of other cases to handle. We are not handling invalid numbers, for example. The program must reject inputs such as "VXL" and "ILV". When we have new examples, we repeat the entire procedure until the whole program is implemented. I will leave that as an exercise for you—we have done enough that we are ready to more formally discuss TDD.

8.2   *Reflecting on our first TDD experience*

Abstractly, the cycle we repeated in the previous section's development process was as follows:

1 We wrote a (unit) test for the next piece of functionality we wanted to implement. The test failed.

2 We implemented the functionality. The test passed.

3 We refactored our production and test code.

This TDD process is also called the *red-green-refactor cycle.* Figure 8.1 shows a popular way to represent the TDD cycle.

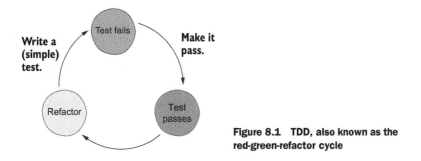

Figure 8.1   TDD, also known as the red-green-refactor cycle

TDD practitioners say this approach can be very advantageous for the development process. Here are some of the advantages:

- *Looking at the requirements first*—In the TDD cycle, the tests we write to support development are basically executable requirements. Whenever we write one of them, we reflect on what the program should and should not do.

  This approach makes us write code for the specific problem we are supposed to solve, preventing us from writing unnecessary code. And exploring the requirement systematically forces us to think deeply about it. Developers often go back to the requirements engineer and ask questions about cases that are not explicit in the requirement.

- *Full control over the pace of writing production code*—If we are confident about the problem, we can take a big step and create a test that involves more complicated cases. However, if we are still unsure how to tackle the problem, we can break it into smaller parts and create tests for these simpler pieces first.

- *Quick feedback*—Developers who do not work in TDD cycles produce large chunks of production code before getting any feedback. In a TDD cycle, developers are forced to take one step at a time. We write one test, make it pass, and reflect on it. These many moments of reflection make it easier to identify new problems as they arise, because we have only written a small amount of code since the last time everything was under control.

- *Testable code*—Creating the tests first makes us think from the beginning about a way to (easily) test the production code before implementing it. In the traditional flow, developers often think about testing only in the later stages of developing a feature. At that point, it may be expensive to change how the code works to facilitate testing.

- *Feedback about design*—The test code is often the first client of the class or component we are developing. A test method instantiates the class under test, invokes a method passing all its required parameters, and asserts that the method produces the expected results. If this is hard to do, perhaps there is a better way to design the class. When doing TDD, these problems arise earlier in the development of the feature. And the earlier we observe such issues, the cheaper it is to fix them.

> **NOTE**   TDD shows its advantages best in more complicated problems. I suggest watching James Shore's YouTube playlist on TDD (2014), where he TDDs an entire software system. I also recommend Freeman and Pryce's book *Growing Object-Oriented Systems Guided by Tests* (2009). They also TDD an entire system, and they discuss in depth how they use tests to guide their design decisions.

8.3   *TDD in the real world*

This section discusses the most common questions and discussions around TDD. Some developers love TDD and defend its use fiercely; others recommend not using it.

As always, software engineering practices are not silver bullets. The reflections I share in this section are personal and not based on scientific evidence. The best way to see if TDD is beneficial for you is to try it!

8.3.1   *To TDD or not to TDD?*

Skeptical readers may be thinking, "I can get the same benefits without doing TDD. I can think more about my requirements, force myself to only implement what is needed, and consider the testability of my class from the beginning. I do not need to write tests for that!" That is true. But I appreciate TDD because it gives me a rhythm to follow. Finding the next-simplest feature, writing a test for it, implementing nothing more than what is needed, and reflecting on what I did gives me a pace that I can fully control. TDD helps me avoid infinite loops of confusion and frustration.

The more defined development cycle also reminds me to review my code often. The TDD cycle offers a natural moment to reflect: as soon as the test passes. When all my tests are green, I consider whether there is anything to improve in the current code.

Designing classes is one of the most challenging tasks of a software engineer. I appreciate the TDD cycle because it forces me to use the code I am developing from the very beginning. The perception I have about the class I am designing is often different from my perception when I try to use the class. I can combine both of these perceptions and make the best decision about how to model the class.

If you write the tests after the code, and not before, as in TDD, the challenge is making sure the time between writing code and testing is small enough to provide developers with timely feedback. Don't write code for an entire day and then start testing—that may be too late.

8.3.2 TDD 100% of the time?

Should we always use TDD? My answer is a *pragmatic* "no." I do a lot of TDD, but I do not use TDD 100% of the time. It depends on how much I need to learn about the feature I am implementing:

- I use TDD when I don't have a clear idea of how to design, architect, or implement a specific requirement. In such cases, I like to go slowly and use my tests to experiment with different possibilities. If I am working on a problem I know well, and I already know the best way to solve the problem, I do not mind skipping a few cycles.
- I use TDD when dealing with a complex problem or a problem I lack the expertise to solve. Whenever I face a challenging implementation, TDD helps me take a step back and learn about the requirements as I go by writing very small tests.
- I do *not* use TDD when there is nothing to be learned in the process. If I already know the problem and how to best solve it, I am comfortable coding the solution directly. (Even if I do not use TDD, I always write tests promptly. I never leave it until the end of the day or the end of the sprint. I code the production code, and then I code the test code. And if I have trouble, I take a step back and slow down.)

TDD creates opportunities for me to learn more about the code I am writing from an implementation point of view (does it do what it needs to do?) as well as from a design point of view (is it structured in a way that I want?). But for some complex features, it's difficult even to determine what the first test should look like; in those cases, I do not use TDD.

We need ways to stop and think about what we are doing. TDD is a perfect approach for that purpose, but not the only one. Deciding when to use TDD comes with experience. You will quickly learn what works best for you.

8.3.3 Does TDD work for all types of applications and domains?

TDD works for most types of applications and domains. There are even books about using it for embedded systems, where things are naturally more challenging, such as Grenning's book *Test Driven Development for Embedded C* (2011). If you can write automated tests for your application, you can do TDD.

8.3.4 What does the research say about TDD?

TDD is such a significant part of software development that it is no wonder researchers try to assess its effectiveness using scientific methods. Because so many people treat it as a silver bullet, I strongly believe that you should know what practitioners think, what I think, and what research currently knows about the subject.

Research has shown several situations in which TDD can improve class design:

- Janzen (2005) showed that TDD practitioners, compared to non-TDDers, produced less-complex algorithms and test suites that covered more.
- Janzen and Saiedian (2006) showed that the code produced using TDD made better use of object-oriented concepts, and responsibilities were better distributed into different classes. In contrast, other teams produced more procedural code.
- George and Williams (2003) showed that although TDD can initially reduce the productivity of inexperienced developers, 92% of the developers in a qualitative analysis thought that TDD helped improve code quality.
- Dogša and Batič (2011) also found an improvement in class design when using TDD. According to the authors, the improvement resulted from the simplicity TDD adds to the process.
- Erdogmus et al. (2005) used an experiment with 24 undergraduate students to show that TDD increased their productivity but did not change the quality of the produced code.
- Nagappan and colleagues (2008) performed three case studies at Microsoft and showed that the pre-release defect density of projects that were TDD'd decreased 40 to 90% in comparison to projects that did not do TDD.

Fucci et al. (2016) argue that the important aspect is writing tests (before or after). Gerosa and I (2015) have made similar observations after interviewing many TDD practitioners. This is also the perception of practitioners. To quote Michael Feathers (2008), "That's the magic, and it's why unit testing works also. When you write unit tests, TDD-style or after your development, you scrutinize, you think, and often you prevent problems without even encountering a test failure."

However, other academic studies show inconclusive results for TDD:

- Müeller and Hagner (2002), after an experiment with 19 students taking a one-semester graduate course on extreme programming, observed that test-first did not accelerate implementation compared to traditional approaches. The code written with TDD was also not more reliable.
- Siniaalto and Abrahamsson (2007) compared five small-scale software projects using different code metrics and showed that the benefits of TDD were not clear.
- Shull and colleagues (2010), after summarizing the findings of 14 papers on TDD, concluded that TDD shows no consistent effect on internal code quality. This paper is easy to read, and I recommend that you look at it.

As an academic who has read most of the work on this topic, I find that many of these studies—both those that show positive effects and those that do not—are not perfect. Some use students, who are not experts in software development or TDD. Others use toy projects without specific room for TDD to demonstrate its benefits. And some use code metrics such as coupling and cohesion that only partially measure code quality. Of course, designing experiments to measure the benefits of a software engineering practice is challenging, and the academic community is still trying to find the best way to do it.

More recent papers explore the idea that TDD's effects may be due not to the "write the tests first" aspect but rather to taking baby steps toward the final goal. Fucci et al. (2016) argue that "the claimed benefits of TDD may not be due to its distinctive test-first dynamic, but rather due to the fact that TDD-like processes encourage fine-grained, steady steps that improve focus and flow."

I suggest that you give TDD a chance. See if it fits your way of working and your programming style. You may decide to adopt it full-time (like many of my colleagues) or only in a few situations (like me), or you may choose never to do it (also like many of my colleagues). It is up to you.

8.3.5 *Other schools of TDD*

TDD does not tell you how to start or what tests to write. This flexibility gave rise to various different schools of TDD. If you are familiar with TDD, you may have heard of the London school of TDD, mockist vs. classicist TDD, and outside-in TDD. This section summarizes their differences and points you to other material if you want to learn more.

In the *classicist school of TDD* (or the *Detroit school of TDD*, or *inside-out TDD*), developers start their TDD cycles with the different units that will compose the overall feature. More often than not, classicist TDDers begin with the entities that hold the main business rules; they slowly work toward the outside of the feature and connect these entities to, say, controllers, UIs, and web services. In other words, classicists go from the inside (entities and business rules) to the outside (interface with the user).

Classicists also avoid mocks as much as possible. For example, when implementing a business rule that would require the interaction of two or more other classes, classicists would focus on testing the entire behavior at once (all the classes working together) without mocking dependencies or making sure to test the units in a fully isolated manner. Classicists argue that mocks reduce the effectiveness of the test suite and make test suites more fragile. This is the same negative argument we discussed in chapter 6.

The *London school of TDD* (or *outside-in TDD*, or *mockist TDD*), on the other hand, prefers to start from the outside (such as the UI or the controller that handles the web service) and then slowly work toward the units that will handle the functionality. To do so, they focus on how the different objects will collaborate. And for that to happen in an outside-in manner, these developers use mocks to explore how the collaboration will work. They favor testing isolated units.

Both schools of thought use the test code to learn more about the design of the code being developed. I like the way Test Double (2018) puts it: "In [the] Detroit school, if an object is hard to test, then it's hard to use; in [the] London school, if a dependency is hard to mock, then it's hard to use for the object that'll be using it."

My style is a mixture of both schools. I start from the inside, coding entities and business rules, and then slowly work to the outside, making the external layers call these entities. However, I favor unit testing as much as possible: I do not like the tests of unit A breaking due to a bug in unit B. I use mocks for that, and I follow all the practices discussed in chapter 6.

I suggest that you learn more about both schools. Both have good points, and combining them makes sense. I recommend Mancuso's 2018 talk, which elaborates on the differences between the schools and how the approaches can be used.

8.3.6   *TDD and proper testing*

Some studies show that TDD practitioners write more test cases than non-TDD practitioners. However, I do not believe that the test suites generated by TDD sessions are as good as the strong, systematic test suites we engineered in the previous chapters after applying different testing practices. The reasoning is simple: when doing TDD, we are not focused on testing. TDD is a tool to help us develop, not to help us test.

Let's revisit figure 1.4 in chapter 1. As I mentioned earlier, TDD is part of "testing to guide development." In other words, you should use TDD when you want your tests to guide you through the development process. When you are finished with your TDD sessions and the code looks good, it is time to begin the effective and systematic testing part of the process I describe: change your focus to testing, and apply specification-based testing, structural testing, and property-based testing.

Can you reuse the tests you created during TDD in the effective and systematic part of the process? Sure. Doing so becomes natural.

Combining TDD and effective testing makes even more sense when both are done in a timely manner. You do not want to TDD something and then wait a week before properly testing it. Can you mix short TDD cycles with short systematic and effective testing cycles? Yes! Once you master all the techniques, you will begin to combine them. The practices I discuss in this book are not meant to be followed linearly—they are tools that are always at your disposal.

Exercises

8.1   This figure illustrates the test-driven development cycle. Fill in the numbered gaps in the figure.

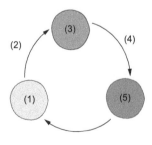

8.2   Which of the following is the least important reason to do TDD?

    A TDD practitioners use the feedback from the test code as a design hint.

    B The practice of TDD enables developers to have steady, incremental progress throughout the development of a feature.

    C As a consequence of the practice of TDD, software systems are tested completely.

    D Using mock objects helps developers understand the relationships between objects.

8.3 TDD has become a popular practice among developers. According to them, TDD has several benefits. Which of the following statements is *not* considered a benefit of TDD? (This is from the perspective of developers, which may not always match the results of empirical research.)

    A Baby steps. Developers can take smaller steps whenever they feel it is necessary.

    B Better team integration. Writing tests is a social activity and makes the team more aware of their code quality.

    C Refactoring. The cycle prompts developers to improve their code constantly.

    D Design for testability. Developers are forced to write testable code from the beginning.

8.4 It is time to practice TDD. A very common practice problem is calculating the final score of a bowling game.

In bowling, a game consists of 10 rounds. In each round, each player has a frame. In a frame, the player can make two attempts to knock over 10 pins with the bowling ball. The score for each frame is the number of pins knocked down, with a bonus for a strike or a spare.

A *strike* means the player knocks over all pins with one roll. In addition to 10 points for knocking down all 10 pins, the player receives a bonus: the total number of pins knocked over in the next frame. Here is an example: [X] [1 2] (each set of [ ] is one frame, and X indicates a strike). The player has accumulated a total of 16 points in these two frames. The first frame scores 10 + 3 points (10 for the strike, and 3 for the sum of the next two rolls, 1 + 2), and the second frame scores 3 (the sum of the rolls).

A *spare* means the player knocks down all pins in one frame, with two rolls. As a bonus, the points for the next roll are added to the score of the frame. For example, take [4 /] [3 2] (/ represents a spare). The player scores 13 points for the first frame (10 pins + 3 from the next roll), plus 5 for the second frame, for a total of 18 points.

If a strike or a spare is achieved in the tenth (final) frame, the player makes an additional one (for a spare) or two (for a strike) rolls. However, the total rolls for this frame cannot exceed three (that is, rolling a strike with one of the extra rolls does not grant more rolls).

Write a program that receives the results of the 10 frames and returns the game's final score. Use the TDD cycle: write a test, make it pass, and repeat.

Summary

- Writing a test that fails, making it pass, and then refactoring is what test-driven development is all about.
- The red-green-refactor cycle brings different advantages to the coding process, such as more control over the pace of development, and quick feedback.
- All the schools of TDD make sense, and all should be used depending on the current context.
- Empirical research does not find clear benefits from TDD. The current consensus is that working on small parts of a feature and making steady progress makes developers more productive. Therefore, while TDD is a matter of taste, using short implementation cycles and testing is the way to go.
- Deciding whether to use TDD 100% of the time is also a personal choice. You should determine when TDD makes you more productive.
- Baby steps are key to TDD. Do not be afraid to go slowly when you are in doubt about what to do next. And do not be afraid to go faster when you feel confident!

Writing larger tests

Most of the code we tested in previous chapters could be tested via unit tests. When that was not possible because, say, the class depended on something else, we used stubs and mocks to replace the dependency, and we still wrote a unit test. As I said when we discussed the testing pyramid in chapter 1, I favor unit tests as much as possible when testing business rules.

But not everything in our systems can (or should) be tested via unit tests. Writing unit tests for some pieces of code is a waste of time. Forcing yourself to write unit tests for them would result in test suites that are not good enough to find bugs, are hard to write, or are flaky and break when you make small changes in the code.

This chapter discusses how to identify which parts of the system should be tested with integration or system tests. Then I will illustrate how I write these tests for three common situations: (1) components (or sets of classes) that should be exercised together, because otherwise, the test suite would be too weak; (2) components that communicate with external infrastructure, such as classes that communicate with databases and are full of SQL queries; and (3) the entire system, end to end.

9.1   *When to use larger tests*

I see two situations where you should use a larger test:

- You have exercised each class individually, but the overall behavior is composed of many classes, and you want to see them work together. Think of a set of classes that calculates the final cost of a shopping cart. You have unit-tested the class responsible for business rule 1 and the class responsible for business rule 2. But you still want to see the final cost of the shopping cart after *all* the rules have been applied to it.
- The class you want to test is a component in a larger plug-and-play architecture. One of the main advantages of object-oriented design is that we can encapsulate and abstract repetitive complexity, so the user only has to implement what matters. Think of a plugin for your favorite IDE (in my case, IntelliJ). You can develop the logic of the plugin, but many actions will only happen when IntelliJ calls the plugin and passes parameters to it.

The following sections show examples of both cases and will help you generalize them.

9.1.1   *Testing larger components*

As always, let's use a concrete example. Suppose we have the following requirement:

> Given a shopping cart with items, quantities, and respective unit prices, the final price of the cart is calculated as follows:
>
> - The final price of each item is calculated by multiplying its unit price by the quantity.
> - The delivery costs are the following. For shopping carts with
>   - 1 to 3 elements (inclusive), we charge 5 dollars extra.
>   - 4 to 10 elements (inclusive), we charge 12.5 dollars extra.
>   - More than 10 elements, we charge 20 dollars extra.
> - If there is an electronic item in the cart, we charge 7.5 dollars extra.

NOTE   The business rule related to delivery costs is not realistic. As a developer, when you notice such inconsistencies, you should talk to the stakeholder, product owner, or whomever is sponsoring that feature. I am keeping this business rule simple for the sake of the example.

Before I begin coding, I think about how to approach the problem. I see how the final price is calculated and that a list of rules is applied to the shopping cart. My experience with software design and design for testability tells me that each rule should be in its own class—putting everything in a single class would result in a large class, which would require lots of tests. We prefer small classes that require only a handful of tests.

Suppose the ShoppingCart and Item classes already exist in our code base. They are simple entities. ShoppingCart holds a list of Items. An Item is composed of a name, a quantity, a price per unit, and a type indicating whether this item is a piece of electronics.

Let's define the contract that all the prices have in common. Listing 9.1 shows the PriceRule interface that all the price rules will follow. It receives a ShoppingCart and returns the value that should be aggregated to the final price of the shopping cart. Aggregating all the price rules will be the responsibility of another class, which we will code later.

Listing 9.1 `PriceRule` **interface**

```
public interface PriceRule {
    double priceToAggregate(ShoppingCart cart);
}
```

We begin with the DeliveryPrice price rule. It is straightforward, as its value depends solely on the number of items in the cart.

Listing 9.2 **Implementation of** `DeliveryPrice`

```
public class DeliveryPrice implements PriceRule {
  @Override
  public double priceToAggregate(ShoppingCart cart) {        Gets the number of items
                                                             in the cart. The delivery
    int totalItems = cart.numberOfItems();    ◁───────────   price is based on this.

    if(totalItems == 0)       ◁───────────        These if statements based
      return 0;                                   on the requirements are
    if(totalItems >= 1 && totalItems <= 3)        enough to return the
      return 5;                                   price.
    if(totalItems >= 4 && totalItems <= 10)
      return 12.5;

    return 20.0;
  }
}
```

NOTE I am using double to represent prices for illustration purposes, but as discussed before, that would be a poor choice in real life. You may prefer to use BigDecimal or represent prices using integers or longs.

With the implementation ready, let's test it as we have learned: with unit testing. The class is so small and localized that it makes sense to exercise it via unit testing. We will apply specification-based and, more importantly, boundary testing (discussed in chapter 2). The requirements contain clear boundaries, and these boundaries are continuous (1 to 3 items, 4 to 10 items, more than 10 items). This means we can test each rule's on and off points:

- 0 items
- 1 item

- 3 items
- 4 items
- 10 items
- More than 10 items (with 11 being the off point)

NOTE Notice the "0 items" handler: the requirements do not mention that case. But I was thinking of the class's pre-conditions and decided that if the cart has no items, the price should return 0. This corner case deserves a test.

We use a parameterized test and comma-separated values (CSV) source to implement the JUnit test.

Listing 9.3   Tests for `DeliveryPrice`

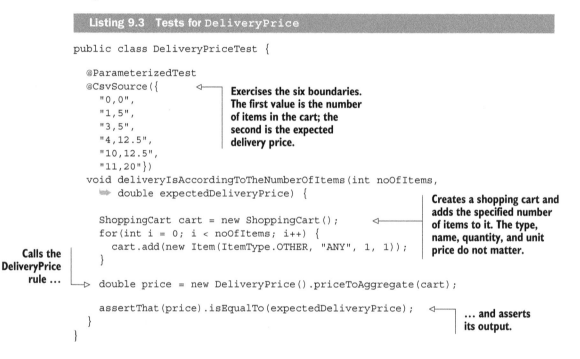

```
public class DeliveryPriceTest {

    @ParameterizedTest
    @CsvSource({
      "0,0",            ◁———┐  Exercises the six boundaries.
      "1,5",                 │  The first value is the number
      "3,5",                 │  of items in the cart; the
      "4,12.5",              │  second is the expected
      "10,12.5",             │  delivery price.
      "11,20"})
    void deliveryIsAccordingToTheNumberOfItems(int noOfItems,
        double expectedDeliveryPrice) {
                                               Creates a shopping cart and
                                               adds the specified number
        ShoppingCart cart = new ShoppingCart();  ◁—  of items to it. The type,
        for(int i = 0; i < noOfItems; i++) {         name, quantity, and unit
          cart.add(new Item(ItemType.OTHER, "ANY", 1, 1));  price do not matter.
        }
        double price = new DeliveryPrice().priceToAggregate(cart);

        assertThat(price).isEqualTo(expectedDeliveryPrice);  ◁——┐ ... and asserts
    }                                                             its output.
}
```
Calls the DeliveryPrice rule ...

Refactoring to achieve 100% code coverage

This example illustrates why you cannot blindly use code coverage. If you generate the report, you will see that the tool does not report 100% branch coverage! In fact, only three of the five conditions are fully exercised: `totalItems >= 1` and `total-Items >= 4` are not.

Why? Let's take the first case as an example. We have lots of tests where the number of items is greater than 1, so the `true` branch of this condition is exercised. But how can we exercise the `false` branch? We would need a number of items less than 1. We have a test where the number of items is zero, but the test never reaches that condition because an early `return` happens in `totalItems == 0`. Pragmatically speaking, we have covered all the branches, but the tool cannot see it.

One idea is to rewrite the code so this is not a problem. In the following code, the implementation is basically the same, but the sequence of `if` statements is written such that the tool can report 100% branch coverage:

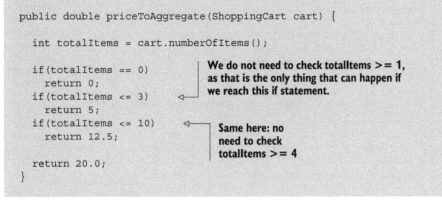

```java
public double priceToAggregate(ShoppingCart cart) {

    int totalItems = cart.numberOfItems();

    if(totalItems == 0)
        return 0;
    if(totalItems <= 3)
        return 5;
    if(totalItems <= 10)
        return 12.5;

    return 20.0;
}
```

We do not need to check totalItems >= 1, as that is the only thing that can happen if we reach this if statement.

Same here: no need to check totalItems >= 4

Next, we implement `ExtraChargeForElectronics`. The implementation is also straightforward, as all we need to do is check whether the cart contains any electronics. If so, we add the extra charge.

Listing 9.4 `ExtraChargeForElectronics` **implementation**

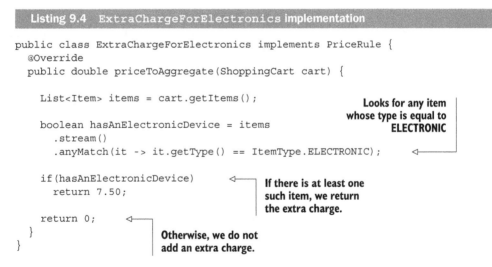

```java
public class ExtraChargeForElectronics implements PriceRule {
  @Override
  public double priceToAggregate(ShoppingCart cart) {

    List<Item> items = cart.getItems();

    boolean hasAnElectronicDevice = items
      .stream()
      .anyMatch(it -> it.getType() == ItemType.ELECTRONIC);

    if(hasAnElectronicDevice)
      return 7.50;

    return 0;
  }
}
```

Looks for any item whose type is equal to ELECTRONIC

If there is at least one such item, we return the extra charge.

Otherwise, we do not add an extra charge.

We have three cases to exercise: no electronics in the cart, one or more electronics in the cart, and an empty cart. Let's implement them in three test methods. First, the following test exercises the "one or more electronics" case. We can use parameterized tests to try this.

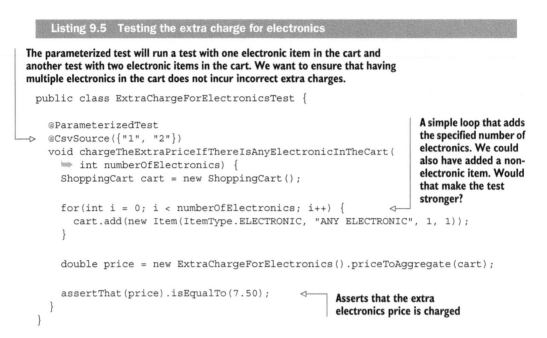

Listing 9.5 Testing the extra charge for electronics

The parameterized test will run a test with one electronic item in the cart and another test with two electronic items in the cart. We want to ensure that having multiple electronics in the cart does not incur incorrect extra charges.

```java
public class ExtraChargeForElectronicsTest {

    @ParameterizedTest
    @CsvSource({"1", "2"})
    void chargeTheExtraPriceIfThereIsAnyElectronicInTheCart(
        int numberOfElectronics) {
        ShoppingCart cart = new ShoppingCart();

        for(int i = 0; i < numberOfElectronics; i++) {
            cart.add(new Item(ItemType.ELECTRONIC, "ANY ELECTRONIC", 1, 1));
        }

        double price = new ExtraChargeForElectronics().priceToAggregate(cart);

        assertThat(price).isEqualTo(7.50);
    }
}
```

A simple loop that adds the specified number of electronics. We could also have added a non-electronic item. Would that make the test stronger?

Asserts that the extra electronics price is charged

We then test that no extra charges are added when there are no electronics in the cart (see listing 9.6).

> **NOTE** If you read chapter 5, you may wonder if we should write a property-based test in this case. The implementation is straightforward, and the number of electronic items does not significantly affect how the algorithm works, so I am fine with example-based testing here.

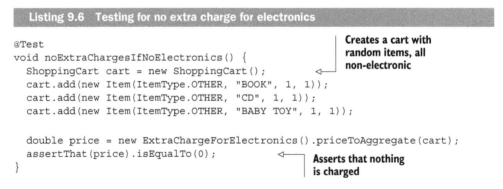

Listing 9.6 Testing for no extra charge for electronics

```java
@Test
void noExtraChargesIfNoElectronics() {
    ShoppingCart cart = new ShoppingCart();
    cart.add(new Item(ItemType.OTHER, "BOOK", 1, 1));
    cart.add(new Item(ItemType.OTHER, "CD", 1, 1));
    cart.add(new Item(ItemType.OTHER, "BABY TOY", 1, 1));

    double price = new ExtraChargeForElectronics().priceToAggregate(cart);
    assertThat(price).isEqualTo(0);
}
```

Creates a cart with random items, all non-electronic

Asserts that nothing is charged

Finally, we test the case where there are no items in the shopping cart.

Listing 9.7 No items in the shopping cart, so no electronics charge

```java
@Test
void noItems() {
    ShoppingCart cart = new ShoppingCart();
```

```
double price = new ExtraChargeForElectronics().priceToAggregate(cart);
assertThat(price).isEqualTo(0);        ◁──┐ The shopping cart is empty,
}                                           so nothing is charged.
```

The final rule to implement is `PriceOfItems`, which navigates the list of items and calculates the unit price times the quantity of each item. I do not show the code and the test, to save space; they are available in the book's code repository.

Let's go to the class that aggregates all the price rules and calculates the final price. The `FinalPriceCalculator` class receives a list of `PriceRules` in its constructor. Its `calculate` method receives a `ShoppingCart`, passes it to all the price rules, and returns the aggregated price.

Listing 9.8 `FinalPriceCalculator` **that runs all the** `PriceRules`

```
public class FinalPriceCalculator {

  private final List<PriceRule> rules;
                                                          Receives a list of
  public FinalPriceCalculator(List<PriceRule> rules) {  ◁─ price rules in the
    this.rules = rules;                                     constructor. This
  }                                                         class is flexible and
                                                            can receive any
                                                            combination of
                                                            price rules.

  public double calculate(ShoppingCart cart) {
    double finalPrice = 0;                        For each price rule,
                                                  gets the price to add
    for (PriceRule rule : rules) {            ◁── to the final price
      finalPrice += rule.priceToAggregate(cart);
    }

    return finalPrice;    ◁──┐ Returns the final
  }                           aggregated price
}
```

We can easily unit-test this class: all we need to do is stub a set of `PriceRules`. Listing 9.9 creates three price rule stubs. Each returns a different value, including 0, as 0 may happen. We then create a very simple shopping cart—its items do not matter, because we are mocking the price rules.

Listing 9.9 Testing `FinalPriceCalculator`

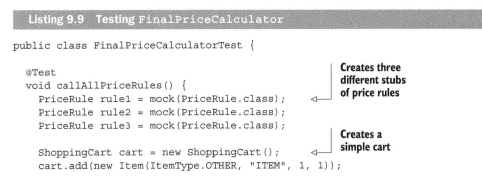

```
public class FinalPriceCalculatorTest {

  @Test                                          Creates three
  void callAllPriceRules() {                     different stubs
    PriceRule rule1 = mock(PriceRule.class);  ◁─ of price rules
    PriceRule rule2 = mock(PriceRule.class);
    PriceRule rule3 = mock(PriceRule.class);
                                                  Creates a
    ShoppingCart cart = new ShoppingCart();   ◁─ simple cart
    cart.add(new Item(ItemType.OTHER, "ITEM", 1, 1));
```

Passes the stubs to the calculator and runs it

```
when(rule1.priceToAggregate(cart)).thenReturn(1.0);
when(rule2.priceToAggregate(cart)).thenReturn(0.0);
when(rule3.priceToAggregate(cart)).thenReturn(2.0);

List<PriceRule> rules = Arrays.asList(rule1, rule2, rule3);
FinalPriceCalculator calculator = new FinalPriceCalculator(rules);
double price = calculator.calculate(cart);

assertThat(price).isEqualTo(3);
    }
}
```

Makes the stubs return different values, given the cart

Given the values we set for the stubs, we expect a final value of 3.

If this is what you envisioned when I posed the requirements, you understand my way of thinking about design and testing. But you may be thinking that even though we tested each of the price rules individually, and we tested the price calculator with stubbed rules, we don't know if these pieces will work when we plug them together.

This is a valid skeptical thought. Why not write more tests? Because our tests already cover all the requirements. Structurally, we have covered everything. In these cases, I suggest writing a larger test that exercises all the classes together. In this case, the larger test will exercise `FinalPriceCalculator` together with all the `PriceRules`. First, let's create a factory class in the production code that is responsible for instantiating the calculator with all its dependencies.

Listing 9.10   `FinalPriceCalculatorFactory`

```
public class FinalPriceCalculatorFactory {

  public FinalPriceCalculator build() {

    List<PriceRule> priceRules = Arrays.asList(
        new PriceOfItems(),
        new ExtraChargeForElectronics(),
        new DeliveryPrice());

    return new FinalPriceCalculator(priceRules);
  }
}
```

Passes the list of PriceRules manually. You can use dependency injection frameworks to do this.

Now all we need to do is to use the factory to build up a real `FinalPriceCalculator` and then give it some inputs. To get started, let's write a test with a shopping cart that has four items (the delivery price is 12.5) and an electronic item (the final price will include the extra charge).

Listing 9.11   A larger test for `FinalPriceCalculator`

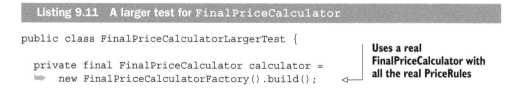

```
public class FinalPriceCalculatorLargerTest {

  private final FinalPriceCalculator calculator =
      new FinalPriceCalculatorFactory().build();
```

Uses a real FinalPriceCalculator with all the real PriceRules

```
@Test
void appliesAllRules() {                                    Builds up a
  ShoppingCart cart = new ShoppingCart();                    shopping cart
  cart.add(new Item(ItemType.ELECTRONIC, "PS5", 1, 299));
  cart.add(new Item(ItemType.OTHER, "BOOK", 1, 29));
  cart.add(new Item(ItemType.OTHER, "CD", 2, 12));
  cart.add(new Item(ItemType.OTHER, "CHOCOLATE", 3, 1.50));

  double price = calculator.calculate(cart);

  double expectedPrice =                                     The prices of
      299 + 29 + 12 * 2 + 1.50 * 3 +                         the items
      7.50 +
      12.5;                        Includes an
                                   electronic
  assertThat(price)                                    Asserts that the
    .isEqualTo(expectedPrice);                         final value matches
}                                                      the shopping cart
}
```

Delivery price

In terms of test code, this is no different from writing a unit test. In fact, based on the definition I gave in chapter 1, I do not consider this an integration test, as it does not go beyond the system's boundaries. This is a larger test that exercises many units.

From a testing perspective, we can apply specification-based, boundary, and structural testing the same way. The difference is that the granularity may be coarser. When testing the DeliveryPrice unit, we only had to think about the rules related to delivery. Now that we are testing all the behavior together (the calculator plus the price rules), the number of combinations is larger.

Specification-based testing in larger tests

Let's look at how I would apply specification-based testing here. I would consider each price rule a category to exercise individually, analogous to the input values of the methods we test in isolation. Therefore, my categories would be *price per item*, *delivery*, and *electronics extra charge*, each with its own partitions. The item itself can also vary. The categories and partitions are as follows:

- Shopping cart:
  - a Empty cart
  - b 1 element
  - c Many elements
- Each individual item:
  - a Single quantity
  - b More than one
  - c Unit price times quantity, rounded
  - d Unit price times quantity, not rounded

(continued)
- Delivery price:
  - a 1 to 3 items
  - b 4 to 10 items
  - c More than 10 items
- Electronics:
  - a Has an electronic item
  - b No electronic items

I would then combine the partitions that make sense, engineer the different test cases, and write them as automated JUnit tests. I will leave that as an exercise for you.

This example shows how much more work it is to test sets of classes together. I use this approach when I see value in it, such as for debugging a problem that happens in production. However, I use these tests in addition to unit tests. I also do not re-test everything. I prefer to use these large component tests as an excuse to try the component with real-world inputs.

9.1.2 *Testing larger components that go beyond our code base*

In the previous example, the large test gives us confidence about the overall behavior of the component, but we could still test each unit individually. In some cases, however, we cannot write tests for units in isolation. Or rather, we can write tests, but doing so would not make sense. Let's look at examples of two small open source projects I coded.

TESTING THE CK TOOL

The first example is a project called CK (https://github.com/mauricioaniche/ck), available on my GitHub page. CK is a tool that calculates code metrics for Java code. To do so, it relies on Eclipse JDT (www.eclipse.org/jdt/), a library that is part of the Eclipse IDE. Among its many functionalities, JDT enables us to build abstract syntax trees (ASTs) of Java code. CK builds ASTs using JDT and then visits these trees and calculates the different metrics.

As you can imagine, CK is highly dependent on how JDT does things. Given an AST, JDT offers clients a way to visit the tree. Clients need to create a class that inherits from ASTVisitor. (Visitor is a popular design pattern for navigating complex data structures.) CK then implements many of these AST visitors, one for each metric.

One of the metrics that CK implements is coupling between objects (CBO). The metric counts the number of other classes the class under analysis depends on. Imagine the fictitious class A in the following listing. This class declares a field of type B and instantiates class C. CK detects the dependency on B and C and returns 2 as the CBO.

Listing 9.12 Fictitious class A that depends on B and C

```
class A {
  private B b;

  public void action() {
    new C().method();
  }
}
```

In listing 9.13, I show a simplified implementation of the CBO metric (you can see the full code on my GitHub). The implementation looks at any declared or used type in the class and adds it to a set. Later, it returns the number of types in the set. Note all the visit methods: they are called by the JDT whenever there is, for example, a method invocation or a field declaration.

Listing 9.13 CBO implementation in CK

I created my own interface, instead of using JDT's ASTVisitor, but it is the same thing.

```
public class CBO implements CKASTVisitor {

    private Set<String> coupling = new HashSet<String>();

    @Override
    public void visit(MethodInvocation node) {
      IMethodBinding binding = node.resolveMethodBinding();
      if(binding!=null)
        coupleTo(binding.getDeclaringClass());
    }

    @Override
    public void visit(FieldDeclaration node) {
      coupleTo(node.getType());
    }

    // this continues for all the possible places where a type can appear...

    private void coupleTo(Type type) {
      // some complex code here to extract the name of the type.
      String fullyQualifiedName = ...;

      addToSet(fullyQualifiedName);
    }
    private void addToSet(String name) {
      this.coupling.add(name);
    }
}
```

Declares a set to keep all the unique types this class uses

If there is a method invocation, gets the type of the class of the invoked method

If there is a field declaration, gets the type of the field

Adds the full name of the type to the set

How can we write a unit test for the CBO class? The CBO class offers many visit methods called by the JDT once the JDT builds the AST out of real Java code. We could try to mock all the types that these visit methods receive, such as MethodInvocation and FieldDeclaration, and then make a sequence of calls to these methods. But in my opinion, that would be too far from what will happen when we run JDT for real.

I do not see a way to unit-test this class without starting up JDT, asking JDT to build an AST out of a small but real Java class, using CBO to visit the generated AST, and comparing the result. So, I used real integration testing in this case.

The test class in listing 9.14 runs CK (which runs JDT) in a specific directory. This directory contains fake Java classes that I created for the sole purpose of the tests. In the code, it is the cbo directory. I have one directory per metric. Because running JDT takes a few seconds, I run it once for the entire test class (see the @BeforeAll method). The test method then asks for the report of a specific class. In the case of the countDifferentDependencies test, I am interested in the coupling of the fake Coupling1 class. I then assert that its coupling is 6.

Listing 9.14   CBOTest

```
public class CBOTest extends BaseTest {          ◁──┐  The BaseTest class provides
                                                     │  basic functionality for all
    @BeforeAll                                       │  the test classes.
    public void setUp() {
        report = run(fixturesDir() + "/cbo");     ◁──┐  Runs JDT on all code in the cbo
    }                                                │  directory. This directory contains
                                                     │  Java code I created solely for
    @Test                                            │  testing purposes.
    public void countDifferentDependencies() {
        CKClassResult result = report.get("cbo.Coupling1");  ◁──┐  CK returns a report,
                                                                 │  which we use to get the
        assertEquals(6, result.getCbo());     ◁──┐              │  results of a specific Java
    }                                            │              │  class we created for this
}                              We expect this class to be       │  test (see listing 9.15).
                               coupled with six classes.
```

To help you better understand why the CBO is 6, listing 9.15 shows the Coupling1 class. This code makes no sense, but it is enough for us to count dependencies. This class uses classes A, B, C, D, C2, and CouplingHelper: that makes six dependencies.

Listing 9.15   Coupling1 fixture

```
public class Coupling1 {

    private B b;    ◁────  B

        public D m1() {   ◁────  D
A  ────▷  A a = new A();
          C[] x = new C[10];    ◁────  C

          CouplingHelper h = new CouplingHelper();   ◁────  CouplingHelper
C2 ────▷  C2 c2 = h.m1();

          return d;
    }
}
```

The `CBOTest` class contains many other test methods, each exercising a different case. For example, it tests whether CK can count a dependency even though the dependency's code is not available (imagine that class `A` in the example is not in the directory). It also tests whether it counts interfaces and inherited classes, types in method parameters, and so on.

It was challenging to come up with good test cases here; and it was not easy to apply specification-based testing, because the input could be virtually any Java class. You may face similar challenges when implementing classes for a plug-and-play architecture. This is a good example of a specific context where we need to learn more about how to test. Testing compilers, which is a related problem, is also a significant area of research.

TESTING THE ANDY TOOL

Another example where I could not write isolated unit tests involved a tool my teaching assistants and I wrote to assess the test suites that our students engineered. The tool, named Andy (https://github.com/cse1110/andy), compiles the test code provided by a student, runs all the provided JUnit tests, calculates code coverage, runs some static analysis, and checks whether the test suite is strong enough to kill mutant versions of the code under test. Andy then gives a grade and a detailed description of its assessment.

Each step is implemented in its own class. For example, `CompilationStep` is responsible for compiling the student's code, `RunJUnitTestsStep` is responsible for executing all the unit tests in the student's submission, and `RunMetaTestsStep` checks whether the test suite kills all the manually engineered mutants we expect it to kill. Figure 9.1 illustrates Andy's overall flow.

If we were to unit-test everything, we would need a unit test for the compilation step, another for the step that runs JUnit, and so on. But how could we exercise the "run JUnit" step without compiling the code first? It is not possible.

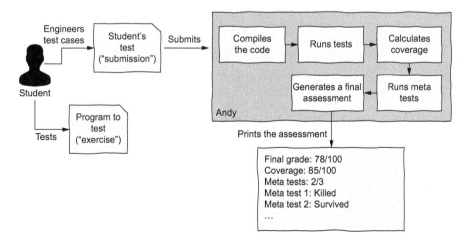

Figure 9.1 Simplified flow of Andy

We decided to use larger tests. For example, the tests that exercise `RunMetaTestsStep` run the entire engine we developed. Thus our test provides a real Java file that simulates the student's submission and another Java file that contains the class under test. Andy gets these files, compiles them, runs the JUnit tests, and finally runs the meta tests.

Listing 9.16 shows one of the tests in the test suite. The `run()` method, which is implemented in the `IntegrationTestBase` test base so all the test classes can use it, runs the entire Andy engine. The parameters are real Java files:

- `NumberUtilsAddLibrary.java`, which contains the code of the class under test
- `NumberUtilsAddOfficialSolution.java`, which contains a possible solution submitted by the student (in this case, the official solution of this exercise)
- `NumberUtilsAddConfiguration.java`, a configuration class that should be provided by the teacher

The `run()` method returns a `Result` class: an entity containing all the results of each step. Because this test case focuses on the meta tests, the assertions also focus on them. In this test method, we expect Andy to run four meta tests—`AppliesMultipleCarries-Wrongly`, `DoesNotApplyCarryAtAll`, `DoesNotApplyLastCarry`, and `DoesNotCheck-NumbersOutOfRange`—and we expect them all to pass.

Listing 9.16 Integration test for the `MetaTests` step

```
public class MetaTestsTest extends IntegrationTestBase {

    @Test
    void allMetaTestsPassing() {              Runs the full
        Result result =                       Andy engine
            run(                      ◁┘
            "NumberUtilsAddLibrary.java",
            "NumberUtilsAddOfficialSolution.java",
            "NumberUtilsAddConfiguration.java");

        assertThat(result.getMetaTests().getTotalTests())
    ▷     .isEqualTo(4);
        assertThat(result.getMetaTests().getPassedMetaTests())
            .isEqualTo(4);
        assertThat(result.getMetaTests())
            .has(passedMetaTest("AppliesMultipleCarriesWrongly"))
            .has(passedMetaTest("DoesNotApplyCarryAtAll"))
            .has(passedMetaTest("DoesNotApplyLastCarry"))
            .has(passedMetaTest("DoesNotCheckNumbersOutOfRange"));
    }
}
```

Asserts that the meta tests step executed as expected

NOTE You may be curious about the `passedMetaTest` method in this test method. AssertJ enables us to extend its set of assertions, and we created one specifically for meta tests. I will show how to do this in chapter 10.

These two examples illustrate situations where unit-testing a class in isolation does not make sense. In general, my advice is to use unit testing as much as possible, because—as

I have said many times before—unit tests are cheap and easy to write. But do not be afraid to write larger tests whenever you believe they will give you more confidence.

9.2 Database and SQL testing

In many of the examples in this book, a Data Access Object (DAO) class is responsible for retrieving or persisting information in the database. Whenever these classes appear, we quickly stub or mock them out of our way. However, at some point, you need to test these classes. These DAOs often perform complex SQL queries, and they encapsulate a lot of business knowledge, requiring testers to spend some energy making sure they produce the expected outcomes. The following sections examine what to test in a SQL query, how to write automated test cases for such queries, and the challenges and best practices involved.

9.2.1 What to test in a SQL query

SQL is a robust language and contains many different functions we can use. Let's simplify and look at queries as a composition of predicates. Here are some examples:

- `SELECT * FROM INVOICE WHERE VALUE < 50`
- `SELECT * FROM INVOICE I JOIN CUSTOMER C ON I.CUSTOMER_ID = C.ID WHERE C.COUNTRY = 'NL'`
- `SELECT * FROM INVOICE WHERE VALUE > 50 AND VALUE < 200`

In these examples, `value < 50`, `i.customer_id = c.id`, `c.country = 'NL'`, and `value > 50 and value < 200` are the predicates that compose the different queries. As a tester, a possible criterion is to exercise the predicates and check whether the SQL query returns the expected results when predicates are evaluated to different results.

Virtually all the testing techniques we have discussed in this book can be applied here:

- *Specification-based testing*—SQL queries emerge out of a requirement. A tester can analyze the requirements and derive equivalent partitions that need to be tested.
- *Boundary analysis*—Such programs have boundaries. Because we expect boundaries to be places with a high bug probability, exercising them is important.
- *Structural testing*—SQL queries contain predicates, and a tester can use the SQL's structure to derive test cases.

Here, we focus on structural testing. If we look at the third SQL example and try to make an analogy with what we have discussed about structural testing, we see that the SQL query contains a single branch composed of two predicates (`value > 50` and `value < 200`). This means there are four possible combinations of results in these two predicates: `(true, true)`, `(true, false)`, `(false, true)`, and `(false, false)`. We can aim at either of the following:

- *Branch coverage*—In this case, two tests (one that makes the overall decision evaluate to `true` and one that makes it evaluate to `false`) would be enough to achieve 100% branch coverage.

- *Condition + branch coverage*—In this case, three tests would be enough to achieve 100% condition + branch coverage: for example, T1 = 150, T2 = 40, T3 = 250.

In "A practical guide to SQL white-box testing," a 2006 paper by Tuya, Suárez-Cabal, and De La Riva, the authors suggest five guidelines for designing SQL tests:

- *Adopting modified condition/decision coverage (MC/DC) for SQL conditions*—Decisions happen at three places in a SQL query: join, where, and having conditions. We can use criteria like MC/DC to fully exercise the query's predicates. If you do not remember how MC/DC coverage works, revisit chapter 3.
- *Adapting MC/DC for tackling nulls*—Because databases have a special way of handling/returning nulls, any (coverage) criteria should be adapted to three-valued logic (true, false, null). In other words, consider the possibility of values being null in your query.
- *Category-partitioning selected data*—SQL can be considered a declarative specification for which we can define partitions to be tested. Directly from Tuya et al.'s paper, we define the following:
  - *Rows that are retrieved*—We include a test state to force the query to not select any row.
  - *Rows that are merged*—The presence of unwanted duplicate rows in the output is a common failure in some queries. We include a test state in which identical rows are selected.
  - *Rows that are grouped*—For each of the group-by columns, we design test states to obtain at least two different groups at the output, such that the value used for the grouping is the same and all the others are different.
  - *Rows that are selected in a subquery*—For each subquery, we include test states that return zero or more rows, with at least one null and two different values in the selected column.
  - *Values that participate in aggregate functions*—For each aggregate function (excluding count), we include at least one test state in which the function computes two equal values and another that is different.
  - *Other expressions*—We also design test states for expressions involving the like predicate, date management, string management, data type conversions, or other functions using category partitioning and boundary checking.
- *Checking the outputs*—We should check not only the input domain but also the output domain. SQL queries may return null or empty values in specific columns, which may make the rest of the program break.
- *Checking the database constraints*—Databases have constraints. We should make sure the database enforces these constraints.

As you can see, many things can go wrong in a SQL query. It is part of the tester's job to make sure that does not happen.

9.2.2 Writing automated tests for SQL queries

We can use JUnit to write SQL tests. All we need to do is (1) establish a connection with the database, (2) make sure the database is in the right initial state, (3) execute the SQL query, and (4) check the output.

Consider the following scenario:

- We have an `Invoice` table composed of a `name` (varchar, length 100) and a `value` (double).
- We have an `InvoiceDao` class that uses an API to communicate with the database. The precise API does not matter.
- This DAO performs three actions: `save()` persists an invoice in the database, `all()` returns all invoices in the database, and `allWithAtLeast()` returns all invoices with at least a specified value. Specifically,
  - `save()` runs INSERT INTO invoice (name, value) VALUES (?,?).
  - `all()` runs SELECT * FROM invoice.
  - `allWithAtLeast()` runs SELECT * FROM invoice WHERE value >= ?.

A simple JDBC implementation of such a class is shown in listings 9.17, 9.18, and 9.19.

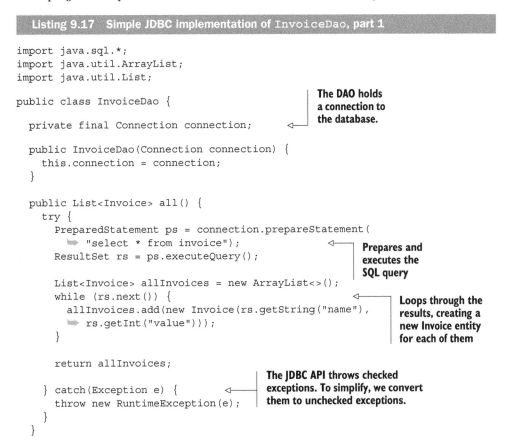

Listing 9.17   Simple JDBC implementation of `InvoiceDao`, part 1

```java
import java.sql.*;
import java.util.ArrayList;
import java.util.List;

public class InvoiceDao {

  private final Connection connection;          ◁──┐ The DAO holds
                                                    │ a connection to
                                                    │ the database.
  public InvoiceDao(Connection connection) {
    this.connection = connection;
  }

  public List<Invoice> all() {
    try {
      PreparedStatement ps = connection.prepareStatement(
          "select * from invoice");             ◁──┐ Prepares and
      ResultSet rs = ps.executeQuery();             │ executes the
                                                    │ SQL query
      List<Invoice> allInvoices = new ArrayList<>();
      while (rs.next()) {                        ◁──┐ Loops through the
        allInvoices.add(new Invoice(rs.getString("name"), │ results, creating a
            rs.getInt("value")));                  │ new Invoice entity
      }                                            │ for each of them

      return allInvoices;
                                        ┌─ The JDBC API throws checked
    } catch(Exception e) {         ◁────┤  exceptions. To simplify, we convert
      throw new RuntimeException(e);     │  them to unchecked exceptions.
    }
  }
}
```

Listing 9.18   Simple JDBC implementation of `InvoiceDao`, part 2

```
public List<Invoice> allWithAtLeast(int value) {
    try {
        PreparedStatement ps = connection.prepareStatement(
            "select * from invoice where value >= ?");
        ps.setInt(1, value);
        ResultSet rs = ps.executeQuery();

        List<Invoice> allInvoices = new ArrayList<>();
        while (rs.next()) {
            allInvoices.add(
                new Invoice(rs.getString("name"), rs.getInt("value"))
            );
        }
        return allInvoices;
    } catch (Exception e) {
        throw new RuntimeException(e);
    }
}
```

> The same thing happens here: we prepare the SQL query, execute it, and then create one Invoice entity for each row.

Listing 9.19   Simple JDBC implementation of `InvoiceDao`, part 3

```
public void save(Invoice inv) {
    try {
        PreparedStatement ps = connection.prepareStatement(
            "insert into invoice (name, value) values (?,?)");

        ps.setString(1, inv.customer);
        ps.setInt(2, inv.value);
        ps.execute();

        connection.commit();
    } catch(Exception e) {
        throw new RuntimeException(e);
    }
}
}
```

> Prepares the INSERT statement and executes it

NOTE   This implementation is a naive way to access a database. In more complex projects, you should use a professional production-ready database API such as jOOQ, Hibernate, or Spring Data.

Let's test the `InvoiceDao` class. Remember, we want to apply the same ideas we have seen so far. The difference is that we have a database in the loop. Let's start with `all()`. This method sends a `SELECT * FROM invoice` to the database and gets back the result. But for this query to return something, we must first insert some invoices into the database. The `InvoiceDao` class also provides the `save()` method, which sends an `INSERT` query. This is enough for our first test.

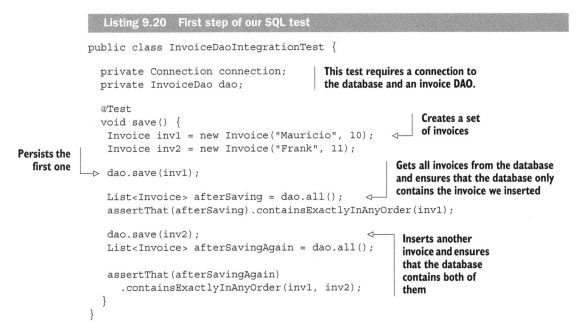

Listing 9.20 First step of our SQL test

```
public class InvoiceDaoIntegrationTest {

    private Connection connection;          This test requires a connection to
    private InvoiceDao dao;                 the database and an invoice DAO.

    @Test
    void save() {                                       Creates a set
      Invoice inv1 = new Invoice("Mauricio", 10);       of invoices
      Invoice inv2 = new Invoice("Frank", 11);
      dao.save(inv1);
                                            Gets all invoices from the database
                                            and ensures that the database only
      List<Invoice> afterSaving = dao.all();   contains the invoice we inserted
      assertThat(afterSaving).containsExactlyInAnyOrder(inv1);

      dao.save(inv2);                                    Inserts another
      List<Invoice> afterSavingAgain = dao.all();        invoice and ensures
                                                         that the database
      assertThat(afterSavingAgain)                       contains both of
        .containsExactlyInAnyOrder(inv1, inv2);          them
    }
}
```

Persists the first one → `dao.save(inv1);`

This test method creates two invoices (`inv1`, `inv2`), persists the first one using the `save()` method, retrieves the invoices from the database, and asserts that it returns one invoice. Then it persists another invoice, retrieves the invoices from the database again, and asserts that now it returns two invoices. The test method ensures the correct behavior of both the `save()` and `all()` methods. The `containsExactlyInAny-Order` assertion from AssertJ ensures that the list contains the precise invoices that we pass to it, in any order. For that to happen, the `Invoice` class needs a proper implementation of the `equals()` method.

In terms of testing, our implementation is correct. However, given the database, we have some extra concerns. First, we should not forget that the database persists the data permanently. Suppose we start with an empty database. The first time we run the test, it will persist two invoices in the database. The second time we run the test, it will persist two new invoices, totaling four invoices. This will make our test fail, as it expects the database to have one and two invoices, respectively.

This was never a problem in our previous unit tests: every object we created lived in memory, and they disappeared after the test method was done. When testing with a real database, we must ensure a clean state:

- *Before the test runs*, we open the database connection, clean the database, and (optionally) put it in the state we need it to be in before executing the SQL query under test.
- *After the test runs*, we close the database connection.

This is a perfect fit for JUnit's `@BeforeEach` and `@AfterEach`, as shown in the following listing.

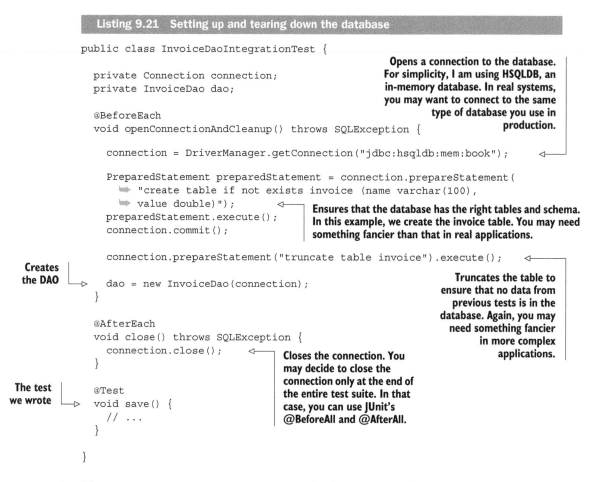

Listing 9.21   Setting up and tearing down the database

```java
public class InvoiceDaoIntegrationTest {

    private Connection connection;
    private InvoiceDao dao;

    @BeforeEach
    void openConnectionAndCleanup() throws SQLException {

        connection = DriverManager.getConnection("jdbc:hsqldb:mem:book");

        PreparedStatement preparedStatement = connection.prepareStatement(
            "create table if not exists invoice (name varchar(100),
             value double)");
        preparedStatement.execute();
        connection.commit();

        connection.prepareStatement("truncate table invoice").execute();

        dao = new InvoiceDao(connection);
    }

    @AfterEach
    void close() throws SQLException {
        connection.close();
    }

    @Test
    void save() {
        // ...
    }

}
```

Opens a connection to the database. For simplicity, I am using HSQLDB, an in-memory database. In real systems, you may want to connect to the same type of database you use in production.

Ensures that the database has the right tables and schema. In this example, we create the invoice table. You may need something fancier than that in real applications.

Creates the DAO

Truncates the table to ensure that no data from previous tests is in the database. Again, you may need something fancier in more complex applications.

Closes the connection. You may decide to close the connection only at the end of the entire test suite. In that case, you can use JUnit's @BeforeAll and @AfterAll.

The test we wrote

The `openConnectionAndCleanup()` method is annotated as `@BeforeEach`, which means JUnit will run the cleanup before every test method. Right now, its implementation is simplistic: it sends a `truncate table` query to the database.

> **NOTE** In larger systems, you may prefer to use a framework to help you handle the database. I suggest Flyway (https://flywaydb.org) or Liquibase (https://www.liquibase.org). In addition to supporting you in evolving your database schema, these frameworks contain helper methods that help clean up the database and make sure it contains the right schema (that is, all tables, constraints, and indexes are there).

We also open the connection to the database manually, using JDBC's most rudimentary API call, `getConnection`. (In a real software system, you would probably ask Hibernate or Spring Data for an active database connection.) Finally, we close the connection in the `close()` method (which happens after every test method).

Let's now test the other method: `allWithAtLeast()`. This method is more interesting, as the SQL query contains a predicate, `where value >= ?`. This means we have different scenarios to exercise. Here we can use all of our knowledge about boundary testing and think of on and off points, as we did in chapter 2.

Figure 9.2 shows the boundary analysis. The on point is the point on the boundary. In this case, it is whatever concrete number we pass in the SQL query. The off point is the nearest point to the on point that flips the condition. In this case, that is whatever concrete number we pass in the SQL query minus one, since it makes the condition false.

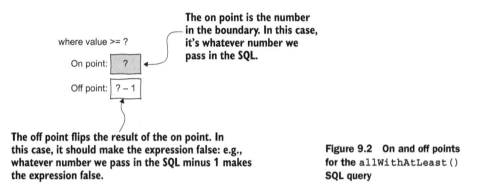

The off point flips the result of the on point. In this case, it should make the expression false: e.g., whatever number we pass in the SQL minus 1 makes the expression false.

Figure 9.2 On and off points for the `allWithAtLeast()` SQL query

The following listing shows the JUnit test. Note that we add an in point to the test suite. Although it isn't needed, it is cheap to do and makes the test more readable:

Listing 9.22 Integration test for the `atLeast` method

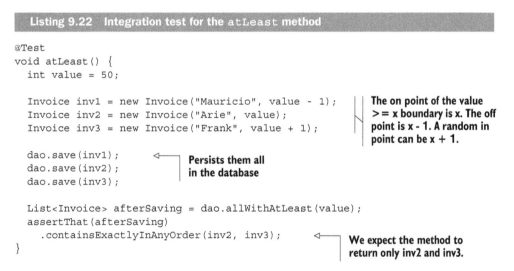

```
@Test
void atLeast() {
  int value = 50;

  Invoice inv1 = new Invoice("Mauricio", value - 1);
  Invoice inv2 = new Invoice("Arie", value);
  Invoice inv3 = new Invoice("Frank", value + 1);

  dao.save(inv1);
  dao.save(inv2);
  dao.save(inv3);

  List<Invoice> afterSaving = dao.allWithAtLeast(value);
  assertThat(afterSaving)
    .containsExactlyInAnyOrder(inv2, inv3);
}
```

The on point of the value >= x boundary is x. The off point is x - 1. A random in point can be x + 1.

Persists them all in the database

We expect the method to return only inv2 and inv3.

The strategy we use to derive the test case is very similar to what we have seen previously. We exercise the on and off points and then ensure that the result is correct. Given where value >= ?, where we concretely replace ? with 50 (see the value variable and the inv2 variable), we have 50 as on point and 49 as off point (value - 1 in inv1).

In addition, we test a single in point. While doing so is not necessary, as we discussed in the boundary testing section in chapter 2, one more test case is cheap and makes the test strategy more comprehensible.

> **NOTE** Your tests should run against a test database—a database set up exclusively for your tests. Needless to say, you do not want to run your tests against the production database.

9.2.3 Setting up infrastructure for SQL tests

In our example, it was simple to open a connection, reset the database state, and so on, but that may become more complicated (or lengthy) when your database schema is complicated. Invest in test infrastructure to facilitate your SQL testing and make sure that when a developer wants to write an integration test, they do not need to set up connections manually or handle transactions. This should be a given from the test suite class.

A strategy I often apply is to create a base class for my integration tests: say, SQL-IntegrationTestBase. This base class handles all the magic, such as creating a connection, cleaning up the database, and closing the connection. Then the test class, such as InvoiceDaoTest, which would extend SQLIntegrationTestBase, focuses only on testing the SQL queries. JUnit allows you to put BeforeEach and AfterEach in base classes, and those are executed as if they were in the child test class.

Another advantage of having all the database logic in the test base class is that future changes will only need to be made in one place. Listing 9.23 shows an implementation example. Note how the InvoiceDaoIntegrationTest code focuses primarily on tests.

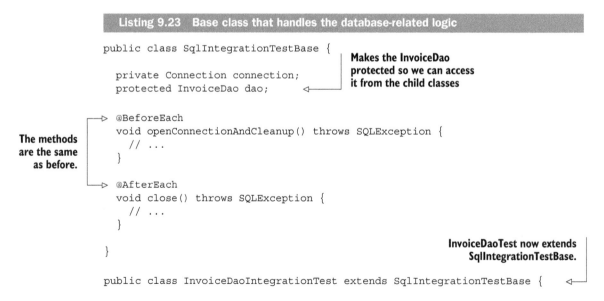

Listing 9.23 Base class that handles the database-related logic

```java
public class SqlIntegrationTestBase {

    private Connection connection;
    protected InvoiceDao dao;           ◁──┐  Makes the InvoiceDao
                                              protected so we can access
                                              it from the child classes

    @BeforeEach
    void openConnectionAndCleanup() throws SQLException {
      // ...
    }

    @AfterEach
    void close() throws SQLException {
      // ...
    }

}

public class InvoiceDaoIntegrationTest extends SqlIntegrationTestBase {   ◁──┘
```

The methods are the same as before.

InvoiceDaoTest now extends SqlIntegrationTestBase.

```
@Test
void save() {
  // ...
}

@Test
void atLeast() {
  // ...
}

}
```

The test class focuses on the tests themselves, as the database infrastructure is handled by the base class.

I will not provide a complete code example, because it changes from project to project. Instead, the following sections list what I do in such an integration test base class.

OPENING THE DATABASE CONNECTION

This means opening a JDBC connection, a Hibernate connection, or the connection of whatever persistence framework you use. In some cases, you may be able to open a single connection per test suite instead of one per test method. In this case, you may want to declare it as static and use JUnit's `BeforeAll` to open and `AfterAll` to close it.

OPENING AND COMMITTING THE TRANSACTION

In more complex database operations, it is common to make them all happen within a transaction scope. In some systems, your framework handles this automatically (think of Spring and its `@Transactional` annotations). In other systems, developers do it by hand, calling something that begins the transaction and later something that commits it.

You should decide on how to handle transactions in your test. A common approach is to open the transaction and, at the end of the test method, commit the transaction. Some people never commit the transaction, but roll it back once the test is over. Because this is an integration test, I suggest committing the transaction for each test method (and not for the entire test class, as we did for the connection).

RESETTING THE STATE OF THE DATABASE

You want all your tests to start with a clean database state. This means ensuring the correct database schema and having no unexpected data in the tables. The simplest way to do this is to truncate every table at the beginning of each test method. If you have many tables, you truncate them all. You can do this by hand (and manually add one `truncate` instruction per table in the code) or use a smarter framework that does it automatically.

Some developers prefer to truncate the tables before the test method, and others after. In the former case, you are sure the database is clean before running the test. In the latter, you ensure that everything is clean afterward, which helps ensure that it will be clean the next time you run it. I prefer to avoid confusion and truncate before the test method.

HELPER METHODS THAT REDUCE THE AMOUNT OF CODE IN THE TESTS

SQL integration test methods can be long. You may need to create many entities and perform more complex assertions. If code can be reused by many other tests, I extract it to a method and move it to the base class. The test classes now all inherit this utility method and can use it. Object builders, frequent assertions, and specific database operations that are often reused are good candidates to become methods in the base class.

9.2.4 *Best practices*

Let's close this section with some final tips on writing tests for SQL queries.

USE TEST DATA BUILDERS

Creating invoices in our earlier example was a simple task. The entity was small and contained only two properties. However, entities in real-world systems are much more complex and may require more work to be instantiated. You do not want to write 15 lines of code and pass 20 parameters to create a simple invoice object. Instead, use helper classes that instantiate test objects for you. These *test data builders,* as they are known, help you quickly build the data structures you need. I will show how to implement test data builders in chapter 10.

USE GOOD AND REUSABLE ASSERTION APIs

Asserting was easy in the example, thanks to AssertJ. However, many SQL queries return lists of objects, and AssertJ provides several methods to assert them in many different ways. If a specific assertion is required by many test methods, do not be afraid to create a utility method that encapsulates this complex assertion. As I discussed, putting it in the base test class is my usual way to go.

MINIMIZE THE REQUIRED DATA

Make sure the input data is minimized. You do not want to have to load hundreds of thousands of elements to exercise your SQL query. If your test only requires data in two tables, only insert data in these two tables. If your test requires no more than 10 rows in that table, only insert 10 rows.

TAKE THE SCHEMA EVOLUTION INTO CONSIDERATION

In real software systems, database schemas evolve quickly. Make sure your test suite is resilient toward these changes. In other words, database evolution should not break the existing test suite. Of course, you cannot (and you probably do not want to) decouple your code completely from the database. But if you are writing a test and notice that a future change may break it, consider reducing the number of points that will require change. Also, if the database changes, you must propagate the change to the test database. If you are using a framework to help you with migration (like Flyway or Liquibase), you can ask the framework to perform the migrations.

CONSIDER (OR DON'T) AN IN-MEMORY DATABASE

You should decide whether your tests will communicate with a real database (the same type of database as in your production environment) or a simpler database (such as an in-memory database). As always, both sides have advantages and disadvantages. Using the same database as in production makes your tests more realistic: your tests will exercise the same SQL engine that will be exercised in production. On the other hand, running full-blown MySQL is much more expensive, computationally speaking, than a simple in-memory database. All in all, I favor using real databases when I am writing SQL integration tests.

9.3 System tests

At some point, your classes, business rules, persistence layers, and so on are combined to form, for example, a web application. Let's think about how a web application traditionally works. Users visit a web page (that is, their browser makes a request to the server, and the server processes the request and returns a response that the browser shows) and interact with the elements on the page. These interactions often trigger other requests and responses. Considering a pet clinic application: a user goes to the web page that lists all the scheduled appointments for today, clicks the New Appointment button, fills out the name of their pet and its owner, and selects an available time slot. The web page then takes the user back to the Appointments page, which now shows the newly added appointment.

If this pet clinic web application was developed using test-driven approaches and everything we discussed in the previous chapters of this book, the developer already wrote (systematic) unit tests for each unit in the software. For example, the `Appointment` class already has unit tests of its own.

In this section, we discuss what to test in a web application and what tools we can use to automatically open the browser and interact with the web page. We also discuss some best practices for writing system tests.

NOTE Although I use a web application as an example of how to write a system test, the ideas in this section apply to any other type of software system.

9.3.1 An introduction to Selenium

Before diving into the best practices, let's get familiar with the mechanics of writing such tests. For that, we will rely on Selenium. The Selenium framework (www.selenium.dev) is a well-known tool that supports developers in testing web applications. Selenium can connect to any browser and control it. Then, through the Selenium API, we can give commands such as "open this URL," "find this HTML element in the page and get its inner text," and "click that button." We will use commands like these to test our web applications.

We use the Spring PetClinic web application (https://projects.spring.io/spring-petclinic) as an example throughout this section. If you are a Java web developer, you are probably familiar with Spring Boot. For those who are not, Spring Boot is the state-of-the-art framework for web development in Java. Spring PetClinic is a simple web application that illustrates how powerful and easy to use Spring Boot is. Its code base contains the two lines required for you to download (via Git) and run (via Maven) the web application. Once you do, you should be able to visit your localhost:8080 and see the web application, shown in figures 9.3 and 9.4.

Figure 9.3   First screenshot of the Spring PetClinic application

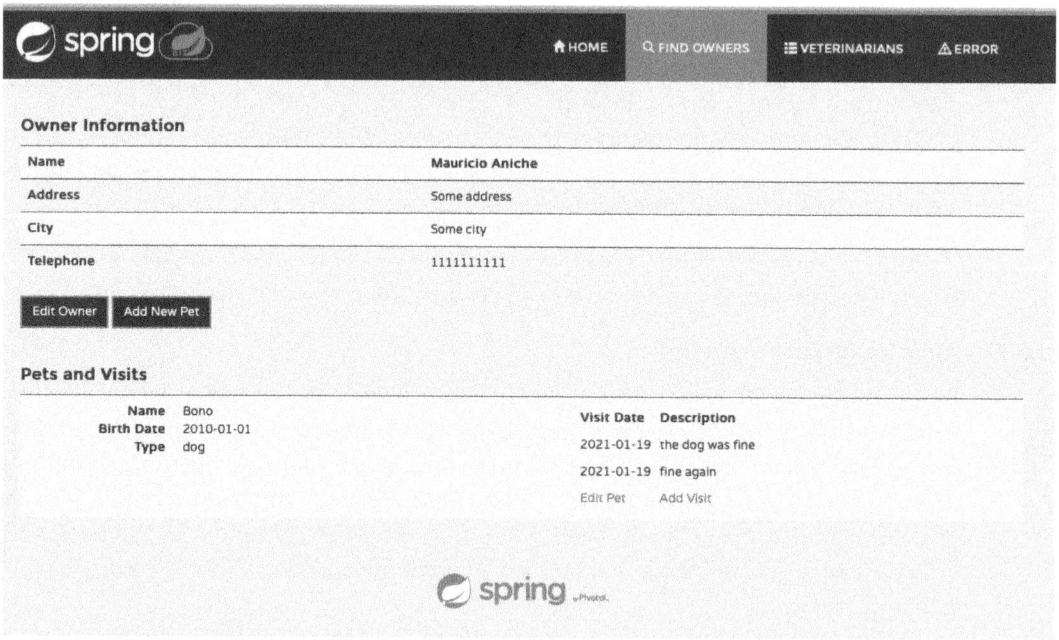

Figure 9.4   Second screenshot of the Spring PetClinic application

Before discussing testing techniques and best practices, let's get started with Selenium. The Selenium API is intuitive and easy to use. The following listing shows our first test.

Listing 9.24 Our first Selenium test

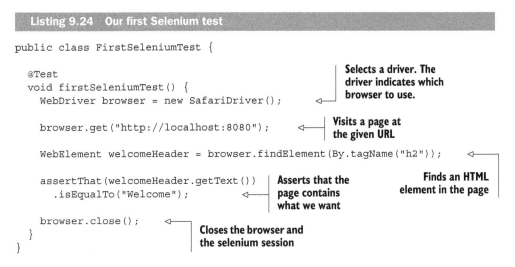

```
public class FirstSeleniumTest {

  @Test
  void firstSeleniumTest() {
    WebDriver browser = new SafariDriver();        ← Selects a driver. The
                                                     driver indicates which
                                                     browser to use.
    browser.get("http://localhost:8080");          ← Visits a page at
                                                     the given URL

    WebElement welcomeHeader = browser.findElement(By.tagName("h2"));  ←

    assertThat(welcomeHeader.getText())   | Asserts that the        Finds an HTML
      .isEqualTo("Welcome");              ← page contains       element in the page
                                          | what we want

    browser.close();   ←
  }                    | Closes the browser and
}                      | the selenium session
```

Let's go line by line:

1 The first line, `WebDriver browser = new SafariDriver()`, instantiates a Safari browser. `WebDriver` is the abstraction that all other browsers implement. If you would like to try a different browser, you can use `new FirefoxBrowser()` or `new ChromeBrowser()` instead. I am using Safari for two reasons:

   a I am a Mac user, and Safari is often my browser of choice.

   b Other browsers, such as Chrome, may require you to download an external application that enables Safari to communicate with it. In the case of Chrome, you need to download ChromeDriver (https://chromedriver.chromium.org/downloads).

2 With an instantiated browser, we visit a URL by means of `browser.get("url");`. Whatever URL we pass, the browser will visit. Remember that Selenium is not simulating the browser: it is using the real browser.

3 The test visits the home page of the Spring PetClinic web app (figure 9.3). This website is very simple and shows a brief message ("Welcome") and a cute picture of a dog and a cat. To ensure that we can extract data from the page we are visiting, let's ensure that the "Welcome" message is on the screen. To do that, we first must locate the element that contains the message. Knowledge of HTML and DOM is required here.

   If you inspect the HTML of the Spring PetClinic, you see that the message is within an h2 tag. Later, we discuss the best ways to locate elements on the page; but for now, we locate the only h2 element. To do so, we use Selenium's `findElement()` function, which receives a strategy that Selenium will use to find the element. We can find elements by their names, IDs, CSS classes, and tag name. `By.tagName("h2")` returns a `WebElement`, an abstraction representing an element on the web page.

4 We extract some properties of this element: in particular, the text inside the `h2` tag. For that, we call the `getText()` method. Because we expect it to return "Welcome", we write an assertion the same way we are used to. Remember, this is an automated test. If the web element does not contain "Welcome", the test will fail.

5 We close the browser. This is an important step, as it disconnects Selenium from the browser. It is always a good practice to close any resources you use in your tests.

If you run the test, you should see Safari (or your browser of choice) open, be automatically controlled by Selenium, and then close. This will get more exciting when we start to fill out forms.

9.3.2 *Designing page objects*

For web applications and system testing, we do not want to exercise just one unit of the system but the entire system. We want to do what we called *system testing* in chapter 1. What should we test in a web application, with all the components working together and an infinite number of different paths to test?

Following what we discussed in the testing pyramid, all the units of the web application are at this point (we hope) already tested at the unit or integration level. The entities in the Spring PetClinic, such as `Owner` or `Pet`, have been unit-tested, and all the queries that may exist in DAOs have also been tested via integration tests similar to what we just did.

But if everything has already been tested, what is left for us to test? We can test the different *user journeys* via web testing. Here is Fowler's definition of a user journey test (2003): "User-journey tests are a form of business-facing test, designed to simulate a typical user's journey through the system. Such a test will typically cover a user's entire interaction with the system to achieve some goal. They act as one path in a use case."

Think of possible user journeys in the Spring PetClinic application. One possible journey is the user trying to find owners. Other possible journeys include the user adding a new owner, adding a pet to the owner, or adding a log entry of the pet after the pet visits the veterinarian.

Let's test one journey: the *find owners* journey. We will code this test using a Page Object pattern. Page objects (POs) help us write more maintainable and readable web tests. The idea of the Page Object pattern is to define a class that encapsulates all the (Selenium) logic involved in manipulating one page.

For example, if the application has a List of Owners page that shows all the owners, we will create a `ListOfOwnersPage` class that will know how to handle it (such as extracting the names of the owners from the HTML). If the application has an Add Owner page, we will create an `AddOwnerPage` class that will know how to handle it (such as filling out the form with the name of the new owner and clicking the button that saves it). Later, we will put all these POs together in a JUnit test, simulate the whole journey, and assert that it went as expected.

When I write Selenium web tests, I prefer to start by designing my POs. Let's begin by modeling the first page of this journey: the Find Owners page. This page is shown in figure 9.5, and the page can be accessed by clicking the Find Owners link in the menu.

We need to type the name of the owner in this HTML field and press the Find Owner button for the search to happen.

Figure 9.5 The Find Owners page

This page primarily contains one interesting thing to be modeled: the "find owners" functionality. For that to work, we need to fill in the Last Name input field and click the Find Owners button. Let's start with that.

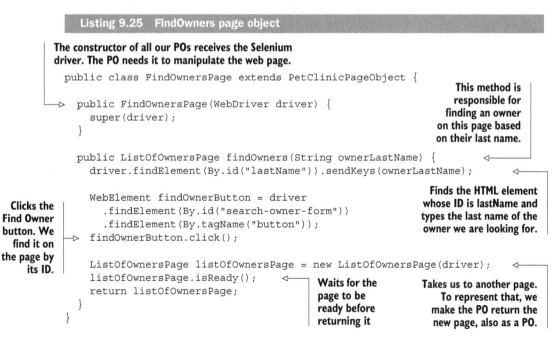

Listing 9.25 FindOwners page object

The constructor of all our POs receives the Selenium driver. The PO needs it to manipulate the web page.

```
public class FindOwnersPage extends PetClinicPageObject {

    public FindOwnersPage(WebDriver driver) {
        super(driver);
    }

    public ListOfOwnersPage findOwners(String ownerLastName) {
        driver.findElement(By.id("lastName")).sendKeys(ownerLastName);

        WebElement findOwnerButton = driver
            .findElement(By.id("search-owner-form"))
            .findElement(By.tagName("button"));
        findOwnerButton.click();

        ListOfOwnersPage listOfOwnersPage = new ListOfOwnersPage(driver);
        listOfOwnersPage.isReady();
        return listOfOwnersPage;
    }
}
```

This method is responsible for finding an owner on this page based on their last name.

Finds the HTML element whose ID is lastName and types the last name of the owner we are looking for.

Clicks the Find Owner button. We find it on the page by its ID.

Waits for the page to be ready before returning it

Takes us to another page. To represent that, we make the PO return the new page, also as a PO.

Let's look at this code line by line:

1 The newly created class `FindOwnersPage` represents the Find Owners page. It inherits from another class, `PetClinicPageObject`, which will serve as a common abstraction for our POs. I show its source code later.

2 Our POs always have a constructor that receives a `WebDriver`. Everything we do with Selenium starts with the `WebDriver` class, which we will instantiate later from a JUnit test method.

3 Methods in this PO represent actions we can take with the page we are modeling. The first action we modeled is `findOwners()`, which fills the Last Name input with the value passed to the `ownerLastName` string parameter.

4 The implementation of the method is straightforward. We first locate the HTML input element. By inspecting the Spring PetClinic web page, we see that the field has an ID. Elements with IDs are usually easy to find, as IDs are unique in the page. With the element in hand, we use the `sendKeys()` function to fill in the input with `ownerLastName`. Selenium's API is fluent, so we can chain the method calls: `findElement(…).sendKeys(…)`.

5 We search for the Find Owner button. When inspecting the page, we see that this button does not have a specific ID. This means we need to find another way to locate it on the HTML page. My first instinct is to see if this button's HTML form has an ID. It does: `search-owner-form`. We can locate the form and then locate a button inside it (as this form has one button).

   Note how we chain calls for the `findElement` method. Remember that HTML elements may have other HTML elements inside them. Therefore, the first `findElement()` returns the form, and the second `findElement` searches only the elements inside the element returned by the first `findElement`. With the button available to us, we call the `click()` method, which clicks the button. The form is now submitted.

6 The website takes us to another page that shows the list of owners with the searched last name. This is no longer the Find Owners page, so we should now use another PO to represent the current page. That is why we make the `findOwners()` method return a `ListOfOwnersPage`: one page takes you to another page.

7 Before we return the newly instantiated `ListOfOwnersPage`, we call an `isReady()` method. This method waits for the Owners page to be ready. Remember that this is a web application, so requests and responses may take some time. If we try to look for an element from the page, but the element is not there yet, the test will fail. Selenium has a set of APIs that enable us to wait for such things, which we will see soon.

We still have more POs to model before writing the test for the entire journey. Let's model the Owners page, shown in figure 9.6. This page contains a table in which each row represents one owner.

Figure 9.6 The Owners page

Our `ListOfOwnersPage` PO models a single action that will be very important for our test later: getting the list of owners in this table. The following listing shows the source code.

Listing 9.26 `ListOfOwners` PO

As we know, all POs receive the
WebDriver in the constructor.

```
public class ListOfOwnersPage extends PetClinicPageObject {
  public ListOfOwnersPage(WebDriver driver) {
    super(driver);
  }

  @Override
  public void isReady() {
    WebDriverWait wait = new WebDriverWait (driver, Duration.ofSeconds(3));
    wait.until(
      ExpectedConditions.visibilityOfElementLocated(
      By.id("owners")));
  }

  public List<OwnerInfo> all() {
    List<OwnerInfo> owners = new ArrayList<>();

    WebElement table = driver.findElement(By.id("owners"));
    List<WebElement> rows = table.findElement(By.tagName(
      "tbody")).findElements(By.tagName("tr"));

    for (WebElement row : rows) {

      List<WebElement> columns = row.findElements(By.tagName("td"));

      String name = columns.get(0).getText().trim();
      String address = columns.get(1).getText().trim();
      String city = columns.get(2).getText().trim();
      String telephone = columns.get(3).getText().trim();
      String pets = columns.get(4).getText().trim();
```

The isReady method lets us know whether the page is ready in the browser so we can start manipulating it. This is important, as some pages take more time than others to load.

The Owners page is considered ready when the list of owners is loaded. We find the table with owners by its ID. We wait up to three seconds for that to happen.

Creates a list to hold all the owners. For that, we create an OwnerInfo class.

Gets the HTML table and all its rows. The table's ID is owners, which makes it easy to find.

For each row in the table ...

... gets the HTML row

Gets the value of each HTML cell. The first column contains the name, the second the address, and so on.

```
        OwnerInfo ownerInfo = new OwnerInfo(
          ⮡ name, address, city, telephone, pets);
        owners.add(ownerInfo);
      }

    return owners;
  }
}
```

Once all the information is collected from the HTML, we build an OwnerInfo class.

Returns a list of OwnerInfos. This object knows nothing about the HTML page.

Let's walk through this code:

1 Our class is a PO, so it extends from `PetClinicPageObject`, which forces the class to have a constructor that receives a `WebDriver`. We still have not seen the `PetClinicPageObject` code, but we will soon.

2 The `isReady()` method (which you can see by the `@Override` annotation is also defined in the base class) knows when this page is loaded. How do we do this? The simplest way is to wait a few seconds for a specific element to appear on the page. In this case, we wait for the element with ID "owners" (the table with all the owners) to be on the page. We tell `WebDriverWait` to wait up to three seconds for the `owners` element to be visible. If the element is not there after three seconds, the method throws an exception. Why three seconds? That was a guess; in practice, you have to find the number that best fits your test.

3 We return to our main action: the `all()` method. The objective is to extract the names of all the owners. Because this is an HTML table, we know that each row is in a `tr` element. The table has a header, which we want to ignore. So, we locate `#owners > tbody > tr` or, in other words, all `tr`s inside `tbody` that are inside the `owners` element. We do this using nested `findElement()` and `findElements()` calls. Note the difference between the two methods: one returns a single element, the other multiple elements (useful in this case, as we know there are many `tr`s to be returned).

4 With the list of rows ready, we iterate over each element. We know that `tr`s are composed of `td`s. We find all `td`s inside the current `tr` and extract the text inside each `td`, one by one. We know the first cell contains the name, the second cell contains the address, and so on. We then build an object to hold this information: the `OwnerInfo` class. This is a simple class with getters only. We also `trim()` the string to get rid of any whitespaces in the HTML.

5 We return the list of owners in the table.

Now, searching for an owner with their surname takes us to the next page, where we can extract the list of owners. Figure 9.7 illustrates the two POs we have implemented so far and which pages of the web application they model.

We are only missing two things. First and foremost, to search for an owner, the owner must be in the application. How do we add a new owner? We use the Add Owner page. So, we need to model one more PO. Second we need a way to visit these pages for the first time.

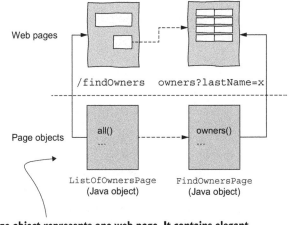

Web pages

/findOwners   owners?lastName=x

Page objects

ListOfOwnersPage   FindOwnersPage
(Java object)   (Java object)

Each page object represents one web page. It contains elegant methods that know how to manipulate the page. Test methods use these page objects to test the web application.

Figure 9.7   An illustration of web pages and their respective POs

NOTE *Much more work* is required to write a test for a single journey than we are used to when doing unit tests. System tests are naturally more expensive to create. But I also want you to recognize that adding a new test becomes easier once you have an initial structure with POs. The high cost comes now, when building this initial infrastructure.

Let's start with adding an owner. The next listing shows the AddOwnerPage PO.

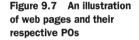

Listing 9.27   .AddOwnerPage page object

```java
public class AddOwnerPage extends PetClinicPageObject {
  public AddOwnerPage(WebDriver driver) {
    super(driver);
  }

  @Override
  public void isReady() {
    WebDriverWait wait = new WebDriverWait (driver, Duration.ofSeconds(3));
    wait.until(
      ExpectedConditions.visibilityOfElementLocated(
      By.id("add-owner-form")));
  }

  public OwnerInformationPage add(AddOwnerInfo ownerToBeAdded) {
    driver.findElement(By.id("firstName"))
      .sendKeys(ownerToBeAdded.getFirstName());
    driver.findElement(By.id("lastName"))
      .sendKeys(ownerToBeAdded.getLastName());
    driver.findElement(By.id("address"))
      .sendKeys(ownerToBeAdded.getAddress());
    driver.findElement(By.id("city"))
      .sendKeys(ownerToBeAdded.getCity());
    driver.findElement(By.id("telephone"))
      .sendKeys(ownerToBeAdded.getTelephone());
```

Again, the PO receives the WebDriver.

The HTML page is ready when the form appears on the screen.

Fills out all the HTML form elements with the data provided in AddOwnerInfo, a class created for that purpose. We find the form elements by their IDs.

```
driver.findElement(By.id("add-owner-form"))        │  Clicks the
    .findElement(By.tagName("button"))             │  Add button
    .click();                                  ◁────┘

OwnerInformationPage ownerInformationPage =
    new OwnerInformationPage(driver);       ◁─────
ownerInformationPage.isReady();                   │  When an owner is added, the web
return ownerInformationPage;                      │  application redirects us to the Owner
  }                                               │  Information page. The method then
}                                                 │  returns the PO of the class we are
                                                  │  redirected to.
```

The implementation should not be a surprise. The isReady() method waits for the form to be ready. The add() method, which is the relevant method here, finds the input elements (which all have specific IDs, making our lives much easier), fills them in, finds the Add Owner button, and returns the PO that represents the page we go to after adding an owner: OwnerInformationPage. I do not show its code, to save space, but it is a PO much like the others we have seen.

Finally, all we need is a way to visit the pages. I usually have a visit() method in my POs to take me directly to that page. Let's add a visit() method to the POs we need to visit: the Find Owner page and the Add Owner page.

Listing 9.28   Adding `visit()` methods to all the POs

```
// FindOwnersPage
public void visit() {
  visit("/owners/find");
}

// AddOwnersPage
public void visit() {
  visit("/owners/new");
}
```

Note that these visit() methods call another visit method in the superclass.

Now it is time to show the PO base class. This is where we put common behavior that all our POs have. Base classes like these support and simplify the development of our tests.

Listing 9.29   Initial code of the PO base class

```
public abstract class PetClinicPageObject {        The base class keeps
                                                   the reference to the
  protected final WebDriver driver;          ◁───  WebDriver.

  public PetClinicPageObject(WebDriver driver) {
    this.driver = driver;
  }                                                The visit method
                                                   should be overridden
  public void visit() {                       ◁─── by the child classes.
    throw new RuntimeException("This page does not have a visit link");
  }
```

```
    protected void visit(String url) {            ◄          Provides a helper
      driver.get("http://localhost:8080" + url);             method for the base
      isReady();                                             classes to help them
    }                                                        visit the page

    public abstract void isReady();              ◄          All POs are forced to implement an isReady
  }                                                          method. Making methods abstract is a nice
  The hard-coded URL can come                                way to force all POs to implement their
  from a configuration file.                                 minimum required behavior.
```

You can make this PO base class as complex as you need. In more involved apps, the base class is more complex and full of helper methods. For now, we have a constructor that receives `WebDriver` (forcing all POs to have the same constructor), a `visit()` method that can be overridden by child POs, a helper `visit()` method that completes the URL with the localhost URL, and an abstract `isReady()` method that forces all POs to implement this functionality.

We now have enough POs to model our first journey. The following listing shows a JUnit test.

Listing 9.30 Our first journey: find owners

```
                                          Creates a concrete WebDriver, the SafariDriver.
                                          Later, we will make this more flexible so our
public class FindOwnersFlowTest {         tests can run in multiple browsers.

  protected static WebDriver driver = new SafariDriver();       ◄

  private FindOwnersPage page = new FindOwnersPage(driver);   ◄──   Creates the
                                                                    FindOwners PO,
  @AfterAll                    When the test suite is done, we      where the test
  static void close() {     ◄  close the Selenium driver. This      should start
    driver.close();            method is also a good candidate
  }                            to move to a base class.

                                          Creates a bunch of owners to
  @Test                                   be added. We need owners
  void findOwnersBasedOnTheirLastNames() {    before testing the listing page.
    AddOwnerInfo owner1 = new AddOwnerInfo(
      "John", "Doe", "some address", "some city", "11111");   ◄
    AddOwnerInfo owner2 = new AddOwnerInfo(
      "Jane", "Doe", "some address", "some city", "11111");
    AddOwnerInfo owner3 = new AddOwnerInfo(
      "Sally", "Smith", "some address", "some city", "11111");
    addOwners(owner1, owner2, owner3);

    page.visit();                        Visits the Find          Looks for all
                                         Owners page              owners with Doe
                                                                  as their surname
    ListOfOwnersPage listPage = page.findOwners("Doe");   ◄
    List<OwnerInfo> all = listPage.all();

    assertThat(all).hasSize(2).                                   Asserts that we find
      containsExactlyInAnyOrder(                                  John and Jane from
      owner1.toOwnerInfo(), owner2.toOwnerInfo());   ◄           the Doe family
  }
}
```

```
private void addOwners(AddOwnerInfo... owners) {
  AddOwnerPage addOwnerPage = new AddOwnerPage(driver);

  for (AddOwnerInfo owner : owners) {
    addOwnerPage.visit();
    addOwnerPage.add(owner);
  }
 }
}
```

The addOwners helper method adds an owner via the Add Owner page.

Let's walk through this code:

1 At the top of the class, we create a static instance of `SafariDriver`, which we enclose in the `@AfterAll` method. To save some time (opening and closing the browser for every test), we only need one instance of `WebDriver` for all the tests in this class. For now, this means our test has the Safari browser hard-coded. Later we will discuss how to make it more flexible so you can run your test suite in multiple browsers.

2 The `findOwnersBasedOnTheirLastNames()` method contains our journey. We create two fake `AddOwnerInfos`: two owners that will be added to the application. For each owner, we visit the Add Owner page, fill in the information, and save. (I created an `addOwners()` private helper method to increase the readability of the main test method.)

3 We visit the Owners page and get all the owners in the list. We expect both newly added owners to be there, so we assert that the list contains two items and they are the two owners we created.

4 `AddOwnerInfo`, the data structure used by `AddOwnerPage`, is different from `OwnerInfo`, the data structure returned by the `ListOfOwnersPage` page. In one, a name is the first name and last name together, and in the other, the first name and last name are separate. We could use a single data structure for both or design them separately. I chose to design them separately, so I needed to convert from one to another. So, I implemented `toOwnerInfo()` in the `AddOwnerInfo` class. It is a simple method, as you see in the next listing.

Listing 9.31 `toOwnerInfo converter` method

```
public OwnerInfo toOwnerInfo() {
  return new OwnerInfo(firstName + " " + lastName, address, city, telephone, "");
}
```

Now, when we run the test, it looks almost like magic: the browser opens, the names of the owners are typed in the page, buttons are clicked, pages change, the browser closes, and JUnit shows us that the test passed. We are finished with our first web Selenium test.

NOTE A good exercise for you is to write tests for other application journeys. This will require the development of more POs!

If you run the test again, it will fail. The list of owners will return four people instead of two, as the test expects—we are running our entire web application, and data is persisted in the database. We need to make sure we can reset the web application whenever we run a test, and we discuss that in the next section.

9.3.3 *Patterns and best practices*

You probably noticed that the amount of code required to get our first system test working was much greater than in previous chapters. In this section, I introduce some patterns and best practices that will help you write maintainable web tests. These patterns come from my own experience after writing many such tests. Together with Guerra and Gerosa, I proposed some of these patterns at the PLoP conference in 2014.

PROVIDE A WAY TO SET THE SYSTEM TO THE STATE THAT THE WEB TEST REQUIRES

To ensure that the Find Owners journey worked properly, we needed some owners in the database. We added them by repeatedly navigating to the Add Owner page, filling in the form, and saving it. This strategy works fine in simple cases. However, imagine a more complicated scenario where your test requires 10 different entities in the database. Visiting 10 different web pages in a specific order is too much work (and also slow, since the test would take a considerable amount of time to visit all the pages).

In such cases, I suggest creating all the required data *before* running the test. But how do you do that if the web application runs standalone and has its own database? You can provide web services (say, REST web services) that are easily accessible by the test. This way, whenever you need some data in the application, you can get it through simple requests. Imagine that instead of visiting the pages, we call the API. From the test side, we implement classes that abstract away all the complexity of calling a remote web service. The following listing shows how the previous test would look if it consumed a web service.

Listing 9.32 **Our test if we had a web service to add owners**

```
@Test
void findOwnersBasedOnTheirLastNames() {
  AddOwnerInfo owner1 = new AddOwnerInfo(
    "John", "Doe", "some address", "some city", "11111");
  AddOwnerInfo owner2 = new AddOwnerInfo(
    "Jane", "Doe", "some address", "some city", "11111");
  AddOwnerInfo owner3 = new AddOwnerInfo(
    "Sally", "Smith", "some address", "some city", "11111");

  OwnersAPI api = new OwnersAPI();      ⟵──── Calls the API. We no longer need to visit
  api.add(owner1);                             the Add Owner page. The OwnersAPI
  api.add(owner2);                             class hides the complexity of calling
  api.add(owner3);                             a web service.

  page.visit();
  ListOfOwnersPage listPage = page.findOwners("Doe");
  List<OwnerInfo> all = listPage.all();
```

```
assertThat(all).hasSize(2).
    containsExactlyInAnyOrder(owner1.toOwnerInfo(), owner2.toOwnerInfo());
}
```

Creating simple REST web services is easy today, given the full support of the web frameworks. In Spring MVC (or Ruby, or Django, or Asp.Net Core), you can write one in a couple of lines. The same thing happens from the client side. Calling a REST web service is simple, and you don't have to write much code.

You may be thinking of security issues. What if you do not want the web services in production? If they are only for testing purposes, your software should hide the API when in production and allow the API only in the testing environment.

Moreover, do not be afraid to write different functionalities for these APIs, if doing so makes the testing process easier. If your web page needs a combination of Products, Invoices, Baskets, and Items, perhaps you can devise a web service solely to help the test build up complex data.

MAKE SURE EACH TEST ALWAYS RUNS IN A CLEAN ENVIRONMENT

Similar to what we did earlier when testing SQL queries, we must make sure our tests always run in a clean version of the web application. Otherwise, the test may fail for reasons other than a bug. This means databases (and any other dependencies) must only contain the bare minimum amount of data for the test to start.

We can reset the web application the same way we provide data to it: via web services. The application could provide an easy backdoor that resets it. It goes without saying that such a web service should never be deployed in production.

Resetting the web application often means resetting the database. You can implement that in many different ways, such as truncating all the tables or dropping and recreating them.

> **WARNING** Be very careful. The reset backdoor is nice for tests, but if it is deployed into production, chaos may result. If you use this solution, make sure it is only available in the test environment!

GIVE MEANINGFUL NAMES TO YOUR HTML ELEMENTS

Locating elements is a vital part of a web test, and we do that by, for example, searching for their name, class, tag, or XPath. In one of our examples, we first searched for the form the element was in and then found the element by its tag. But user interfaces change frequently during the life of a website. That is why web test suites are often highly unstable. We do not want a change in the presentation of a web page (such as moving a button from the left menu to the right menu) to break the test.

Therefore, I suggest assigning proper (unique) names and IDs to elements that will play a role in the test. Even if the element does not need an ID, giving it one will simplify the test and make sure the test will not break if the presentation of the element changes.

If for some reason an element has a very unstable ID (perhaps it is dynamically generated), we need to create any specific property for the testing. HTML5 allows us to create extra attributes on HTML tags, like the following example.

> **Listing 9.33 HTML element with a property that makes it easy to find**

```
<input type="text"
id="customer_\${i}"
name="customer"
data-selenium="customer-name" />
```

It is easy to find the HTML element that has a data-selenium attribute with customer-name as its value.

If you think this extra property may be a problem in the production environment, remove it during deployment. There are many tools that manipulate HTML pages before deploying them (minification is an example).

NOTE Before applying this pattern to the project, you may want to talk to your team's frontend lead.

Visit every step of a journey only when that journey is under test

Unlike unit testing, building up scenarios on a system test can be complicated. We saw that some journeys may require the test to navigate through many different pages before getting to the page it wants to test.

Imagine a specific page A that requires the test to visit pages B, C, D, E, and F before it can finally get to A and test it. A test for that page is shown here.

> **Listing 9.34 A very long test that calls many POs**

```
@Test
void longest() {
  BPage b = new BPage();
  b.action1(..);
  b.action2(..);

  CPage c = new CPage();
  c.action1(..);

  DPage d = new DPage();
  d.action1(..);
  d.action2(..);

  EPage e = new EPage();
  e.action1(..);

  FPage e = new FPage();
  f.action1(..);

  // finally!!
  APage a = new APage();
  a.action1();

  assertThat(a.confirmationAppears()).isTrue();
}
```

Calls the first PO

Calls a second PO

Calls a third PO, and so on

Note how long and complex the test is. We discussed a similar problem, and our solution was to provide a web service that enabled us to skip many of the page visits. But if visiting all these pages is part of the journey under test, the test should visit each one. If one or two of these steps are not part of the journey, you can use the web services.

ASSERTIONS SHOULD USE DATA THAT COMES FROM THE POs

In the Find Owners test, our assertions focused on checking whether all the owners were on the list. In the code, the `FindOwnersPage` PO provided an `all()` method that returned the owners. The test code was only responsible for the assertion. This is a good practice. Whenever your tests require information from the page for the assertion, the PO provides this information. Your JUnit test should not locate HTML elements by itself. However, the assertions stay in the JUnit test code.

PASS IMPORTANT CONFIGURATIONS TO THE TEST SUITE

The example test suite has some hard-coded details, such as the local URL of the application (right now, it is localhost:8080) and the browser to run the tests (currently Safari). However, you may need to change these configurations dynamically. For example, your continuous integration may need to run the web app on a different port, or you may want to run your test suite on Chrome.

There are many different ways to pass configuration to Java tests, but I usually opt for the simplest approach: everything that is a configuration is provided by a method in my `PageObject` base class. For example, a `String baseUrl()` method returns the base URL of the application, and a `WebDriver browser()` method returns the concrete instance of `WebDriver`. These methods then read from a configuration file or an environment variable, as those are easy to pass via build scripts.

RUN YOUR TESTS IN MULTIPLE BROWSERS

You should run your tests in multiple browsers to be sure everything works everywhere. But I don't do this on my machine, because it takes too much time. Instead, my continuous integration (CI) tool has a multiple-stage process that runs the web test suite multiple times, each time passing a different browser. If configuring such a CI is an issue, consider using a service such as SauceLabs (https://saucelabs.com), which automates this process for you.

9.4   *Final notes on larger tests*

I close this chapter with some points I have not yet mentioned regarding larger tests.

9.4.1   *How do all the testing techniques fit?*

In the early chapters of this book, our goal was to explore techniques that would help you engineer test cases systematically. In this chapter, we discuss a more orthogonal topic: how large should our tests be? I have shown you examples of larger component tests, integration tests, and system tests. But regardless of the test level, engineering good test cases should still be the focus.

When you write a larger test, use the requirement and its boundaries, the structure of the code, and the properties it should uphold to engineer good test cases. The challenge is that an entire component has a much larger requirement and a much larger code base, which means many more tests to engineer.

I follow this rule of thumb: exercise everything at the unit level (you can easily cover entire requirements and structures at the unit level), and exercise the most important behavior in larger tests (so you have more confidence that the program will work when the pieces are put together). It may help to reread about the testing pyramid in section 1.4 in chapter 1.

9.4.2 *Perform cost/benefit analysis*

One of the testing mantras is that a good test is cheap to write but can capture important bugs. Unit tests are cheap to write, so we do not have to think much about cost.

Larger tests may not be cheap to write, run, or maintain. I have seen integration test suites that take hours to run—and cases where developers spend hours writing a single integration test.

Therefore, it is fundamental to perform a simple cost/benefit analysis. Questions like "How much will it cost me to write this test?" "How much will it cost to run?" "What is the benefit of this test? What bugs will it catch?" and "Is this functionality already covered by unit tests? If so, do I need to cover it via integration tests, too?" may help you understand whether this is a fundamental test.

The answer will be "yes" in many cases. The benefits outweigh the costs, so you should write the test. If the cost is too high, consider simplifying your test. Can you stub parts of the test without losing too much? Can you write a more focused test that exercises a smaller part of the system? As always, there is no single good answer or golden rule to follow.

9.4.3 *Be careful with methods that are covered but not tested*

Larger tests exercise more classes, methods, and behaviors together. In addition to all the trade-offs discussed in this chapter, with larger tests, the chances of covering a method but not testing it are much higher.

Vera-Pérez and colleagues (2019) coined the term *pseudo-tested methods*. These methods are tested, but if we replace their entire implementation with a simple `return null`, tests still pass. And believe it or not, Vera-Pérez and colleagues show that pseudo-tested methods happen in the wild, even in important open source projects. This is another reason I defend both unit tests *and* larger tests, used together to ensure that everything works.

9.4.4 *Proper code infrastructure is key*

Integration and system tests both require a decent infrastructure behind the scenes. Without it, we may spend too much time setting up the environment or asserting that behavior was as expected. My key advice here is to invest in test infrastructure. Your infrastructure should help developers set up the environment, clean up the environment, retrieve complex data, assert complex data, and perform whatever other complex tasks are required to write tests.

9.4.5 *DSLs and tools for stakeholders to write tests*

In this chapter, we wrote the system tests ourselves with lots of Java code. At this level, it is also common to see more automation. Some tools, such as the Robot framework (https://robotframework.org) and Cucumber (https://cucumber.io), even allow you to write tests in language that is almost completely natural. These tools make a lot of sense if you want others to write tests, too, such as (non-technical) stakeholders.

9.4.6 *Testing other types of web systems*

The higher we go in levels of testing, such as web testing, the more we start to think about the frameworks and environment our application runs in. Our web application is responsive; how do we test for that? If we use Angular or React, how do we test it? Or, if we use a non-relational database like Mongo, how do we test it?

Testing these specific technologies is far beyond the scope of this book. My suggestion is that you visit those communities and explore their state-of-the-art tools and bodies of knowledge. All the test case engineering techniques you learn in this book will apply to your software, regardless of the technology.

SYSTEM TESTS IN SOFTWARE OTHER THAN WEB APPLICATIONS

I used web applications to exemplify system tests because I have a lot of experience with them. But the idea of system testing can be applied to any type of software you develop. If your software is a library or framework, your system tests will exercise the entire library as the clients would. If your software is a mobile application, your system tests will exercise the mobile app as the clients would.

The best practices I discussed still apply. Engineering system tests will be harder than engineering unit tests, and you may need some infrastructure code (like the POs we created) to make you more productive. There are probably also specific best practices for your type of software—be sure to do some research.

Exercises

9.1 Which of the following recommendations should you follow to keep a web application testable? Select all that apply.

    A Use TypeScript instead of JavaScript.

    B Make sure the HTML elements can be found easily from the tests.

    C Make sure requests to web servers are performed asynchronously.

    D Avoid inline JavaScript in an HTML page.

9.2 Which of the following statements is true about end-to-end/system testing?

    A End-to-end testing cannot be automated for web applications and therefore has to be performed manually.

    B In web testing, end-to-end testing is more important than unit testing.

    C End-to-end testing can be used to verify whether the frontend and back-end work together well.

    D End-to-end tests are, like unit tests, not very realistic.

9.3 Which of the following is true about page objects?

    A POs abstract the HTML page to facilitate the engineering of end-to-end tests.

    B POs cannot be used in highly complex web applications.

    C By introducing a PO, we no longer need libraries like Selenium.

    D POs usually make the test code more complex.

9.4 Which of the following are important recommendations for developers who are engineering integration and system test suites? Choose all that apply.

    A What can be tested via unit testing should be tested via unit testing. Use integration and system tests for bugs that can only be caught at that level.

    B It is fundamental for developers to have a solid infrastructure to write such tests, as otherwise, they would feel unproductive.

    C If something is already covered via unit testing, you should not cover it (again) via integration testing.

    D Too many integration tests may mean your application is badly designed. Focus on unit tests.

9.5 Which of the following can cause web tests to be flaky (that is, sometimes pass, sometimes fail)? Choose all that apply.

    A AJAX requests that take longer than expected

    B The use of LESS and SASS instead of pure CSS

    C The database of the web app under test is not being cleaned up after every test run

    D Some components of the web app were unavailable at the time

Summary

- Developers benefit from writing larger tests, ranging from testing entire components together, to integrating with external parties, to entire systems.
- Engineering larger tests is more challenging than writing unit tests, because the component under test is probably much bigger and more complex than a single unit of the system.
- All the test case engineering techniques we have discussed—specification-based testing, boundary testing, structural testing, and property-based testing—apply to larger tests.
- Investing in a good test infrastructure for large tests is a requirement. Without it, you will spend too much time writing a single test case.

Test code quality

10

This chapter covers

- Principles and best practices of good and maintainable test code
- Avoiding test smells that hinder the comprehension and evolution of test code

You have probably noticed that once *test infected*, the number of JUnit tests a software development team writes and maintains can become significant. In practice, test code bases grow quickly. Moreover, we have observed that Lehman's law of evolution, "Code tends to rot, unless one actively works against it" (1980), also applies to test code. A 2018 literature review by Garousi and Küçük shows that our body of knowledge about things that can go wrong with test code is already comprehensive.

As with production code, *we must put extra effort into writing high-quality test code bases so they can be maintained and developed sustainably.* In this chapter, I discuss two opposite perspectives of writing test code. First, we examine what constitutes good and maintainable test code, and best practices that can help you keep complexity under control. Then we look at what constitutes problematic test code. We focus on key *test smells* that hinder test code comprehension and evolution.

I have discussed some of this material informally in previous chapters. This chapter consolidates that knowledge.

10.1 Principles of maintainable test code

What does good test code look like? There is a great deal of literature about test code quality, which I rely on in this section. Much of what I say here can be found in the works of Langr, Hunt, and Thomas (2015); Meszaros (2007); and Beck (2019)—as always, with my own twist.

10.1.1 Tests should be fast

Tests are a developer's safety net. Whenever we perform maintenance or evolution in source code, we use the feedback from the test suite to understand whether the system is working as expected. The faster we get feedback from the test code, the better. Slower test suites force us to run the tests less often, making them less effective. Therefore, good tests are fast. There is no hard line that separates slow from fast tests. You should apply common sense.

If you are facing a slow test, consider the following:

- Using mocks or stubs to replace slower components that are part of the test
- Redesigning the production code so slower pieces of code can be tested separately from fast pieces of code
- Moving slower tests to a different test suite that you can run less often

Sometimes you cannot avoid slow tests. Think of SQL tests: they are much slower than unit tests, but there is not much you can do about it. I separate slow tests from fast ones: this way, I can run my fast tests all the time and the slow tests when I modify the production code that has a slow test tied to it. I also run the slow tests before committing my code and in continuous integration.

10.1.2 Tests should be cohesive, independent, and isolated

Tests should be as cohesive, independent, and isolated as possible. Ideally, a single test method should test a single functionality or behavior of the system. *Fat tests* (or, as the test smells community calls them, *eager tests*) exercise multiple functionalities and are often complex in terms of implementation. Complex test code reduces our ability to understand what is being tested at a glance and makes future maintenance more difficult. If you face such a test, break it into multiple smaller tests. Simpler and shorter tests are better.

Moreover, tests should not depend on other tests to succeed. The test result should be the same whether the test is executed in isolation or together with the rest of the test suite. It is not uncommon to see cases where test B only works if test A is executed first. This is often the case when test B relies on the work of test A to set up the environment for it. Such tests become highly unreliable.

If you have a test that is somewhat dependent on another test, refactor the test suite so each test is responsible for setting up the whole environment it needs. Another tip that helps make tests independent is to make sure your tests clean up their messes: for example, by deleting any files they created on the disk and cleaning up values they inserted into a database. This will force tests to set up things themselves and not rely on data that was already there.

10.1.3   Tests should have a reason to exist

You want tests that either help you find bugs or help you document behavior. You *do not* want tests that, for example, increase code coverage. If a test does not have a good reason to exist, it should not exist. Remember that you must maintain all your tests. The perfect test suite is one that can detect all the bugs with the minimum number of tests. While having such a perfect test suite is impossible, making sure you do not have useless tests is a good start.

10.1.4   Tests should be repeatable and not flaky

A *repeatable* test gives the same result no matter how many times it is executed. Developers lose their trust in tests that present flaky behavior (sometimes pass and sometimes fail, without any changes in the system or test code).

Flaky tests hurt the productivity of software development teams. It is hard to know whether a flaky test is failing because the behavior is buggy or because it is flaky. Little by little, flaky tests can make us lose confidence in our test suites. Such lack of confidence may lead us to deploy our systems even though the tests fail (they may be broken because of flakiness, not because the system is misbehaving).

The prevalence and impact of flaky tests in the software development world have increased over time (or, at least, we talk more about them now). Companies like Google and Facebook have publicly talked about problems caused by flaky tests.

A test can become flaky for many reasons:

- *Because it depends on external or shared resources*—If a test depends on a database, many things can cause flakiness. For example, the database may not be available at the moment the test is executed, it may contain data that the test does not expect, or two developers may be running the test suite at the same time and sharing the same database, causing one to break the test of the other.
- *Due to improper time-outs*—This is a common reason in web testing. Suppose a test has to wait for something to happen in the system: for example, a request coming back from a web service, which is then displayed in an HTML element. If the web application is slower than normal, the test may fail because it did not wait long enough.
- *Because of a hidden interaction between different test methods*—Test A somehow influences the result of test B, possibly causing it to fail.

The work of Luo et al. (2014) also shed light on the causes of flaky tests. After analyzing 201 flaky tests in open source systems, the authors noticed the following:

- Async wait, concurrency, and test order dependency are the three most common causes of flakiness.
- Most flaky tests are flaky from the time they are written.

- Flaky tests are rarely due to the platform-specifics (they do not fail because of different operating systems).
- Flakiness is often due to dependencies on external resources and can be fixed by cleaning the shared state between test runs.

Detecting the cause of a flaky test is challenging. Software engineering researchers have proposed automated tools to detect flaky tests. If you are curious about such tools and the current state of the art, I suggest that you read the following:

- The work of Bell et al. (2018), who proposed DeFlaker, a tool that monitors the coverage of the latest code changes and marks a test as flaky if any new failing test did not exercise any of the changed code.
- The work of Lam et al. (2019), who proposed iDFlakies, a tool that executes tests in random order, looking for flakiness.

Because these tools are not fully ready, it is up to us to find the flaky tests and fix them. Meszaros has made a decision table that may help you with that task. You can find it in his book (2007) or on his website (http://xunitpatterns.com/Erratic%20Test.html).

10.1.5 Tests should have strong assertions

Tests exist to assert that the exercised code behaved as expected. Writing good assertions is therefore key to a good test. An extreme example of a test with bad assertions is one with *no* assertions. This seems strange, but believe it or not, it happens—not because we do not know what we are doing, but because writing a good assertion can be tricky. In cases where observing the outcome of behavior is not easily achievable, I suggest refactoring the class or method under test to increase its observability. Revisit chapter 7 if you need tips for how to do so.

Assertions should be as strong as possible. You want your tests to fully validate the behavior and break if there is any slight change in the output. Imagine that a method `calculateFinalPrice()` in a `ShoppingCart` class changes two properties: `finalPrice` and the `taxPaid`. If your tests only ensure the value of the `finalPrice` property, a bug may happen in the way `taxPaid` is set, and your tests will not notice it. Make sure you are asserting everything that needs to be asserted.

10.1.6 Tests should break if the behavior changes

Tests let you know that you broke the expected behavior. If you break the behavior and the test suite is still green, something is wrong with your tests. That may happen because of weak assertions (which we have discussed) or because the method is covered but not tested (this happens, as discussed in chapter 9). Also recall that I mentioned the work of Vera-Pérez and colleagues (2019) and the existence of pseudo-tested methods.

Whenever you write a test, make sure it will break if the behavior changes. The TDD cycle allows developers to always see the test breaking. That happens because the behavior is not yet implemented, but I like the idea of "let's see if the test breaks if the behavior does not exist or is incorrect." I am not afraid of purposefully introducing a bug in the code, running the tests, and seeing them red (and then reverting the bug).

10.1.7 *Tests should have a single and clear reason to fail*

We love tests that fail. They indicate problems in our code, usually long before the code is deployed. But the test failure is the first step toward understanding and fixing the bug. Your test code should help you understand what caused the bug.

There are many ways you can do that. If your test follows the earlier principles, the test is cohesive and exercises only one (hopefully small) behavior of the software system. Give your test a name that indicates its intention and the behavior it exercises. Make sure anyone can understand the input values passed to the method under test. If the input values are complex, use good variable names that explain what they are about and code comments in natural language. Finally, make sure the assertions are clear, and explain why a value is expected.

10.1.8 *Tests should be easy to write*

There should be no friction when it comes to writing tests. If it is hard to do so (perhaps writing an integration test requires you to set up the database, create complex objects one by one, and so on), it is too easy for you to give up and not do it.

Writing unit tests tends to be easy most of the time, but it may get complicated when the class under test requires too much setup or depends on too many other classes. Integration and system tests also require each test to set up and tear down the (external) infrastructure.

Make sure tests are always easy to write. Give developers all the tools to do that. If tests require a database to be set up, provide developers with an API that requires one or two method calls and voilà—the database is ready for tests.

Investing time in writing good test infrastructure is fundamental and pays off in the long term. Remember the test base classes we created to facilitate SQL integration tests and all the POs we created to facilitate web testing in chapter 9? This is the type of infrastructure I am talking about. After the test infrastructure was in place, the rest was easy.

10.1.9 *Tests should be easy to read*

I touched on this point when I said that tests should have a clear reason to fail. I will reinforce it now. Your test code base will grow significantly. But you probably will not read it until there is a bug or you add another test to the suite.

It is well known that developers spend more time reading than writing code. Therefore, saving reading time will make you more productive. All the things you know about code readability and use in your production code apply to test code, as well. Do not be afraid to invest some time in refactoring it. The next developer will thank you.

I follow two practices when making my tests readable: make sure all the information (especially the inputs and assertions) is clear enough, and use test data builders whenever I build complex data structures.

Let's illustrate these two ideas with an example. The following listing shows an Invoice class.

Listing 10.1 Invoice class

```
public class Invoice {

  private final double value;
  private final String country;
  private final CustomerType customerType;

  public Invoice(double value, String country, CustomerType customerType) {
    this.value = value;
    this.country = country;
    this.customerType = customerType;
  }

  public double calculate() {        <-- The method we will soon test.
    double ratio = 0.1;                  Imagine business rule here.

    // some business rule here to calculate the ratio
    // depending on the value, company/person, country ...

    return value * ratio;
  }
}
```

Not-very-clear test code for the calculate() method could look like the next listing.

Listing 10.2 A not-very-clear test for an invoice

```
@Test
void test1() {
  Invoice invoice = new Invoice(new BigDecimal("2500"), "NL",
  ➥ CustomerType.COMPANY);
  double v = invoice.calculate();
  assertThat(v).isEqualTo(250);
}
```

At first glance, it may be hard to understand what all the information in the code means. It may require some extra effort to see what this invoice looks like. Imagine an entity class from a real enterprise system: an Invoice class may have dozens of attributes. The name of the test and the name of the cryptic variable v do not clearly explain what they mean. It is also not clear if the choice of "NL" as a country or "COMPANY" as a customer type makes any difference for the test or whether they are random values.

A better version of this test method could be as follows.

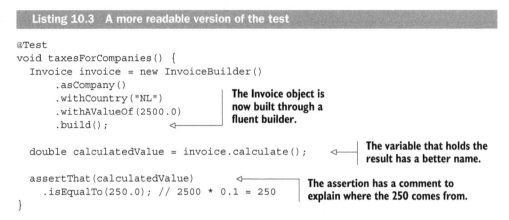

Listing 10.3   A more readable version of the test

```
@Test
void taxesForCompanies() {
  Invoice invoice = new InvoiceBuilder()
      .asCompany()
      .withCountry("NL")                    The Invoice object is
      .withAValueOf(2500.0)                 now built through a
      .build();                             fluent builder.

  double calculatedValue = invoice.calculate();    The variable that holds the
                                                    result has a better name.

  assertThat(calculatedValue)
    .isEqualTo(250.0); // 2500 * 0.1 = 250    The assertion has a comment to
}                                              explain where the 250 comes from.
```

First, the name of the test method—taxesForCompanies—clearly expresses what behavior the method is exercising. This is a best practice: name your test method after what it tests. Why? Because a good method name may save developers from having to read the method's body to understand what is being tested. In practice, it is common to skim the test suite, looking for a specific test or learning more about that class. Meaningful test names help. Some developers would argue for an even more detailed method name, such as taxesForCompanyAreTaxRateMultipliedByAmount. A developer skimming the test suite can understand even the business rule.

Many of the methods we tested in previous chapters, while complex, had a single responsibility: for example, substringsBetween in chapter 2, or leftPad in chapter 3. We even created single parameterized tests with a generic name. We did not need a set of test methods with nice names, as the name of the method under test said it all. But in enterprise systems, where we have business-like methods such as calculateTaxes or calculateFinalPrice, each test method (or partition) covers a different business rule. Those can be expressed in the name of that test method.

Next, using InvoiceBuilder (the implementation of which I show shortly) clearly expresses what this invoice is about: it is an invoice for a company (as clearly stated by the asCompany() method), "NL" is the country of that invoice, and the invoice has a value of 2500. The result of the behavior goes to a variable whose name says it all (calculatedValue). The assertion contains a comment that explains where the 250 comes from.

InvoiceBuilder is an example of an implementation of a *test data builder* (as defined by Pryce [2007]). The builder helps us create test scenarios by providing a clear and expressive API. The use of fluent interfaces (such as asCompany().withAValueOf()...) is also a common implementation choice. In terms of its implementation, Invoice-Builder is a Java class. The trick that allows methods to be chained is to return the class in the methods (methods return this), as shown in the following listing.

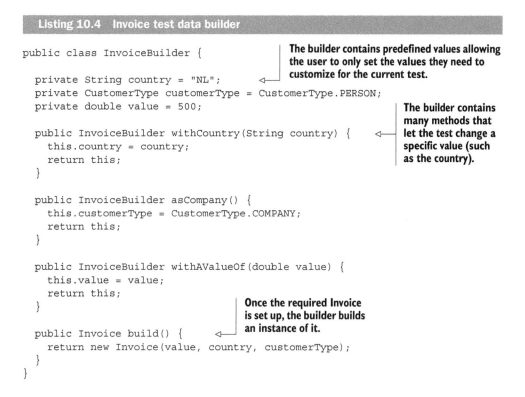

Listing 10.4   Invoice test data builder

```
public class InvoiceBuilder {

  private String country = "NL";
  private CustomerType customerType = CustomerType.PERSON;
  private double value = 500;

  public InvoiceBuilder withCountry(String country) {
    this.country = country;
    return this;
  }

  public InvoiceBuilder asCompany() {
    this.customerType = CustomerType.COMPANY;
    return this;
  }

  public InvoiceBuilder withAValueOf(double value) {
    this.value = value;
    return this;
  }

  public Invoice build() {
    return new Invoice(value, country, customerType);
  }
}
```

> The builder contains predefined values allowing the user to only set the values they need to customize for the current test.

> The builder contains many methods that let the test change a specific value (such as the country).

> Once the required Invoice is set up, the builder builds an instance of it.

You should feel free to customize your builders. A common trick is to make the builder build a common version of the class without requiring the call to all the setup methods. You can then, in one line, build a complex invoice, as you see in the next listing.

Listing 10.5   Building an invoice with a single line

```
var invoice = new InvoiceBuilder().build();
```

In such a case, the build method (without any setup) will always build an invoice for a person with a value of 500.0 and "NL" as the country (see the initialized values in InvoiceBuilder).

Other developers may write shortcut methods that build other common fixtures for the class. In listing 10.6, the anyCompany() method returns an Invoice that belongs to a company (and the default value for the other fields). The fromTheUS() method builds an Invoice for someone in the U.S.

Listing 10.6   Other helper methods in the builder

```
public Invoice anyCompany() {
  return new Invoice(value, country, CustomerType.COMPANY);
}
```

```
public Invoice fromTheUS() {
  return new Invoice(value, "US", customerType);
}
```

Building complex test data is such a recurrent task that frameworks are available to help, such as Java Faker (https://github.com/DiUS/java-faker) for the Java world and factory_bot (https://github.com/thoughtbot/factory_bot) for Ruby. I am sure you can find one for your programming language.

Finally, you may have noticed the comment near the assertion: 2500 * 0.1 = 250. Some developers would suggest that the need for this comment indicates the code requires improvement. To remove the comment, we can introduce explanatory variables: in listing 10.7, we use the `invoiceValue` and `tax` variables in the assertion. It is up to you and your team members to agree on the best approach for you.

Listing 10.7   Making the test more readable via explanatory variables

```
@Test
void taxesForCompanyAreTaxRateMultipliedByAmount() {
    double invoiceValue = 2500.0;        ◁───┐  Declares the
    double tax = 0.1;                         │  invoiceValue and
                                              │  tax variables

    Invoice invoice = new InvoiceBuilder()
        .asCompany()
        .withCountry("NL")
        .withAValueOf(invoiceValue)      ◁───┐  Uses the variable instead
        .build();                             │  of the hard-coded value

    double calculatedValue = invoice.calculate();

    assertThat(calculatedValue)               │  The assertion uses the
        .isEqualTo(invoiceValue * tax);  ◁───┤  explanatory variables instead
}                                             │  of hard-coded numbers.
```

To sum up, introducing test data builders, using variable names to explain the meaning of information, having clear assertions, and adding comments where code is not expressive enough will help developers better comprehend the test code.

10.1.10 Tests should be easy to change and evolve

Although we like to think that we always design stable classes with single responsibilities that are closed for modification but open for extension (see Martin [2014] for more about the Open Closed Principle), in practice, that does not always happen. Your production code will change, and that will force your tests to change as well.

Therefore, your task when implementing test code is to ensure that changing it will not be too painful. I do not think it is possible to make it completely painless, but you can reduce the number of points that will require changes. For example, if you see the same snippet of code in 10 different test methods, consider extracting it. If a change happens and you are forced to change that code snippet, you now only have to change it in 1 place rather than 10.

Your tests are coupled to the production code in one way or another. That is a fact. The more your tests know about how the production code works, the harder it is to change them. As we discussed in chapter 6, a clear disadvantage of using mocks is the significant coupling with the production code. Determining how much your tests need to know about the production code to test it properly is a significant challenge.

10.2 Test smells

In the previous sections, we discussed some best practices for writing good test code. Now let's discuss test smells. The term *code smell* indicates symptoms that may indicate deeper problems in the system's source code. Some well-known examples are *Long Method*, *Long Class*, and *God Class*. Several research papers show that code smells hinder the comprehensibility and maintainability of software systems (such as the work by Khomh and colleagues [2009]).

While the term has long been applied to production code, our community has been developing catalogs of smells that are specific to test code. Research has also shown that test smells are prevalent in real life and, unsurprisingly, often hurt the maintenance and comprehensibility of the test suite (Spadini et al., 2020).

The following sections examine several well-known test smells. A more comprehensive list can be found in *xUnit Test Patterns* by Meszaros (2007). I also recommend reading the foundational paper on test smells by Deursen and colleagues (2001).

10.2.1 Excessive duplication

It is not surprising that code duplication can happen in test code since it is widespread in production code. Tests are often similar in structure, as you may have noticed in several of the code examples in this book. We even used parameterized tests to reduce duplication. A less attentive developer may end up writing duplicate code (copy-pasting often happens in real life, as Treude, Zaidman, and I observed in an empirical study [2021]) instead of putting some effort into implementing a better solution.

Duplicated code can reduce the productivity of software developers. If we need to change a duplicated piece of code, we must apply the same change in all the places where the code is duplicated. In practice, it is easy to forget one of these places and end up with problematic test code. Duplicating code may also hinder the ability to evolve the test suite, as mentioned earlier. If the production code changes, you do not want to have to change too much test code. Isolating duplicated code reduces this pain.

I advise you to refactor your test code often. Extracting duplicate code to private methods or external classes is often a good, quick, cheap solution to the problem. But being pragmatic is key: a little duplication may not harm you, and you should use your experience to judge when refactoring is needed.

10.2.2   *Unclear assertions*

Assertions are the first thing a developer looks at when a test fails. A good assertion clearly reveals its reason for failure, is legible, and is as specific as possible. The test smell emerges when it is hard to understand the assertions or the reason for their failure.

There are several reasons for this smell to happen. Some features or business rules are so complex that they require a complex set of assertions to ensure their behavior. In these situations, we end up writing complex assert instructions that are not easy to understand. To help with such cases, I recommend writing customized assert instructions that abstract away part of the complexity of the assertion code, and writing code comments that explain quickly and in natural language what those assertions are about. The latter mainly applies when the assertions are not self-explanatory. Do not be afraid to write a comment in your code if it will help future developers understand what is going on.

Interestingly, a common best practice in the test best practice literature is the "one assertion per method" strategy. The idea is that a test with a single assertion can only focus on a single behavior, and it is easier for developers to understand if the assertion fails. I strongly disagree with this rule. If my test is cohesive enough and focuses on a single feature, the assertions should ensure that the entire behavior is as expected. This may mean asserting that many fields were updated and have a new value. It may also mean asserting that the mock interacted with other dependencies properly. There are many cases in which using multiple assertions in a single test is useful. Forcing developers to have a single assertion per test method is extreme—but your tests also should not have useless assertions.

Frameworks often offer the possibility of doing *soft assertions*: assertions that do not stop the test if they fail but are reported only at the very end of the test execution (which is still considered a failed test). For example, AssertJ offers this ability (http://mng.bz/aDeo).

Finally, even if you know what to assert for, picking the right assertion method provided by whatever test framework you are using can make a difference. Using the wrong or not ideal assert instruction may lead to imprecise assertion error messages. I strongly suggest using AssertJ and its extensive collection of assertions.

10.2.3   *Bad handling of complex or external resources*

Understanding test code that uses external resources can be difficult. The test should ensure that the resource is readily available and prepared for it. The test should also clean up its mess afterward.

A common smell is to be optimistic about the external resource. Resource optimism happens when a test assumes that a necessary resource (such as a database) is readily available at the start of its execution. The problem is that when the resource is not available, the test fails, often without a clear message that explains the reason. This can confuse developers, who may think a new bug has been introduced in the system.

To avoid such resource optimism, a test should not assume that the resource is already in the correct state. The test should be responsible for setting up the state itself. This can mean the test is responsible for populating a database, writing the required files to the disk, or starting up a Tomcat server. This setup may require complex code, and you should also make your best effort to abstract away such complexity by, for example, moving such code to other classes (like `DatabaseInitialization` or `TomcatLoader`) and allowing the test code to focus on the test cases.

Another common test smell happens when the test assumes that the resource is available all the time. Imagine a test method that interacts with a web service, which may be down for reasons we do not control. To avoid this test smell, you have two options: avoid depending on external resources by using stubs and mocks or, if the test cannot avoid using the external dependency, make the test suite robust enough. For example, make your test suite skip that test when the resource is unavailable, and provide an alert explaining why that was the case. This may seem counterintuitive, but remember that developers trust their test suites. Having a single test fail for the wrong reasons can make you lose confidence in the entire test suite.

From a readability perspective, it should be easy to understand all the (external) resources required and used by the test. Imagine that a test requires a test file in some directory. If the file is not there, the test fails. A first-time developer may have difficulty understanding this prerequisite. Avoid having such mystery guests in your test suite. The test code should be explicit about all its external dependencies.

10.2.4 *Fixtures that are too general*

A *fixture* is the set of input values used to exercise the component under test. As you may have noticed, fixtures are the stars of the test method, as they derive naturally from the test cases we engineer using any of the techniques we have discussed.

When testing more complex components, you may need to build several different fixtures: one for each partition you want to exercise. These fixtures can then become complex. And to make the situation worse, while tests are different from each other, their fixtures may intersect. Given this possible intersection among the different fixtures, as well as the difficulty with building complex entities and fixtures, you may decide to declare a large fixture that works for many different tests. Each test would then use a small part of this large fixture.

While this approach may work, and the tests may correctly implement the test cases, they quickly become hard to maintain. Once a test fails, you will find yourself with a large fixture that may not be completely relevant for that particular failing test. You then must manually filter out parts of the fixture that are not exercised by the failing test. That is an unnecessary cost.

Making sure the fixture of a test is as specific and cohesive as possible helps you comprehend the essence of a test (which is, again, highly relevant when the test starts to fail). Build patterns (focusing on building test data) can help you avoid generic fixtures. More specifically, the Test Data Builder pattern we discussed is often used in the test code of enterprise applications. Such applications often deal with creating complex sets of interrelated business entities, which can easily lead developers to write general fixtures.

10.2.5 *Sensitive assertions*

Good assertions are fundamental in test cases. A bad assertion may result in a test not failing when it should. However, a bad assertion may also cause a test *to fail when it should not*. Engineering a good assertion statement is challenging—even more so when components produce fragile outputs (outputs that change often). Test code should be as resilient as possible to the implementation details of the component under test. Assertions also should not be oversensitive to internal changes.

In the tool we use to assess students' submissions (https://github.com/cse1110/andy), we have a class responsible for transforming the assessment results into a message (string) that we show in our cloud-based IDE. The following listing shows the output for one of our exercises.

Listing 10.8   An example of the output of our tool

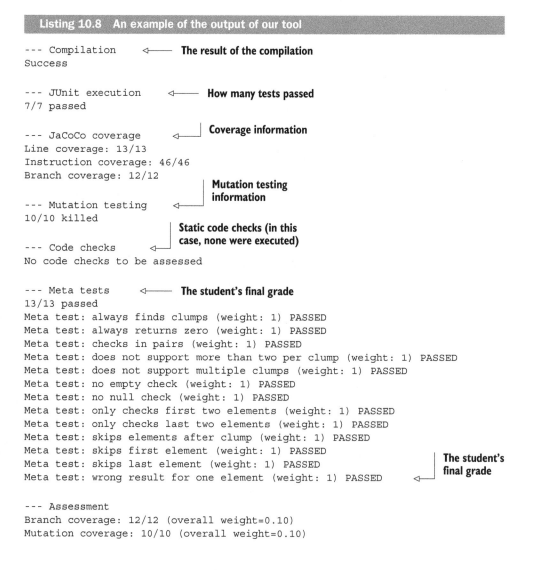

```
--- Compilation        ◁——— The result of the compilation
Success


--- JUnit execution    ◁——— How many tests passed
7/7 passed

--- JaCoCo coverage    ◁——┐ Coverage information
Line coverage: 13/13
Instruction coverage: 46/46
Branch coverage: 12/12
                         ┌── Mutation testing
                         │   information
--- Mutation testing   ◁──┘
10/10 killed
                       ┌── Static code checks (in this
                       │   case, none were executed)
--- Code checks        ◁──┘
No code checks to be assessed


--- Meta tests         ◁——— The student's final grade
13/13 passed
Meta test: always finds clumps (weight: 1) PASSED
Meta test: always returns zero (weight: 1) PASSED
Meta test: checks in pairs (weight: 1) PASSED
Meta test: does not support more than two per clump (weight: 1) PASSED
Meta test: does not support multiple clumps (weight: 1) PASSED
Meta test: no empty check (weight: 1) PASSED
Meta test: no null check (weight: 1) PASSED
Meta test: only checks first two elements (weight: 1) PASSED
Meta test: only checks last two elements (weight: 1) PASSED
Meta test: skips elements after clump (weight: 1) PASSED
Meta test: skips first element (weight: 1) PASSED            ┌── The student's
Meta test: skips last element (weight: 1) PASSED            │   final grade
Meta test: wrong result for one element (weight: 1) PASSED ◁─┘


--- Assessment
Branch coverage: 12/12 (overall weight=0.10)
Mutation coverage: 10/10 (overall weight=0.10)
```

```
Code checks: 0/0 (overall weight=0.00)
Meta tests: 13/13 (overall weight=0.80)

Final grade: 100/100
```

If we write tests without thinking too much, we end up writing lots of assertions that check whether some string is in the output. And given that we will write many test cases for many different outputs, our test suite will end up with lots of statements like "assert output contains Final grade: 100/100".

Note how sensitive this assertion is. If we change the message slightly, the tests will all break. Making assertions that are less sensitive to small changes is usually a good idea.

In this situation, we have no other option than to assert that the string matches what we have. To sort this out, we decided to create our own set of assertions for each part of the message we need to assert. These assertions enable us to decouple our test code from the strings themselves. And if the message changes in the future, all we will need to do is change our assertion.

In listing 10.9, the `reportCompilationError` test method ensures that we show the proper message to the student when they submit a solution that does not compile. We create a `Result` object (representing the final assessment of the student solution) with a compilation error. We then call the method under test and get back the generated string message.

Listing 10.9 A test that uses our own assertions

Creates a Result in which we tell the student that there is a compilation error in their solution

```
@Test
void reportCompilationError() {

    Result result = new ResultTestDataBuilder()
        .withCompilationFail(
            new CompilationErrorInfo(
                "Library.java", 10, "some compilation error"),
            new CompilationErrorInfo(
                "Library.java", 11, "some other compilation error")
    ).build();

    writer.write(ctx, result);            ←─── Calls the method
    String output = generatedResult();         under test and gets
                                               the generated message

    assertThat(output)            ←─────── Asserts that the message is as we expect.
        .has(noFinalGrade())              Note, however, our set of assertions:
        .has(not(compilationSuccess()))   noFinalGrade, compilationSuccess, and
        .has(compilationFailure())        so on. They decouple our test from the
        .has(compilationErrorOnLine(10))  concrete string.
        .has(compilationErrorOnLine(11))
        .has(compilationErrorType("some compilation error"))
        .has(compilationErrorType("some other compilation error"));
}
```

The trick happens in the assertions. Note the many assertions we created: noFinal-Grade() ensures that the final grade is not displayed, compilationErrorOnLine(10) ensures that we tell the student there is a compilation error on line 10, and so on. To create these assertions, we use AssertJ's extension capabilities. All we need to do is create a method that returns AssertJ's Condition<?> class. The generic type should be the same as the type of the object on which we are performing the assertion. In this case, the output variable is a string, so we need to create a Condition<String>.

The implementation of the compilationErrorOnLine assertion is shown in listing 10.10. If a compilation error happens, we print "- line <number>: <error message>". This assertion then looks for "- line <number>" in the string.

Listing 10.10 compilationErrorOnLine assertion

```
public static Condition<String> compilationErrorOnLine(int lineNumber) {
  return new Condition<>() {
    @Override
    public boolean matches(String value) {
      return value.contains("- line " + lineNumber);
    }
  };
}
```

Makes the method static, so we can statically import it in the test class

Checks whether value contains the string we are looking for

Back to the big picture: make sure your assertions are not too sensitive, or your tests may break for no good reason.

Exercises

10.1 Jeanette hears that two tests are behaving strangely. Both of them pass when executed in isolation, but they fail when executed together.

Which one of the following is *not* the cause of this problem?

 A The tests depend on the same external resources.

 B The execution order of the tests matters.

 C Both tests are very slow.

 D They do not perform a cleanup operation after execution.

10.2 Look at the following test code. What is the most likely test code smell that this piece of code presents?

```
@Test
void test1() {
  // web service that communicates with the bank
  BankWebService bank = new BankWebService();

  User user = new User("d.bergkamp", "nl123");
  bank.authenticate(user);
  Thread.sleep(5000); // sleep for 5 seconds

  double balance = bank.getBalance();
  Thread.sleep(2000);
```

```
Payment bill = new Payment();
bill.setOrigin(user);
bill.setValue(150.0);
bill.setDescription("Energy bill");
bill.setCode("YHG45LT");

bank.pay(bill);
Thread.sleep(5000);

double newBalance = bank.getBalance();
Thread.sleep(2000);

// new balance should be previous balance - 150
Assertions.assertEquals(newBalance, balance - 150);
}
```

    A Flaky test

    B Test code duplication

    C Obscure test

    D Long method

10.3 RepoDriller is a project that extracts information from Git repositories. Its integration tests use a lot of real Git repositories (that are created solely for the test), each with a different characteristic: one repository contains a merge commit, another contains a revert operation, and so on.

Its tests look like this:

```
@Test
public void test01() {

  // arrange: specific repo
  String path = "test-repos/git-4";

  // act
  TestVisitor visitor = new TestVisitor();
  new RepositoryMining()
    .in(GitRepository.singleProject(path))
    .through(Commits.all())
    .process(visitor)
    .mine();

  // assert
  Assert.assertEquals(3, visitor.getVisitedHashes().size());
  Assert.assertTrue(visitor.getVisitedHashes().get(2).equals("b8c2"));
  Assert.assertTrue(visitor.getVisitedHashes().get(1).equals("375d"));
  Assert.assertTrue(visitor.getVisitedHashes().get(0).equals("a1b6"));
}
```

Which test smell *might* this piece of code suffer from?

    A Condition logic in the test

    B General fixture

     c Flaky test

     D Mystery guest

10.4 In the following code, we show an actual test from Apache Commons Lang, a very popular open source Java library. This test focuses on the static `random()` method, which is responsible for generating random characters. An interesting detail in this test is the comment `Will fail randomly about 1 in 1000 times`.

```
/**
 * Test homogeneity of random strings generated --
 * i.e., test that characters show up with expected frequencies
 * in generated strings.  Will fail randomly about 1 in 1000 times.
 * Repeated failures indicate a problem.
 */
@Test
public void testRandomStringUtilsHomog() {
  final String set = "abc";
  final char[] chars = set.toCharArray();
  String gen = "";
  final int[] counts = {0, 0, 0};
  final int[] expected = {200, 200, 200};
  for (int i = 0; i < 100; i++) {
    gen = RandomStringUtils.random(6,chars);
    for (int j = 0; j < 6; j++) {
      switch (gen.charAt(j)) {
        case 'a': {counts[0]++; break;}
        case 'b': {counts[1]++; break;}
        case 'c': {counts[2]++; break;}
        default: {fail("generated character not in set");}
      }
    }
  }
  // Perform chi-square test with df = 3-1 = 2, testing at .001 level
  assertTrue("test homogeneity -- will fail about 1 in 1000 times",
    chiSquare(expected,counts) < 13.82);
}
```

Which one of the following statements is incorrect about the test?

     A The test is flaky because of the randomness that exists in generating characters.

     B The test checks for invalidly generated characters and also checks that characters are picked in the same proportion.

     c The method being static has nothing to do with its flakiness.

     D To avoid flakiness, a developer should have mocked the `random()` function.

10.5 A developer observes that two tests pass when executed in isolation but fail when executed together.

     Which of the following is the least likely fix for this problem (also known as Test Run War)?

    A Make each test runner a specific sandbox.

    B Use fresh fixtures in every test.

    c Remove and isolate duplicated test code.

    D Clean up the state during teardown.

Summary

- Writing good test code is as challenging as writing good production code. We should ensure that our test code is easy to maintain and evolve.

- We desire many things in a test method. Tests should be fast, cohesive, and repeatable; they should fail for a reason and contain strong assertions; they should be easy to read, write, and evolve; and they should be loosely coupled with the production code.

- Many things can hinder the maintainability of test methods: too much duplication, too many bad assertions, bad handling of complex (external) resources, too many general fixtures, too many sensitive assertions, and flakiness. You should avoid these.

Wrapping up the book

This chapter covers
- Revisiting what was discussed in this book

We are now at the end of this book. The book comprises a lot of my knowledge about practical software testing, and I hope you now understand the testing techniques that have supported me throughout the years. In this chapter, I will say some final words about how I see effective testing in practice and reinforce points that I feel should be uppermost in your mind.

11.1 Although the model looks linear, iterations are fundamental

Figure 11.1 (which you saw for the first time back in chapter 1) illustrates what I call *effective software testing*. Although this figure and the order of the chapters in this book may give you a sense of linearity (that is, you first do specification-based testing and then move on to structural testing), this is not the case. You should not view the proposed flow as a sort of testing waterfall.

Software development is an iterative process. You may start with specification-based testing, then go to structural testing, and then feel you need to go back to specification-based testing. Or you may begin with structural testing because the

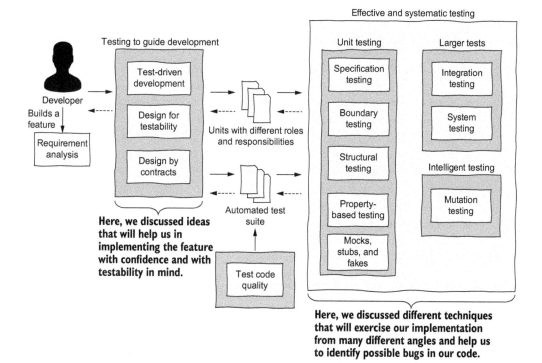

Figure 11.1 Flow of a developer who applies effective and systematic testing. The arrows indicate the iterative nature of the process; we may go back and forth between techniques as we learn more about the program under development and test.

tests that emerged from your TDD sessions are good enough. There is nothing wrong with customizing the process to specific cases.

As you become more experienced with testing, you will develop a feeling for the best order in which to apply the techniques. As long as you master them all and understand the goals and outputs of each, that will come naturally.

11.2 Bug-free software development: Reality or myth?

The techniques explore the source code from many different perspectives. That may give you the impression that if you apply them all, no bugs will ever happen. Unfortunately, this is not the case.

The more you test your code from different angles, the greater the chances of revealing bugs you did not see previously. But the software systems we work with today are very complex, and bugs may happen in corner cases that involve dozens of different components working together. Domain knowledge may help you see such cases. So, deeply understanding the business behind the software systems you test is fundamental in foreseeing complex interactions between systems that may lead to crashes or bugs.

I am betting all my chips on *intelligent testing*. I do not talk much about it in this book, although it appears in figure 11.1. Intelligent testing is all about having computers explore software systems for us. In this book, we automated the process of test execution. Test case engineering—that is, thinking of good tests—was a human activity. Intelligent testing systems propose test cases for us.

The idea is no longer novel among academics. There are many interesting intelligent testing techniques, some of which are mature enough to be deployed into production. Facebook, for example, has deployed Sapienz, a tool that uses search-based algorithms that automatically explore mobile apps, looking for crashes. And Google deploys fuzz testing (generating unexpected inputs to programs to see if they crash) on a large scale to identify bugs in open source systems. And the beauty of the research is that these tools are not randomly generating input data: they are getting smarter and smarter.

If you want to play with automated test case generation, try EvoSuite for Java (www.evosuite.org). EvoSuite receives a class as input and produces a set of JUnit tests that often achieve 100% branch coverage. It is awe-inspiring. I am hoping the big software development companies of this world will catch up with this idea and build more production-ready tools.

11.3 *Involve your final user*

This book focuses on *verification*. Verification ensures that the code works as we expect. Another angle to consider is *validation*: whether the software does what the user wants or needs. Delivering software that brings the most value is as essential as delivering software that works. Be sure you have mechanisms to ensure that you are building the right software in your pipeline.

11.4 *Unit testing is hard in practice*

I have a clear position regarding unit testing versus integration testing: you should do as much unit testing as possible and leave integration testing for the parts of the system that need it. For that to happen, you need code that is easily tested and designed with testability in mind. However, most readers of this book are not in such a situation. Software systems are rarely designed this way.

When you write new pieces of code that you have more control over, be sure you code in a unit-testable way. This means integrating the new code with hard-to-test legacy code. I have a very simple suggestion that works in most cases. Imagine that you need to add new behavior to a legacy class. Instead of coding the behavior in this class, create a new class, put the new behavior in it, and unit-test it. Then, in the legacy class, instantiate the new class and call the method. This way, you avoid the hassle of writing a test for a class that is impossible to test. The following listing shows an example.

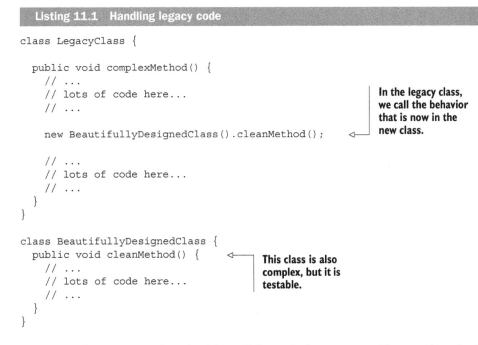

Listing 11.1 Handling legacy code

```
class LegacyClass {

  public void complexMethod() {
    // ...
    // lots of code here...
    // ...

    new BeautifullyDesignedClass().cleanMethod();

    // ...
    // lots of code here...
    // ...
  }
}

class BeautifullyDesignedClass {
  public void cleanMethod() {
    // ...
    // lots of code here...
    // ...
  }
}
```

In the legacy class, we call the behavior that is now in the new class.

This class is also complex, but it is testable.

You may, of course, need to do things differently for your specific case, but the idea is the same. For more information on handling legacy systems, I suggest Feather's book (2004). I also suggest reading about the anti-corruption layer idea proposed by Evans (2004).

11.5 Invest in monitoring

You do your best to catch all the bugs before we deploy. But in practice, you know that is impossible. What can you do? Make sure that you detect the bugs as soon as they happen in production.

Software monitoring is as important as testing. Be sure your team invests in decent monitoring systems. This is more complicated than you may think. First, developers need to know what to log. This may be a tricky decision, as you do not want to log too much (to avoid overloading your infrastructure), and you do not want to log too little (because you will not have enough information to debug the problem). Make sure your team has good guidelines for what should be logged, what log level to use, and so on. If you are curious, we wrote a paper showing that machine learning can recommend logs to developers (Cândido et al., 2021). We hope to have more concrete tooling in the future.

It is also difficult for developers to identify anomalies when the system logs millions or even billions of log lines each month. Sometimes exceptions happen, and the software is resilient enough to know what to do with them. Developers log these exceptions anyway, but often the exceptions are not important. Therefore, investing in ways to identify exceptions that matter is a pragmatic challenge, and you and your team should invest in it.

11.6   *What's next?*

There is still much to learn about software testing! This book did not have space to cover these important topics:

- *Non-functional testing*—If you have non-functional requirements such as performance, scalability, or security, you may want to write tests for them as well. A 2022 book by Gayathri Mohan, *Full Stack Testing* (https://learning.oreilly.com/library/view/full-stack-testing/9781098108120) has good coverage of these type of tests.

- *Testing for specific architectures and contexts*—As you saw in chapter 9, different technologies may require different testing patterns. If you are building an API, it is wise to write API tests for it. If you are building a VueJS application, it is wise to write VueJS tests. Manning has several interesting books on the topic, including *Testing Web APIs* by Mark Winteringham (www.manning.com/books/testing-web-apis); *Exploring Testing Java Microservices*, with chapters selected by Alex Soto Bueno and Jason Porter (www.manning.com/books/exploring-testing-java-microservices), and *Testing Vue.js Applications* by Edd Yerburgh (www.manning.com/books/testing-vue-js-applications).

- *Design for testability principles for your programming language*—I mostly discussed principles that make sense for object-oriented languages in general. If you are working with, for example, functional languages, the principles may be somewhat different. If we pick Clojure as an example, Phil Calçado has a nice blog post on his experiences with TDD in that language (http://mng.bz/g40x), and Manning's book *Clojure in Action* (www.manning.com/books/clojure-in-action-second-edition) by Amit Rathore and Francis Avila has an entire chapter dedicated to TDD.

- *Static analysis tools*—Tools such as SonarQube (www.sonarqube.org) and Spot-Bugs (https://spotbugs.github.io/) are interesting ways to look for quality issues in code bases. These tools mostly rely on static analysis and look for specific buggy code patterns. Their main advantage is that they are very fast and can be executed in continuous integration. I strongly suggest that you become familiar with these tools.

- *Software monitoring*—I said you should invest in monitoring, which means you also need to learn how to do proper monitoring. Techniques such as A/B testing, blue-green deployment, and others will help you ensure that bugs have a harder time getting to production even if they made it through your thorough testing process. The blog post "QA in Production" by Rouan Wilsenach is a good introduction to the subject (https://martinfowler.com/articles/qa-in-production.html).

Have fun testing!

appendix
Answers to exercises

Chapter 1

1.1 The goal of systematic testing, as its name says, is to engineer test cases in a more systematic way, rather than simply following gut feelings. Systematic testing gives engineers sound techniques to engineer test cases out of requirements, boundaries, and source code.

1.2 The *absence-of-errors fallacy*. While the software does not have many bugs, it does not give users what they want. In this case, the verification is good, but the developers need to work on the validation.

1.3 B. Exhaustive testing is impossible in most cases.

1.4 D. Test early is an important principle, but it is definitely not related to the problem of only doing unit tests. All the other principles can help developers understand that using different types of testing is important.

1.5 A. The pesticide paradox fits the discussion best. The development team has high code coverage, but they need to apply different techniques.

1.6 A. The primary use of integration tests is to find mistakes in the communication between a system and its external dependencies.

1.7 A.

1.8 A.

1.9 B.

Chapter 2

2.1 D. This is a functional testing technique. There is no need for the source code.

2.2 Possible actions:

- We should treat "no filename with this name" and "omitted" as exceptional and test them just once.
- We should treat pattern size "empty" as exceptional and test it just once.
- We should treat "pattern is improperly quoted" as exceptional and test it just once.
- We should constrain the options in the "occurrences in a single line" category to happen only if "occurrences in the file" are either exactly one or more than one. It does not make sense to have no occurrences in a file and one pattern in a line.

2.3 There are no right or wrong answers to this exercise. It shows that many of the decisions we make are based on what we know about the system—or, in this case, what we assume about the system. When context kicks in, there may be more possible invalid test cases than those in the boundaries.

Regardless of the decisions you make as a tester about specific invalid test cases, it is important to justify those decisions. For example:

- Do we need to test negative numbers separately from positive numbers? Based on the specification, there's no reason to do so. If you look at the source code (assuming you have access to the source code), does it make you feel that this test is necessary?
- Do we need to test trailing zeroes? If the user inputs a string that is converted later, testing may be important.
- Do we need to test extreme numbers like `Integer.MAX_VALUE` or pass a `long` or `float`?
- Do we need to test with a string consisting of only one letter or more than two letters? If there's no input validation, unintended behavior may occur.
- Do we need to test lowercase letters? Maybe the program can't distinguish between lower- and uppercase letters.

Here are some examples of possible invalid partitions:

- `[Integer.MIN_VALUE, 999]`
- `[4001, Integer.MAX_VALUE]`
- `[A, B]`
- `[N, Z]`
- `[0, 999]`
- `[AAA, ZZZ]`

2.4 We can group the tests cases in their partitions:

- Divisible by 3 and 5: T1, T2
- Divisible by just 3 (not by 5): T4

- Divisible by just 5 (not by 3): T5
- Not divisible by 3 or 5: T3

Only the partition where the number is divisible by both 3 and 5 has two tests. Therefore we can only remove T1 or T2.

2.5 A. The on point can be read from the condition: 570. The on point makes the condition true. So, the off point should make the condition false: 571.

2.6 The on point is 10. Here we are dealing with an equality. The value can go both up and down to make the condition false. As such, we have two off points: 9 and 11.

Chapter 3

3.1 B.

- Lines 2–4, 6, and 8 are always covered.
- The condition in line 4 is true, so line 5 is also covered.
- The condition in line 6 is false with `right=21`, so line 7 is not covered.
- The condition on line 8 is false (note that `left` has been changed). Therefore, line 9 is not covered, but lines 10 and 11 are.

In total, 8 of the 10 lines are covered, so the line coverage is $8/10 \times 100 = 80\%$.

3.2 Example of a test suite that achieves 100% line coverage:

```
@Test
public void removeNullInListTest() {
    LinkedList<Integer> list = new LinkedList<>();

    list.add(null);

    assertTrue(list.remove(null));
}

@Test
public void removeElementInListTest() {
    LinkedList<Integer> list = new LinkedList<>();

    list.add(7);

    assertTrue(list.remove(7));
}

@Test
public void removeElementNotPresentInListTest() {
    LinkedList<Integer> list = new LinkedList<>();

    assertFalse(list.remove(5));
}
```

Note that many test suites achieve 100% line coverage; this is just an example.

You should have three tests. At least one test is needed to cover lines 5 and 6 (*removeNullInListTest*, in this case). This test will also cover lines 2–4.

Second, you need a test for lines 12–13 (`removeElementInListTest`). This test also covers lines 9–11. A third test is needed to cover line 17 (`removeElementNotPresent-InListTest`).

3.3 C. You need at least one test to cover the `true` branch of the decision in line 2. Then, with another test, you can make the decisions in lines 2 and 12 `false`. Add another test to cover the `false` branch of the decision in line 16. Finally, an additional test is needed to cover the `true` branch of the decision in line 16. This gives you a minimum of four tests.

3.4 A and B.

3.5 The table for the given expression is as follows:

Test	A	B	Result
1	F	F	F
2	F	T	F
3	T	F	T
4	T	T	T

From this table, we can deduce sets of independence pairs for each of the parameters:

- A: `{ (1, 3), (2, 4) }`
- B: `{ (empty) }`

There is no independence pair for B. Thus it is not possible to achieve MC/DC coverage for this expression.

Since there is no independence pair for B, this parameter does not affect the result. You should recommend that the developer restructure the expression without using B, making the code easier to maintain.

This example shows that software testers can contribute to code quality not only by spotting bugs but also by suggesting changes that result in better maintainability.

3.6 D. The loop in the method makes it impossible to achieve 100% path coverage. You would have to test all possible iterations. For the other answers, you can come up with a test case that makes it possible: `"aXYa"`.

3.7 A is true. Statement D, about basic condition coverage, is false, although "full condition coverage" does subsume branch coverage as it combines both branch and conditional coverage.

3.8 A.

3.9 D. All the alternatives are incorrect.

- There are no studies that affirm that structural testing should be preferred over specification-based tests.
- We need good requirements, but they do not need to be formal models.
- Boundary analysis can be done with the specification or the source code.

Chapter 4

4.1 D.

4.2 The existing pre-conditions are *not* enough to ensure the property of the removed assertion. The post-condition ensured that the returned value was never `null`. The pre-conditions ensure that `board` itself cannot be `null` and that `x` and `y` are in its range. But it does not ensure that values in `board` are not `null`. To have the same guarantee, the class would need an invariant that ensures that no place in `board` is `null`.

4.3 B.

4.4 C.

4.5 Static methods do not have invariants. Class invariants are related to the entire object, while static methods do not belong to any object (they are stateless). So, the idea of (class) invariants does not apply to static methods.

4.6 A.

Chapter 5

5.1 In example-based testing, tests use one concrete instance (out of often infinite possibilities). In property-based testing, tests define the property that needs to hold, and the testing framework generates random inputs, looking for an input that would break the property.

5.2 There are two clear properties: strings that are palindromes should return `true`, and strings that are not palindromes should return `false`. For the first property, the property-based test can generate a random string and then concatenate it with its reversed value. The program should return `true` for those. For the second property, the property-based test can generate a random string. The program should return `false` for those.

There are a few caveats to pay attention to. For the first property, we also need to consider palindromes that have an odd length. Imagine that we generate the random string "abc". "abccba" is a palindrome, but "abc*X*cba" is also a palindrome, where "*X*" is any character. Making the test also generate palindromes with odd lengths is a nice way to test such a boundary.

For the second property, you can add some random letters in the generated string to ensure that the string is not a palindrome. These random letters should be different from the characters the string is generated with. Otherwise, the random generation may generate a palindrome by chance, which would mistakenly break the test.

5.3 Fuzzing or fuzz testing is all about exercising the program with invalid, unexpected, and random data to see if it crashes. Property-based testing also generates random data, but always with the goal of exercising a property. The test should pass with the random data. With fuzzing, we try random inputs until the test crashes. Fuzzing is a major area of research, and these tools are getting smarter by the day. You can read more about it in *The Fuzzing Book* (www.fuzzingbook.org).

Chapter 6

6.1 Fakes have real, working implementations of the class they simulate. However, they usually do the same task in a much simpler way.

Stubs provide hard-coded answers to the calls that are performed during the test. Unlike fakes, stubs do not have a working implementation.

Mock objects act like stubs but are preconfigured to know what kind of interactions should occur with them.

6.2 A.

6.3 C.

6.4 C.

6.5 Anything that is infrastructure-related, too complex, or too slow is a good candidate to be replaced by mocks. On the other hand, entity classes, simple utility functions, and data holders are not commonly mocked.

6.6 No set answer.

Chapter 7

7.1

- Developer 1: Observability
- Developer 2: Controllability
- Developer 3: Controllability

7.2 The ones to be prioritized are 1 and 3. As we discussed in the chapter, it is very important to keep the domain and infrastructure separated for testability. How would you write a unit test for a piece of code that contains business rules and talks to a database or an external API?

Regarding option 2, because the focus is to write unit tests, dependencies such as databases will be mocked. Thus the size of the database does not matter.

Regarding option 4, testing classes with many attributes and fields requires extra effort because the tester has to instantiate and set values for all these fields. However, this does not prevent you from writing tests.

7.3 To test the `runBatch` method of `OrderDeliveryBatch` (for example, in a unit test), you need to be able to use mocks or stubs for at least the `orderBook` and `delivery` objects.

In the current implementation, this is not possible, as you cannot change `order-Book` or `delivery` from outside the class. In other words, you want to improve controllability to improve testability.

If you allow the dependencies to be injected, you will be able to use mocks and stubs. Therefore, you should consider *dependency injection.*

7.4 The implementation currently lacks controllability. You cannot change the values that `Calendar` gives in the method because its `getInstance` method is static. Although newer versions of Mockito can mock static methods, try to avoid them as much as possible.

A solution would be to either receive `Calendar` as a parameter of the method or inject a `Clock`, which is a layer on top of `Calendar` (or whatever other Date class you prefer).

7.5 No set answer.

Chapter 8

8.1 Look at figure 8.1.

8.2 C. Although a few studies show that the number of tests written by TDD practitioners is often greater than the number of tests written by developers not practicing TDD, this is not the main reason developers use TDD. Of the alternatives, this is the least important. All the other choices are more important reasons, according to the TDD literature.

8.3 B.

8.4 No set answer.

Chapter 9

9.1 B and D.

9.2 C.

9.3 A.

9.4 A and B.

C is wrong. There may be cases where you want to cover the same piece of code via unit and integration testing. They catch different bugs.

D is also wrong. Some types of applications benefit more from integration testing, and in those cases, more integration tests should be used. That said, not being able to write unit tests when they are the best choice may indicate deeper design issues.

9.5 A, C, and D.

Chapter 10

10.1 C.

10.2 A.

10.3 D. This test requires the existence of a Git repo to work. Although this is explicit in the test, a developer may need to understand what this Git repo looks like to understand a possible test failure. Thus this test suffers from a *mystery guest*.

This test is unlikely to be flaky. The Git repository used in the test will never change. It is also unlikely that Git will change its behavior. Everything runs in a single thread, so there are no concurrency issues.

10.4 D. The test is about testing the generator and its homogeneity; if we mock the random function, the test loses its purpose.

10.5 C.

References

Aniche, Maurício, and Marco Aurélio Gerosa. 2015. "Does Test-Driven Development Improve Class Design? A Qualitative Study on Developers' Perceptions." *Journal of the Brazilian Computer Society* 21 (1): 1–11.

Aniche, Maurício, Eduardo Guerra, and Marco Aurélio Gerosa. 2014. "Improving Code Quality on Automated Tests of Web Applications: A Set of Patterns." In *21st Conference on Pattern Languages of Programs (PLOP)*.

Aniche, Maurício, Christoph Treude, and Andy Zaidman. 2021. "How Developers Engineer Test Cases: An Observational Study." *Transactions on Software Engineering (TSE)*. https://arxiv.org/abs/2103.01783.

Arguelles, Carlos, Marko Ivankovic, and Adam Bender. 2020. "Google Testing Blog: Code Coverage Best Practices." https://testing.googleblog.com/2020/08/code-coverage-best-practices.html.

Baeldung, Eugen. 2020. "The Dao Pattern in Java." www.baeldung.com/java-dao-pattern.

Beck, Kent. 2002. *Test-Driven Development: By Example*. Addison-Wesley Professional.

Beck, Kent. 2019. "Test Desiderata." https://medium.com/@kentbeck_7670/test-desiderata-94150638a4b3.

Beck, Kent, and Erich Gamma. 1998. "JUnit Test Infected: Programmers Love Writing Tests." *Java Report* 3 (7).

Bell, Jonathan, Owolabi Legunsen, Michael Hilton, Lamyaa Eloussi, Tifany Yung, and Darko Marinov. 2018. "DeFlaker: Automatically Detecting Flaky Tests." In *2018 IEEE/ACM 40th International Conference on Software Engineering (ICSE)*, 433–444. IEEE.

Beller, Moritz, Georgios Gousios, Annibale Panichella, Sebastian Proksch, Sven Amann, and Andy Zaidman. 2019. "Developer Testing in the IDE: Patterns, Beliefs, and Behavior." *IEEE Transactions on Software Engineering* 45 (3): 261–284.

Black, Rex, Erik van Veenendaal, and Dorothy Graham. 2012. *Foundations of Software Testing ISQTB Certification*, 3rd ed. Cengage Learning EMEA.

Bloch, Joshua. 2008. *Effective Java (The Java Series)*. Prentice Hall PTR.

Boehm, Barry W., and Philip N. Papaccio. 1988. "Understanding and Controlling Software Costs." *IEEE Transactions on Software Engineering* 14 (10): 1462–1477.

Bouwers, Eric, Joost Visser, and Arie Van Deursen. 2012. "Getting What You Measure." *Communications of the ACM* 55 (7).

Cândido, Jeanderson, Jan Haesen, Maurício Aniche, and Arie van Deursen. 2021. "An Exploratory Study of Log Placement Recommendation in an Enterprise System." In *Proceedings of the 2021 Mining Software Repositories Conference*. ACM.

Chen, Yiqun T., Rahul Gopinath, Anita Tadakamalla, Michael D. Ernst, Reid Holmes, Gordon Fraser, Paul Ammann, and René Just. 2020. "Revisiting the Relationship Between Fault Detection, Test Adequacy Criteria, and Test Set Size." In *Proceedings of the 35th IEEE/ACM International Conference on Automated Software Engineering*. IEEE.

Chilenski, John Joseph. 2001. "Investigation of Three Forms of the Modified Condition Decision Coverage (MCDC) Criterion." DOT/FAA/AR-01/18. United States Federal Aviation Administration, Office of Aviation Research.

Cockburn, Alistair. 2005. "Hexagonal Architecture." https://alistair.cockburn.us/hexagonal-architecture/.

Dogša, Tomaž, and David Batič. 2011. "The Effectiveness of Test-Driven Development: An Industrial Case Study." *Software Quality Journal* 19 (4): 643–661.

Encyclopedia.com. 2020. "Roman Numerals: Their Origins, Impact, and Limitations." https://www.encyclopedia.com/science/encyclopedias-almanacs-transcripts-and-maps/roman-numerals-their-origins-impact-and-limitations.

Erdogmus, Hakan, Maurizio Morisio, and Marco Torchiano. 2005. "On the Effectiveness of the Test-First Approach to Programming." *IEEE Transactions on Software Engineering* 31 (3): 226–237.

Evans, Eric. 2004. *Domain-Driven Design: Tackling Complexity in the Heart of Software*. Addison-Wesley Professional.

Feathers, Michael. 2004. *Working Effectively with Legacy Code*. Pearson.

Feathers, Michael. 2008. "The Flawed Theory Behind Unit Testing." https://michaelfeathers.typepad.com/michael_feathers_blog/2008/06/the-flawed-theo.html.

Feathers, Michael. 2013. "The Deep Synergy Between Testability and Good Design." https://www.youtube.com/watch?v=4cVZvoFGJTU.

Feathers, Michael, and Steve Freeman. 2009. "Test Driven Development: Ten Years Later." InfoQ. http://www.infoq.com/presentations/tdd-ten-years-later.

Ferrari, Fabiano Cutigi, Alessandro Viola Pizzoleto, and Jeff Offutt. 2018. "A Systematic Review of Cost Reduction Techniques for Mutation Testing: Preliminary Results." In *Proceedings of the IEEE International Conference on Software Testing, Verification and Validation Workshops (ICSTW)*. IEEE.

Fowler, Martin. "ClockWrapper." https://martinfowler.com/bliki/ClockWrapper.html.

Fowler, Martin. 2003. "User Journey Test." www.martinfowler.com/bliki/UserJourneyTest.html.

Fowler, Martin. 2005. "Command-Query Separation." www.martinfowler.com/bliki/CommandQuerySeparation.html.

Fowler, Martin. 2007. "Mocks Aren't Stubs." martinfowler.com/articles/mocksArentStubs.html.

Fowler, Martin. 2021. "On the Diverse and Fantastical Shapes of Testing." martinfowler.com/articles/2021-test-shapes.html.

Freeman, Steve, and Nat Pryce. 2009. *Growing Object-Oriented Software, Guided by Tests*. Pearson Education.

Freeman, Steve, Tim Mackinnon, Nat Pryce, and Joe Walnes. 2004. "Mock Roles, Not Objects." In *Companion to the 19th Annual ACM SIGPLAN Conference on Object-Oriented Programming Systems, Languages, and Applications*, 236–246. ACM.

Fucci, Davide, Hakan Erdogmus, Burak Turhan, Markku Oivo, and Natalia Juristo. 2016. "A Dissection of the Test-Driven Development Process: Does It Matter to Test-First or to Test-Last?" *IEEE Transactions on Software Engineering* 43 (7): 597–14.

Gamma, E., R. Helm, R., Johnson, and J. Vlissides. 1993. "Design Patterns: Abstraction and Reuse of Object-Oriented Design." In *European Conference on Object-Oriented Programming*, 406–431.

Garousi, Vahid, and Barış Küçük. 2018. "Smells in Software Test Code: A Survey of Knowledge in Industry and Academia." *Journal of Systems and Software* 138: 52–81.

George, Boby, and Laurie Williams. 2003. "An Initial Investigation of Test Driven Development in Industry." In *Proceedings of the 2003 ACM Symposium on Applied Computing*, 1135–1139. ACM.

Google. 2016. "OSS-Fuzz: Continuous Fuzzing for Open Source Software." https://github.com/google/oss-fuzz.

Gopinath, Rahul, Carlos Jensen, and Alex Groce. 2014. "Code Coverage for Suite Evaluation by Developers." In *Proceedings of the 36th International Conference on Software Engineering*. IEEE.

Grenning, James W. 2011. *Test Driven Development for Embedded C*. Pragmatic Bookshelf.

Hammarberg, Marcus, and Joakim Sundén. 2014. *Kanban in Action*. Manning Publications.

Harman, Mark, and Peter O'Hearn. 2018. "From Start-Ups to Scale-Ups: Opportunities and Open Problems for Static and Dynamic Program Analysis." In *IEEE 18th International Working Conference on Source Code Analysis and Manipulation (SCAM)*, 1–23. IEEE.

Hayhurst, Kelly J. 2001. "A Practical Tutorial on Modified Condition/Decision Coverage." https://shemesh.larc.nasa.gov/fm/papers/Hayhurst-2001-tm210876-MCDC.pdf.

Hermans, Felienne. 2021. *The Programmer's Brain: What Every Programmer Needs to Know About Cognition*. Manning Publications.

Hipp, Richard. 2021. "The Untold Story of SQLite." https://corecursive.com/066-sqlite-with-richard-hipp.

Hutchins, Monica, Herb Foster, Tarak Goradia, and Thomas Ostrand. 1994. "Experiments on the Effectiveness of Dataflow- and Control-Flow-Based Test Adequacy Criteria." In *Proceedings of 16th International Conference on Software Engineering*. IEEE.

Inozemtseva, Laura, and Reid Holmes. 2014. "Coverage Is Not Strongly Correlated with Test Suite Effectiveness." In *Proceedings of the 36th International Conference on Software Engineering*. IEEE.

Janzen, David S. 2005. "Software Architecture Improvement Through Test-Driven Development." In *Companion to the 20th Annual ACM SIGPLAN Conference on Object-Oriented Programming, Systems, Languages, and Applications*, 240–241. ACM.

Janzen, David S., and Hossein Saiedian. 2006. "On the Influence of Test-Driven Development on Software Design." In *19th Conference on Software Engineering Education & Training (CSEET'06)*, 141–148. IEEE.

Jeng, Bingchiang, and Elaine J. Weyuker. 1994. "A Simplified Domain-Testing Strategy." *ACM Transactions on Software Engineering and Methodology (TOSEM)* 3 (3): 254–270.

Kaner, Cem, Sowmya Padmanabhan, and Douglas Hoffman. 2013. *The Domain Testing Workbook*. Context Driven Press.

Khomh, Foutse, Massimiliano Di Penta, and Yann-Gael Gueheneuc. 2009. "An Exploratory Study of the Impact of Code Smells on Software Change-Proneness." In *16th Working Conference on Reverse Engineering*, 75–84. IEEE.

Lam, Wing, Reed Oei, August Shi, Darko Marinov, and Tao Xie. 2019. "iDFlakies: A Framework for Detecting and Partially Classifying Flaky Tests." In *12th IEEE Conference on Software Testing, Validation and Verification (ICST)*, 312–322. IEEE.

Langr, Jeff, Andy Hunt, and Dave Thomas. 2015. *Pragmatic Unit Testing in Java 8 with JUnit*. Pragmatic Bookshelf.

Lehman, Meir M. 1980. "Programs, Life Cycles, and Laws of Software Evolution." *Proceedings of the IEEE* 68 (9): 1060–1076.

Liskov, Barbara H., and Jeannette M. Wing. 1994. "A Behavioral Notion of Subtyping." *ACM Transactions on Programming Languages and Systems (TOPLAS)* 16 (6): 1811–1841.

Liskov, Barbara. 1987. "Keynote Address—Data Abstraction and Hierarchy." In *Addendum to the Proceedings on Object-Oriented Programming Systems, Languages, and Applications*. ACM.

Luo, Qingzhou, Farah Hariri, Lamyaa Eloussi, and Darko Marinov. 2014. "An Empirical Analysis of Flaky Tests." In *Proceedings of the 22nd ACM SIGSOFT International Symposium on Foundations of Software Engineering*, 643–653. ACM.

Mancuso, Sandro. 2018. "Does TDD Lead to Good Design?" https://www.youtube.com/watch?v=KyFVA4Spcgg&t=195s.

Mao, Ke. 2018. "Sapienz: Intelligent Automated Software Testing at Scale." 2018. https://engineering
.fb.com/2018/05/02/developer-tools/sapienz-intelligent-automated-software-testing-at-scale.

Marick, Brian. 2014. "Ten Years of TDD." http://c2.com/cgi/wiki?TenYearsOfTestDrivenDevelopment.

Martin, Robert C. 1996. "The Dependency Inversion Principle." *C++ Report* 8 (6).

Martin, Robert C. 2014. "The Open Closed Principle." https://blog.cleancoder.com/uncle-bob/2014/
05/12/TheOpenClosedPrinciple.html.

Martin, Robert C. 2014. "The Single Responsibility Principle." https://blog.cleancoder.com/uncle-bob/
2014/05/08/SingleReponsibilityPrinciple.html.

Martin, Robert C. 2018. *Clean Architecture: A Craftsman's Guide to Software Structure and Design*. Prentice
Hall.

Martin, Robert C., and Micah Martin. 2006. *Agile Principles, Patterns, and Practices in C#*. Prentice Hall
PTR.

Meszaros, Gerard. 2007. *XUnit Test Patterns: Refactoring Test Code*. Pearson Education.

Meyer, Bertrand. 1992. "Applying 'Design by Contract'." *Computer* 25 (10): 40–51.

Meyer, Bertrand. 1997. *Object-Oriented Software Construction*, vol. 2. Prentice Hall Englewood Cliffs.

Micco, John. 2016. "Flaky Tests at Google and How We Mitigate Them." https://testing.googleblog.com/
2016/05/flaky-tests-at-google-and-how-we.html.

Mockito. 2019. "How to Write Good Tests." https://github.com/mockito/mockito/wiki/
How-to-write-good-tests.

Müeller, Matthias M., and Oliver Hagner. 2002. "Experiment About Test-First Programming." *IEEE
Proceedings—Software* 149 (5).

Nagappan, Nachiappan, E. Michael Maximilien, Thirumalesh Bhat, and Laurie Williams. 2008. "Realiz-
ing Quality Improvement Through Test Driven Development: Results and Experiences of Four
Industrial Teams." *Empirical Software Engineering* 13 (3): 289–302.

Namin, Akbar Siami, and James H. Andrews. 2009. "The Influence of Size and Coverage on Test Suite
Effectiveness." In *Proceedings of the 18th International Symposium on Software Testing and Analysis*. IEEE.

Netflix. 2020. "Ready for Changes with Hexagonal Architecture." https://netflixtechblog.com/
ready-for-changes-with-hexagonal-architecture-b315ec967749.

Oracle. 2020. Java Language Specification: The assert Statement. https://docs.oracle.com/javase/specs/
jls/se15/html/jls-14.html#jls-14.10.

Osherove, Roy. 2009. *The Art of Unit Testing: With Examples in .NET*. Manning Publications.

Ostrand, Thomas J., and Marc J. Balcer. 1988. "The Category-Partition Method for Specifying and Generating Functional Tests." *Communications of the ACM* 31 (6): 676–686.

Parsai, Ali, and Serge Demeyer. 2020. "Comparing Mutation Coverage against Branch Coverage in an
Industrial Setting." *International Journal on Software Tools for Technology Transfer* 22 (4): 365–388.

Petrovic, Goran, and Marko Ivankovic. 2018. "State of Mutation Testing at Google." In *Proceedings of the
40th International Conference on Software Engineering: Software Engineering in Practice*. IEEE.

Pezzè, Mauro, and Michal Young. 2008. *Software Testing and Analysis: Process, Principles, and Techniques*.
John Wiley & Sons.

Pryce, Nat. 2007. "Test Data Builders: An Alternative to the Object Mother Pattern." www.natpryce.com/
articles/000714.html.

Regehr, John. 2014. "Use of Assertions." https://blog.regehr.org/archives/1091.

Schaffer, André. 2018. "Testing of Microservices." https://engineering.atspotify.com/2018/01/11/
testing-of-microservices.

Schröter, Adrian, Thomas Zimmermann, and Andreas Zeller. 2006. "Predicting Component Failures at
Design Time." In *Proceedings of the 2006 ACM/IEEE International Symposium on Empirical Software Engineering*. ACM.

Schuchert, Brett L. 2013. "DIP in the Wild." www.martinfowler.com/articles/dipInTheWild.html.

Shatnawi, Raed, and Wei Li. 2006. "An Investigation of Bad Smells in Object-Oriented Design." In *Third International Conference on Information Technology: New Generations (ITNG'06)*, 161–165. IEEE.

Shore, James. 2014. "Let's Play: Test-Driven Development." https://www.youtube.com/playlist?list=PL0CCC6BD6AFF097B1.

Shull, Forrest, Grigori Melnik, Burak Turhan, Lucas Layman, Madeline Diep, and Hakan Erdogmus. 2010. "What Do We Know About Test-Driven Development?" *IEEE Software* 27 (6): 16–19.

Siniaalto, M., and P. Abrahamsson. 2007. "Does Test-Driven Development Improve the Program Code? Alarming Results from a Comparative Case Study." In *IFIP Central and East European Conference on Software Engineering Techniques*, 143–156.

Spadini, Davide, Maurício Aniche, Magiel Bruntink, and Alberto Bacchelli. 2019. "Mock Objects for Testing Java Systems." *Empirical Software Engineering* 24 (3): 1461–1498.

Spadini, Davide, Martin Schvarcbacher, Ana-Maria Oprescu, Magiel Bruntink, and Alberto Bacchelli. "Investigating Severity Thresholds for Test Smells." 2020. In *Proceedings of the 17th International Conference on Mining Software Repositories*. ACM.

Test Double. 2018. "London School TDD." https://github.com/testdouble/contributing-tests/wiki/London-school-TDD.

Trautsch, Fabian, Steffen Herbold, and Jens Grabowski. 2020. "Are Unit and Integration Test Definitions Still Valid for Modern Java Projects? An Empirical Study on Open-Source Projects." *Journal of Systems and Software* 159.

Tuya, Javier, M. José Suárez-Cabal, and Claudio De La Riva. 2006. "A Practical Guide to SQL White-Box Testing." *ACM SIGPLAN Notices* 41 (4): 36–41.

Tuya, Javier, M. José Suárez-Cabal, and Claudio De La Riva. 2006. "SQLMutation: A Tool to Generate Mutants of SQL Database Queries." In *Second Workshop on Mutation Analysis (Mutation 2006—ISSRE Workshops 2006)*. IEEE.

Van Deursen, Arie, Leon Moonen, Alex Van Den Bergh, and Gerard Kok. 2001. "Refactoring Test Code." In *Proceedings of the 2nd International Conference on Extreme Programming and Flexible Processes in Software Engineering*.

Van Deursen, Steven, and Mark Seemann. 2019. *Dependency Injection: Principles, Practices, and Patterns.* Manning Publications.

Vera-Pérez, Oscar Luis, Benjamin Danglot, Martin Monperrus, and Benoit Baudry. 2019. "A Comprehensive Study of Pseudo-Tested Methods." *Empirical Software Engineering* 24 (3): 1195–1225.

Vocke, Ham. 2018. "The Practical Testing Pyramid." https://martinfowler.com/articles/practical-test-pyramid.html.

Wilsenach, Rouan. 2017. "QA in Production." https://martinfowler.com/articles/qa-in-production.html.

Winters, Titus, Tom Manshreck, and Hyrum Wright. 2020. *Software Engineering at Google: Lessons Learned from Programming Over Time.* O'Reilly Media.

Yandrapally, Rahulkrishna, and Ali Mesbah. 2021. "Mutation Analysis for Assessing End-to-End Web Tests." In *Proceedings of the 37th International Conference on Software Maintenance and Evolution*. IEEE.

Yu, Chak Shun, Christoph Treude, and Maurício Aniche. 2019. "Comprehending Test Code: An Empirical Study." In *Proceedings of the 2019 IEEE International Conference on Software Maintenance and Evolution (ICSME)*. IEEE.

Zarechneva, Julia. 2021. "Reinventing the QA Process." https://blog.picnic.nl/reinventing-the-qa-process-25854fee51f3.

Zeller, Andreas, Raul Gopinath, Marcel Böhme, Gordon Fraser, and Christian Holler. 2022. *The Fuzzing Book.* CISPA Helmholtz Center for Information Security.

index